QUEER TWIN CITIES

Twin Cities GLBT

QUEER

MINNESOTA

UNIVERSITY OF MINNESOTA PRESS
Minneapolis
London

Oral History Project

TWIN CITIES

EDITORIAL BOARD OF THE TWIN CITIES GLBT ORAL HISTORY PROJECT

Michael David Franklin • Larry Knopp • Kevin P. Murphy • Ryan Patrick Murphy
Jennifer L. Pierce • Jason Ruiz • Alex T. Urquhart

The poem "Just Because" is printed by permission of Elise Matthesen; copyright Elise Matthesen.

Published by the University of Minnesota Press
111 Third Avenue South, Suite 290
Minneapolis, MN 55401-2520
http://www.upress.umn.edu

Library of Congress Cataloging-in-Publication Data
Queer Twin Cities / Twin Cities GLBT Oral History Project.
p. cm.
Includes bibliographical references and index.
ISBN 978-0-8166-5320-1 (hc : alk. paper)
ISBN 978-0-8166-5321-8 (pb : alk. paper)
1. Lesbians—Minneapolis and St. Paul Metropolitan Area (Minn.)—History.
2. Gays—Minneapolis and St. Paul Metropolitan Area (Minn.)—History. I.
Twin Cities GLBT Oral History Project (Minn.)
HQ75.6.U52M566 2010
306.76′609776579—dc22

2010026226

Printed in the United States of America on acid-free paper
The University of Minnesota is an equal-opportunity educator and employer.

17 16 15 14 13 12 11 10 10 9 8 7 6 5 4 3 2 1

CONTENTS

ACKNOWLEDGMENTS

Like many collaborative research projects, this one entailed a great deal of time, effort, and innovative thought from all seven of us on the Editorial Board of the Twin Cities GLBT Oral History Project. This book is also the product of many more people who donated their time and talents to the Oral History Project and to *Queer Twin Cities,* some of whom we want to officially thank here.

This book and the GLBT Oral History Project would not have been possible without the efforts of Dorthe Troeften. As a doctoral candidate in the Department of English at the University of Minnesota in 2003, she devised a transgender oral history project and persisted to secure Institutional Review Board approval, no small feat. Building on this momentum over the next few years, she generously mentored people on how to conduct, think, and write about oral history as well as how to advocate for trans participants who shared their lives with us. Indeed, Dorthe exemplified what it means to be an activist–intellectual who sees the social and personal transformative possibilities of oral history: in her work she reached out to and allied herself with local trans groups, and she never lost sight of the needs of participants and how they could best benefit from oral history. Her many contributions to the project are deeply appreciated and vitally shaped this book. Roderick Ferguson advised Dorthe on the initial summer project and provided important feedback in its early stages.

This project was made possible by funding received from the University of Minnesota, including two Graduate Research Partnership Program summer grants, which got the project started by inspiring collaboration between faculty and graduate students in the College of Liberal Arts. Jennifer L. Pierce received a Schochet Research Award from the GLBT

Programs Office at the University of Minnesota, and undergraduate students Danielle Kasprzak and Joel Kinder were awarded grants from the Undergraduate Research Opportunity Program. We have been fortunate to receive the support of several sympathetic administrators at the university: Dean Jim Parente, Dean Steven Rosenstone, and Associate Dean Robert B. McMaster all granted funds to keep this project going.

Several administrative units and departments at the university were key in supporting the project, especially the departments of American studies (and its chair, Riv-Ellen Prell); gender, women, and sexuality studies (Joanna O'Connell, chair); and history (M. J. Maynes, chair). Colleen Hennen from the Department of American Studies worked particularly diligently on logistics; this book would not have been possible without her help. She kept us laughing throughout the sometimes daunting process of maintaining funding. Staff and faculty at the Institute for Advanced Study also provided crucial logistical support, especially Ann Waltner, Susannah L. Smith, Jeanne Kilde, Karen Kinoshita, and Angie Hoffman-Walter. We thank the departments of English, sociology, and anthropology at the University of Minnesota and the departments of American studies and gender and sexuality studies at Macalester College for support of project activities.

Also at the University of Minnesota, we thank the Schochet Center for GLBT Studies and the Gay, Lesbian, Bisexual, Transgender, Ally Programs Office, in particular Anne Phibbs, whose unflagging support and guidance for the program have been critical. Jean-Nickolaus Tretter not only was an interview subject but provided extensive archival help. He has been a friend to this project from its very beginning, as has Beth Zemsky, formerly with the university.

At the University of Minnesota Press, we appreciate the encouragement and support of senior acquisitions editor for regional studies, Todd Orjala, and of editorial director Richard Morrison. We are grateful to Barrie Jean Borich, David Churchill, Lisa Duggan, Molly McGarry, and the anonymous reviewers who supported our initial proposal with the Press. Anne Enke, who provided thoughtful feedback as an outside reviewer of our manuscript, improved this work in ways great and small.

Several special undergraduate students were crucial in getting the Oral History Project started and keeping it alive through the years. Ann McKenzie, our first intern, started this oral history and worked tirelessly to keep it active; many of the oral historical sources used in these chapters are the results of her work. We are also thankful to Danielle Kasprzak for hard work on the Oral History Project and extensive research for this book. She dedicated countless hours of labor transcribing interviews, among many other administrative tasks. Her own senior project for the departments of English and American studies at the University of Minnesota helped to shape several chapters; she deserves far more credit than this small acknowledgment. Mike Carioliano helped with the project when he was an undergraduate at the University of Minnesota, as did Ryan Li Dahlstrom and Joel Kinder.

Several of our colleagues made intellectual contributions to this book, including Andrea Robertson Cremer, Caley Horan, Kathleen Hull, Polly Reed Myers, Tiffany Muller Myrdahl, Tim Ortyl, and N'Jai-An Patters. We thank them for helping this book take shape. Many activists and important scholars of gender and sexuality shared their expertise as guest speakers for the Oral History Project over the years, including Nan Alamilla Boyd, Hector Carrillo, Lisa Duggan, Anne Enke, Jim Hubbard, Scott Morgensen, Sarah Schulman, and Susan Stryker. Their ideas are woven through the following chapters.

Finally, dozens of individuals shared their inspiring, brave, hilarious, and heart-breaking stories with the Twin Cities GLBT Oral History Project. This book is dedicated to them.

INTRODUCTION QUEER TWIN CITIES

Jennifer L. Pierce

Gus Van Sant's film *Milk,* a chronicle of Harvey Milk's career and the first Hollywood portrayal of a gay political movement, provoked mixed reactions from activists, scholars, and a spectrum of lesbian, gay, bisexual, and transgender (LGBT)–identified individuals. Some celebrated the wide exposure of Milk's story, while others criticized its historical accuracy. In Minnesota, debate focused on two scenes involving a gay Minnesota teen. In the first, Milk advises the desperate and suicidal young man to get out of town and catch the first bus to San Francisco. This important scene is structured so that viewers will identify with the hope of Milk's movement and empathize with the desperation of gay teens "trapped" in the Midwest. This empathy and identification come full circle when later in the film the audience meets the "liberated" Minnesotan working in Los Angeles as a gay activist.

The notion that San Francisco and L.A. have functioned as cities of gay salvation while the Midwest is the place of gay suicidal despair should sit uneasily with a Minnesota audience. The Twin Cities, after all, have a history of gay radical activism as long and deep as that found in coastal cities. The film's use of the "boy from Minnesota" to position cities like San Francisco as cosmopolitan sites of salvation in a national geography marked by intolerance, fear, and repression continues to circulate in our own time.[1] This trope elides the rich and complex traditions of queer organizing and sociality in the Midwest and other "flyover" states. Further, it assumes that Minnesota's history has followed a normative gendered and sexual trajectory in contrast to San Francisco's seemingly more dynamic and transgressive history.

In claiming the Twin Cities as "queer," this volume provides an alternative account that challenges these assumptions in two important ways. First, we show that Minnesota had its own active and visible movement of LGBT people who fought for rights and created a political movement that was *both* connected to *and* unique from those on the coast. Second, we examine how sexuality, particularly in its transgressive expressions, has shaped people's lives in Minnesota from the late nineteenth century to the present. By sexuality, we refer not only to a range of identities—straight, queer, lesbian, bulldagger, gay, transgender, and bisexual, among others—but also to a range of meanings, desires, norms, behaviors, and relationships that operate within regimes of power across time and place.[2] Rather than treating identities or communities as singular and historically coherent—as in "the gay community"—the following chapters illuminate how sexual politics has organized social relationships in differing and contradictory ways over time.

What this means is that queer desire, love, and sex are only some of the many forms of sexuality considered here. To take one interesting historical example, in the late nineteenth century health officials and moral reformers attempted to regulate the sexuality of immigrant lumberjacks by discouraging their forays into Minneapolis to visit prostitutes and drinking establishments. According to one historical account, "Free from booze, professional gamblers and prostitutes, protected from all the parasites and dangers of the outside world, the camps were in every sense a true home to these displaced men of that era."[3] Paradoxically, the very logging camps reformers imagined would protect these men from the dangers of sex in the city were also spaces where men transgressed the bounds of "respectable" gender and sexual expression. Within these all-male environments, some men dressed as women, presumably to please themselves or attract other men, while others lived together as couples. Although the existing historical evidence is certainly suggestive, we do not know definitively whether these men had sex with one another (see chapter 3). Nevertheless, their interactions and relationships constitute social relations that clearly depart from dominant sexual and gender norms of the time period. Our focus on sexuality as an organizing principle allows us to capture the complex workings of male homosociality in an industry that was crucial to the economic development of the region.

Theorizing sexuality as a principle of social organization also illuminates how sexual identities create and give meaning to other identities. As Brandon Lacy Campos, one of the panelists involved in the roundtable discussion in this volume, points out, sexuality often has different meanings and salience in communities of color than among white gay men. For instance, in Latino communities, men may have sex with other men, but many are unlikely to adopt a gay identity or to consider themselves part of an LGBT community (chapter 4). Similarly, Megan MacDonald argues that American Indians who identify as "two-spirit" have organized their own political groups separate from white mainstream LGBT organizations because of their unique history of colonization (chapter 6). MacDonald quotes Beth Brant, a Mohawk woman, who prefers the term "two-spirit" because she does not want to make "distinctions between sexuality and spirituality."[4] As Brant puts it, "our sexuality has been colonized, sterilized, whitewashed . . . what the dominant culture has never been able to comprehend is that spirit/sex/prayer/flesh/religion/natural is who I am as a Two-Spirit."[5] These examples demonstrate not only that the category LGBT has different meanings to different groups of people, but that sexuality also produces meaning as it intersects with other identities. In this light, sexuality represents a constitutive element not just of LGBT community history, but also of Latino history, American Indian history, women's history, and many other domains we might assume are distinct from or unrelated to sexual pasts.

Theorizing sexuality as a principle of social organization also enables us to see how sexuality structures social relationships. At the level of meaning, terms such as "prostitute," "welfare queen," "teen mother," and "AIDS risk" invoke imagined relationships between morally "good" and "bad" gendered and sexual subjects such as "good girls" versus "sluts, " "working families" versus "tangles of pathology," or "domestic partner" versus "pedophile." At the same time, these sexualized terms have animated and transformed national debates that have had far-reaching social and economic consequences for immigrants, poor people, men of color, and the inner city. Battles over who engages in the "right" types of private and public sex have not only structured the formation and marginalization of LGBT communities, but they have also fueled initiatives to close the borders, end welfare, criminalize and incarcerate an entire generation of young men of color, and transfer wealth from rural and urban areas to racially segregated suburban spaces. Understanding the ways that sexuality—and LGBT community and politics—are interwoven with and organize these broader dynamics is one purpose of this volume.

Finally, imagining sexuality as an organizing principle across time and place means that the stories we tell are always changing. As mentioned earlier, lumberjacks who cross-dressed and lived as couples experienced a degree of tolerance in logging camps at the turn of the twentieth century. Interestingly, by the 1950s, bars catering to "sex deviates" (the term for homosexuals in this historical moment) were tolerated by the police in Minneapolis, but not if their patrons chose to cross-dress in these spaces (see chapters 3 and 7). By the 1960s, gender nonconformity had become a psychiatric diagnosis called "gender identity disorder." Trans people had to submit to this diagnosis and edit their sexual desires and histories of gender performance accordingly in order to obtain medical authorization for reassignment surgery (chapter 2). As these historical examples suggest, meanings and assumptions about sexuality and about gender change dramatically over the twentieth century, but not in a neat linear progression from oppression to liberation that we might imagine.

Understandings of sexuality also shift from place to place within the same historical moment. For instance, the 1950s cross-dressing bar patrons who faced police harassment in Minneapolis discovered that if they crossed the river and went to the same kinds of places in St. Paul, they typically did not (chapter 7). Sexuality can also carry widely divergent meanings for different constituencies. For example, in the 1980s, one feminist group proposed an antipornography ordinance in the city of Minneapolis, one it understood within the context of civil rights. For these women, the production and sale of pornography was not a moral obscenity issue, but a patriarchal form of violence that oppressed women and denied them their civil rights (chapter 8). For other feminists who opposed the ordinance, it signified censorship and a violation of freedom of speech. For many gay men, it was seen as complicit in the state regulation of gay male sexualities associated with the AIDS pandemic. And for at least one sex-industry worker, the ordinance was understood as a middle-class "icky-poo disdain" for her labor. As all these examples suggest, theorizing sexuality as a malleable principle of social organization means that sexuality is not a fixed basis for exploitation or liberation, but rather an ongoing incitement to politics.

While sexual politics affecting queer and other subjectivities is the analytic focus of this volume, the place we examine is the Twin Cities. For those unfamiliar with Minnesota, the Twin Cities are one metropolitan area, but the differences between the state capital, St. Paul, and the economic capital, Minneapolis, are stark. Although they adjoin one another, are connected by the Mississippi River, and share many of the same east–west streets, the few miles that separate the downtown districts seem far more imposing. Jokes about needing your passport to travel from one to the other, that St. Paul is a suburb of Minneapolis, and stories of lifelong residents of one city who have never been to the other are common. The differences in queer life are equally apparent. An annual Pride celebration occurs in Minneapolis, which is home to the vast majority of the metropolitan area's gay bars, restaurants, bookstores, coffee shops, beaches, and AIDS services and organizations. If one asks where the gay neighborhood is, many will respond that it lies in Minneapolis. Additionally, the history of Minneapolis is actually a story of two cities; St. Anthony, founded first, was annexed by Minneapolis in 1872. When you add to this the extensive suburban rings, a queer narrative of the Twin Cities becomes even more difficult. The metropolitan region in which they are situated is the largest between Seattle to the west and Chicago to the east. But with a population of only 3.2 million (the sixteenth-largest metropolitan region in the United States), the Twin Cities have, by some measures, the third-largest Pride celebration. Furthermore, only about one-fourth of the metropolitan area's population lives in "The Cities," as Minneapolis and St. Paul are known regionally. So, queer life in the Twin Cities is as suburban as it is urban.

Although many of the chapters in this volume do focus on LGBT life stories in Minneapolis and St. Paul, we argue that the Twin Cities function more as an eclectic seat of queer life for a far larger region, as opposed to the center of all queer life. Indeed, the many distinct features of the Twin Cities presented us with a wide range of challenges. Because Minneapolis and St. Paul are different cities in different counties, they differ significantly in terms of law and geography. Their proximity to each other, however, makes them in many ways inseparable. Thus the story of sexuality in the Twin Cities is an amalgamation of local, city, state, and regional histories that cannot be abstracted from one another.

What this means is that the chapters to follow take us to disparate physical and temporal locations. They feature not only lumber workers in northern Minnesota and moral reformers in Minneapolis during its formative years, but also suburbs in the post–World War II era, female impersonators in bars in Minneapolis and St. Paul in the 1950s, police brutality and murders of gay men in the Loring Park neighborhood of Minneapolis in the 1970s, alleged "sex rings" in the suburbs and the rise of the AIDS pandemic in the 1980s, and the more recent experiences of young queer activists of color. Some chapters tell stories of same-sex love and others tell stories of sexuality in the accounts sex workers, welfare recipients, AIDS activists, antipornography feminists, founders of bisexual political organizations, and two-spirit organizers.

Our interest in how sexuality is constituted and makes meaning about queer relations in the Twin Cities grows out of a collective project whose origins can be traced to a pair of 2003 research proposals, developed by Jason Ruiz and Dorthe Troeften, graduate students in American studies and English, respectively, at the University of Minnesota, and professors Kevin P. Murphy and Roderick Ferguson, to conduct oral histories with individuals who identified as gay, lesbian, bisexual, or transgender. These projects were motivated by the paucity of oral histories focusing on queer life in the region and the desire to produce a community resource that could be made available to researchers, activists, and others interested in the history of queer life in the Upper Midwest. The project later grew into the Twin Cities Gay Lesbian Bisexual Transgender Oral History Project (OHP), a collective of students, faculty, and community researchers dedicated to collecting and preserving the life histories of those who formed queer identities in the metropolitan area of Minneapolis and St. Paul.

Since the project began in 2003, we have collected nearly one hundred life stories, which are to be housed in the Tretter Collection in GLBT Studies in the Elmer L. Andersen Library at the University of Minnesota. We purposefully designed our methodology to seek diversity among our narrators. ("Narrators" is a term used by oral historians to emphasize that the people who tell their life stories are active participants in the research process.)[6] By diversity we refer not only to race, gender, and particular queer identities, but also to modes of public life. Achieving that goal proved difficult; the challenges faced in that regard are discussed in the first two chapters of this volume. Activists and business owners have told us their stories, but so too have individuals who are *not* political leaders, public figures, or entrepreneurs. Several of our narrators live in Minneapolis's most radical neighborhoods, but have lived queerness in a largely domestic, private manner. Many self-identified as gay or lesbian in their teens or as young adults, while others "came out" in their late sixties. In fact, we talked to sixty-year-olds who had never engaged in same-sex activity but who nevertheless strongly identified as gay or lesbian. We also talked to seventy-year-olds who had engaged in same-sex activity for decades but were reluctant to claim identity categories that one might attach to such behavior. Some narrators have lived their entire lives in the Twin Cities, while others grew up here, traveled widely, and then returned.

Over time, project participants expanded the range of methodologies employed, incorporating archival and other forms of ethnographic research into the collective research endeavor. The following chapters demonstrate this breadth; they draw not only from collected life histories but from a range of other sources. The chapters take many different forms and draw from many different disciplines, including history, sociology, and geography as well as interdisciplinary fields such as feminist studies and American studies. Some are explicitly historical and grounded primarily in archival sources from the Minnesota Historical Society or the Tretter Collection at the University of Minnesota, while others are close readings of only one or several oral histories. Still others are pointedly theoretical, deploying evidence from life stories, other interviews, or fieldwork, and one is presented in a roundtable format. Thematically, they all explore a number of questions about sexuality as a form of social organization. Some address the dilemmas of using sexual identity as a basis for community. Others focus on how sexuality and gender have been used to police the boundaries of space and place. Still others examine how sexuality is intertwined within the broader context of political economy and national politics. All, we believe, offer something important both theoretically and empirically. Together, they enhance and enrich not just local and regional queer archives, but understandings of sexuality, queer sex, and historical and sociospatial relations more broadly.

In the first chapter, "Queering Oral History: Reflections on the Origins of the Twin Cities GLBT Oral History Project," Jason Ruiz describes the inception of the Twin Cities Gay, Lesbian, Bisexual, and Transgender Oral History Project (OHP), detailing the intellectual agenda behind it as well as tactical decisions that shaped how we gathered interviews in the initial year of the project. For instance, he explains why we felt compelled to use "GLBT" to name the project despite our own political inclinations and preferences for the term "queer." In outlining the methodological foundations of the project, he also points to some of the institutional obstacles we encountered in establishing an archive for queer oral history. For example, any research project conducted at the University of Minnesota involving human subjects must secure approval from the Institutional Review Board (IRB). Charged with protecting human subjects in university research, historically IRBs have played an important regulatory role in establishing standards for ethical research. At times, however, we found the board's regulatory role at odds with our own intellectual, political, and ethical commitments. Minnesota's IRB, for instance, considers self-identified lesbian, gay, and bisexual individuals to be less vulnerable than people who identify as trans or who otherwise challenge gender norms, a distinction between more and less vulnerable with which many of us were uncomfortable because we understood it as potentially pathologizing trans people.

In chapter 2, "Calculating Risk: History of Medicine, Transgender Oral History, and the Institutional Review Board," Michael David Franklin puts transgender participants in the Oral History Project and their complex relationship with the University of Minnesota's IRB at the center of his analysis. By placing correspondence from the IRB concerning our application for recruiting research participants in conversation with the history of medicalization surrounding "gender identity disorder," Franklin sheds important light on the ways the university continues to regulate research on gender variance and sexuality. In response to our initial application, the IRB expressed concern that conducting oral histories might be upsetting for participants with memories of trauma living as a trans person in a social world hostile to gender nonconformity and sexual difference. Paradoxically, the very institution that now sought to protect an "at risk" or "vulnerable" population from harm is the same one that originally produced the diagnostic category "gender identity disorder," pathologizing individuals who identified as trans. By juxtaposing the "IRB's concern about the distress of transgender oral history participants and the clinic's domestication of unruly embodiments of gender and sexuality in the 1960s and 1970s," Franklin reveals the university's legacy of "risk management."

Moving from some of our methodological considerations and dilemmas, chapter 3, "Sexuality in the Headlines: Intimate Upheavals as Histories of the Twin Cities," explores the shifting meanings of sexuality in public debates over a broad expanse of time—the past 120 years. In doing so, Ryan Patrick Murphy and Alex T. Urquhart chart the changing relationship between sexual narratives, government, the economy, and various social groups in the Twin Cities by taking "snapshots" of three different time periods. Their first snapshot documents how sexuality served to organize social relationships for economic productivity between 1880 and 1920. In telling stories about sexuality, such as the value of masculine bonding and labor in the logging camps of northern Minnesota or the dangers of prostitution and alcohol consumption for idle men on the streets of Minneapolis, preachers, moral reformers, and civic leaders encouraged social relationships that enhanced economic productivity. As Murphy and Urquhart find, these narratives of virtue and vice were as likely to laud homosocial relationships—possibly even homosexual relationships—as they were to demonize heterosexual lives that fell outside the boundaries of the nuclear family, thereby challenging the assumption that homosexuality has been uniformly repressed in the past.

Murphy and Urquhart's second snapshot traces the increased visibility and regulation of nonnormative sexual and gender identities between 1945 and 1975. Following World War II, the federal government created a number of social programs that transformed urban geographies and social relationships: expansive suburbs were built, millions of families sent their children to college for the first time, and unemployment, disability, and retirement insurance aided the most vulnerable sectors of the workforce. As the state identified populations and provided them with assistance—veterans, the elderly, the poor, the disabled—it also deepened distinctions along all modes of social difference, especially those pertaining to race, gender, and sexuality. In this intensifying differentiation between black and white, rich and poor, immigrant and native-born, and women and men, GLBT identities began to emerge as the basis for a unique and visible community. With this visibility came repression, a backlash that fueled ongoing violence against gay and gender-nonconforming people, but also invigorated new political movements to meet these challenges.

In the third and final snapshot of chapter 3, Murphy and Urquhart follow unrest in the Twin Cities between 1980 and the year 2000, tracing the relationship between sexual narratives and neoliberal policy reforms of privatization.[7] Here they examine the sexual controversies of the 1980s that spawned both the *Bowers v. Hardwick* Supreme Court decision that upheld state sodomy laws and Minnesota's proposed "public sexual conduct law," showing how stories inciting fear of "sexual transgressors" helped distribute power and wealth upwards, while taking them away from marginalized groups. Social policies of the 1980s had serious consequences for queer people, especially for those who were poor, women, or people of color. Deep cuts to social programs by the Reagan administration made it more difficult for marginalized groups to access state-subsidized health coverage, housing, child care, and job training. And as public commitment to social welfare dwindled, the state's ability to effectively respond to the

AIDS crisis evaporated. At the same time, homosexual and gender-non-conforming populations were ensnared in the ongoing backlash against the "sexual revolution" of the 1960s, with "headline-making outcry against perverts, pedophiles, and prostitutes inflaming a new repression of queers as sexual transgressors." Struggling for an effective response to this new round of sexual demonization in an age of economic austerity, leaders of the gay and lesbian rights movement worked to domesticate queer lives by framing their sexuality as inherently adult, monogamous, and private in order to distinguish themselves from "the specter of perverts, pedophiles, and prostitutes" making headlines in the Twin Cities and across the nation. Although such activism won fundamentally important workplace, housing, and political protections for GLBT people, as Murphy and Urquhart point out, the increasing tendency to link gay rights to gay couples' consumerism and domesticity also reinforced the broader conservative push for private solutions to social problems.

The next three chapters focus on the sometimes fraught relationship between sexual identity and community. Communities, particularly queer communities, have often been romanticized as "safe spaces" of support and belonging that somehow exist outside of capitalism as an economic system and other structural forms of inequality such as racism, sexism, and heterosexism.[8] By contrast, the following chapters illuminate how exclusions pose a challenge to such utopian understandings of community and, at times, can serve as the basis for successful organizing. In chapter 4, "The Myth of the Great White North: Claiming Queer People of Color Histories in the Twin Cities (A Roundtable Discussion)," eight local activists including Jason Ruiz, a member of the OHP collective, underscore the many ways that normative or "white-only" understandings of the "gay community" serve to exclude queers of color. Organized by Charlotte Karem Albrecht, Brandon Lacy Campos, and Jessica Giusti and presented in the form of an edited transcript from a roundtable discussion, "a literal historical narrative," it provides both the theoretical framework for the conversation and the critical self-reflection about the contemporary politics of being queer in the Twin Cities produced through the discussion. Scholars and activists alike have long argued that the acronym "GLBT" carries with it a history of racial and class exclusions.[9] As the panelists point out, this is also a problem when GLBT serves as the basis for naming historical subjects. Their frank and articulate discussion of racism addresses one of the central challenges posed by organizing around identity categories such as gay or lesbian.

In chapter 5, "A Single Queer Voice with Polyphonic Overtones: Elise Matthesen and the Politics of Subjectivity in the Twin Cities," Mark Soderstrom also addresses the problem of assuming that the gay or lesbian community will "encompass the variety of its constituents." To do so, he provides a close reading of one OHP life history, that of Elise Matthesen. Like many other OHP narrators, Matthesen grew up in a rural area and moved to the Twin Cities as a young adult. She married in 1981, "a union she acquiesced to because she didn't believe people like her, that is, bisexual, existed." She left her marriage after a year, got involved in the lesbian and various women's communities in the Twin Cities area, and cofounded a local bisexual organization, Biwimmin Welcome. Matthesen identifies herself in multiple ways and through many different communities: as a woman, a bisexual, a Midwesterner, a "farm kid," a participant in science-fiction fandom and writing, a performer in local Renaissance fairs, a member of the recovery movement, and a polyamorous woman. Although Matthesen's personality, sexuality, and activism are all expressed within this complex web of communities and identities, she has not always found support of her multiple identifications. For example, her description of her relationship with the larger lesbian communities in Minneapolis is one of participation and yet marginalization as a bisexual woman. As Soderstrom points out, Matthesen's life story is an important challenge to the conventional lesbian "coming out" story in which a misunderstood homosexual youth leaves the countryside for the city where she finds sex, love, and community acceptance of her queer identity. At the same time, however, Matthesen's life story resists reduction to a single standpoint or community, "her life is enriched, not impoverished, by the multiplicity of her liminal communities," which ensure that though Matthesen may be in many ways an "outsider" to the mainstream, she is never alone.

In chapter 6, "Two-Spirits Organizing: Indigenous Two-Spirit Identity in the Twin Cities Region," Megan L. MacDonald examines sexual identity and community in a different context, that of GLBT Two-Spirit indigenous people in the Twin Cities. Because the Twin Cities have been an urban magnet for indigenous populations from across the United States, Canada, and, increasingly, Mexico, they have also served as a fertile ground for GLBT Two-Spirit organizing, with the advent of groups such as the Indigenous Peoples Task Force and American Indian Gays and Lesbians, both in 1987. As MacDonald finds, GLBT Two-Spirit people face many of the challenges that the mainstream queer community does. But their historical experiences of dealing with U.S. colonialism and racism have led to distinctive forms of activism and community support. Detailing the uniqueness of this activism, MacDonald highlights the pivotal role activists have played in the sustenance of GLBT Two-Spirit community and well-being in the last twenty years.

The following two chapters focus on sexuality, gender, and the regulation of space. In chapter 7, "Skirting Boundaries: Queer Bar Cultures in the Postwar Twin Cities," Amy M. Tyson explores queer spaces in the Twin Cities in the 1950s. Although many historical accounts depict the 1950s as a time of sexual repression, characterized by police raids in bars and other public spaces, Tyson finds by contrast that law enforcement authorities in the Twin Cities were more accommodating. Bars patronized by "sex deviates" could not be closed simply because of their clientele. Although this might suggest that the Twin Cities were somehow exceptional, in the sense of being relatively tolerant with respect to how law enforcement reckoned with queer public spaces, Tyson also finds that this ostensible tolerance hinged on the ability of occupants in these spaces to perform a normative understanding of gender and sexuality. Bars per se were not policed, for example, but the spectacle of cross-dressing was. At midcentury, Minneapolis may not have been able to "close bars because of deviates," but throughout the 1950s, police were quick to act whenever gender nonconformity was more publicly performed.

Pamela Butler examines the regulation of sexuality in public spaces in a more recent historical moment with a very different set of social actors in chapter 8, "Sex and the Cities: Reevaluating 1980s Feminist Politics in Minneapolis and St. Paul." Specifically, she focuses on adult entertainment theaters and bookstores frequented by straight and gay men and the antipornography feminist campaigns targeted against them during the 1980s. In depicting this campaign, the popular media portrayed all feminists as opponents of free speech, a portrayal that Butler argues equates feminism with a particular brand of antipornography feminism, thereby erasing a wide range of feminists, including civil libertarians, academics, and others who campaigned and spoke out *against* antipornography legislation. At the same time, Butler also challenges accounts that described antipornography feminists as puritanical about sex and aligned with the Christian

Right. She finds instead that the sexual politics of antipornography feminists in the Twin Cities was complex, including both stereotypical white middle-class prudery *and* a radical sexual politics that embraced women's right to sexual pleasure. Moreover, while the feminist campaign against pornography had some goals in common with the Christian Right, actual collaboration between the two groups was rare. In fact, Minneapolis right-wing Christian organizations actually denounced the antipornography ordinance because of its association with radical and lesbian feminists.

Butler also brings to light significant conflicts and exclusions that have been ignored in other accounts of the campaign in Minneapolis. For example, in the case of lesbian and gay activists in the Twin Cities, the antipornography movement exacerbated tensions between them. As radical and lesbian feminisms flourished in private spaces such as coffee houses, the Minneapolis police cracked down with arrests for indecent exposure in public spaces that disproportionately affected poor people, trans people, and people of color. The fifteen adult bookstores in Minneapolis—the same bookstores antipornography feminists were working to shut down—were a central site for these arrests. Thus, while a few gay men were supportive of the feminist antipornography movement, antipornography feminism was largely seen by gay men as complicit in the state regulation of public sex and gay male sexualities. Like gay men, sex workers both straight and gay were also subject to these police crackdowns. Furthermore, in spite of their obvious connection to the pornography industry, sex workers were not included in feminist debates about pornography, resulting in feelings of alienation and distrust. As Butler suggests, these problems compel us to think more productively about the politics of space in building successful coalitions around the many iterations of sexuality.

The next two chapters focus on the relationship between sexuality and political economy. In her now-classic feminist essay "The Traffic in Women," anthropologist Gayle Rubin links sex to political economy through the exchange of women in kinship systems.[10] As she argues, the exchange of women through marriage was a means of increasing wealth for men, maintaining heterosexual relationships, and subordinating women. Ryan Patrick Murphy's chapter, "The Gay Land Rush: Race, Gender, and Sexuality in the Life of Post-Welfare Minneapolis," illuminates how sexual narratives operate within a capitalistic economic system to bolster the financial opportunities of gay men, while disadvantaging others. Here, Murphy identifies the rhetoric real-estate agents and developers used to associate profitable gentrification with the gay community. As one of the developers he interviews tells him, "gays are great owners, and really add value to the buildings and to the neighborhood." Murphy's chapter moves beyond a simple story about gays contributing to gentrification, however, by arguing that the "Gay Land Rush" in the Twin Cities is also one of "accumulation by dispossession."[11] In other words, as gay men rush to buy up new luxury condos, poor people and people of color are further marginalized in the shifting geography of the urban landscape.

For local policy makers, sexual understandings of the causes of poverty—child rearing outside of marriage, lack of sexual restraint, and the failure to commit to monogamy—serve to rationalize new public policy initiatives that redistribute wealth, land, and resources upward and out of poor urban neighborhoods. In this light, loft and condominium ownership in the Twin Cities becomes an increasingly prevalent, private "solution" to the public crisis of racialized urban poverty that has intensified with the demise of the welfare state. Strikingly, it is a sexual narrative about the "GLBT community linking its identity to boutiques, banks, and BMWs" that becomes a means to "revitalize" these same neighborhoods. Rather than concluding on a pessimistic note, however, Murphy's identification of these two narratives suggests that sexuality can become the basis for a new form of political mobilization that builds new alliances across class and racial lines, thus interrupting the sexual justifications for an increasingly regressive local and national policy agenda.

In chapter 10, "Private Cures for a Public Epidemic: Target(ing) HIV and AIDS Medications in the Twin Cities," Alex T. Urquhart and Susan Craddock link local cases and spaces—the Minnesota AIDS Walk organized by the Minnesota AIDS Project (MAP) and the conflict surrounding the University of Minnesota's HIV/AIDS drug Abacavir—to national politics, illustrating how these cases manifest changing relationships to the state, community, queer politics, and disease. Using interviews, their own activist experiences, and archival research, Urquhart and Craddock argue in the first case study that AIDS walks emerged as a way to raise awareness about HIV/AIDS, to make specific political and economic demands upon the state for better funding and institutional support for prevention and treatment programs, and for expedited biomedical research on vaccines and antiretroviral drugs. However, as AIDS walks have evolved, there has been a greater emphasis on their need to raise funds for HIV prevention programs from community agencies rather than the state, and to boost a dwindling recognition of AIDS as a relevant political issue. In the second case study, their analysis of the University of Minnesota's AIDS drug Abacavir shows the same dwindling visibility of AIDS as an issue relevant to a wide public constituency. Here, their argument provides an illustration of a contentious relationship among university biomedical research, corporate dictates, and the accountability to a nebulously defined "public" whose political validity is even more tenuous. What both cases make clear is that the mobilization of economic resources in the private sector, rather than the imperative that the government respond to an ongoing public health emergency, now guides contemporary responses to AIDS, and that this neoliberal shift generates new conjugations of disenfranchisement and community politics that directly translate into AIDS morbidity and mortality.

There is a tendency in many contemporary GLBT political groups to tell the story of queer history as a progressive narrative: one that recounts a past of struggle and oppression that is ultimately overcome by a triumphal present of acceptance and integration. In the volume's concluding chapter, "Gay Was Good: Progress, Homonormativity, and Oral History," Kevin P. Murphy draws from the interviews with OHP participants to critically interrogate the assumptions underlying this narrative. As he demonstrates, narrators themselves challenge the notion that life was worse "back then" and so much better now. They express at once loss and ambivalence in connection with this present moment of seeming progress, inclusion, and normalization. Some narrators, for instance, see the contemporary politics of "assimilation" as part of a broader, conservative embrace of "security" that works against the liberatory and communal goals of queer life on the Left in the 1970s.

Murphy proposes that these narratives of disappointment and loss be read "as expressions of the melancholy of homonormativity" or as symptoms of the psychological and political costs of moving away from a historical position of exclusion to one of inclusion. For example, the political costs include an implicit valuing of particular kinds of lives and lifestyles (i.e., white, middle-class professional gays and lesbians in nuclear families) while obscuring the continued degradation of those outside the mainstream such as the poor, people of color, the nonmonogamous, and gender nonconformists. For Murphy, an analysis of the melancholy of homonormativity opens up "possibilities for developing a coalitional politics that, rather than insisting on 'pride' and 'progress,' galvanizes feelings of exclusion, alienation, and disaffection to critique the injustices of neoliberal governance from the margins."

Murphy's chapter speaks to many of the themes contained in this volume: the varying and contradictory meanings of sexuality over time and place, skepticism about historical narratives of GLBT progress, and an insistence on politics that moves beyond a singular focus on gay identity. Indeed, as many of the chapters show, imagining the potential connections across various axes of sexual meaning and difference—single mothers of color, gay condo dwellers, sex workers, lesbians, transsexuals, and other sexual dissidents—opens up new political possibilities for building coalitions across race and class lines, connections we might miss if sexuality were not our analytic focus.

Notes

Thanks to Ryan Patrick Murphy and Alex T. Urquhart who through both writing and discussion helped clarify my writing about our theoretical framework for this volume. I am also grateful to Alex for his felicitous description of the Twin Cities and the "hook" for this chapter, which I have used with his permission here. Larry Knopp and Kevin P. Murphy's superb editing skills greatly improved this chapter.

1 Bradley Campbell, "Harvey Milk and the Boy from Minnesota," *City Pages*, January 14, 2009, http://blogs.citypages.com/blotter/2009/01/harvey_milk_and.php; accessed 11/12/09.

2 Our theoretical framework derives from the work of Michel Foucault, *The History of Sexuality* (New York: Vintage Books, 1990). It also follows from the work of historian Leila Rupp, who uses the terms "'same sex love and sexuality' to describe a wide variety of desires and emotional behaviors throughout American history." See Leila Rupp, *A Desired Past: A Short History of Same-Sex Love in America* (Chicago: University of Chicago Press, 1999), 7.

3 John Zitur, Greg Scherer, Mark Scherer, and Scherer Brothers Lumber Company, *In the Camps: In Their Own Words—Lumberjacks and Their Stories* (Minneapolis: Scherer Brothers Lumber Co., 1988), 1.

4 Beth Brant, *Writing as Witness* (Toronto: Women's Press, 1994), 55.

5 Ibid., 60.

6 The term "narrator," connoting an agentic authorial voice, is often compared to terms such as "interviewee," "interview subject," and "data" that not only are more passive descriptors, but are also tied to empiricist epistemological projects. See Mary Jo

Maynes, Jennifer L. Pierce, and Barbara Laslett, *Telling Stories: The Use of Personal Narratives in the Social Sciences and in History* (Ithaca, N.Y.: Cornell University Press, 2008), 15.

7 For an important discussion of neoliberalism that informs many chapters in this volume, see Lisa Duggan, *The Twilight of Equality? Neoliberalism, Cultural Politics, and the Attack on Democracy* (Boston: Beacon, 2003).

8 For an excellent critique of the ways the term "community" has been romanticized, see Miranda Joseph, *Against the Romance of Community* (Minneapolis: University of Minnesota Press, 2002).

9 For a particularly elegant and somewhat different take on this issue, see Roderick A. Ferguson, "Sissies at the Picnic: The Subjugated Knowledges of a Black Rural Queer," in Hokulani Aikau, Karla Erickson, and Jennifer L. Pierce, eds., *Feminist Waves, Feminist Generations: Life Stories from the Academy* (Minneapolis: University of Minnesota Press, 2007), 188–96.

10 Gayle Rubin, "The Traffic in Women: Notes on the 'Political Economy' of Sex," in Rayna Reiter, ed., *Toward an Anthropology of Women* (New York: Monthly Review Press, 1975).

11 Gillian Patricia Hart, *Disabling Globalization: Places of Power in Post-Apartheid South Africa* (Berkeley: University of California Press, 2002), 39.

1. QUEERING ORAL HISTORY REFLECTIONS ON THE ORIGINS OF THE TWIN CITIES GLBT ORAL HISTORY PROJECT

Jason Ruiz

As the authors of the following chapters illustrate, the Twin Cities of Minneapolis and St. Paul share a long history as the social, cultural, and political hubs for lesbian, gay, bisexual, transgender (LGBT) and other queer life in the Upper Midwest. In the 1970s, for example, "Gay House" served as a model for neighborhood resource centers across the nation. In the same decade, the lesbian coffee shop and co-op movements provided spaces to gather and organize and were a highly visible part of life in South Minneapolis. Although it might be an overstatement to call the Twin Cities "the San Francisco of the Midwest," as some locals are fond of saying, it is undeniable that Minneapolis and St. Paul have long drawn sizable queer populations from rural Minnesota and surrounding states. Many moved here for the simple (but not easy) fact that they wanted to live outside of the confines of their small towns and the surveillance of their families. These queer migrants mixed with the locals to forge vibrant social networks—located in bars, parties, cruising spots, theaters, and behind closed doors. Ricardo Brown's memoir *The Evening Crowd at Kirmser's,* to cite another example, tells the author's even earlier story as gay man in the 1940s by focusing on the community of patrons that frequented a particular St. Paul nightspot.[1] Brown offers what historians would call a "microhistory," an extremely local (and in this case highly personal) study through which we can make larger historical inferences. Alternately heartbreaking and hilarious, Brown's stories testify to the existence of vibrant queer life in the Twin Cities before LGBT politics took to the streets.

Even so, very little oral historical evidence had been collected about gays and lesbians in Minnesota when this project was founded. Although scholars such as Anne Enke, whose work compares urban lesbian communities in the Midwest, have collected important oral historical evidence, there have been extraordinarily few places for the scholar, student, or activist interested in local queer history to turn to hear the stories of Minnesota's queer past.[2] And in a culture that discourages intergenerational dialogue between queer youth and their elders (a common complaint from the older interviewees in this project), it has been difficult for younger generations to hear about queer life here in the voices of those who lived it. Although oral history research has gained legitimacy among historians over the past few decades and is an obvious route for data collection for the many younger queer scholars who have entered graduate programs across the country, we were also surprised that there seemed to be so few large-scale queer oral history projects under way.

Origins

Professor Kevin Murphy and I were awarded a grant from the Graduate Research Partnership Program for 2003, intended to encourage collaboration between faculty and graduate students in the College of Liberal Arts at the University of Minnesota. It was the summer following my second year as a PhD student in American studies. Initially conceptualizing a project involving research with existing queer oral historical sources, we were perplexed when we found that, even with such a robust history, no one had systematically gathered and preserved queer life histories. Brown's memoir aside, the only primary sources with which we might have worked were located at the Minnesota Historical Society, which—despite its vast holdings—housed only twelve recorded oral histories with LGBT-identified individuals. Although the quality of the twelve interviews was high, the quantity was insufficient to draw broad conclusions about the history of the queer Twin Cities. We surmised that our project needed to shift in focus: we would collect the histories ourselves. We decided to try to build an archive where one did not exist, a community resource that could be made available to researchers, activists, and everyday people interested in the history of queer life in the Upper Midwest.

Thus, partially out of frustration with the dearth of oral historical evidence, we founded the project that would later become the Twin Cities GLBT Oral History Project (OHP), a collective of student, faculty, and community researchers interested in collecting and preserving the life histories of those who formed queer identities and communities in the Minneapolis–St. Paul metropolitan area in the latter half of the twentieth century. This chapter, focused on the early stages of the OHP, provides a twofold introduction to the project: first, it will detail the origins of the project, including the intellectual and tactical decisions that helped shape how we gathered interviews during its initial year; second, it will gesture at the types of historical questions that I hope our project will stimulate in readers of this book and in future generations of researchers who might be interested in the queer Twin Cities.

Shortly after we conceived the project, Professor Murphy and I contacted Dorthe Troeften, a graduate student in English at the university. Troeften, who was being advised in summer research by Roderick Ferguson (also from the Department of American Studies), was particularly interested in transgender identity and community formation in Minnesota and had already begun some preliminary research to prepare herself for conducting interviews with local trans-identified people. Troeften recognized the compatibility of our new projects and, like us, was eager to pool our resources and start working together. Given her interest in transgender studies, we decided that Troeften would focus on the transgender part of the project. In other words, the "T" was separated from the "G," "L", and "B" parts of our project for reasons based on logistics and academic interests rather than to suggest that gender and sexuality are easily separated. Though we felt self-conscious about this arrangement, not wanting to further marginalize or alienate trans folks from other queers, it did help us—for better or worse—to navigate the trickier aspects of institutional approval and community politics. For the long term, we envisioned a collective for ourselves and others who might be interested in oral history research and local queer history, regardless of gender, sexual identity, or institutional status. Undergraduate volunteers Danielle Kasprzak, Mike Carioliano, and Ann McKenzie (our first volunteer, who served as an intern and would go on to pursue a PhD of her own in history at the University of Maryland) were instrumental in launching the project at this early stage.

A primary step in the early stages of the process was securing permission from the Institutional Review Board (IRB), the office charged with protecting the human subjects of all university research. IRBs emerged on university campuses in the 1960s and 1970s as responses to an ugly history of mistreatment of human subjects (like the infamous Tuskegee syphilis study that denied its subjects—poor black sharecroppers—due care from 1932 to 1972); they are administered on each campus by a faculty committee and regulated by the federal government.[3] The primary purpose of all IRBs is to ensure that researchers secure informed consent from their subjects, making sure that they are fully aware of the risks (and sometimes benefits) associated with their participation in the study. One cannot deny that informed consent is a good thing.

But the relationship between those employing oral historical methodologies and institutional review boards has often been uneasy, with many oral historians refuting the idea that those telling their histories qualify as "human subjects" in the same vein as, say, subjects participating in clinical drug trials. This controversy forces us think about the nature of conducting oral history, whether oral histories constitute data (as the IRBs claim) or our collective knowledge about the past. In June 2006, the American Association of University Professors (AAUP) released a report claiming that institutional review boards threaten the academic freedom of oral historians.[4] The Oral History Association now advises on its Web site that researchers avoid their institutions' IRB offices altogether, saying that "oral historians should take the policy statement to their chairs, deans, provosts or other administrators responsible for institutional compliance with federal regulations."[5] In his chapter in this volume, Michael David Franklin reflects upon the particular challenges of acquiring clearance to work with transgender populations and what this process has to say about the construction of trans people as a highly medicalized "vulnerable population."

This was one of those instances in which the institutional separation of our project from Troeften's had real consequences. Comparatively speaking, the IRB considered self-identified lesbian, gay, and bisexual individuals to be less vulnerable than people who identified as trans or who otherwise challenged gender norms, so we breezed through the approval process while Troeften haggled over why, exactly, oral histories with trans people were riskier. This designation between more and less vulnerable research participants raised concerns about institutional perceptions of gay, lesbian, and bisexual subjects versus transgender people. We were particularly concerned that the IRB's concern over trans subjects reflected the categorization of transgender people as pathological—that is, suffering from "gender identity disorder." Franklin delineates these concerns and what they mean for the production of transgender subjectivities in his contribution to this book.

From these beginnings, the collective has grown to include several dozen volunteers (some of whom have been compensated at times, either in the form of graduate research assistantships or hourly wages for special services like transcription). These volunteers have collected hundreds of hours of taped interviews over the years. In fact, many of the contributors to this volume have worked with the project in some capacity, whether as interviewers, transcribers, grant writers, or in other roles. The collective is an eclectic mix of students, community members, and academics with diverse areas of expertise and interest. Some of us are native Minnesotans and some are transplants (I fall into the latter category, having moved to the Twin Cities in 1997 and away in 2008).

The origins of this project reflect, in a sense, the very roots of GLBT/queer studies, which has tended to focus on the development of local communities. Historian Marc Stein has effectively argued that local historiography not only enhances queer studies but has been crucial to the development of the field. Even so, the relationship between local studies and the broader field has sometimes been fraught. Stein writes:

> Microhistorical details may fascinate those who know the region, but bore others. Local boosterism and competitive rivalries have led to hyperbolic claims about which were the queerest places and which the most challenging for queers (and, by extension, queer researchers). Moreover, professional pressures to demonstrate national significance have encouraged premature pronouncements about the typical, atypical, or prototypical aspects of local phenomena. Nevertheless, for twenty years local history has been the field's dominant genre.[6]

Although this depiction of local history's dominance in the field of LGBT studies elides the ascendance of queer theory to the academic study of sexuality, Stein is correct to suggest that it is the local studies that have garnered the most popular attention. Books such as George Chauncey's *Gay New York* are not only influential in the academy, but have proven tremendously popular for academic works.[7] Later in this chapter, I will argue that we should be careful not to separate community studies from queer theory, but first I want to offer some further explanation regarding the methodologies and outlooks that we employed in putting together this piece of local history.

Methodologies and Outlooks

From the start, we have approached the life stories that we collect as texts rather than historical truth. We never saw this to be an empirical project. This is not to say that we do not want the oral histories that we collect to add to the historical record (for, housed at the Tretter Collection in GLBT Studies at the University of Minnesota's Elmer L. Andersen Library, they will continue to be used this way), but to highlight the fact that we see the life stories that we collect to reflect the murky relationships between history, memory, and the construction of identity. Our participants' memories are never stable, discrete objects that we can measure; more often, they contradict themselves—not to mention the other participants. But, like Elizabeth Kennedy and Madeline Davis, pioneering queer oral historians mentioned below, we see that *how* people construct their life narratives is significant to history itself.[8] It is in this sense that I think that our project extends beyond history and into the terrain of queer studies; instead of identifying, categorizing, or defining the gay and lesbian Twin Cities, the Oral History Project has since its inception been more interested in asking *how one begins to think of himself or herself* as gay or lesbian.

In order to get at this complex question, the methodologies that we have employed have been more flexible than rigid. This means that the questions that we have asked our interviewees have fluctuated to reflect the agendas of the interviewers, the needs and desires of the interview subjects, and changes in the fields of GLBT and queer studies. I say so without fear that I will expose our failures at objectivity, for no one in the collective has suffered from the illusion that our task is to gather empirical evidence. Interviews and life stories are never static, but living things that have tended to take shape before our very eyes. This is to say that we have embraced the subjective nature of oral history research; in fact, some of us sought out this project as a refuge from the academy's ever-increasing focus on the empirical truth. The spontaneous questions that we ask have sometimes shocked, appalled, aroused, and saddened us, but have always grown out of the fact that telling one's life story is not a matter of reporting facts and figures but is itself subject to the murkiness of memory, the stubbornness of secrets, and the narrative quirks of those doing the telling. I remember an interview that Ann McKenzie and I conducted with a man in his seventies named Herb in his tiny Minneapolis apartment. Toward the end of a seven-hour conversation (conducted over two sessions in 2004), Herb told us the story of his longtime partner dying in his arms. Ann and I cried along with Herb as he told us that his partner, his body and mind ravaged with the final stages of AIDS, did not recognize him in his final moments, asking, "Who are you?" This is where research protocols get complicated, where it is made evident that narrative and affect, not data, drive the oral historical project. "Only your best friend, kid," was Herb's teary reply as he relayed it to us.

Surely Ann and I could not sustain our pose as dispassionate observers in a moment like this; as much as we were tempted to pose as objective researchers, we needed to respond to Herb's emotional state and to acknowledge our own responses to the charged emotional places to which Herb's stories took us. We turned off the recorder and, along with Herb, took a few minutes to compose ourselves. Herb, like many who shared their stories with us, spoke to the fact that queer history always begins with what is personal and frequently—for lack of a better term—messy. With our willingness to accommodate the messiness of life narratives in mind, I want to address a few of the practical choices that we made while putting this project together. Although we developed a flexible interview style, some of the protocols that we developed (and to which we always stuck, however emotional some interviews became) deserve a mention here.

Participants

A major decision that we made in the beginning was simply deciding to whom we should talk. The notion of a definable, discernible "GLBT community" is a fiction, given the porosity of identity and experience. We knew that there would be individuals who, no matter how "transparent" we found their behaviors, would never self-identify as GLBT—and that there would be GLBT-identified folks who transgressed our personal biases regarding who "counts" as lesbian, bisexual, gay, or transgendered. The only way to avoid letting our presumptions define the GLBT community was to allow for self-definition in terms of identification with the community and its corresponding identity categories. With great trepidation, we began to think of ourselves as a project by and for the GLBT community, even though those of us who were involved from the beginning (and just about everyone who got involved later) suspected that no such thing really existed. Of course, we knew that lots of people think of themselves as part of a coherent, cohesive community, but we also felt that the very idea of community is much more complicated than we could capture in a project title.[9] Even as I write this, years later, I'm not sure that it makes sense to call it a "GLBT Oral History Project," but I do so for the sake of clarity.

To recruit participants, we placed an ad in a free weekly alternative newspaper, posted flyers in bars and coffee shops frequented by LGBT clientele, handed out postcards at the Minneapolis pride parade, and received some coverage in the local queer publication. People also heard about us through word of mouth and from postings on listservs. Others heard about the project from their friends who we interviewed. Perhaps in retrospect we were lucky that the first interview subjects trickled in rather slowly (it certainly did not feel lucky at the time), for it allowed us to interview every single person who approached us in the first year of the project. Most of the original pool of participants—which many oral historians call "narrators"—wanted to tell us the complete stories of their lives. Others came to us with specific agendas or even wanted to narrate *other* people's lives. The reader should note that the essays in this book draw from both the original interviews collected under the auspices of the Twin Cities GLBT Oral History Project and other interviews that were collected to meet the needs of individual authors' specific projects. Alex Urquhart and Susan Craddock, for example, conducted interviews with individuals who had specific expertise or experience with the HIV/AIDS Drug Assistance Program and could not rely upon the body of interviews conducted under the auspices of the Oral History Project (see chapter 10).

We were, for practical reasons, not very picky about whom we interviewed during the early phase of the project: as long as potential narrators identified as bisexual, gay, lesbian, or queer at some point in their lives or saw themselves as somehow a part of the GLBT Twin Cities, we were glad to talk to them. But we did limit our participation in a couple of important ways. First, we chose to interview gay-, lesbian-, and bisexual-identified individuals over the age of fifty. We felt that it was important to talk to participants whose memories—especially memories of their sexual selves—reached back before the advent of the U.S. gay and lesbian movement. Whereas the history of the movement in the Twin Cities still inhabits a comparatively significant part of the popular memory, LGBT-identification in the Twin Cities prior to the 1970s is less understood. Dorthe Troeften, however, did not enact such age limits because of the relatively smaller size of the transgender community (and because of the needs of her dissertation, which was less bounded by the time frame in which Professor Murphy and I were interested), requiring only that trans narrators be eighteen years old because IRB guidelines are particularly strict in regard to minors and the topic of transgender children has, to say the least, been controversial in recent years.

Second, we also limited participation to those who had lived in the Twin Cities for at least thirty years so that those whom we interviewed would have long-standing memories of the cities. This project is intrinsically tied to a particular place (and the spaces that queers carved out for themselves within this place), so we wanted to ensure that we interviewed individuals with deep connections to the Twin Cities. Although we were aware of and highly interested in the experiences of rural queer Minnesotans, we limited our geographic scope to Minneapolis, St. Paul, and their suburbs for practical reasons—much to the chagrin of several writers of angry e-mails, who felt slighted by our exclusive attention to "The Cities." These e-mailers did have a point, because rural queers always seem to be at the margins of queer history, but, as a small band of volunteers with recorders, the vast state of Minnesota was simply and regrettably beyond our range of vision.[10]

Most participants were interviewed in their own homes. We initially toyed with the idea talking with participants in more neutral locations, such as coffee shops, or in a more controllable environment, such as an office at the university, but decided that it would be ideal to interview our participants in the setting in which they would be most relaxed. Relinquishing control of the sound environment has paid off: partners pop in and out of scenes, cats purr on their owners' laps, and phones ring. These are the sounds of the everyday lives of those that we interview. The one interview that I conducted on the university campus felt slightly sterile, as if neither the interviewee nor I could fully relax.

As a part of informed consent, all of the participants in the Oral History Project have the right to remain anonymous. From our first contact, we told potential narrators that we would be using their first name only if requested or that they could choose to use a pseudonym in the interview. If the subject chose a pseudonym, we would only know the person by that name and would destroy any communications that linked the real name from the chosen name. This "de-identification" is standard protocol and required by the IRB to protect subjects, but an overwhelming majority of all of the research participants throughout the years have chosen to use their real names. We asked narrators to identify themselves when we started the recording process; most proudly stated their whole name into the microphone as if they were consciously and purposefully inscribing themselves into the archive. When I asked interviewees why they would choose to use their real names, which I usually did informally after the interview, many told me that they had struggled for years to be "out" to themselves and the world, so it meant a lot for them to go "on the record." It was my sense that they felt compelled to give the archive "the official story." Others told me that, since they did not have children, recording their real name would mean that their stories did not fade away when they died—that the archive represented a link between themselves and posterity.

Concerning Identity and Community

The narrators from the original pool immediately challenged commonly held assumptions about the boundaries of gay, lesbian, and bisexual categories. Indeed, in that first year we talked to sixty-year-olds who had never engaged in same-sex activity but whose identities were firmly gay or lesbian and seventy-year-olds who had engaged in same-sex activity for decades but were reluctant to adhere to any of the identity categories that one might attach to such behavior. We also talked to individuals who decided to use their interviews as a platform for coming out: I remember conducting an interview on a freezing Minnesota night with a very nervous man who had only recently told his wife and adult children that he was gay. He saw talking with the Oral History Project as a step in the coming out process. Folks with these sexual and broader personal histories complicate what we mean by "GLBT history." We never shied away from these complicated queer subjectivities but embraced them for their potential to challenge us to think in new ways about the definitions of identity and community.

While planning the project and still heavily recruiting participants in that first year, we wrestled with the tricky politics of nomenclature. Most of us working on the project are aligned with queer studies and/or politics. For almost three decades, queer studies has fixated on the social construction of homosexuality in the late nineteenth century and, later, the advent of gay and lesbian identities in the twentieth century as ways to organize and politicize sexual difference. The field is dedicated to deconstructing and denaturalizing the idea that "the homosexual," in Foucault's terms, is a discrete "species."[11] How, then, do we undertake a project like this one, which requires that individuals see themselves as belonging to categories of homosexuality (i.e., gay, lesbian, or bisexual), while retaining a critical stance?

Many of us who were involved in the early stages of the project had rejected the categories of gay, lesbian, and bisexual in our personal and intellectual lives as too rigid and self-consciously constructed for our uses. As a group, then, we struggled over whether we could legitimately label ourselves a "GLBT" oral history project when these were not the categories with which we were personally aligned. We were reluctant to reify categories that we saw as flimsily constructed, politically problematic, increasingly commodified, questionably racialized, and just too narrow to adequately reflect the sexual diversity of the Twin Cities.[12] We did, however, recognize the political and cultural salience of these categories to the population with whom we wanted to work, so we faced a conundrum. Even though we hoped for a world where sexual categories will lose their power over us, we felt that it was overly optimistic to assume that we are "postidentity"—that such categories as lesbian, gay, bisexual, and transgender no longer matter for those whose life stories we sought to collect. For the majority of our participants, to call oneself gay or lesbian is a political act, one that they alternately see as "radical" and "defiant" or simply "natural." This meant that we had to suspend our doubts regarding the "realness" of homosexuality and gay identity to acknowledge the very real roles that these identifications played in the everyday lives of our participants.

There are also some practical reasons that we made the decision to use terms like "gay" and "lesbian" instead of "queer." So far in this chapter I have used the terms "queer" and "GLBT" pretty much interchangeably, but doing so in the field is a lot trickier. For example, many older gay men have a very different relationship to calling themselves or being called "queer" than most young gay men do. Whereas my generation has often claimed to use the term "queer" to ameliorate the strictures of modern identity categories, many of our participants used "gay" to liberate and affirm themselves in a homophobic culture. Strangely, the very term that my generation has embraced because of its flexibility and inclusiveness is a source of painful memories for older men. I remembered attending a workshop my second year of college at the newly renamed Queer Student Cultural Center, in which a professor emeritus old enough to be our grandfather chastised my fellow students and me for what he saw as our uncritical adoption of "queer" as an identity under which to organize. While I remained committed to the use of "queer" as a personal and intellectual framework when I got involved in this project (and today), I also had individuals like our workshop leader and the generational differences between us in mind when we were deciding the labels that we would attach to the project. We wanted to attract the largest possible pool of participants, so Professor Murphy and I decided that it was important to use terms that would resonate with men and women of a certain age.

Similar to our reluctance to reinforce lesbian, gay, bisexual, and transgender as stable identity categories, we were ambivalent about the term "community" while launching the project. As the queer of color activists whose voices make up the roundtable discussion included in this volume attest, the idea of a GLBT community is also problematic in terms of whom it leaves out: who, exactly, it fails to represent as a part of "the community" and whose voices have been silenced or erased in imagining a singular community that claims to encompass all those who identify as transgender, lesbian, bisexual, gay, or queer. Queer people of color—myself included—along with other groups marginalized by the dominant modes of queer history, often complain that queer history has most often been told as white gay (male) history. The roundtable discussion that Charlotte Karem Albrecht, Brandon Lacy Campos, and Jessica Giusti organized for inclusion in chapter 4 challenges that paradigm.

Historical Interventions

I mentioned that age was one of the limits that we set for participation as an interviewee in the project. Being over the age of fifty certainly did not qualify one as a "community elder," but it did improve the chances that participants would have been aware of their sexual preferences before 1969, a major milestone in the production of North American (and some say global) queer identity categories. A main goal of the project, from my point of view, is to explore—from a particularly Midwestern perspective—the dominant paradigms in queer historiography, including the intense interest in the story of the Stonewall Riots and the idea that gay liberation has a linear history and specific starting point.[13] In June 1969, New York Police Department officers raided the Stonewall Inn, a gay bar in Greenwich Village. The patrons of the place and eventually others, as we know from the much-repeated story, rioted for several days against the police, publicly demanding their right to assemble in a queer space. In subsequent decades, Stonewall has taken on almost mythic proportions as a metanarrative for GLBT identity formation in the United States, and has come to represent national, even universal, liberation for some activists who advocate a global gay identity. The historical actors and political effects of the riots continue to be hotly debated and are beside the point of my argument here; I am less interested in what actually transpired at Stonewall and in other milestones in queer history and more interested in how they function in the historical and popular imaginations. For some, gay liberation starts at Stonewall and ends with gay marriage equality.

But some scholars have argued against the paradigmatic status of the riot. While acknowledging the significance of the event, they also point toward the shortcomings of the concept that gay and lesbian politics and community formation on a large scale grew out of Stonewall. Martin F. Manalansan IV, for example, has turned to Filipino diasporic communities to challenge the idea that Stonewall meant liberation for all and that alternative (i.e., ethnic) articulations of queerness that do not adhere to the strictures and structures of gay and lesbian identity formation are somehow less developed than North American LGBT identities.[14] Manalansan forces us to rethink activists' assertions that "GAY IS GLOBAL" or, as the T-shirts and bumper stickers claim, "WE'RE EVERYWHERE," by demonstrating the ways that subjects might draw from—and then choose to use or reject—elements of mainstream LGBT cultures.

For our project, we were eager to hear how queer communities formed in the Twin Cities even before the increased visibility of sexual minorities in the late 1960s. John D'Emilio's analysis of homophile societies in *Sexual Politics, Sexual Communities* inspired us to ask how queer people lived out their sexual desires and identities prior to Stonewall.[15] We were eager, in other words, for interviews that would debunk the three myths of pre-1970s queer life that George Chauncey describes in *Gay New York:* the myths that pre-Stonewall queers were shrouded in isolation, invisibility, and silence.[16] We wondered if we could apply recent innovations in queer history and historiography like Chauncey's to the context of the Twin Cities. Did queers in the Twin Cities feel isolated, invisible, and silent prior to 1969?

Local histories are a logical place to turn in undoing these myths. This intervention is not new, but began with the first works of what we now call LGBT/queer studies, such as Esther Newton's early ethnographic work in Kansas City and Cherry Grove, a beach resort, on Fire Island in New York. In more recent work, Elizabeth Kennedy and Madeline Davis's *Boots of Leather, Slippers of Gold: The History of a Lesbian Community* used oral history methods to argue that Buffalo, New York, had an established lesbian community as far back as the 1940s. Victor Silverman and Susan Stryker, in an example from documentary film, suggest in *Screaming Queens: The Riot at Compton's Cafeteria* that a 1966 altercation in and outside a café popular with queer—especially transgender—patrons in the tenderloin district of San Francisco can be read to challenge dominant GLBTQ scholarship.[17] Like Kennedy and Davis, the directors (who are scholars and activists in addition to filmmakers) show us that there is ample historical evidence to counter the Stonewall master narrative—if we are willing to listen. Other notable examples of local works that make this intervention are Nan Alamilla Boyd's *Wide Open Town* and Lillian Faderman and Stuart Timmons's more recent *Gay L.A.*[18] These scholars and their work suggest how, by turning to local articulations of queer community formation, we can begin to rethink accepted narratives of community formation and gay liberation. We did not want the Twin Cities GLBT Oral History Project to be merely a local replay of these histories, but we did draw inspiration from the ways in which these projects intervene in dominant historical narratives by drawing from the life narratives.

Many of our narrators have themselves described the ways in which their lives as queer-identified men and women challenge the Stonewall paradigm. Some of the most personally satisfying moments for me have been those in which our participants have contested, through their own life stories, the idea that queers in the Midwest owed their liberation to those in Greenwich Village. For example, a number of our participants were active as students in FREE (Fight Repression of Erotic Expression), one of the nation's first gay student groups—founded just one month before Stonewall at the University of Minnesota. As members of FREE, our participants remember such activities as attending university dances en masse in same-sex couples (a move that anticipated the "guerrilla queer bar" trend thirty years later) and advocating against campus police harassment of queer students. These memories of FREE can help us to rethink the singularity of the Stonewall narrative in the story of gay and lesbian politics. In listening to such stories, a larger network of gay and lesbian politics that emerged in the twentieth century becomes visible, and we can begin to tell the more complicated story of queer identity and community formation than the oversimplified story of Stonewall provides.

Listening to the narrators also reminds us that we must exercise caution when attaching political identities to our subjects' adoptions of terms like "gay" and "lesbian" to describe their sexual identities. Like many of our early narrators, an interviewee named Robert couldn't even remember Stonewall in relation to his memories of the exciting social milieu that he found in Minneapolis: "I have trouble remembering what year it was," he said. ". . . '69? No, we were too busy partying at the Gay Nineties and Sutton's and Tony's [all local bars frequented by men who had sex with other men]. We weren't being harassed by the cops." Robert speaks to an argument that Amy Tyson makes in chapter 7 of this volume, that Minneapolis queer bar cultures were mostly tolerated by local authorities; Tyson explains that the myth of isolation simply does not hold water in the local context. Although Robert's focus on partying over politics may or may not be typical, most of the narrators attest personally to the fact that Stonewall was not a moment of universal consequence for queers. This is not to say that Stonewall was not a galvanizing moment for the start of a national GLBT movement or that Minnesota queers were blissfully unaware of early queer organizing, but that we must look beyond the dominant narratives to understand how the politics of sexuality shapes individual lives.

For Midwesterners of the 1950s and 1960s, political and personal identity formation was as much—if not more—a matter of local consequence. Certainly, national controversies surrounding homosexuality, especially Anita Bryant's Save Our Children campaign in 1977, resonated with queers in the Twin Cities, but we must also look to the ways in which the demands of local everyday life often eclipsed matters of national concern. Our participants adopted various identities and played many (sometimes contradictory) social roles in 1969: they describe themselves as having been students, activists, tomboys, farm boys, good girls, professionals, partiers like Robert, life partners, self-defined sluts, and on and on. And while some clearly identify the riots in New York or the nationwide protests against Bryant as defining moments in their lives, the national LGBT movement (and its many, often conflicting, movements within that movement) did not always mirror local realities. This book's focus on local history's relationship to that broader history reflects this dynamic relationship between national trends and local lived experience.

One of my favorite questions that we asked in the early interviews addressed our participants' perceptions of whether it was easier to be a queer youth today or when they were younger. Their answers often defied the trajectory (from oppression to liberation) of widely accepted narratives of queer history. To my great surprise as I conducted interviews, many participants remember the 1940s and 1950s in idyllic terms and worried for contemporary queer youth. It can be argued whether this is historical truth or the invention of their memories and life narratives, but it is telling that they do not unilaterally assume that it is easier to be queer today than it was in the 1950s. Chuck, a participant in his sixties, said:

> I'm amazed. Every Sunday, a lot of young people come to church. And I look at them, and I think, "Your life is so much easier at your age now than it was for me when I was your age." And yet I realized they also have other challenges. There wasn't AIDS when I came out, which is a big thing that [even] the youngest gay/lesbian/bisexual/transgender person has to deal with. So, while I had my set of hard things, they've got theirs. . . . As an older gay person, there are many places that I went to as a younger person that I couldn't go to now. It would not be safe. Now I'm amazed I wasn't killed. I've put myself in harm's way so often, and at the time I didn't think twice about it. But now, as a senior, I do. I guess taking up with strangers years ago wasn't as dangerous as it is now.

Chuck, who had been a promiscuous younger man, illustrates that we can not take for granted that gay liberation made the personal lives of younger gay men any easier—he sees himself as actually having had *more* sexual freedom than a young man coming of age today. He contrasted his experiences living as a young adult in San Francisco in the late 1970s with those who became active after the onslaught of AIDS to illustrate that queer history is not a linear path toward progress.

In another example of this logic, Judy, a fifty-nine-year-old lesbian-identified interviewee, put it this way when asked what message she would have for young queers today:

> I think I would want to tell people that it's very dangerous to take for granted your freedom because it can be taken away, and it might be. So it's important to remember that it's not given that people will allow you to live your life freely. You know, I think, I see the way the Pride celebration is going more toward being a commercial event that doesn't have much to do with our culture. With celebrating our culture, with the politics of our culture, it's about other things and I think that's dangerous. It really is. I think we can lose our freedom. Women can lose the right to abortion. We can lose the right to be out.

Whereas Chuck contrasted his experiences from those of today's youth in terms of sex and personal safety, Judy was more politically conscious: she worries that "women can lose the right to abortion. We can lose the right to be out," acknowledging that the politics of sexuality does not move unidirectionally toward progress, but ebbs and flows in changing cultural tides. Like Judy and Chuck, many of our narrators acknowledge that younger queers, although more vocal than older generations and more likely to see themselves reflected in dominant political and popular cultures, face an entirely new set of political and personal concerns. Perhaps more provocatively, they articulate the uneven terrain of queer politics and history in the twentieth century, helping to dismantle a rigid narrative of gay and lesbian history from oppression to liberation. This book is dedicated to them.

Notes

Thanks to the Graduate Research Partnership Program at the University of Minnesota's College of Liberal Arts for the initial funding of this project and to Jennifer L. Pierce for offering thorough and thoughtful editorial guidance on this chapter. I would also like to thank Dorthe Troeften, Ann McKenzie, and Danielle Kasprzak for keeping the Oral History Project alive in its earliest stages and Anne Enke for thoughtful and thorough feedback on a draft of this essay. Most especially I want to acknowledge the generous and unflagging support that Kevin P. Murphy has provided since the start of this project and to the dozens of queer men and women whom I interviewed for the Twin Cities GLBT Oral History Project.

1 Ricardo J. Brown, *The Evening Crowd at Kirmser's: A Gay Life in the 1940s* (Minneapolis: University of Minnesota Press, 2001).

2 Anne Enke, *Finding the Movement: Sexuality, Contested Space, and Feminist Activism* (Durham, N.C.: Duke University Press, 2007).

3 See Jennifer Howard, "Oral History under Review," *Chronicle of Higher Education*, vol. 53, issue 12 (November 2006): A14.

4 The report is titled "Research on Human Subjects: Academic Freedom and the Institutional Review Board" and echoed a report filed by the AAUP in 2000. See the AAUP Web site: http://www.aaup.org/AAUP/About/committees/committee+repts/CommA/ResearchonHumanSubjects.html (accessed May 21, 2007).

5 http://omega.dickinson.edu/organizations/oha/org_irbquestion.html (last accessed May 21, 2007).

6 Marc Stein, "Theoretical Politics, Local Communities: The Making of U.S. LGBT Historiography," *GLQ: A Journal of Lesbian and Gay Studies* (2005) 11(4): 605–25.

7 George Chauncey, *Gay New York: Gender, Urban Culture, and the Making of the Gay Male World, 1890–1940* (New York: Basic Books, 1994).

8 Elizabeth Kennedy and Madeline Davis, *Boots of Leather, Slippers of Gold: The History of a Lesbian Community* (New York: Penguin Books, 1994).

9 See Miranda Joseph, *Against the Romance of Community* (Minneapolis: University of Minnesota Press, 2002), for a particularly rousing critique of the idea and politics of community.

10 See directors Jamie A. Lee and Dawn Mikkelson's film *Treading Water* (St. Paul: Aquaries Media, 2001) for a fascinating portrait of contemporary queer life in rural Minnesota. Will Fellows also documented the lives of gay-identified men in the Midwest in *Farm Boys: Lives of Gay Men from the Rural Midwest* (Madison: University of Wisconsin Press, 1996).

11 Michel Foucault, *The History of Sexuality: Volume I: An Introduction* (New York: Knopf, 1990), 43.

12 This is not to say that *queer* would have been an unproblematic terminological choice. The recent cultural turn in which *queer* stands in for *LGBT* (see *Queer Eye for the Straight Guy* and *Queer As Folk*) exemplifies the extent to which *queer* has been normalized and commodified within U.S. popular culture.

13 For scholarly examples of the centrality of the Stonewall narrative, see Martin Duberman, Martha Vicinus, and George Chauncey, eds., *Hidden from History: Reclaiming the Gay and Lesbian Past*, reissue ed. (New York: Plume, 1990), and Martin Duberman, *Stonewall* (New York: Penguin, 1994). For cinematic examples of the Stonewall myth

in action, see the documentaries *Before Stonewall* and *After Stonewall* and the narrative film *Stonewall.*

14 See Martin F. Manalansan IV, "In the Shadows of Stonewall: Examining Gay Transnational Politics and the Diasporic Dilemma," in David Lloyd and Lisa Lowe, eds., *The Politics of Culture in the Shadow of Capital* (Durham, N.C.: Duke University Press, 1997), and his *Global Divas: Filipino Gay Men in the Diaspora* (Durham, N.C.: Duke University Press, 2003).

15 John D'Emilio, *Sexual Politics, Sexual Communities: The Making of a Homosexual Minority in the United States, 1940–1970* (Chicago: University of Chicago Press, 1983).

16 Chauncey, *Gay New York,* 6.

17 Esther Newton, *Cherry Grove, Fire Island: Sixty Years in America's First Gay and Lesbian Town* (Boston: Beacon, 1993); Elizabeth Kennedy and Madeline Davis, *Boots of Leather, Slippers of Gold: The History of a Lesbian Community* (New York: Penguin, 1994); and Victor Silverman and Susan Stryker, directors, *Screaming Queens: The Riot at Compton's Cafeteria* (Frameline, 2005).

18 Nan Alamilla Boyd, *Wide Open Town: A History of Queer San Francisco to 1965* (Berkeley and Los Angeles: University of California Press, 2005), and Lillian Faderman and Stuart Timmons, *Gay L.A.: A History of Sexual Outlaws, Power Politics, and Lipstick Lesbians* (New York: Basic Books, 2006).

2. CALCULATING RISK HISTORY OF MEDICINE, TRANSGENDER ORAL HISTORY, AND THE INSTITUTIONAL REVIEW BOARD

Michael David Franklin

In June 2005, my colleague Dorthe Troeften and I drove to a modest retirement community on the outskirts of Minneapolis to pay a visit to Carol, a white transgender woman in her late seventies who had contacted the Twin Cities GLBT Oral History Project (OHP) in order to contribute her life story. As we all sat around her living room for roughly two hours, Carol shared her life with us: memories of her experimentations with cross-dressing as a child in upstate Minnesota, of her overseas military service during the Korean War, of her overlapping experiences in public as a male printer and in private as a transvestite in a small Minnesota town in the late 1950s. In order to be, as she put it, "more free" to be Carol, she moved in 1961 to Minneapolis, and it was there that she would purchase at a downtown bookstore issues of the magazine *Transvestia.* A periodical devoted to the heterosexual male-to-female transvestite, *Transvestia* contained personal ads through which Carol befriended other transvestites in the Twin Cities. Soon she found herself in the company of these friends driving eastward to Madison, Wisconsin, or farther on to Chicago, to attend regional meetings for the national transvestite sorority that she had joined.

Two months later, in August 2005, Dorthe and I along with our colleague Ryan Li Dahlstrom visited the home of Julian, a white middle-aged transgender man who with his partner generously prepared dinner for us before sharing his life story. He recalled how as a youth he, in his words, "wanted something more" out of life than his situation presented him, specifically in the form of access to knowledge about and experiences with cultures and people who weren't white, middle-class, and straight. At the age of seventeen in the early 1980s, he recalled how he became aware of his desire for women and his identification as a lesbian, an awakening that motivated him to travel to Minneapolis to feminist coffeehouses to, according to him, "find people like me." These yearnings led him into an adult life in the Twin Cities that unfolded around activism: his involvement in the first lesbian band in Minneapolis, his participation with the Lesbian Avengers as a self-identified "very butch dyke," his response to the devastation of HIV/AIDS on gay and lesbian social scenes he inhabited, his past work as a carpenter and current work as a nurse. All of his experiences, he suggested, reflected in some way his guiding principle that "pain is a motivator" to challenge operations of power that perpetuate exploitation and discrimination by participating in political action firmly rooted in the embodied experiences of oppressed people. One recent expression of this personal ethos is his activism with the Minnesota Transgender Health Coalition, an organization that aims to educate health-care providers about ways to offer safe and affirmative health-care services for trans and gender-nonconforming people.

Although the two snapshots offered here only scratch the surface of everything shared, Carol's and Julian's stories nevertheless breathe life into two strands of the transgender history of the Twin Cities.[1] Despite the differences between Carol's and Julian's lives, as they moved in vastly different social circles and had access to different kinds of politics and cultures, a key similarity worth considering is the process of oral history methodology itself. Carol's oral history resisted any simple linear structure; Dorthe's and my questions and Carol's sudden recollections created a rich autobiographical mosaic that wove through a number of experiences, from reflections on her situation as the only transgender woman living at a gender-normative retirement community to memories of her visits to a Lake Street shop owned by her friend, a female dwarf dressmaker, in whom she confided her transvestism and from whom she purchased dresses during the mid-1960s. Similarly, Julian's story emerged out of an interactive process of questions and remembrances, guided by the major events in his life but textured with such fond and seemingly unrelated recollections as watching when he was a child the jiggle of his grandmother's flabby arms while she kneaded bread dough. All in all, neither life story was a neatly wrapped package that was simply handed over to Dorthe and Ryan Li and me; each was as complex in its revelation as in its substance.

I start with an observation about these oral histories' enunciation because their openness and range sharply contrast with the constraints within which trans and gender-nonconforming people have traditionally expressed themselves to the university. I specifically refer here to the history of transsexual medicine in the United States. Dealing with the establishment of university-based gender identity clinics in the 1960s and 1970s, trans people historically were required to walk a tightrope of cross-gender identification as narrowly theorized by medical authorities if they had any hopes of accessing medical technologies of reassignment and securing authorization for their new gender identities. In other words, trans people had little choice but to submit themselves to the psychopathology called "gender identity disorder" and to edit their desires and histories accordingly if they were to be legitimated before the eyes of medicine and the law. Since the privatization of transsexual health-care services in the early 1980s, and especially with the rise of transgender studies and the transgender rights movement emerging in the early 1990s, we might assume that the university regulation of gender nonconformity is now in the past, that a new era is upon us, one abounding with liberated trans politics, cultures, and voices. Yet, in this chapter I hesitate to embrace institutional alliance as a skeleton key for unlocking liberation partly because of what I recognize as the endurance of the university's regulation. In order to explore the productive potential of this recognition, this chapter assesses the conditions of possibility for transgender oral history at the University of Minnesota by examining the OHP in the light of the medical history of gender nonconformity.

In her essay "Sex Change, Social Change: Reflections on Identity and Institutions," Viviane Namaste asserts that the criminalization of transsexuality is politically and epistemologically a useful starting point for measuring the influence that different institutions have had on the organization of everyday life for transsexuals. Drawing from her ethnographic research with transsexual women who lived and worked as cabaret artists and sex workers in Montreal during the 1960s and 1970s, Namaste spotlights the vast scope of the legal, medical, and social intolerance of transsexuality of the recent past: the injustices and harsh abuses inflicted by policemen and judges against transsexual women arrested for prostitution or cross-dressing in public or even "disturbing the peace." The medical correlate of this legal intolerance was the criminalization of voluntary surgical castration. Clinics were legally prohibited from providing this service at the request of the patient, yet at the same time they required the absence of testicles before they would admit male-bodied women into their reassignment programs. Namaste argues, "it is in a critical examination of this criminalization of transsexual lives that we can better understand both the lived experiences of transsexuals in the past, and the ways in which specific institutions—health, law, social services—have an impact on how people can, or cannot, change sex."[2] She is interested, then, in how official institutions implicitly relied upon the criminalization of transsexuality, and specifically how many transsexual women would turn to black-market surgeons or friends for the purpose of castration, how many of them had little choice but to weather the hardships of sex work if they wanted to raise enough money for genital conversion surgery. Thus, for Namaste, the social gains recently made by trans people emerge out of this historical backdrop of criminalization and institutional discrimination. Progress can never be as easy as washing one's hands of past oppressions when many transsexual, transgender, and gender-nonconforming people's everyday lives are still variously subjugated by the fluxing powers of racism and capitalism. Rather, no matter how extensive its gains, a contemporary politics of trans enfranchisement in Canada and the United States is forever tethered to this dynamic between the institution and the transsexual.

How, then, might we use the historical particularity of transsexual medicine to assess how the university has domesticated gender nonconformity into an intelligible mode of personhood? And how might we see transgender oral history as both an artifact of this domestication and a mode of embodied knowledge whose potential for critical rupture lies precisely within the incoherence that so concerns the university? In light of Namaste's intervention and her call for activists and scholars to keep the criminalization of transsexuality at the heart of any political plan of action regarding gender-nonconforming people, I want to approach these questions by thinking about the relationship between the university and trans people as one characterized by a history of pathologization. In order to make sense of why the University of Minnesota's Institutional Review Board (IRB) required a separate application for oral history research with transgender participants, we should consider the importance of the diagnostic category of "gender identity disorder" and the conceptual grounds that it has consecrated within the university.[3] The institutionally mandated sequestration of transgender people as a vulnerable population in need of special protection constitutes a regulatory procedure that paradoxically invites the collection of transgender oral histories. To put this paradox simply, regulation and constraint are not inimical to knowledge production in this instance, but rather catalyze it: we are able to establish with the university's blessing a public history project that aims to give voice to those trans people washed over by the silent tides of heteronormative and homonormative historiography precisely because of the institutional inroads made by gender nonconformity's study and medicalization in the 1960s and 1970s. Thus, bringing an examination of IRB correspondence into conversation with the history of transsexual medicine not only creates a unique vantage point for looking at a transgender oral history project at the University of Minnesota, but I argue that it also represents a vital history for evaluating how the university as an institution productively regulates sexuality and other embodied modes of difference.[4]

To begin seeing transgender oral history in this light, we should first appraise the purpose and origins of institutional review boards. An IRB can be broadly described as a formal committee charged with the responsibility of approving and monitoring any study involving human subjects based on the ethical soundness and scientific integrity of that study. Ethical guidelines for this process of review prioritize the safety, well-being, and rights of human research participants through the procurement of their informed consent. If the population in question is determined to be incapable of giving full informed consent because of their age, mental health, or precarious legal status—such as children, adults with developmental disabilities, prisoners, drug users, or undocumented immigrants—extra precautions must be taken on the part of the researcher to ensure that participants are protected and treated respectfully and justly. If the risks of studying individual participants and/or their communities are judged to outweigh the gains in knowledge, approval is withheld and research cannot commence. As stated on the Web site for the University of Minnesota's Institutional Review Board, "any University research that uses humans, human tissue, surveys of human subjects, or human subjects' records requires IRB review."[5] Thus, although standards of review are modeled after biomedical and psychological research, any university-based research that derives information about humans from living human beings must secure IRB approval.

This is not to suggest that social-scientific or oral history projects are incapable of violating the trust or rights of participants, but rather to underscore how the institutional directive to review human research has manifested in response to a precedent of biomedical abuse. Indeed, literature about the need for IRB oversight regularly invokes a history of the exploitation of marginalized populations in the name of science. This legacy begins with the Nuremburg Trials, in which Nazi physicians who medically experimented on Jews and other concentration camp prisoners during World War II were prosecuted as war criminals. The Nuremburg Trials generated a system of ethical guidelines for scientific research on humans called the Nuremburg Code. From the 1940s onward, this code of ethics was variously implemented and updated throughout the West. It specifically underwent revision and expansion in the United States in the 1960s and 1970s, when social unrest galvanized increasingly strident public conversations about the responsibilities of institutions to their subjects. This critical discourse arguably became the most heated with the public exposure of the infamous Tuskegee syphilis study, a biomedical project from 1932 to 1972 that researched the effects of untreated syphilis on black male sharecroppers in the American South. The public outrage inflamed by the Tuskegee study kicked off a domino effect of federal interventions into the management of human experimentation, particularly the 1974 passage of the National Research Act and its subsequent establishment of the National Commission for the Protection of Biomedical and Behavioral Research. The commission sought to investigate how a project like Tuskegee could continue unchallenged for forty years, and from its findings it issued the Belmont Report, which asserted that respect for humans, beneficence, and justice were three principles fundamental to scientific research. The Belmont Report consolidated a code of ethics designed to balance the protection of human research subjects with an institutional will to knowledge predominantly exercised within biomedical realms. Since its publication in 1978, it continues to be a touchstone for the organization and operation of IRBs in the United States.[6]

What are the limits of a biomedically calibrated ethical code when applied to a research proposal for the collection of oral histories from people who embody a medicalized mode of difference? To put it more precisely, how does the transgender participant's marked status as a medicalized subject factor into the IRB's calculation of the proposed research's potential risk? In the initial correspondence between my colleague Dorthe Troeften and the IRB in the summer of 2003, negotiations occurred over how to properly interact with those transgender people wanting to participate in what would become the OHP. The IRB sparred with Troeften about how to best safeguard the identities and autonomy of transgender participants, as well as what language to use to target that population. Two specific examples demonstrate this. First, when prompted in her fourteen-page application, Troeften designated the level of risk to the transgender participant population as not greater than minimal, basing her rationale on her objection to the medicalization of cross-gender identification. Furthermore, she carefully laid out how participant identities would be protected and how participants' choices would be respected regarding the handling of oral history recordings and transcripts. In a response letter to Troeften that expressed concern and withheld approval until revisions were made to the application, the IRB stipulated that the risks were greater than minimal, that "one might become upset during or after participation in your study" and "could reveal information that [would] identify them in a way they [would] regret."[7] And despite Troeften's explicitly stated desire to create a public archive of audio-recorded transgender oral histories, the IRB further argued that the "tapes should be destroyed immediately upon transcription" in anticipation of participants' regrets.[8]

In examining Troeften's exchanges with the IRB, it is revealed that the institutional logic of the IRB butts heads with the methods and purpose of the OHP in a way that suggests a particular transgender subject formation that the IRB imagines. Indeed, Troeften engages out of necessity in a liberal discourse of visibility and inclusion, of seeking out and giving voice to a marginalized population who otherwise would be rendered multiply invisible by a hetero-gendered social system. She engages in this discourse of liberation, this discourse that promises to emancipate gender-nonconforming people from the shackles of medicalization, because the IRB's community-based logic requires the configuration of transgender people as such: noteworthy for the uniqueness of their life experiences, but constructed as vulnerable and pathologized through the medicalization of their cross-gender identification as "gender identity disorder" in the fourth revised edition of the *Diagnostic and Statistical Manual of Mental Disorders*. The transgender population's dependence on the medical and therapeutic establishments to treat their presumed disorder by certifying their identities—the perceived core of their vulnerability—outweighs all else. In this instance, then, the discursive silence of everyday transgender lives warrants attention and remedy, according to the IRB's logic, yet the terms of inviting transgender voices to narrate their life histories are highly policed. Transgender participants become important to the university and the community at large because of their embodied gender knowledges, yet the rationale motivating the IRB to grant Troeften's project ultimate approval configures transgender people's gender nonconformity as apolitical, as a potential personal and institutional risk that, if carefully managed, can yield insights for everyone in the name of celebrating diversity.

The rights and privacy of research subjects must be a priority for any researcher, especially when interacting with those participants from marginalized communities scarred with histories of abuse and neglect at the hands of investigating institutions. Nevertheless, this correspondence shows how in rightfully prioritizing the protection of and respect for trans participants, the IRB imagines the collection of transgender oral histories as a process fraught with risk. That is, through its benevolent vigilance the IRB expresses concern about how oral history might take an unexpected turn, might stir up unpleasant emotions, might distress or anger the participant with memories of the trauma of living as a trans person in an aggressively hetero-gendered and heteronormative world, memories that in their recollection might, I should add, unexpectedly and even unintentionally offer critiques of the social and economic conditions responsible for such trauma. The history of transsexual medicine can offer us a precedent for such institutional anxiety about the eruptive possibilities of gender nonconformity. Particularly, this history demonstrates how in clinically studying transsexuality, the university theorized gender variance as a risk to both social and personal stability in an effort to justify its interventions.

From the mid-1960s until the 1980s, transsexual medicine underwent significant changes that correlate with broader political, economic, social, and cultural developments in the United States. The gender identity clinic is a key institution that indexes these broader transformations. By November 1966 when Johns Hopkins University established the United States' first gender identity clinic, a theory of gender—a concept that emerged out of Johns Hopkins clinical studies of intersexuality in the 1950s—was on its way to becoming the dominant medical explanation for transsexuality. Historian Susan Stryker argues that the formation of the Johns Hopkins clinic, which was followed by clinics at the University of Minnesota in 1967 and other private and public research universities well into the 1970s, was an early watershed moment for the professionalization of transsexual medicine. Designed to reassign a limited number of carefully prescreened, predominantly female-identified male-bodied candidates, the gender identity clinic was an interdisciplinary initiative with the primary purpose of researching the corrective treatment of transsexuality and the secondary purpose of easing the suffering of transsexuals. Assumed in the clinic's formative logic was the need to standardize transsexual health-care services to ensure the safety of transsexuals. Prior to 1966, transsexuals purchased transitioning services from practitioners whose reputations were advertised either by word of mouth among transsexual social networks or by the popular press's coverage of transsexuality. This under-the-table model of consumer medicine, in which an array of hormones and surgical procedures were commodities delivered upon payment with few to no questions asked, could not guarantee consistently high-quality services from doctor to doctor. But it did allow transsexuals with the proper financial means the freedom to choose and access those technologies that they deemed necessary for their health.[9] Transsexuality in this framework, then, manifested as the bastard offspring of subjugated self-knowledge and illegitimate medical enterprise.

If prior to 1966 transsexuality was the illicit result of an unorthodox union, the gender identity clinic paved the way for its recognition as a medical condition via an institutional imperative for intelligibility. When the popular press sensationally publicized in the 1950s and 1960s the mutilation of transsexuals by opportunistic back-alley surgeons, the ensuing stigmatization of on-demand transsexual health care occasioned the institutionalization of transsexual medicine. Surgical violence against transsexuals was justification for university-affiliated professionals in the mid-1960s to invoke and act upon "an ethical concern . . . that transsexual clients could be better served if the proper authorities developed objective criteria for managing their care."[10] Stryker contends that this shift toward a national network of standardized transsexual health care was not just a paternalistic dismissal of transsexuals' self-knowledge about their own physical and mental health. It also signaled a broader "attempt at the social-scientific regulation of culture through academically sanctioned expert opinion, an anxious effort to control potentially destabilizing social expressions of sexuality and gender in the context of sexual revolution and a burgeoning feminist movement."[11] Producing transsexuals as subjects who needed institutional shelter from violence and the incoherence of cross-gender identification, yet who emblematized the errant forces that threatened revolution, the clinic was an apparatus to discipline the nonconformity that galvanized political ferment and to diagnose the insurgencies that convulsed the nation and undermined authority. The clinic sought to study a small number of selected patients chosen to test how well gender-

'U' doctors study 29 patients in sex-change cases

By Lewis Cope
Staff Writer

Twenty-nine male-into-female sex-change operations were performed at the University of Minnesota Hospitals between 1966 and 1969 in one of the pioneer research programs in this field.

"The heart of the whole thing is the 10-year followup study of these patients" now in progress said Dr. Donald W. Hastings, the psychiatrist who directed the study.

"If someone were to ask, 'Do you or do you not recommend this surgery?' I would say I would want to talk to you in five years" after there has been more time to study these patients' adjustments to the new life, Dr. Hastings said.

He did note that:

■ Nine of the 29 patients have married. Three of them have been divorced, which Dr. Hastings noted would not be particularly surprising for any group of that size.

■ "We've had no suicides" in the group. Transsexuals who have not had surgery — because of their burning desire to change sex — have a high suicide rate.

■ "We have not had anyone say they were sorry they had the operation."

Dr. Donald Hastings

■ Looking at individual cases, however, "there have been results ranging from spectacular to relatively poor." One patient now holds a teaching position "at the professorial level," for example, but others have had serious social-adjustment problems.

Dr. Hastings emphasized that more time is needed to study the patients' lives from four standpoints — their social, sexual, emotional and economic adjustments.

"We started the program because there was nothing else we could offer such patients," Dr. Hastings said. However, he added, "I'm open minded" about what the study's final findings will be.

The study group, supported by research funds, now is closed to new patients.

New cases would be accepted on a regular private-patient basis, Dr. Hastings said. This means any new patients now would be expected to pick up the bill for their extensive hospitalization and care.

No new patients have been admitted on that basis so far.

The Transsexual Research Project at the University of Minnesota Medical School was the second of its kind in the United States and was distinguished by its research into the long-term effects of gender reassignment. Unlike the national media bonanza surrounding Johns Hopkins University's announcement of its gender identity clinic in 1966, the attention paid to Minnesota's clinic was predominantly local in origin and civil in tone, as illustrated in this article published on November 21, 1972. From the University of Minnesota Archive; courtesy of the Minneapolis Star Tribune.

reassignment technologies helped one assimilate to social norms. Central to these patients' medical treatment and to the clinic's knowledge production was the grafting of intelligibility onto the transsexual, the diagnostic rendering of transsexuality as an intrinsic disorder capable of amelioration through hormonal and surgical therapies.[12]

Out of an ethical concern, then, the clinic produced gender-nonconforming individuals as a potential liability to the social order, as a potential threat to themselves, and thus their cross-gender identification as a *risk* to be managed and remade as intelligible. Central to this process of assuming the stewardship of gender nonconformity in an effort to render it—and by extension, gender-variant people—coherent and assimilative was gender's differentiation from sexuality. Indeed, a driving force of the clinic was the codification of those personal experiences we now readily label as "gender" from the morass of eroticism seen to pulse within insurgencies beyond the clinic gates. The history of transsexual medicine is a history of haunting, of anxious proclamations of pure origins that work to occlude gender's communion with sexuality by discretely articulating cross-gender identification through an intersection of social hierarchies of race, class, and citizenship. Historian Joanne Meyerowitz has traced how in their move to use the concept of gender to explain reassignment, transsexuals and doctors in the Cold War United States shared a stake in the presupposition that gender developmentally preceded sexuality, that only a coherent gender in harmony with one's mind and body would inaugurate one's mature (hetero)sexuality, that anything construed as sexuality in one's life prior to transitioning was described as traumatic or unwanted or altogether absent, and thus that gender had to be theorized and espoused discretely in order to ratify the desire for and the medical dispensation of reassignment technologies.[13] Moreover, Sandy Stone describes the political and discursive effects of deploying an ideology of gender discreteness in her landmark essay "The *Empire* Strikes Back: A Posttranssexual Manifesto" when she explains how transsexuals who needed the medical establishment's cooperation with transitioning could express themselves only through a strict script of lifelong, unceasing, hypernormative, and asexual cross-gender identification, a script in which even presurgical masturbation would be grounds to refuse treatment.[14]

Gender emerges from this institutional history, then, as a newly identified dimension of personhood denuded of its erotic components, of its sexual meanings. Out of the need to neutralize the risk posed by transsexuality, the clinic consolidated cross-gender identification as a phenomenon that in diagnostic form deferred its sexual dimensions. This is not to suggest that desire, fantasy, and sexual practice were absent from the lives of transsexuals at this time, but rather to acknowledge that sexuality was judged in this clinical context to be the seat of risk if it was not properly expressed. For example, some transsexuals during the 1960s and 1970s who sought medical and legal recognition in the United States more easily gained doctors' cooperation if they convincingly embodied a normative gender formation forged at the intersection of whiteness, middle-class propriety, and heterosexuality.[15] Such an embodiment was not only seen by the medical establishment to improve the likelihood of a transsexual's productive contribution to society through legal, gainful employment in a wage labor economy, the yardstick of a transsexual's posttransition success.[16] This embodiment of intersecting privileges has also been used by some transsexuals to argue in courts and to the public at large that they are ordinary, respectable, and self-sufficient citizens of the nation-state who therefore deserve equal rights before the law.[17] Many transsexuals were denied treatment altogether by doctors during this period because of their inability to assimilate to dominant social conventions of race, class, nationality, and sexuality that the clinic sought to reproduce: aspirants of color, aspirants living in poverty, aspirants in prison or selling sex on the streets, undocumented immigrant aspirants, and lesbian, bisexual, and gay aspirants. Even those middle-class transsexuals who successfully passed through the clinic in order to establish lives in their preferred genders did not escape association with risk altogether. The overwhelming need shared by the clinic and some transsexuals to sequester gender from its sexual meanings resulted, after all, in response to the anxious opinion common within popular as well as medical and legal discourses that transsexuals were self-loathing homosexuals, or miscreants who desired to become the opposite sex for base purposes. In sum, transsexual sexuality in this historical moment was granted a very small arena in which any expression short of heterosexual love, vanilla sex, and marriage threatened the foundation of a transsexual's gender claims.

What I am trying to get at in recounting this history is how, despite gender's primary separation from sexuality, other differences were always already at play at an institutional level that in turn had repercussions in the everyday lives of trans people. If this history tells us anything, it is that social vectors of race, class standing, nationality, and citizenship status underpinned the transsexual aspirant's ability (or lack thereof) to claim and realize her or his preferred gender.[18] Instead of limiting our sight to the two dimensions of gender and sexuality when considering the history of transsexual medicine, we must continue to expand our vision kaleidoscopically to discern the geometries of intersecting modalities that underwrote gender's distillation from biological sex and sexuality, and that, moreover, informed the clinic's affirmative management of transsexuality as an intelligible medical condition. And we must begin to critically measure and understand how the university has come to use the language of risk as a tool to deal with people who are not the presumed beneficiaries of its efforts, people whose bodies, lives, and communities have been objects of scientific scrutiny precisely because they deviate from the normative vectors of society that silently course through the university's procedures and stated mission.

In his essay "Administering Sexuality; or, the Will to Institutionality," social theorist Roderick A. Ferguson queries how the university has operated in the interest of global capitalism. It is in this analytic context that we can begin to see how the language of risk, exemplified by the emergence of transsexual medicine, works as an instrument of the university. For Ferguson, the late 1960s is a significant moment for understanding this transformation, because from 1966 to 1970, marginalized student groups traditionally underserved or ignored altogether by public institutions demanded changes that would facilitate their greater inclusion, representation, and autonomy within university settings. As with the clinical response to transsexuals, universities made changes in policy, enrollments, and curriculum to satisfy these demands. In short, the card deck of institutional power was reshuffled at the instigation of the students. Ferguson is particularly interested in thinking about how and why this reshuffling transformed the university: to summarize his argument, events in the late 1960s inaugurated a new way in which the university approached social differences traditionally held in its peripheries, if not altogether excluded. Instead of exclusion or repression, the university conditionally ushered the protesters through the gates and into its hallowed halls. That is, instead of suppressing the rebukes of angry female students and students of color, the universities addressed their grievances by incorporating them, by establishing new departments, by courting nontraditional students and faculty, by allocating resources in an effort to appease. Ferguson writes: "differences that were often articulated as critiques of the presumed benevolence of political and economic institutions become absorbed within an administrative ethos that recast those differences as testaments to the progress of the university."[19] To put this another way, the university incorporated incarnations of those differences that were amenable to institutional order, logic, and authority.

Taking his cue from social theorist Michel Foucault, Ferguson identifies this new kind of institutional power as that which is affirmative and goes on to delineate how this power operates through the affirmative articulations of difference with political and economic reverberations. Drawing from cultural theorist Stuart Hall, he argues:

> If contemporary globalization . . . incorporates differences as a way to neutralize any ruptural possibilities, we might say that the administrative university unmarks and reabsorbs difference, one of the familiar imprints of globalization. We can think of this moment as unleashing a new mode of power, one characterized generally by the commodification of difference as part of

> an emergent global capital, and specifically as part of the university's own efforts to incorporate and commodify differences of race and gender.[20]

In this passage Ferguson proposes that developments in global capitalism over the last forty years have required the university's neutralization and incorporation of difference in an effort to align its interests with those of capital, in an effort to justify its enduring importance to increasingly dissatisfied and disenfranchised constituencies. Thus, the university's institutionalization of difference, rife with the potential to skewer and quake the intersecting hegemonies that lubricate the political and economic mechanisms of capitalism, also signals a history of the formation of institutional subjects representative of such differences.

Central to Ferguson's assessment of this moment is Foucault's theory that power is productive, that power is a force that fluxes and coalesces through institutions and their subjects to rule not just by repression, but to rule also through the inducement of pleasure, the formation of knowledge, and the sanctioning of certain embodiments and practices. For Foucault, sexuality is a force of power that constitutes and affirms modern subjects, and Ferguson uses this observation to illuminate how the university produces obedient subjects through an imperative to administrate sexuality within institutional realms. The emergence, then, of institutional subjects who function as symbols of the university's benevolence and progress is evident over the course of the university's evolution throughout the twentieth century. Although Ferguson focuses on how the humanities have weathered the transformation undergone by the university, risk becomes a crucial modality for gauging how the university incorporates disruptive subjects into its shoals in order to sustain its position within the dominant social order as the heart of knowledge production.

To think about the language of risk as a tool of the university, we might consider an observation by anthropologist Patricia A. Marshall about the consequences of the overzealous institutional review of research:

> While [IRBs] perform an important role in providing oversight for human subjects' protections, they are, in fact, gatekeepers for the implementation of studies. Without their approval, [one's] research cannot move forward. In the current environment of regulatory controversy, reports of research ethics abuses, and revisions of existing guidelines, IRBs may be inclined to interpret

> rules and make decisions based on fear—that their institution might be sued, that their institution might have all research activities shut down by the "feds" for lack of oversight.[21]

Marshall notes how the ethical evaluation of human subject studies can be steered by an institutional fear that takes on economic undertones, that imagines the fallout of litigation and federal intervention as toxic to the university's integrity and self-proclaimed mission of excellence. The fear of mishandling populations deemed to be at greater than minimal risk does not become an occasion for the university to devise more progressive and innovative community-based models of research, but rather to doggedly withhold approval in the name of protection. Thus, the process of risk management calibrated by this fear anticipates and lays the groundwork for the IRB's assessment of a transgender oral history project.

To return to the same response letter that I quoted earlier, we can see the productive regulation of cross-gender identification through the IRB's instructions to Troeften to adjust the language from a flyer that called for participants. In the flyer Troeften invites participation by stating that the medical establishment denies the multiplicity of transgender lives, that the category of transgender erases the sexual. In response, the IRB asserts that the language in this paragraph and throughout the flyer is "leading and therefore will bias your sample" and "needs to be rewritten in more neutral language."[22] The terms on which the OHP supposedly ruptures the silence that occludes the public articulation of transgender experiences, the terms on which those transgender voices are allowed to confidently speak into the microphone for themselves, for the sake of history, for the education of us all, inside and outside of the university—all of these stipulations asserted by the IRB suggest how the medical establishment's continued stake in managing cross-gender identification indirectly impacts the framework of an oral history project that politically aligns itself with trans communities. The IRB's anxious investment in the transgender population as at risk and in need of institutional shelter ultimately works to repackage and reinscribe the pathologization of gender nonconformity. The IRB's alibi for policing the recruitment and inclusion of transgender voices is an alibi of multiculturalism, not an alibi of sexuality.

I invoke this correspondence and situate it within a genealogy of gender nonconformity not to critique Troeften or the OHP, but rather to point

Addendum: Script for informing possible subjects about the study:

"Trans/action: Transgender Oral Histories and the Transformation of Gender Studies"
Dorthe Troeften

***

ARE YOU A TRANSGENDERED PERSON?
DO YOU WANT TO TELL YOUR STORY?

GLBT Oral History Research Project seeks volunteers to tell the story of their experiences as transgendered people in our culture, and especially in relation to the medical establishment.

The researcher is a Doctoral Candidate in the English Department at the University of Minnesota who is interested in how our culture's gender norms shape the experiences of transgendered people. The researcher is non-transgendered but a respectful ally of transgendered people.

Believing that the official story that is being told about transgender as a disorder sets the terms for the life conditions of transgendered people and that it glosses over the complexity and multiplicity of transgendered experiences, the researcher wishes to gather the oral histories of a variety of transgendered people to show the multiplicity of transgendered life.

If you wish to share your story, it will be incorporated into the researcher's doctoral dissertation, and in future publications about the multiplicity of transgendered experiences. Also if you wish, your story can be made available as part of the Jean-Nickolaus Tretter Collection in the GLBT Oral History Archive, housed in the Anderson library at the University of Minnesota.

You can thereby work with the researcher toward the increased visibility and understanding of transgender in the public at large.

If you agree to be part of this study you will be asked to meet at least once for an interview about your experiences as a transgendered person. You will be asked open questions so that you at all times can choose what information to disclose. If at any point you are uncomfortable with a question, you are free to not answer it.

Participating in this study is entirely voluntary; you can withdraw at any time. The researcher wishes for this interview process to be a positive experience where you tell your story because you want to share it and in the way you want to share it.

If you are interested in participating, or you have questions, please feel free to contact the researcher at: [illegible]

***

Dorthe Troeften's original flyer to recruit oral history participants as it was submitted for IRB review.

toward how even the OHP's agenda to critique such pathologizing legacies and logics through oral history methodology must consider the grounds of its inception. Troeften acknowledges this critical intervention in her application to the IRB when she identifies two objectives of her study: the production of narratives that run counter to transsexual autobiographies in which medicine liberates the autobiographical subject from the prison of the "wrong body"; and the demonstration that transgender lives are no less overdetermined than any others, that the medical model of cross-gender identification is just one of many forces that constitutes transgender subject formations. And oral history participants themselves variously criticize in their oral histories the institutional oversight and authorization of transsexual and transgender identities.[23] These narrations in their scope, in their defiance of the paternalistic label of vulnerable and their assertion of the pains and joys of their lives, suggest, then, a way that institutional regulation is an incomplete process, that trouble flashes in the peripheries—and that the imperative of informed consent and the overproduction of the individual participant in IRB literature must be levied with the complexity of the everyday.

I have juxtaposed the University of Minnesota IRB's concern about the distress of transgender oral history participants and the clinic's domestication of unruly embodiments of gender and sexuality in the 1960s and 1970s in order to spotlight an institutional legacy of risk management. Recent conversations in transgender studies contend that the practice of risking incoherence in culture and everyday life signals a promising way for trans people to resist the pressures of assimilation and to creatively incite meaningful change in a politics of the local.[24] But, as we have seen, the university has maintained a proactive interest in benevolently calculating risk to abet its handling of certain communities and its self-organization around market aspirations. And it is our critical attention to the uses of risk that allows us to think about transgender oral history as a recent manifestation of power granted by the university in this moment of contemporary globalization.

Notes

This chapter is dedicated to the memory of my mother, Kay Franklin. Special thanks to Dorthe Troeften for making transgender oral history at the University of Minnesota.

1 This impressive and important history includes the establishment of the second gender reassignment program in the United States at the University of Minnesota Medical School in 1967; the collaboration between transsexual activist Diana Slyter and local cisgender gay men to successfully revise the definition of a Minneapolis anti-discrimination civil rights ordinance to encompass gender variance in 1975, the first such legal inclusion in the United States that was followed by St. Paul in 1990; and the enactment of a pioneering state law modeled after the Minneapolis and St. Paul codes that banned discrimination against transgender people in 1993. For a longer history of transgender civil rights in Minnesota, see Paisley Currah and Shannon Minter, *Transgender Equality: A Handbook for Activists and Policymakers,* http://www.thetaskforce.org/downloads/reports/reports/TransgenderEquality.pdf (accessed on March 24, 2008).

For more on the University of Minnesota's Transsexual Research Project, see Donald W. Hastings, "Inauguration of a Research Project on Transsexualism in a University Medical Center," in *Transsexualism and Sex Reassignment,* ed. Richard Green and John Money (Baltimore: Johns Hopkins University Press, 1969), 243–51; Donald Hastings, "Experience at the University of Minnesota with Transsexual Patients," in *Proceedings of the Second Interdisciplinary Symposium on Gender Dysphoria Syndrome,* ed. Donald R. Laub and Patrick Gandy (Stanford, Calif.: Stanford University Medical Center, 1973), 234–36. And for information about a landmark 1977 lawsuit successfully filed by Margaret Dierdre O'Hartigan against the state of Minnesota to fund her genital conversion surgery through Medicaid, see "Medicaid Funding for Transsexual Surgery," *Minnesota Law Review* 63 (1979): 1037–54.

2 Viviane Namaste, "Sex Change, Social Change: Reflections on Identity and Institutions," in *Sex Change, Social Change: Reflections on Identity, Institutions, and Imperialism* (Toronto: Women's Press, 2005), 15.

3 Elsewhere in this book Jason Ruiz explains how the Oral History Project came to secure IRB approval to work with cisgender lesbian, gay, and bisexual participants. See chapter 1.

4 This chapter draws from writings about neoliberalism, that political philosophy, market practice, and mode of governance that activists, economists, and theorists have increasingly used to define developments in capitalism ascending in the 1960s and continuing in various manifestations into the twenty-first century. I see my chapter entering into this discourse in its consideration of how the history of medicine and later transgender oral history signal two different moments of incorporation on the part of the university in its response to progressive social movements. That is, my chapter offers a genealogy of an institutional response to scattered mobilizations that rallied around the transformation of the embodied self and the actualization of its

attendant desires for social life as a particular gender in defiance of birth assignment. This response, as I argue, trussed the trans subject in order to give her or him a social and institutional viability, as well as to produce an intelligible knowledge about gender and its vagaries, distinct from sexuality. Yet, this response is part of a broader context in which dominant social and economic forces sought to cater to the individual in their push to dismantle the welfare state and privatize formerly public resources in the name of market competition.

For more about this context and particularly how risk management becomes a key strategy of the institutional governance of the self under neoliberal capitalism, see Nikolas Rose, "Governing 'Advanced' Liberal Democracies," in *Foucault and Political Reason*, ed. Andrew Barry, Thomas Osborne, and Nikolas Rose (Chicago: University of Chicago Press, 1996), 37–64. For an alternative analysis of neoliberalism that gauges its political and economic consequences at the level of subject formation in excess of institutions, see Wendy Brown, "Neoliberalism and the End of Liberal Democracy," in *Edgework: Critical Essays on Knowledge and Politics* (Princeton, N.J.: Princeton University Press, 2005), 37–59.

5 "Protecting Human Subjects Guide: 2. What Is Subject to Review?" http://www.research.umn.edu/irb/guide/humanGuide2.cfm (accessed on March 31, 2008)

6 For an overview of IRB history and protocol, see *Institutional Review Board: Management and Function*, ed. Elizabeth A. Bankert and Robert J. Amdur (Sudbury, Mass.: Jones and Bartlett, 2006), especially Robert J. Amdur and Elizabeth A. Bankert, "The Institutional Review Board: Definition and Federal Oversight," 24–25; and Amy L. Davis, "The Study Population: Women, Minorities, and Children," 129–33.

7 Letter to Dorthe Troeften from the University of Minnesota Institutional Review Board, June 10, 2003, 1.

8 Ibid.

9 Susan Stryker, "Portrait of a Transfag Drag Hag as a Young Man: The Activist Career of Louis G. Sullivan," in *Reclaiming Genders: Transsexual Grammars at the Fin de Siecle*, ed. Kate More and Stephen Whittle (London: Cassell, 1999), 69.

10 Ibid.

11 Ibid.

12 For more on the history of the gender identity clinic in the United States and particularly how gender ideologies codified within the clinical sector shaped and informed transsexual and transgender identities in the 1980s, see Anne Bolin, "Transcending and Transgendering: Male-to-Female Transsexuals, Dichotomy, and Diversity," in *Third Sex, Third Gender: Beyond Sexual Dimorphism in Culture and History*, ed. Gilbert Herdt (New York: Zone Books, 1996), 447–85, especially 452–56.

13 Joanne Meyerowitz, *How Sex Changed: A History of Transsexuality in the United States* (Cambridge: Harvard University Press, 2002), 98–129.

14 Sandy Stone, "The *Empire* Strikes Back: A Posttranssexual Manifesto," in *Body Guards: The Cultural Politics of Gender Ambiguity,* ed. Julia Epstein and Kristina Straub (New York: Routledge, 1991), 280–304.

15 Meyerowitz, *How Sex Changed,* 224–26.

16 For an analysis of the transsexual as an agent of neoliberal capitalism whose bodily transformation has been understood and legitimated through a vocabulary of market productivity, see Dan Irving, "Normalized Transgressions: Legitimizing the Transsexual Body as Productive," *Radical History Review* 100 (winter 2008): 38–59.

17 For more on some transsexuals' recent uses of embodied racial, gender, and sexual privilege to successfully claim full citizenship to the Australian nation-state, see Aren Z. Aizura, "Of Borders and Homes: The Imaginary Community of (Trans)Sexual Citizenship," *Inter-Asia Cultural Studies* 7:2 (2006): 289–309.

18 This holds true for the Oral History Project's archive of transgender oral histories. A common reason that many gender-nonconforming people of color gave to Dorthe Troeften about why they would not contribute their life stories (even though they supported the project) was that their nonwhiteness would narratively manifest in ways that would disclose their identities to people familiar with the trans social network of the Twin Cities. In other words, anonymity would be difficult, if not impossible, for them in a predominantly white trans scene. Thus, the vast majority of transgender oral histories collected to date have been from participants who are white U.S. citizens.

19 Roderick A. Ferguson, "Administering Sexuality; or, the Will to Institutionality," *Radical History Review* 100 (winter 2008): 162–63.

20 Ibid., 162.

21 Patricia A. Marshall, "Human Subjects Protections, Institutional Review Boards, and Cultural Anthropological Research," *Anthropological Quarterly* 76:2 (2003): 273.

22 Letter to Troeften from IRB, 1.

23 Phyllis and Barbara both discuss how to navigate society as trans women by finding opportunity within institutional cracks to construct socially viable gender identities. Kara has in the past bypassed a transphobic and cost-prohibitive medical establishment by purchasing black market hormones, a strategy she herself acknowledged came with its own health risks. And Aaron has discussed how his readings of queer theory have allowed him to critically identify the ways that institutions have constrained his practices and politics as a transmasculine queer person.

24 For example, see Jean Bobby Noble, *Sons of the Movement: FtMs Risking Incoherence on a Post-Queer Cultural Landscape* (Toronto: Women's Press, 2006).

3. SEXUALITY IN THE HEADLINES

INTIMATE UPHEAVALS AS HISTORIES OF THE TWIN CITIES

Ryan Patrick Murphy and Alex T. Urquhart

The following pages present a century's worth of headline-making public debates about sexuality in Minnesota. Intimate tales from the archives at the Minnesota Historical Society, the University of Minnesota's Tretter Collection of GLBT history, the region's largest daily newspapers, and the Twin Cities GLBT Oral History Project shed light on the political, economic, and social forces shaping the events depicted here. Although modern concepts of identity such as lesbian, bisexual, transgender, and gay dot these pages, the following is not a comprehensive queer family album. Telling a single, coherent story of the Twin Cities GLBT past might have us ask the following questions: What was life like for us on the bustling streets of turn-of-the-twentieth century downtown Minneapolis? Where were we during World War II? How did our community weather the social upheavals of the 1960s?

Although it would certainly illuminate long-repressed accounts of the Twin Cities' past, presenting a single story of GLBT history might also cover up how stereotypes, wives' tales, theories, jurisprudence, and government policies about sex have changed dramatically over time. To shed light on ways that the meaning of homosexual sex and gender transgressions have shifted over decades, we have taken snapshots of three different time periods, aiming to figure out how sexuality was an organizing principle for society in each instance. Although they span 120 years of Minnesota history, the snapshots are by no means random. Instead, each captures a distinct relationship between the government, the economy, and social groups in the Twin Cities.

Snapshot 1 shows how sexuality organized social relationships for productivity between 1880 and 1920. This forty-year period was not only the peak of European immigration to the Midwest, but a time when Minnesota became a national and global economic power by exploiting the abundant natural resources in its farm fields, pine forests, sandstone quarries, and iron mines. Stories about sex—whether in the context of masculine bonding and labor in the logging camps of northern Minnesota or of prostitutes serving idle men on Minneapolis streets—helped harness this productive capacity. These narratives of virtue and vice were as likely to laud homosocial—and dare we say homosexual—relationships as they were to demonize heterosexual lives that fell outside the boundaries of the nuclear family, challenging assumptions that homosexuality has been universally and uniformly repressed in the past.

Fast-forwarding to Minnesota's breakneck postwar economic boom, snapshot 2 documents how sexuality organized society for visibility between 1945 and 1975. Haunted by memories of economic depression and war, the government began to take an active role in managing social relations to stave off the fascist and socialist challenges that arose during the interwar period. The resulting social programs transformed urban geographies and social relationships: expansive suburbs were built, millions of families sent their kids to college for the first time, and unemployment, disability, and retirement insurance aided the most vulnerable sectors of the workforce. But as the state identified populations to provide with assistance—veterans, the elderly, the poor, the disabled—it deepened distinctions along all modes of social difference, especially those pertaining to race, gender, and sexuality. In this intensifying differentiation between black and white, rich and poor, immigrant and native-born, and women and men, GLBT identities began to emerge as the basis for a unique and visible community. With this visibility came repression, a backlash that fueled ongoing violence against gay and gender-nonconforming people, but that invigorated new political movements to meet these challenges.

Snapshot 3 covers unrest in the Twin Cities between 1980 and the year 2000, tracing how sexuality organized society for privatization. In the autumn of 1973, the United States entered its deepest and longest recession since the Great Depression of the 1930s. A new generation of conservative politicians, intellectuals, and business leaders prescribed cutting taxes and eliminating social programs in an effort to jump-start the flagging economy, allowing the free market—rather than the government—to solve society's problems. Sexual narratives, especially those drawing on anxieties of race and poverty, helped justify the transition from public to private policy solutions. Prostitutes, single mothers of color, and families on welfare were demonized as undeserving recipients of state aid. Meanwhile, an increasingly organized gay and lesbian rights movement worked to differentiate queer people from other sexually scapegoated groups, containing gay sex in the privacy of the bedroom and in committed, monogamous relationships. Although such activism won fundamentally important workplace, housing, and political protections for LGBT people, the increasing tendency to link gay rights to gay couples' consumerism and domesticity reinforced the broader conservative push for private solutions to social problems.

While the following pages provide a cacophony of sexual information, their silences are sometimes as deafening as their din. Although debates about masculinity and femininity, racial identity, gender nonconformity, and poverty sustain the discussion, propertied white men figure disproportionately as subjects of these narratives. Lesbians, trans-identified people, and queers of color are distinctly underrepresented as oracles of information. These gaps largely stem from the power dynamics that regulate access to public conversations, and therefore to historic preservation. Politicians, police, public health officials, corporate elites, and the leaders of LGBT institutions—positions that have been overwhelmingly likely to be white and male, especially during the time periods of these snapshots—dominate the means of communication and representation. But rather than allowing the unequal nature of representation to suppress historical inquiry, this chapter and this book turn the spotlight on such silences, asking new questions and offering alternate research methods to tell different tales of sexuality and the Twin Cities.

Snapshot 1: The Era of Productive Homosociality, 1880–1920

Between 1880 and 1920, the Twin Cities gained global recognition as a center of commerce and industry. Propelled by booming timber, grain, and iron-ore mining industries, Minneapolis and St. Paul entrenched themselves as the political and economic seat of the northern plains. While extraction of Minnesota's natural resources brought the region enviable wealth, it also triggered breakneck population growth, rapid urbanization, and intensifying immigration. Public health, religious, financial, legal, and

Two "gay blades" sun themselves at the beach on Harriet Island, 1900. Courtesy of the Minnesota Historical Society.

political institutions struggled to manage the social and political anxieties accompanying these changes. In particular, labor-intensive industries required large populations of single male workers, a labor formation that deviated from the social and familial norms of the era. While their bodies and toil symbolized Minnesota's robust economic horizons, single men's lives also raised concerns about vice, sexual degeneracy, and moral decay. Stories, ideas, and policies about sexuality and gender helped resolve these tensions. Close consideration of such practices disrupts assumptions that civic and religious organizations, the judiciary, and corporations were universally and uniformly homophobic and repressive in the turn-of-the-century Twin Cities. While they demonized workingmen's fraternizing and imbibing—especially in presumably heterosexual venues like brothels and saloons—such institutions simultaneously venerated homosocial spaces as foundations of prosperity and productivity, tempering anxieties about homosexuality in the process. The following pages record some of these headline-making tales, documenting representations of gender and sexuality that became "acceptable" in the pursuit of a healthier and wealthier Minnesota.

Until clear-cutting exhausted white pine forests at the end of the 1920s, demand to cut, process, and transport timber brought thousands of lumbermen from Canada and the northeastern United States to Minnesota. At the industry's apex in 1900, one year's culling of Minnesota white pine could have built "nearly 600,000 two-story homes or a boardwalk nine feet wide encircling the world at the equator."[1] During the period, twenty thousand men worked in temporary tarpaper logging camps across northern Minnesota, while thousands of others staffed attendant industries.[2] Logging shacks slapped together on jagged hillsides carved out of the forest epitomize the Minnesota wilderness yet underscore the absence of stable homes and traditional family structures in the lives of lumber workers.[3] Long hours on the job, constant demands to pack up and move toward remaining stands of white pine, and extremely harsh northern Minnesota winters meant that women and children rarely accompanied loggers during the weeks and months that they worked. Work in the timber industry offered little chance for marriage, a fixed household, child rearing, and gender segregated domestic labor that defined nineteenth-century bourgeois society. Middle-class women's prescribed roles as child bearer, domestic worker, and moral leader for the family were structurally impossible in this booming industry. The bulk of these workers' contact with women occurred not in the refuge of the home and the family—spaces that in the lumber camp context were entirely homosocial—but on their days off in towns and cities, and often in the context of alcohol and prostitution.

Given these social and sexual patterns, political, economic, and cultural institutions embraced the homosocial structure of the lumber camp as the place where workingmen were made into productive citizens, a conclusion that generated new definitions of appropriate domestic relations. Although the camps did not produce a male-headed household supplemented by female domestic work and child rearing, they required the same types of labor and social stewardship normally performed by women. While this included cooking and cleaning, the camps also needed to reproduce the "moralizing" influences of the wife and family, values that helped ensure productivity and order (18). To accomplish such regulation, lumber

Close quarters and long winters defined the lives of these men in 1887 at one of the smaller lumber camps that littered upper Minnesota at the turn of the century. Courtesy of the Minnesota Historical Society.

companies reorganized workingmen's time around working, eating, sleeping, and religious observance to discourage the entertainments commonly associated with such industries—drinking, gambling, and visiting prostitutes (20). Preachers known as "sky pilots," for example, would travel between camps offering moral education to the men, often extolling close male bonds and condemning the corrupting influence of women (ibid.).

Although corporate, civic, and religious leaders worked to chasten lumbermen's lives and desires, a number of sexual and gender transgressions became possible and even normalized in this all-male environment. An industry inspector reported one such instance when asked about the presence of women in the camps. In his tenure moving from camp to camp in the early part of the twentieth century, the agent remembered that female labor was almost nonexistent, even taboo (30). In one instance, he was surprised when he found a camp that had a female cook. The inspector's initial shock over the unexpected appearance of a woman subsided when he realized the cook was actually a man who dressed as a woman. The camp inspector remembered, "After supper that night, the cook came into the office dressed up in women's clothing with lipstick on, face painted

The Lumber Jack SKY PILOT

F. E. HIGGINS

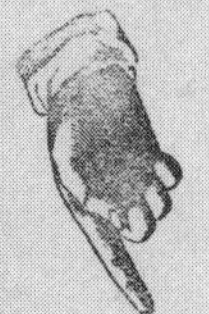

Will Speak

AT ______________________

SUCJECT -- My Experience for Seventeen Years Among the Men of the Lumber Camps.

Sky pilots were responsible for providing moral and social guidance to male lumberjacks during the long isolating winters. This announcement for a visit from a sky pilot was from 1909. Courtesy of the Minnesota Historical Society.

Lumberjacks would often spend their entire paycheck on booze or lose it while gambling in scenes like the one here in Northome, Minnesota, in 1903. Some lumberjacks suspected that lumber companies hired professional gamblers as a way to force the men to return to the camps early. Courtesy of the Minnesota Historical Society.

and powdered, and wearing rings. He visited a short while with Dale and myself. . . . Dale told me later that the cook stayed all winter and turned out very fine meals" (28).

The same official also documented a cook whose gender he could never establish. "There was another cook at the horse camp of the Virginia Rainy Lake Company east of Cusson who dressed as a man while cooking, but when the men met him in town, he was dressed like a woman, and they never did know if he was a man or a woman" (ibid.) This account raises a number of intriguing questions: Was this a man who was having sex with other men in town? Was this a woman who passed as a man and was able to benefit from the relatively substantial wages that being a lumber camp cook provided, and doubly profited from the attendant sexual industries of the camp town? After all, as cooks were among the highest-paid camp residents, and as the timber industry as a whole paid better wages than many industries, workingmen could often afford sexual pleasures for sale

People dressed in the clothing of the opposite sex at this costume party in the Twin Cities in 1910. Courtesy of the Minnesota Historical Society.

while away from camp. Regardless of who this person was, because s/he could be inserted into the narrative of the homosocial family of the lumber industry, this person was able to violate a number of bourgeois ideas about gender and family.

Although inspectors' reports never explicitly confronted the topic of homosexuality, the stories told about lumberjacks convey a distinct sense of love and companionship between workers. And while visits to brothels were a regular occurrence, this was "kind of a no, no" for the lumber "family" social order.[4] The narrative of lumberjack culture and productivity required that companionship, whether sexual or not, be found with other men. A laborer's "only companion and confidant can ever be another oversized, tobacco chewing, bean farting, fanny kicking lumberjack" (1). These male companions were sometimes given sexualized nicknames like "broad-assed Ole" (2), and names similar to the explicitly sexual titles for madams in town like "Pretty Peggy" or "Big Tit Tilly" (16). It was even a common practice in the industry's later years for young single men to live in small shacks with an older male peer (20). Lumberjacks' lives complicate orthodox understandings of relationships between work and leisure, between productive and destructive endeavors, between normalcy and deviance, and between homosexuality and all of these binaries. In this regime of sexuality one could have sex with a man, live with a man, even have a lifelong male companion and not necessarily have it called into question. This is, perhaps, one reason why historical accounts of sexual acts are hard to find. The signs that men were developing intimate bonds, passing friendships, sharing rooms, living together, and even having sex with one another were normalized by the demands of the lumber industry.

MURDEROUS MEN AND DANGEROUS PROSTITUTES

During an era when manual labor enabled homosocial bonds and corresponding gender and sexual transgressions, explicit narratives of homosexual sex generated undeniable controversy. But in perhaps the most widely publicized example of male homosexuality from the early-twentieth-century Twin Cities, when an itinerant worker murdered his male lover and that lover's mother, alcoholism—not homosexuality—bore the brunt of the blame for the deadly scenario. In 1906, William Williams, an attractive twenty-eight-year-old steamfitter, murdered sixteen-year-old John Keller and the boy's mother in St. Paul.[5] Williams insisted that he accidentally shot the two after an argument over moving to Winnipeg with Keller, a move the boy's mother opposed. The two men had been sleeping together in Keller's bed at his family's residence at the time of the murder, an apparently common occurrence over the course of their two-year relationship.

Although the prosecution highlighted Williams and Keller's intimacy, there was little discussion or scandal about the sex between the two men. In the course of the trial, the prosecutor attempted to introduce the impropriety of their relationship first when questioning the origins of the conflict between Williams and Keller's mother. "'Is it not a fact that you left because they insisted on John sleeping in another room?' asked the prosecutor. 'No that is a lie,' shouted Williams in a fury of anger."[6] The second attempt by the prosecutor to make homosexuality the issue on trial was in a discussion of the origin of their relationship. Williams and Keller met when they began working together at a fort in Montana. Williams told the court that he and Keller left to escape squalid living conditions that forced them to live together in a tiny shed. The prosecution retorted that discomfort over their intimacy generated the pair's departure from the camp.

These instances were the extent of the public record about Williams's sexuality as a source of outrage or shame. The prosecutor's frustrations over failing to paint Williams pink stems from his attempt to do so in a context where homosociality was fairly normalized. After all, extraction industries required men to live together intergenerationally and in close quarters for extended periods of time. The prosecution was able to evoke the discomfort that surrounded these practices, but failed to make male intimate relations the operative category of deviance or a secret whose exposure would guarantee conviction. Twin Cities daily papers, for example, regularly reported that Keller and Williams's relationship had been intimate for two years. Furthermore, despite the fact that their sex lives appeared to be public record, neither Williams nor his younger lover were ever charged with sodomy, a sexual practice that was criminalized in Minnesota in 1891. In fact, the antisodomy statute was rarely, if ever, enforced.[7] To enforce sodomy laws would have required the state of Minnesota to draw attention to the practices and lifestyles, whether sexual or not, of the tens of thousands of men who were living and working together throughout the state. Policing sodomy would not only make homosexuality deviant, it would inscribe deviance onto the homosocial relationships that industries required as they harvested Minnesota's natural resources.

While the prosecutor attempted and failed to make homosexuality the main motivation in the killing, the defense succeeded at casting alcohol in that role. Expert witness testimony from doctors verified alcohol abuse by both Williams and Keller's mother, placing an alleged mental disorder on center stage. The disorder in question was not homosexuality, the nascent socioscientific category of same-sex sexual deviance, but "alcoholic mania."[8] In the end, the jury found Williams guilty of two counts of second-degree murder, a capital crime. Although the jury eventually handed down a death sentence, it extensively deliberated before reaching a verdict and struggled with the validity of Williams's defense, even asking the judge for clarification on the aggregation of murder charges while pondering a diminished sentence.

The Williams case was never widely rendered a story of a "gay murderer." There is no homosexual panic or community outrage documented in the historical record. Williams's hanging continues to be a site of scrutiny and intrigue not because it memorializes a turn-of-the-twentieth-century same-sex love affair gone wrong, but because it was the last execution performed in Minnesota and a catalyst for the abolition of the death penalty in the state. Williams's executioners miscalculated the stretching properties of the rope used in the hanging, a mistake that allowed Williams's neck to withstand the fall from the platform, and which meant that he would remain alive for nearly fifteen minutes as he hung in agony from the gallows. Three deputies were forced to hold the rope taut to guarantee Williams's suffocation. The "public outcry against the botched hanging was severe,"[9] challenging any assumptions that accusations of homosexuality surrounding the case yielded public vengeance and a desire for suffering. The violence of the execution only added to sympathy Williams acquired just moments earlier when, according to one published report, he gave "a dignified speech in which he proclaimed his innocence. He said the murdered boy was the best friend he had ever had."[10]

Although sexuality took a back seat to drunkenness as the primary explanatory factor for Williams's rage, stories about sexuality—and their relationship to drunkenness and prostitution—were hypervisible in public debates over urban spaces where itinerant workers like Williams and Keller spent their time. As religious, corporate, and state institutions lauded masculine homosocial spaces of labor for their productivity, they railed against the Minneapolis neighborhoods where many workingmen spent time between jobs or on layoff. Most infamously scorned was Bridge Square, Minneapolis's "skid row," which ran from First Avenue North to Fifth Avenue South and between First and Fourth Streets. The district was home to scores of single-room occupancy flophouses, downscale restaurants with complimentary food as a vehicle to enhance alcohol sales, cheap hotels, unlicensed saloons known as "blind pigs," and a variety of gambling establishments scattered between warehouses and other industrial structures.[11] Saloons like the Olsen Dance Hall were places where "men and dancing girls mixed within a rowdy atmosphere, caresses were freely given, and rushes were made to private stalls adjoining the saloon's bar at regular intervals." Police and city officials condemned watering holes like Olsen's as dens of sexual excess and deviance,[12] making alcohol consumption, heterosexual prostitution, and interracial sex the centerpieces of their antivice agenda. Arrests for prostitution and drunkenness abound in the police records during the period that Williams stood trial. It was also common for alcohol to be used as a defense. In a murder of one man by another, the defendant insisted during sentencing, "Judge, I want you to take my oath. I am never going to touch another drop of liquor so long as I live, and I want you to swear me to that."[13]

Maurer's Saloon, 507 Washington Avenue North, was one of many saloons on Washington Avenue that catered to the thousands of working and out-of-work men in Minneapolis in 1919. Courtesy of the Minnesota Historical Society.

The most threatening manifestations of vice emerged when race collided with alcohol and female sexuality. Although Minneapolis never became a termination point during the "great migration," Minnesota political, economic, and cultural institutions had close ties to the Midwest cities integral to the great migration of African Americans from the South. Chicago, Detroit, and Pittsburgh became destinations for Minnesota's natural resources and these lines of commerce channeled fears of Minnesota becoming a destination for Southern blacks. The overrepresentation of African American sex workers in the archive documents the transportation of anxieties about race alongside records of grain tonnage exports and lodging ledgers. Police and newspaper archives, for example, repeatedly point to an alleged "crime spree" by a group of African American "alley workers" in Bridge Square in 1907. Documenting the arrest of one such woman, police reports described her as "one of the numerous colored prostitutes who hang around South Washington, robbing white men."[14] The record of another arrest for vagrancy during the same time period described a woman in custody as "one of the gang of colored prostitutes who prey on drunken [farm]hands, etc. in South Minneapolis."[15]

While heterosexual prostitution and alcohol-related crimes litter police and court records, homosexuality and sodomy only appear when the crime includes transgressions against children. William Hennings, who ran a North Side store at 624 20th Avenue North and a lodging house downtown at 1023 Hennepin Avenue, was charged with immoral conduct with boys in 1907. The officer noted that Hennings was "abusing them in an unnatural way," and "at the time of arrest, [he] was found offering boys $1.00 to go to his room with him for that purpose." Hennings was sentenced to ninety days in the City Workhouse.[16] Once again, homosexuality did not mark this incident as exceptional. Although police were clearly enforcing lines of deviance between children and adults, they were not explicitly drawing distinctions between homosexuality and heterosexuality, a phenomenon particularly apparent in the state's decision not to charge Hennings with sodomy.

Although Bridge Square may not have been publicly condemned as a site of homosexual perversion, the social phenomena of the neighborhood transgressed prevailing conventions of gender, sexuality, and bourgeois sensibility. Waitresses carting whiskey to the unemployed, women barkeeps throwing drunks out of their businesses with their brute strength, and women supporting themselves in the sex trade violated prescribed gender roles. Temperance crusaders railed against the "moral toboggan slide" or the degradation of young women alcoholics and cocaine addicts on the streets of Bridge Square. For example, at the dedication of a flagpole in the first phase of a 1917 beaux arts urban renewal project aiming to pave over the blighted areas, the Daughters of the American Revolution declared that the skid row of Bridge Square was finally being thrown into "the dustbin of history."[17] After decades of attempting to reform this area, demolition emerged as the only cure.

FROM SEXUAL DEMOLITION TO SEXUAL REFORMATION

As the urban sexual cultures of the late nineteenth and early twentieth centuries generated widespread anxiety and public outcry, social reformers and state institutions crafted a number of new tactics to control and manage these sexual challenges and to make men and women productive members of society. Homosocial spaces and relationships were centerpieces of such responses. As we saw in the management of lumberjacks and other itinerant workers, the homosocial world of labor made working-class and immigrant men into morally chaste and industrious model citizens.[18] For women, the homosocial environment of the family was the foundation of appropriate womanhood. Although deeply informed by nineteenth century bourgeois domestic ideals, model families of the period did not necessarily involve heterosexual relations and a single male provider as head of household. Instead, settlement houses, such as the Pillsbury House, flourished in the Twin Cities (and throughout the urban United States) to teach women about appropriate domestic and family relations in the first half of the twentieth century. They did so via a homosocial community of women and mothers, rather than by reproducing the heterosexual nuclear family.

In what we now know as the first wave of feminist activism, middle-class white women built political power by highlighting their role as the stewards of morality. As women were responsible for guiding the family's moral compass, first-wave feminists argued that women were uniquely positioned to challenge the corrupting influences of urban, industrial capitalism and the political institutions controlled by this economic system.[19] The notion that men were economic providers while women guaranteed the moral stability of the home would guide women's participation in a number of social movements, translating women's domestic authority to the domestic affairs of the nation. Cleaning up gambling, alcohol, prostitution, and poverty in the pubic world became an extension of women's domestic duties. Domesticity as a solution to the anxieties of the urbanizing and industrializing Twin Cities lent political legitimacy to settlement houses and other feminist reform movements.

While political organizing around the private sphere heavily references heterosexual nuclear family ideals, we often elide the ways that women's authority in these matters grew out of homosocial institutions like the Wells Memorial Settlement House women's basketball team. After all, settlement houses shaped ideas about "good women"—as they applied to both the private household of the family and the public household of politics—not through women's interactions with or dependence upon men, but via homosocial relations with other women. Ironically, institutions aiming to reinforce social norms leaving middle-class white women dependent on men and contained in domestic, monogamous spaces

Women's basketball team organized through the Wells Memorial Settlement House, 1922. Photograph by Lee Brothers; courtesy of the Minnesota Historical Society.

allowed some early-twentieth-century Twin Cities women to live, work, and politic largely independent of men's immediate authority.

While settlement houses tended to be organized by and for women, one Twin Cities institution focused on the protection of young men and boys. Lying six blocks southeast of the "gateway district"—as skid row had been renamed during the 1917 renewal efforts—at 620 South 7th Street, the Wartburg was incorporated under the Lutheran Hospice and Benevolent Association in 1925. The organization described itself as a "residential club" performing "preventative work" in the lives of young men.[20] At the Wartburg, a surrogate nuclear family structure aimed to turn orphaned or wayward youth into upstanding men. As the organization put it, "We want to replace as near as possible the Christian parental home and personally be the 'pals' of the young men, giving them counsel and advice in a friendly spirit."[21] A Lutheran pastor would serve as father alongside the "matron of our institution." The Wartburg aimed to provide "a home for men to protect, aid and safeguard young men who come to our city and to render the services of a Good Samaritan to all those who need in particular Christian love."[22] Well aware that agricultural and resource extraction industries frequently left young, unskilled male laborers idle and unemployed on Minneapolis's streets, Wartburg administrators feared that corresponding poverty and boredom would drive impressionable youth into a life of crime. Rather than imagining itself as a charity, the Wartburg was explicitly designed to provide a moral compass that would aid the boys in returning to the workforce. One supporter noted, "I have seen the Reverend time and again, pat the boys on the back when they came in from looking for work and tell them to keep up their courage."[23] In "a real home to single men"[24] the tenants would be better suited to becoming good productive members of society. Without the benefits of their home, the organization argued that "there is a class of young men from good homes in this and foreign lands, that get stranded in this city and whom it would be a pity to send into the environments or associations of some other organisations."[25]

"Knowing that the private home was the great character builder," the Wartburg did its best to create a nuclear family. It even attempted to establish gendered relations. This is most evident in the Wartburg's reliance on "hospice mothers," the women performing domestic labor for the boys living in the facility. The Wartburg highlighted the necessity of such gendered labor of matronly Lutheran women—the very basis of the heterosexual nuclear family—as it solicited funds from public and private donors:

> Home without a mother would be an impossibility. Without her it would become a mere boarding house. The hospice is fortunate in having the assistance of the Women's Auxiliary. In fact, its homelike character is largely due to these ladies. It betrays the touch of a woman's hand. The Auxiliary furnishes the pillows, sheets, quilts, blankets, curtains—all those things that lie in the province of womanhood. Nothing can be nobler than to be a mother to motherless boys. Nothing sweeter than to furnish his home. The auxiliary meets on the last Monday of each month at the hospice. It welcomes quests and desires nothing more than to win more ladies to aid in their labor of love.[26]

The organization believed that the heterosocial context of the family prepared men to be good citizens. Innovating on the settlement-house movement's tradition of providing family-like services to young people in need, the Wartburg deployed a heterosocial model of reform rather than a homosocial one. The Wartburg wanted to reproduce the nuclear family for its residents, while the settlement-house movement was designed to train women through interaction with other women.

If we were to assume that the heterosexual norms of the nuclear family were the primary basis for a morally chaste and productive society, we would expect that the Wartburg would have been wildly successful. Yet success was something the Wartburg saw little of. The institution could not raise the private capital it needed for operations and repayment of the debt incurred in acquiring startup capital. Every year it tried and failed to acquire funds from the United Way, the city of Minneapolis, and the state of Minnesota.[27] It hobbled along on the limited funds it was able to raise until it was forced to close its doors because of financial insolvency. While civic leaders and activists in feminist and other reform movements reiterated the need to clean up vice and eradicate Minneapolis's moral crisis, the nuclear family model of social services offered by the Wartburg appears to have gotten little traction. Officials agreed that employment and labor were solutions to the crime and vice problem, but they did not necessarily see the nuclear family as a basis for providing diligent and industrious workers. Funding denials from the state and private organizations claimed that the Wartburg did not provide a service that differed in any substantive way from the shelters Minneapolis already ran. The Wartburg frequently responded that it was the only home for boys able to offer a nuclear family environment. Authorities dismissed this answer, insisting that hard work—rather than nuclear family relations—was most important to building good character in young men. Young men transitioned from "tramps" to "citizens" when they moved from idleness to laboring.[28]

The management of sexual and gendered lives at the turn of the century exemplifies that productivity often trumped nascent constructions of the nuclear heterosexual family as the prescribed foundation of modern society. The prevalence of elite efforts to intervene in alcohol consumption, gambling, and prostitution via the chastening power of labor, the relatively unremarkable coverage of homosexuality at the center of Minnesota's final execution, and veneration of all-women's space in settlement houses and other Progressive Era reform movements expose the presumed curative power of homosocial relations in the early-twentieth-century Twin Cities. Because male homosociality was so closely tied to productivity and single male relations with women to alcoholism and decline, moral reformers largely failed to vilify same-sex connections between men or women. In the process, spaces opened for gender transgression and homosexual desire to abound with relatively little public notice or outcry.

Snapshot 2: The Politics of Sexuality and Visibility at Midcentury, 1945–1975

> We were really a part of American history in that I was born in St. Paul proper. We lived over near my grandmother's house, actually. And she had eight children. My mother was the oldest of those. We were a part of that family so I grew up as a young child within a really large, extended Irish Catholic family. And then in 1953, my mom and dad moved us to Richfield, which was just being built then. We had a brand-new house. That suburb was just brand-new. The end of Richfield was 78th Street, which really was a demarcation between civilized land and undeveloped farmland. And 78th Street is now 494. Now, I used to ride my bike out to there, and everything ended. It was just fields and dirt roads after that. So, we were all a part of that movement to the suburbs and that whole change in the fifties of everybody's lifestyle. We then separated from my grandmother's house and became this little nuclear family. So my younger siblings who were born in the late fifties were raised in a very different environment than I was. I recognize that as a loss, that loss of that extended family. I see that going forward, that we are ever more isolated.

This quote from Judy (January 13, 2004) tracks a major physical and ideological movement in sexual, gender, and family formations of the Twin Cities and the United States in the mid-twentieth century. Judy's narration demonstrates the real-life impacts of that period's social and economic policies, particularly in relation to newly vigorous state support for an idealized nuclear family. As Judy reflects on the changes in her life and family, we are reminded that the norms emerging at midcentury were not organic and timeless but entangled with a vast movement of ideas, people, and resources aimed at reorganizing society. Hardly a mere reflection of "the way things were" in an innocent 1950s America, the nuclear family was a consequence of the concerted actions of elected officials, corporate leaders, the police and military, and the scientific and academic communities. These people and institutions focused public policy on the family and its constitutive elements—marriage, monogamy, domesticity, racial segregation, single-family home ownership, and automobile transportation. This construction of normative heterosexuality not only prescribed where, how, and which people should be having sex and reproducing, but also identified and defined those who failed or refused to comply with these norms: the prostitute, the single woman, the homosexual, and the gender nonconformist.

While notions of progress, productivity, and the need to "tame the frontier" frequently challenged ideals of monogamy and domesticity in the early twentieth century, postwar reinvestment in family raised the stakes of punishment for those transgressing the newly fomented norms and of the rewards for subscribing to them. It would be inaccurate to say that the nuclear family was an entirely new institution, or that deviations from the nuclear ideal were widely accepted in the period before World War II. Government and corporate demands for compliance with nuclear family ideals are well documented prior to the 1940s. Indeed, "welfare capitalism," the dominant approach to labor-management relations between 1900 and 1920, positioned the family as the site where a person learned to be a productive and responsible worker. But as evidence from the turn of century suggests, the needs of labor often trumped the ideas of the family when family stood in the way of the types of labor required.[29] What was new about state intervention after 1930 was the increased power of the government to act. In response to major social and political crises, including the massive global Great Depression, Western governments more thoroughly and aggressively regulated big business, labor, health and welfare, and the built environment. In the United States, as elsewhere in the West, the nuclear family served as a primary technology to accomplish such regulation. As historian Margot Canaday has shown, the postwar era saw the development of a "straight state," which created a range of policies and regulations that richly rewarded heterosexual familial formations at the same time that it defined the homosexual as unworthy of full citizenship.[30] This process certainly played out in the Twin Cities. With low-interest loans for brand-new houses in pristine Bloomington, Richfield, and Brooklyn Park, with lavish shopping malls like "the Dales," and with expansive grocery stores like Byerly's and Applebaum's, Twin Citians complying with the suburban, nuclear family paradigm were richly rewarded. At the same time, pathologizing research by doctors and psychologists, "blue discharges" from the armed services, and increasing police harassment on the streets of St. Paul and Minneapolis generated new intimidation for those deviating from the nuclear family.

This section analyzes archival sources and oral histories to trace the multiple ways that nonnormative sexual and gender expression became "visible" in the postwar Twin Cities—both through the stigmatizing and often repressive attention of state institutions and the dominant culture, and via attempts to claim rights, political power, and access to public space by Twin Citians challenging society's demand for heterosexuality. We analyze the U.S. Army's efforts to examine and organize soldiers' sex lives, and the corresponding suspicions cast on local working-class women living outside the nuclear family. We explore queer memories of suburbanization, reflecting on narratives of blatant discrimination and isolation, but also on the encounters and alliances these people formed. The essay closes with the rise of a wave of sexuality- and gender-based repression on the streets of inner-city St. Paul and Minneapolis in the 1970s. As trans and gay Twin Citians built publicly identifiable relationships, households, businesses, bars, and political movements, antagonisms intensified between these groups and a dominant culture assuming that the heterosexual nuclear family was the necessary foundation of a stable and prosperous society. While such tension spawned widespread harassment and physical violence against queer people, it also inspired the vigorous new activist movements flourishing by 1980.

SEXUAL MANEUVERS IN THE ARMY CAMPS

Mid-twentieth-century sexual repression often involved direct intervention by state agencies in sexual matters. Government institutions—including police forces and the military—embarked on new efforts to discover, define, and repress young men's and women's sex lives in the New Deal and World War II era. These interventions frequently targeted specific populations outside the nuclear family. For example, in the summer of 1940, Minnesota hosted an estimated forty thousand troops on training maneuvers at the U.S. Army's Camp Ripley, located north of the Twin Cities in between the cities of St. Cloud and Brainerd. Anticipating the influx of young men, state and local authorities in alliance with the American Social Hygiene Association (ASHA) devised a comprehensive program to prevent syphilis and gonorrhea. Although the control of syphilis and gonorrhea was fundamentally a medical intervention—treatment with Salversan and

Men posing with artillery during military maneuvers at Camp Ripley in 1940. Courtesy of the Minnesota Historical Society.

penicillin, prophylaxis, and condoms—it also generated symbols around proper and improper sexuality and underscored the nuclear family as the primary organizing principle of society. It is a moment where we can see the ways that "medicine is not just affected by social, economic, and political variables—it is embedded in them."[31] Controlling the spread of a sexually transmitted infection also involved attempts to control the way people had sex and understood their own sexual and gender identities.

This regulation of sexuality is evident in the range of preventive measures undertaken by the ASHA and the military at Camp Ripley. In addition to the normal public health infrastructure—treatment, exams, and prophylaxis—the state also worked to manage the sexual activity that might occur during the maneuvers. Officials hired four undercover agents to assist in the apprehension of prostitutes.[32] They surveyed "all resorts, cabin camps, et cetera" and obtained "the names and addresses of all female employees" in the area to "prevent the influx of ringers."[33] Additionally, the registers of all hotels, cabin camps, and resorts were "carefully checked to determine the type of patronage the licensee was catering to and to determine whether or not these rooms were available for

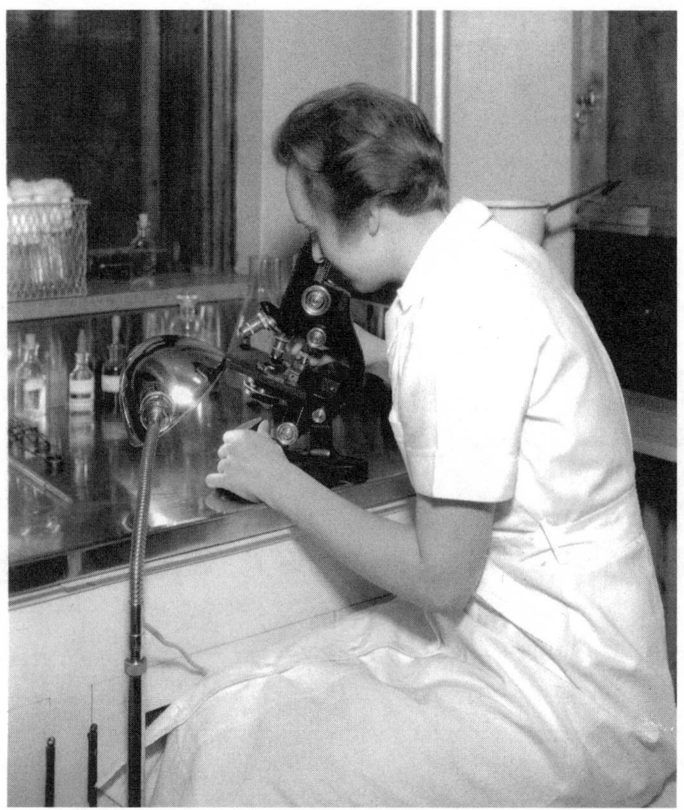

Lab technician performing syphilis diagnostic in 1940 at a Minneapolis clinic. Courtesy of the Minnesota Historical Society.

rental more than once each night." Officials interviewed all soldiers who tested positive for syphilis in order to ascertain the source of infection.

The program placed a special burden on women who worked nearby, condemning labor outside of the home as potentially deviant. Whether a hotel front-desk clerk, a waitress, or a domestic worker, labor performed by women outside the heterosexual nuclear family was often conflated with prostitution, and thus held the potential to perpetuate physical disease, social disorder, and even aid to Axis forces.[34]

The surveillance of women workers exposes the degree to which the control of information had become critically important to regulating and repressing sexuality by the mid-twentieth century. The ability to know and quantify individuals' sexual intimacies allowed the state to both identify and control modes of sexual pleasure. Such information facilitated the increasingly visible campaign by the state to fashion proper sexual subjects in the immediate postwar era. For example, the U.S. Armed Forces' ability to discover and catalog the "truth" of soldiers' sex lives became the basis for the "blue discharges," ferreting "homosexuals" from the military, which augmented both an anticommunist agenda demonizing queers and the institutionalization of the heterosexual nuclear family by excluding soldiers acting on same-sex desire from veterans' benefits for housing, education, and welfare.[35]

SUBURBANIZATION AND THE RACE AND GENDER POLITICS OF FAMILY IN THE MID-TWENTIETH-CENTURY TWIN CITIES

Given the increased state regulation and policing of sexuality in the mid-twentieth century and during the height of the Cold War, one might assume that repression, silence, and invisibility predominated in the Twin Cities. In part, this was the case. Chris recalls the ominous sexual silences from a Twin Cities childhood during the period:

> I remember when this woman from our church came to visit. She would always visit by herself, and I asked mom where her husband was. And my mom would just look at me "like that." And I would bring it up again. My mom finally just sort of mouthed to me (whispering) "She's divorced!" I mean it was like she couldn't even say the word *divorce* out loud. Being divorced was a shameful thing. So being queer didn't come up at all. That was completely taboo.[36]

Lynda offers a similarly repressive narrative when describing sexuality in Abbotswood, Wisconsin, the town her parents called home:

> It was a heck of a lot scarier at that time. I mean, now everybody knows someone who's gay, or most everyone. And it's not a big issue. But at that time I can't think of anyone I could have talked to about it.[37]

While virtually all Twin Citians who were later active in openly queer or GLBT circles note dramatic changes in public sexual cultures during and after the 1960s, many also remind us that sexual possibilities outside the heterosexual nuclear family were many during the mid-twentieth century. Recalling his youth and adolescence in the Minneapolis northern suburb of Columbia Heights in the 1960s, Gary recalls that "homosexuality was absolutely invisible unless you really, really looked for it."[38] Gary's comments reveal a fascinating paradox of Cold War sexuality in the Twin Cities: a queerness that was both visible and invisible.

State efforts to bolster the heterosexual nuclear family and render sexual transgressions invisible during the period were certainly significant. Nowhere were these processes more visible than in the construction of the suburbs of the Twin Cities. The population of the central cities of Minneapolis and St. Paul peaked in the 1950 census, with federal programs aimed at returning veterans beginning to depopulate the city despite robust economic growth in the region. Homeward-bound GIs were granted significant federal assistance for higher education and job training, as well as government-guaranteed low-interest home mortgages via the newly formed Federal Housing Administration (FHA). FHA loans allowed a multiplicity of young couples to build both their net worth and commitment to the nuclear family in developments springing out of the prairie grass on the outskirts of the city, including Richfield and Edina to the Twin Cities' southwest, Maplewood and Woodbury on the east, and Brooklyn Park and Columbia Heights on the northwest.

Although suburbanization offered a wealth of opportunities to some Twin Citians, race, gender, sexuality, and class were systematically mobilized to deny access to pristine new landscapes. Racist lending practices by private banks and the federal government and racially restrictive building legislation ensured that the mushrooming suburbs were restricted to whites only. The legal denial of FHA loans to people of color formally excluded them from suburban home ownership—the most lucrative financial tool of the twentieth century—thereby initiating a mass upstreaming of financial and political resources into the hands of middle-class whites.[39] In addition, the mandate to build the interstate highway system perpetuated confiscation by eminent domain of the lowest-value urban land, which in the Twin Cities meant the dynamiting of the long-standing Rondo Neighborhood, the African American business district in St. Paul. The destruction of Rondo and parts of the Phillips neighborhood in Minneapolis meant the collapse of family businesses owned by people of color, interrupting opportunities for generational wealth.

To bolster efforts to racially reengineer the landscape, suburbanization made the heterosexual nuclear family the primary ordering institution

The location is not specified for this photograph taken in the Twin Cities in 1968, and it remains unidentifiable given the thousands of houses and streets with similar appearances throughout the inner-ring suburbs. Photograph by Norton & Peel; courtesy of the Minnesota Historical Society.

of society. Private builders developed lines of modest-sized, single-family homes for sale at reasonable prices to white families with FHA backing. Retail infrastructure was kept separate from residential space, requiring a car for access. Daily activities were therefore spent in private space, either inside the home, the yard, the car, or the shopping center, a significant departure from the multiplicity of social and sexual interactions of early-twentieth-century urban social formations. These domestic economies were sustained by salaries and benefits provided to largely white male workforces in both the union and management sectors of the burgeoning manufacturing economy. Heterosexual marriage became compulsory for many white middle-class women needing access to housing, health, and retirement benefits and consumer economies otherwise denied them in a sexist economy.

Despite the state's insistence on heterosexuality, domesticity, and appropriate masculinity and femininity, both the pristine and private built environment, and the deafening silences around sexuality, opened new spaces for queer connections. Respondent Lynda recalls bringing lovers from her years at the University of Wisconsin-River Falls, just east of the Twin Cities suburbs, on summer visits to her parents' house:

> I mean my mother understood my connection with Krista and she didn't discourage it at all. And even with my friend from college who I brought home a number of times, she never freaked out about it. Maybe she even knew something was going on. I don't know . . .[40]

Lynda recalls a moment when she at once was repressed into silence, unable to discuss intimate relationship with her mother, but also offered a domestic space inside her parents' home where queer friendship and romance could flourish. Silence opened a space for sexual connections, making queerness "invisible unless you looked for it."

Other queer Twin Citians explicitly distanced themselves from repressive narratives about the urban spaces and family formations of the mid-twentieth century. Ted was a mixed-race queer adolescent in a Jewish section of inner city North Minneapolis in the 1950s. While the construction of the suburbs and interstate highway system fostered both racial segregation and the nuclear family, Ted recalls multiple ways that his social world as a youth resisted this discipline:

> At the time there were the "homosexuals" and all I knew was they were supposed to be bad. But I had a few friends who were like I was—boys who were effeminate, and hung around the girls a lot. We were a mixed-race group of girls and boys that were all friends. I had a lover that was kind of a secret in junior high. We would sneak around. I met him swimming because the boys would swim naked back in those days. And it seemed like we liked each other's bodies and we started fooling around. I was excited . . . it was good feelings when we were around each other even though we weren't allowed to be open about it.[41]

Ted explicitly refuses to connect his departure from dominant norms of the time—being a mixed-race African American and American Indian feminine boy with a Jewish lover in a largely white Protestant city in the 1950s—to a narrative of repression. While he notes that public embrace of gay identity would have been unthinkable during his childhood, Ted repeatedly interrupts assumptions that these silences were inherently oppressive. "I didn't really struggle with the situation. I accepted what I was. It was just the way I was made and I never tried to change how I was made." Ted further rejects a narrative of trauma around his mother's move to suburban Coon Rapids, a largely segregated bedroom community of Minneapolis, after the death of his father in the late 1960s. "It wasn't a big transition," he argued, placing Coon Rapids in a continual process of movement in his life—between his father's African American and American Indian roots on the shores of Lake Mille Lacs, his white mother's family farm in northern Minnesota, and his home in the Twin Cities. "The move just felt like going back and forth to the farm." On both urban and suburban landscapes, Ted was able to produce a queer social world by forging sexual connections that were "invisible unless you looked for them."

Ted's personal life on the suburban landscape became even more significant as he transitioned to adulthood, and as gay identity became more visible both in national politics and for Ted personally. In 1972, twenty-nine-year-old Ted adopted a two-week-old baby girl. Although this was his first child, parenting was nothing new to Ted as he had helped his mother raise many of her twenty-one foster children. Yet his becoming an adoptive parent as a single gay man of color in Anoka County, a northwest suburban enclave that had long dissented from the social-welfare consensus of the Democratic-Farmer-Labor Party (DFL) and had been among the most conservative in the state, was unprecedented. The adoption occurred two decades before adoption rights became central to mainstream gay politics, and occurred with strikingly little fanfare:

> I just filled out the paperwork and was interviewed by the social workers to start the process. During the investigation process there was some homophobic opposition from some of my family in California. In the court they came in with all the gay stereotypes—about how we're not good parents. But the court overruled it and said I was a fit parent.

Ted's domestic life dramatically departed from nuclear family norms: he raised his child as a single parent with help from his mother while he worked. While public policy reshaped the Twin Cities around white suburban heterosexual domestic life, Ted's story illustrates that this political and economic project also produced social lives that exceeded and rejected these norms.

The lives and experiences of Ted, Gary, and Lynda exemplify the new forms of difference produced by the ascendance of the nuclear family paradigm. Some people could gain access to the privileges of suburban domesticity as long as they kept silent or "made it invisible unless you looked for it." For others, like Ted, who could not evade the markers of his nonnormativity and were categorically denied any opportunity to be "invisible unless you look for it," the inaccessibility of the nuclear family mandate offered the impetus to build a life outside white, middle-class, heterosexual domesticity.

"ANOTHER GAY MURDER!" LONG, HOT SUMMERS OF VIOLENCE IN THE TWIN CITIES

While Ted took full advantage of queer visibilities emerging on the suburban landscape of the 1960s, new challenges faced those claiming these newly prevalent identities. While many Oral History Project narrators struggled with and flourished amid suburban life, a new wave of repression faced gay and trans people on the streets of Minneapolis and St. Paul's central neighborhoods in the early 1970s. Although individual actors perpetuated most of the violence, the state's indifference to the outbreak—and in some cases the active participation of police and elected officials in it—tacitly endorsed the wave of repression and allowed it to intensify. By 1980, when four dozen gay and trans people had been murdered during the preceding decade, it appeared that to deviate from nuclear family norms—whether as a gender-nonconforming person, a poor or homeless person, or a person of color—could cost a person his or her life.

This unprecendented wave of brutality began in the late 1970s. On the evening of June 5, 1979, for example, Terry Knudsen, a white gay man who was the maitre d' of the Minneapolis Athletic Club restaurant, was walking through Loring Park at 1:15 a.m. after a postwork cocktail with friends. Knudsen was approached by two men and brutally beaten. By 7 a.m. the next morning, Knudsen was in Hennepin County Medical Center, missing his right eye, with his brain crushed against the left side of his skull. The beating was the sixth attack in a single week on a gay or trans person in Loring Park. That same week, bouncers at the Gay 90's and Saloon gay bars reported the nightly presence of a group of at least fifteen juveniles terrorizing the patrons of these establishments. The bouncers alleged that firefighters using the parking lot of the Gay 90's as a staging area looked on in amusement, yelling antigay slurs at bar patrons rather than intervening in the crimes.[42]

After a week of brutal attacks and police indifference Terry Knudsen died of his injuries on June 14, 1979. That same morning, the body of thirty-one-year-old white gay man Les Benscotter was found in his St. Paul apartment naked and strangled. Benscotter had left University Avenue's Townhouse Bar late the night before and hitchhiked home. The words "FAGS WILL DIE" were scrawled in toothpaste on a bookcase next to Benscotter's beaten and maimed body.[43] In the six years following Knudsen's attack, physical and political violence aimed at those outside white, suburban, middle-class, heterosexual domesticity would leave more than forty dead in Minneapolis, St. Paul, and the suburbs.[44]

With more than forty people dead, police were more likely to arrest the targets of this violence than the perpetrators. While murders went unsolved, more than five thousand individuals were arrested in the half-decade following the Knudsen killing, primarily via entrapping patrons and sex workers in adult bookstores and theaters, bathhouses, and public parks. Repression by police and public officials was particularly evident in a raid on downtown Minneapolis's Big Daddy's bathhouse just three weeks after the Knudsen and Benscotter killings, on June 28, 1979. At 4 a.m., John Locke, the head of the vice squad and later Minneapolis police chief, stormed the bathhouse with Deputy Mayor Erv Dauphin. Witnesses accused the officials of being "rude, offensive, and drunk." Although Dauphin never admitted to being present on the raid, many of the arrested patrons testified to his presence in public condemnations of the event. The highly unusual inclusion of a civilian elected official in a 4 a.m. raid on a public sexual space led many to believe these public servants acted during their own evening of drinking in downtown bars. Locke had vowed in a press conference the very evening before to "clean up" the city. Those arrested at Big Daddy's argued that the drunken bust seemed to be his first, though strikingly unsuccessful, effort toward implementing this initiative.[45] When confronted about procedures deployed in the bust, and about the fact that no prostitution was found inside, Locke snapped, "I didn't catch anybody in the act, but I know that place is a whorehouse for men."[46]

Locke's statements illustrate police and public officials' tendency to blame gay and trans people, sex workers, and people of color for the violence committed against them. Just two months before Les Benscotter's

Publisher: Bruce S. Brockway
Editors: Bruce S. Brockway
Alan Stombaugh

Associate Editor
Thom Higgins

Volume 1, Number 4 August 1, 1979

EXTRA!

Deputy Mayor Raids Gay Bath

Likes to Play Cop

By Bruce Brockway and Thom Higgins

Amid widespread dissatisfaction in the Gay community with both the office of Minneapolis mayor Al Hofstede and the Minneapolis Police Department, evidence was uncovered Tuesday intimately linking Hofstede's top aide, Erv Dauphin, with the recent police raid on a gay-serving Minneapolis steambath.

There had been early speculation soon after the 4 A.M. raid at Big Daddy's Steambath, 3 N. 7th Street last June 28 that standard police procedures had been suspended for the event. Witnesses to the raid had reported that three men identifying themselves as police officers had forcibly entered the bath, conducted themselves in a "rude, offensive, and drunken" manner, and evicted patrons they found on the premises. Yet Minneapolis Police Vice Squad head Sergeant John Locke, interviewed the next day by Frank Allen of the Minneapolis Star, claimed that only two officers had been involved in the roust, and admitted he had led the "inspection".

An interdepartmental affair

Early this week, *Positively Gay* uncovered evidence that the third "officer" had actually been a high-level official from the Mayor's office, and Monday several witnesses to the raid positively identified a photo of Deputy Mayor Erv Dauphin as that of the previously unidentified third "officer".

Tuesday, Dauphin refused to affirm or deny the allegations but defended the raid on the grounds that it had been a fire inspection. (A routine inspection had been made eighteen days prior to the raid by the Minneapolis Fire Inspection Department.) And Dauphin praised the new Vice Squad head: "(John) Locke and I have been friends for fifteen years. When that place (Big Daddy's) was a gym, we both used to work out there. Box, I mean."

Locke refused to comment on Dauphin's part in the Big Daddy's incident.

Mayor confirms involvement

Late Wednesday afternoon, Mayor Hofstede admitted to *Positively Gay*'s Bruce Brockway that his top aide had participated in the Big Daddy's shake-out, but did not state whether that action was "on the job". "Erv did say he went along on that raid", the Mayor confessed. In answer to witnesses charges that Dauphin was "obviously intoxicated", the Mayor replied: "Erv doesn't drink, so he couldn't have been drunk. He hasn't been drinking since about a month before that raid. Erv understands that he does strange things when he drinks, so he doesn't drink anymore."

Deputy Mayor Erv Dauphin

Since previously the incident had been thought to involve only members of the Minneapolis Police Department, the investigation of complaints filed by Big Daddy's patrons had been left in the hands of the Police Internal Affairs Unit. As Dauphin is a civilian, it is possible that his involvement will bring the Minneapolis City Attorney's office into the investigative process. Impersonating an officer is a misdemeanor under Minnesota Statutes.

Hofstede has been increasingly unpopular of late in the Gay community, largely because of what many see as his inability to control his police and his refusal to face the Gay community in a public forum. The situation was aggravated last weekend, when Hofstede bowed out of appearing at the "No More Assaults" Conference at Government Center in response to the recent killing of a Gay man, Terry Knudsen. The Police Department is also out of favor with Gays now in the light of the Knudsen murder and the inability of the police to close the case.

Whorehouse or firetrap?

Vice's Locke added to the growing discontent with his department on June 29th, when he told the Minneapolis Star: "I didn't catch anybody in the act this time, but as far as I'm concerned, that place (Big Daddy's) is a whorehouse for men . . . we will go back and lock the place up." And "I don't have to have a warrant. I can go in anywhere and inspect anything anytime I want." His inspection authority was based, Locke said, on Big Daddy's being a "licensed establishment".

Bath owner William Batson confirmed last week that Big Daddy's is not and never has been a license holder. The business was inspected in February, 1977, by the Minneapolis Building Inspector and given a use permit. But the city has no ordinance authority to license steambaths, and no steambath in Minneapolis is licensed.

Gary Grefenberg, Co-Chair of the Minnesota Committee for Gay Rights, first heard rumors of Dauphin's involvement about ten days ago but opposed *Positively Gay*'s publishing the charges, saying "We wanted to use that information on Erv to force the Mayor to make some positive public statements." Asked why ten days hadn't sufficed to bring Hofstede to that position, Grefenberg replied, "But the Mayor doesn't even know we know yet."

Small potatoes

Others in the Gay community wondered why relatively small Big Daddy's had been the target of the raid instead of Minneapolis' largest bath, the Locker Room Health Club. At the last meeting of the Minneapolis Civil Rights Commission, Kevin Mossier questioned Police Chief Elmer Nordlund on the matter, describing the Locker Room as "a supermarket of sin compared to Big Daddy's". But perhaps a Gay Male member of that audience had the best answer: "There'd be a riot if they raided that place . . . and you know it."

Positively Gay, *the Twin Cities primary gay and lesbian community newspaper in 1979, ran a special "extra edition" of the monthly paper in August dedicated to Big Daddy's raid. Deputy Mayor Erv Dauphin graced the cover as the centerpiece of a story by well-known local activists Bruce Brockway and Thom Higgins. Bruce Brockway and Thom Higgins, "Deputy Mayor Raids Gay Bath,"* Positively Gay *1, no. 4, August 1, 1979, 1. Courtesy of the Jean-Nickolaus Tretter Collection, University of Minnesota Libraries.*

death, Robert Allan Taylor was murdered in a St. Paul apartment in a similarly violent situation. On February 24, 1980, eighteen-year-old David Houle was acquitted of Taylor's murder, despite the fact that the jury acknowledged that Houle had accompanied Taylor to his apartment and beaten Taylor to death. The jury ruled that the killer's actions were in self-defense, a part of thwarting "unwanted sexual advances." Refusing a person's sexual advances by killing him thus became a legally acceptable solution to a proposed sexual exchange.[47]

In response to a climate of indifference from state institutions, activists from across the Twin Cities mobilized to interrupt the violence and identify the ways that gender, race, and poverty perpetuated it. On December 20, 1986, for example, American Indian leaders held a protest march through the largely Indian Phillips neighborhood to confront a wave of brutal, unsolved murders, including one that claimed the life of Phyllis Olson, who had been active on the gay bar scene since the early 1970s. A subsequent political summit and conference was coordinated by veteran American Indian Movement activist Bill Means as well as American Indian lesbian and longtime police accountability activist Janice Command. Activists eulogized American Indian murder victims, providing details on a wealth of unsolved cases. Nine of forty-eight murder victims in Minneapolis in 1986 were American Indian, ten times the proportion of Indians in the population. In addition, 31 percent of the city's ongoing unsolved murders had indigenous victims. Many of the murders involved the extreme violence that queer activists were also confronting, such as the murder of Phillips neighborhood resident Mary Rose Villebrun, who was thrown from a moving pickup truck onto a Twin Cities freeway by her white attacker.[48]

Soft-peddling the racial inequities of policing and punishment, Minneapolis Police Chief Anthony Bouza responded to the Phillips march by claiming that as indigenous populations grappled with chemical dependency and poverty, their lifestyle made them more likely to be the victims and perpetrators of crimes. Police Captain Jack McCarthy was even more specific, arguing that pervasive alcohol abuse caused the extreme levels of violence facing American Indians in Minneapolis.[49] Public officials argued that alleged social pathologies—drinking excessively or using drugs, going to bars, engaging in sex work, going home with strangers—ultimately caused anti-Indian violence. Within the logic of such a framework, the killing of a person like Phyllis Olson—who lacked a permanent address, who may have been a sex worker, who was American Indian, and who frequented gay establishments—was regarded as a natural consequence of her lifestyle.[50] Such arguments not only served to blame Olson for her own demise, but also to imply that those living outside the norms of straight, white, suburban, middle-class domesticity were undeserving of police time and attention.

Legal and law-enforcement response to headline-making murders of the late 1970s and early 1980s corroborates activists' assertions that the state naturalized, trivialized, and dismissed violence against queers, the poor and homeless, and people of color. Minneapolis police refused to label Mary Louise Villebrun's death a murder, instead rendering it an alcohol-related "accident," even though they determined that she had been sexually assaulted before she was thrown from a moving vehicle and killed. The situation was similar across the river in St. Paul, where the police department declined to automatically investigate Les Benscotter's death as a murder despite the scrawling of "FAGS WILL DIE" above his severely beaten body. "Unless toxicology reports indicate foul play, we don't have a murder," noted St. Paul Police Captain Gerald Kissling. He later noted at the same press conference, "It's getting so that if a homosexual, Negro, or Chicano gets killed, you hear all this stuff about the cops not doing their jobs. When a WASP gets killed, nobody says anything. I'm getting pretty damn sick of all these pressure groups." Although Kissling was forced to retract this statement, no one challenged his subsequent remark that the Benscotter case was "on the back burner." Nor did the press clarify that unlike the situation facing Villebrun, Benscotter, and others, there were no unsolved, unprosecuted murder cases against WASPs at the time he made his statement.[51] Activists, on the other hand, were well aware of the "back burner" nature of these cases. Jon Moore, the owner of the Saloon, a prominent downtown Minneapolis gay bar, publicly noted that no police detective had ever approached the bar as a part of any murder investigation, even though it was widely known that many of the victims and perpetrators were among the bar's regulars.[52]

Benscotter's and Villebrun's killings expose the high price that some people were forced to pay for deviating from mid-twentieth-century suburban nuclear family norms. As these pages show, the terms and corresponding costs of such deviation have varied dramatically across time and space, whether enforced upon single working women, people with homosexual affinities in the suburbs, patrons of gay bars and bathhouses, or those racially and economically marked as poor, of color, or queer on the

Positively Gay *ran this cartoon as the centerpiece of the July 1979 cover story that charged police and public officials with a tepid and dismissive response to the murder of Les Benscotter. Bruce Brockway, "Meeting/March/Vigil Draws 1200,"* Positively Gay *1, no. 3, July 1, 1979, 1. Courtesy of the Jean-Nickolaus Tretter Collection, University of Minnesota Libraries.*

streets of Minneapolis. But as the police, policy makers, doctors, mortgage brokers, and real-estate developers worked to make these differences hypervisible and economically salient, these groups claimed such visibility as a basis for new political movements. Indeed, such differences were foundational to the feminist, antiracist, and queer activism that reshaped the Twin Cities and beyond after 1960.

Snapshot 3: Out of the Streets and into the Bedrooms, 1980–2000

On the afternoon of June 30, 1986, an angry crowd of nearly five hundred protesters gathered outside the Federal Building on South 4th Street in downtown Minneapolis. Earlier that day, the U.S. Supreme Court upheld the Georgia "sodomy laws" in its decision in the case *Bowers v.*

Hardwick, allowing dozens of states to continue to criminalize oral or anal sex between consenting adults in private space. Activists insisted that the *Bowers* ruling was yet another attack on a population already reeling from a string of three dozen aggravated murders of gay and gender-nonconforming people in the Twin Cities area, and from the inept and dismissive government response to the AIDS pandemic that had reached crisis proportions locally.[53] Although *Bowers* clearly censured the increasingly organized gay rights movement of the mid-1980s, its immediate consequences were ambiguous. After all, not a single person had been charged or convicted of violating the Minnesota sodomy law during the widely reported police crackdown on queer Twin Citians between 1979 and 1985, even though five thousand people had been arrested.[54] During that period of repression, law enforcement focused its attention on sexual acts occurring in public, accusing people of offenses like indecent exposure, soliciting prostitution, and lewd and lascivious behavior. The state largely ignored sex acts taking place in the confines of private homes, and never turned to the sodomy statute as a means to regulate sexual culture and behavior. Nevertheless, gay leaders understood that the Supreme Court's reaffirmation of the inherent criminality of homosexual sex acts could derail efforts for the equality of the gay and lesbian community under the law. If political opponents could claim that sex crimes are the foundation of gay and lesbian identity, then the municipal equal rights ordinances, housing and employment discrimination protections, and domestic partner benefits programs the lesbian and gay movement had begun to win would all be jeopardized.

Prominent Twin Cities activists scrambled to craft a new agenda in the wake of the Court's ruling, focusing efforts on rebuffing *Bowers'* intrusion into gays' and lesbians' private sexual lives. During the 1987 session of the Minnesota Legislature, Karen Clark and Allan Spear, Minnesota's first and only openly lesbian and gay officials elected to state government offices, introduced the "public sexual conduct law." The bill was a horse trade, performing two political tasks. First, it struck down Minnesota's sodomy law, legalizing all sex that was consensual, between adults, and occurring in private space. Second, it created a new misdemeanor for a crime called "public sex," giving police new powers to seek out and arrest anyone having sex in a car, alleyway, park, open lot, or other public venue.[55] The political compromise sought to engage and accommodate growing public controversy over sexual transgressions in the city, creating new penalties for

Putting the spotlight on "public sexual conduct," the Star Tribune, *Minneapolis's largest daily paper, ran a cover story on gay cruising in Loring Park on a Sunday in 1989. The feature included this dimly lit, film noir-esque depiction of "car cruising" along Spruce Place near Oak Grove Street. Brian Peterson,* Star Tribune, *September 29, 1989, 1A. Courtesy of the* Minneapolis Star Tribune.

those participating in public sexual cultures in exchange for legal protection for consenting adults having sex in private.

The following pages take up the sexual controversies of the 1980s that spawned both the *Bowers* decision and the proposed "public sexual conduct law," tracing how stories' ideas about sex helped distribute power and wealth to some people, and take them away from others. The 1980s were undeniably a daunting decade for queer people, especially for those who were poor, women, or people of color. Reduced enforcement of equal employment opportunity laws by the Reagan administration denied marginalized groups access to high-paying careers long restricted to elite white men. Deep cuts to social programs made it more difficult to access state-subsidized health coverage, housing, child care, and job training. And as public commitment to social welfare dwindled, the state's ability to effectively respond to the AIDS crisis evaporated. At the same time, homosexual and gender-nonconforming populations were ensnared in the ongoing backlash against the "sexual revolution" of the 1960s, with headline-making outcry over perverts, pedophiles, and prostitutes inflaming new repression of queers as sexual transgressors. Struggling for an effective response to a new round of sexual demonization in an age of economic austerity, leaders of the gay and lesbian rights movement worked to domesticate queer lives—attempting to frame their sexuality as inherently adult, monogamous, and private—to disentangle themselves from the specter of perverts, pedophiles, and prostitutes making headlines in the Twin Cities and across the nation. These pages explore the context and motivations for efforts to shift queer lives and politics out of the streets and into the bedrooms, a move that extended political and economic resources to gays and straights having monogamous sex in private, and stripped them away from people unwilling or unable to comply with the new mandate for domestication.

SEX PANIC I: RACE, PROSTITUTION, AND HIV

While the *Bowers* decision reaffirmed the government's right to referee sex in private space—allowing the state to burst into the bedroom to thumbs-up straight sex in the missionary position and to blow the whistle on anal and oral penetration—the bulk of what had become a relentless media din about sexuality in the Twin Cities in the mid-1980s revolved around intimate encounters in public. Just two months before *Bowers,* for example, local CBS affiliate WCCO ran the first prime-time television exposé on the AIDS pandemic in Minnesota. The feature's apparent purpose was to document local people's journeys through the crisis, but the bulk of the discussion revolved around the sensationalized—and later debunked—narrative of Fabian Bridges, someone who had never been a permanent resident of the Twin Cities. Bridges was a young African American gay man publicly accused of being a prostitute who knowingly spread AIDS in Ohio and Texas before he died. Playing up Bridges's pathologies and its own benevolence, WCCO noted that it had given Bridges cash to cover lodging and incidentals for the interview, and that he squandered the money at a gay bathhouse, one of Minneapolis's most vilified public sex venues.[56]

The exoticizing and demonizing sex and race politics of the WCCO piece were reproduced in the Twin Cities' most widely circulating daily newspaper in a series of cover stories on another sex worker during the same period. On April 2, the *Star Tribune* claimed that Minneapolis resident Ronda Williams was the first woman prostitute known to carry the HIV virus, accusing Williams of intentionally spreading AIDS by refusing to cease having sex for money, and by failing to inform her clients of her HIV status.[57] Presumably to protect an unsuspecting public from Williams's careless disregard for their safety, journalists published her home address, and convinced the Minneapolis Police Department to release Williams's mug-shot photograph. These shards of personal information revealed Williams to be an African American woman from the poorest census tracts of near-North Minneapolis, the neighborhood with the highest crime and poverty rates in the state. Boiling 1980s race- and class-based anxieties about gang-related violence, drug dealing, welfare dependency, matriarchal families, and prostitution in African American urban spaces fueled hyperbolic accounts of Williams's personal, sexual, and working life. "When an AIDS carrier becomes a public menace," barked the headline of one *Star Tribune* story condemning Williams as an "immediate, imminent, and present danger to the public health, " and quoting a Hennepin County prosecutor who compared Williams to "someone down the street carrying a bomb."[58]

While racist stereotypes about the violence and sexual excesses of African American life produced dehumanizing portrayals of both Bridges and Williams, their stories were particularly threatening to white and middle-class publics because prostitution was a space where AIDS could cross boundaries between poor and elite people, between people of color and whites, and between public sexual encounters and private nuclear families. A March 1986 *Star Tribune* cover story on Stan Borman, a white gay male sex worker for the escort service Minneapolis Men, explicitly stoked these fears. Borman had come forward to WCCO television news immediately after the Bridges documentary aired, claiming he had sex with more than a thousand clients while knowing he was infected with HIV, and that four of his coworkers had already died from AIDS. During the *Star Tribune* interview, Borman admitted that many of his partners were bisexual men with wives and children. Secret trysts between Borman and anonymous husbands meant that white, middle-class suburban Twin Cities families would no longer be exempt from the AIDS pandemic once assumed to be safely contained within gay male, prostitute, drug addict, and immigrant populations.[59]

SEX PANIC II: THE "JORDAN SEX RING"

The racialized specter of the HIV-positive prostitute from the streets of Minneapolis intentionally spreading disease to the private spaces of the white suburbs was the latest in a string of perceived threats to the nuclear family after the social upheavals of the 1960s. The Twin Cities had long been a center of such anxieties, particularly in terms of presumed links between child endangerment and homosexuality. In 1977, conservative activist and citrus industry publicist Anita Bryant brought her "Save Our Children" campaign to St. Paul after that city passed a gay and lesbian civil rights ordinance. Although the Bryant uproar scared the public enough to repeal the ordinance, no one was able to positively connect the cultural shifts of the sexual revolution that Bryant assailed—whether those shifts involved homosexuality, polyamory, swinging single culture, or other departures from the containment of sexuality in the nuclear family—to actual child sexual abuse.

This all changed in the Twin Cities in the summer of 1984, when a trailer park nestled into the banks of the Minnesota River in the quiet suburban community of Jordan began to make international headlines. In the late fall of 1983, two young Jordan girls told authorities that they had been sexually abused by an adult male in their community.[60] The girls' story quickly caught the attention of Kathleen Morris, the accomplished thirty-seven-year-old Scott County Attorney who had made headlines a year earlier prosecuting the Cermak family sexual abuse case, where a grandfather was proven to have molested fifteen young relatives. Cermak prosecutors relied heavily on testimony from child victims, with Morris's innovative use of anatomically correct dolls to solicit child accounts of sex abuse becoming standard procedure in other cases after Morris's success.[61] Such interview techniques with the Jordan girls and others in the area revealed a grizzly pattern that media outlets quickly termed "the Jordan sex ring." Morris and other prosecutors believed that two "interlocking rings," each consisting of up to thirty-five adults, systematically coordinated the sexual exploitation and abuse of as many as sixty children. The rings allegedly hosted sex parties where children were abused, where satanic sexual rituals took place, and where sex was so violent that authorities feared young children had been murdered. Throughout early and mid-1984, three waves of arrests, beginning with low-income families in Jordan's trailer park and later branching out into suburban subdivisions, landed twenty-four Jordan parents in jail. Twenty-six children were placed in protective custody, with authorities diagnosing abuse severe enough to warrant moving children to foster homes far away from the Twin Cities suburbs, creating new names and identities for many of the children, and preventing any contact between children and their families in Jordan.[62]

Media outlets and government institutions scrambled to respond to the alleged Jordan sex ring, a response that seemed all the more urgent as the Jordan case unfolded at the same time as California's McMartin Preschool scandal, where school officials were alleged to have coordinated the systematic sexual assault of scores of children in day care in 1983. The Jordan sex ring investigation, for example, spawned a three-day conference in September 1986, where two hundred professionals from across the world gathered at Breezy Point Resort on the sandy shores of north central Minnesota's Pelican Lake to craft a strategy to manage what they saw as an explosive problem of child sexual abuse. Press coverage exhaustively reported their disturbing findings. A *Minneapolis Star Tribune* cover story from October 1986 began with the ominous line, "Child molesters are every parent's fear. They can be neighbors, cousins, uncles, pediatricians, school teachers, or fathers." The conference coverage publicized profiles of potential predators, providing extensive and often inflammatory and confusing statistics. One study, for example, found that most predators also exhibited a host of other deviant sexual tendencies, such as 20 percent of predators who raped adult women and 28 percent of predators who were exhibitionists. Another found that eight-year-olds were more arousing to predators than any other age group. Media coverage raised concerns that a range of seemingly innocent practices of daily life in Minnesota were in fact warnings of child molestation.[63] A pair of low-cut jeans, a tight halter top, or a revealing swimsuit could be the sign of an exhibitionist predator. A group of eight-year-olds playing tag or hide-and-seek at a local playground could silently arouse scores of local molesters. To help challenge this seemingly widespread problem, the state of Minnesota and the federal government upped their contribution to nearly $1 million per year to "Project Impact," a program that, according to the *Star Tribune,* "aimed to protect Minnesota's most precious resource: children."

SEX PANIC III: THE CHILDREN'S THEATER

Initial media coverage of the "Jordan sex ring" repeatedly noted the white working-class background of many of the accused, as well as their trailer park dwellings and employment as retail clerks, civil servants, and low-level law-enforcement staff, social locations that became an easy basis for ridicule and dismissal by elite Twin Citians in Minneapolis and the western suburbs. The safe separation of upscale Twin Cities spaces from the Jordan furor was quickly shattered in the summer of 1984, however, as a new child molestation scandal broke out in Minneapolis's stately Fair Oaks Park neighborhood at the world-renowned Children's Theater. That summer, a Bureau of Criminal Affairs probe and Hennepin County grand jury charged the founder of the Children's Theater and five other staff members with sexually abusing up to a dozen young male actors, and for failing to report that abuse. The organization's leader, widely heralded as an artistic genius who had helped to remake the Twin Cities theater scene in the 1970s, was alleged to have had inappropriately close relationships with many young protégés, hosting private house parties where liquor was widely distributed and having a string of sexual relationships with actors that ranged from forced fondling to long-term sexual intimacy. Overnight, the Children's Theater acting school—a crown jewel of Minnesota's longstanding social-democratic commitment to the arts and culture—became a house of ill repute in the public consciousness, feared to have linked recruitment and casting of teen actors to their willingness to be sexual with the executive director. Although the alleged victims were far different from those in Jordan—mostly fifteen- and sixteen-year-olds, whereas the alleged Jordan victims were mostly of preschool age—discourses of "sexual predator" and "child molester" pervaded coverage of both cases. Even the motif of a "sex ring" pervaded both scandals, with a Children's Theater board member publicly insisting that "there were concentric circles of people who were in complicity," linked together in a ring of denial that excused and obscured the rampant proliferation of child molestation at one of Minneapolis's most prestigious cultural institutions.[64]

When the Supreme Court handed down the *Bowers* decision in June 1986, coverage in Minnesota was nearly drowned out as the fallout from the Williams and Bridges AIDS prostitution scares, the Children's Theater scandal, and the "Jordan sex ring" were at the top of the nightly news. *Bowers* merely added another sexual category—sodomy—to a spectrum of vulgar consequences of the moral turpitude of the sexual revolution, from prostitution to sex parties to exhibitionism to intergenerational sex. Yet, by mid-1986, the investigation of the "Jordan sex ring" revealed something even more disturbing than the allegations. Although one resident of the

Valley Green mobile home park in Jordan pleaded guilty to sexual abuse charges and was eventually sentenced to forty-five years in jail, the first couple to stand trial in the Jordan case was found innocent by a jury. After the presentation of what proved to be extremely unreliable evidence by the prosecution, charges were subsequently dropped against all twenty-one remaining defendants, making the individual who initially confessed the only person ever convicted of having sexual relations with children in the Jordan case, and raising deep questions about how one abuse conviction could be turned into a story of "two interlocking rings" of up to seventy perpetrators of sex crimes against children. Twenty-two of the twenty-six children removed from Jordan families were returned after some children had been in foster care for more than three years, and after parents were cleared of all charges.[65]

EXPLAINING SEX PANICS WITH ANTIFEMINISM

By early 1986, in a stream of letters to the editor and television news interviews, Minnesotans began to demand an explanation for how Scott County prosecutors had become so carried away—how seemingly isolated events of sexual abuse had been turned into interlocking rings of satanic and murderous sex. Kathleen Morris, the Scott Country Attorney and driving force behind the investigation, quickly became persona non grata. Working to retract their own sensationalization of sex parties in Jordan, media outlets quickly played up Morris's often erratic, obsessive, and megalomaniacal public persona, deploying misogynistic caricatures that the public would soon see in Glenn Close's lead in 1987's *Fatal Attraction,* or Kathy Bates's performance in 1990's *Misery.* A September 1987 exposé in the Sunday *Star Tribune,* for example, deeply personalized the controversy over Morris's handling of the Jordan case. The seven thousand-word essay detailed her background as a conservative Southern Methodist in rural Illinois who vigorously opposed drinking, smoking, and premarital sex, as well as her rise to power as a young, single (except for a short marriage), childless attorney defending children's rights. The story chronicled Morris's famously violent public outbursts, including twice spitting in the face of a colleague in her Scott County office, frequently calling the Jordan defendants "pukes," and once shouting within earshot of the press, "I'm sick to death of things like the presumption of innocence!" Interviews also played up her disconcertingly predictable descent into tears whenever she spoke of allegedly abused children, and her tendency to color stories with dramatic evidence of ongoing ritualized sexual abuse in Jordan. She told the *Star Tribune,* for example, about a Scott County Fair run-in with a mother whose daughter had recently been returned from foster care, insinuating that the woman continued to violently repress the girl's attempt to reveal the truth. "Suddenly, from the other side of the woman, her six-year-old

Scott County Attorney Kathleen Morris became the lightning rod for the fallout from the "Jordan Sex Ring." The Star Tribune *captured Morris in her office for a Sunday magazine cover story as the controversy peaked in September 1987. Stormi Greener,* Star Tribune, *September 6, 1987: 1SM. Courtesy of the* Minneapolis Star Tribune.

daughter appeared, exclaiming, 'Mommy, Mommy, it's Kathleen!' And she slapped her. And, of course, she shut up and didn't say anything else," Morris ominously recalled.[66]

The spotlight on Kathleen Morris's apparent obsessiveness and instability in the wake of the "Jordan sex ring" distracts attention from the large extent to which the public, the media, the police, child advocates, psychologists, and prosecutors believed and bought into Morris's narrative with little or no evidence to prove that anything had happened. This tendency to see sexual threats where they failed to exist extended beyond the charged domain of child endangerment. Ronda Williams, for example, was still alive in 2002 despite having been accused of spreading HIV to her clients in 1986. Living with AIDS for seventeen years would have been nearly impossible for anyone who contracted the disease five years before the first rudimentary AIDS drugs became available, not to mention for a woman whose race, poverty, and line of work would have made it extremely difficult to access the health care necessary to manager her disease. Nevertheless, the assumption that Williams was on the street spreading HIV year after year after year helped propel watershed legislation that would have made it a crime to transmit HIV in Minnesota. The 1994 bill made it a felony punishable by up to five years in prison to engage in behavior that has been "demonstrated epidemiologically to transmit HIV, knowing or having reason to know that the behavior might result in transmission of HIV."[67] The bill's retributive framework would have invalidated existing public health efforts to fight the disease, as criminalization of transmission would have likely discouraged people from getting tested and from informing sex partners of their HIV status. Although the bill failed to emerge from committee in the state senate, it was wildly popular on the floor of the house, and passed with an initial vote of 106 to 25.

1980S SEX PANICS AND THE FUTURE OF GLBT POLITICS

While the sex panics of the 1980s may have been paranoid and—at least in the Ronda Williams and Jordan cases—largely in people's heads, they have had a lasting impact on sexual politics in the Twin Cities, and especially on the strategies and desires of queer social movements. In the wake of the *Bowers* decision, activists worked to rescue gay and lesbian identity and community from the troubled waters of AIDS-spreading

Minnesota: police power for AIDS?

Law changes sought to force compliance

Analysis by Tim Campbell

If the Minnesota Commissioner of Health, Sr. Mary Madonna Ashton, has her way, Minnesota will see some law changes in 1987 which will give her department new powers to control people's private sexual behavior. The direction of the proposed law changes will be designed to make contact tracing easier from the legal standpoint.

Such actions are probably not surprising in light of the potential devastation of the AIDS epidemic.

To wrap up the AIDS report as of the end of 1986, the U.S. Center for Disease Control counts 29,304 total cases of diagnosed AIDS by its strict definition. Roughly 16,230 of those cases have already died. The remainder are expected to die within 18 months of their diagnosis.

The State of Minnesota, which ranks 23rd in the nation, has reported 155 official cases of AIDS. 83 of them have died

Illustration adapted from a Cavello© drawing

near majority of the population that the government has no business in bedrooms looking for sin. Are we now going to turn around and say "It's ok for the government to sneak into the bedroom to search for sickness?"

Forget it! No branch of the government has any business in anyone's bedroom with police power. The right to privacy is valid even in a plague. The right to control over one's own body is valid even in a plague. Let's not forget the principles behind our politics. Never.

AIDS can only be transmitted through sex and needle sharing. Competent human beings have the right to take this risk. This is fundamental.

Right now, we would be hard pressed to prove that any one is an active carrier of killer AIDS. Anyone who is ignoring AIDS is responding to the uncertainty of our information about risk, at least in part.

The government needs to build its case better, further its research, and persuade with advertising and other eduction. The government should not be using police power to create a smoke screen around the way it

Tim Campbell, editor of the GLC Voice, *the monthly paper that replaced* Positively Gay *in the early 1980s, extensively covered and criticized government efforts to monitor the sex practices of people with AIDS and criminalize the transmission of the HIV virus. This early feature appraises HIV-related proceedings in the 1986 session of the Minnesota Legislature. Tim Campbell, "Minnesota: Police Power for AIDS?"* GLC Voice *156, January 5, 1987, 1. Courtesy of the Jean-Nickolaus Tretter Collection, University of Minnesota Libraries.*

prostitutes, murderous child-abusing sex parties, and man-boy sex at the Children's Theater. In the process, local leaders shifted focus away from the streets—spending less time defending public cultural and sexual venues like downtown bathhouses, adult bookstores, and cruising spots in Loring Park—and into the bedroom, framing queer sex as the business of monogamous, adult couples in the privacy of their own homes. The push to privatize and domesticate homosexual and gender-nonconforming bodies, sexualities, and politics is evident in the "public sexual conduct law" and subsequent legislation. After Spear, Clark, and others failed to garner enough support to move their compromise forward in the legislature, local activist Barbara Carlson made a similar pact the center of her 1989 race for Minneapolis City Council. Carlson had been a close associate of Thom Higgins, Brian Coyle, and other prominent 1970s gay activists. Her latest proposal offered to tie Coyle's longtime bid for domestic partner benefits for city employees to a new proposal to ban cruising in Loring Park.[68]

The cruising ordinance would have made it illegal to drive past any given point in Loring Park more than three times in an evening, effectively banning "car cruising," a common public sexual practice in cold northern climates. Like the "public sexual conduct law," Carlson's horse trade gave the police new power to monitor, document, and interrupt public sexual acts, while it extended new medical, vacation, and retirement benefits to those able to legally prove they lived in committed, domestic, monogamous relationships. Although the partner benefits trade-off garnered widespread support from the gay and straight political establishment, it drew immediate fire from grassroots activists, who came together in a group called FAGS—Friends Against Gay Suppression—and argued that the proposal was an intentional criminalization of long-standing queer public sexual culture in Loring Park. FAGS organized get-out-the-vote efforts and support rallies against Carlson, a key element in defeating her bid for City Council as well as blocking the anticruising initiative.[69]

By 1990, all Minnesota legislative efforts to provide new rights for monogamous couples in exchange for further criminalization of public sex had failed. Law enforcement continued to police intimate encounters in parks, bookstores, and alleyways using laws against indecent exposure, lewd and lascivious behavior, and prostitution, while sodomy laws sat unenforced until the 2003 Supreme Court decision *Lawrence v. Texas* officially decriminalized many queer sexual practices in private space. Although the sex panics of the 1980s seemed to have faded into distant memory, their residue drives a continuing shift in mainstream GLBT politics. After all, Ronda Williams was a lightning rod for AIDS hysteria in Minnesota at its apex in 1986, fear mongering that had a disproportionate impact on gay men. But Williams's name or story never appeared in the gay press, either during her original character assassination or during the Minnesota Legislature's subsequent attempt use her life to make HIV transmission into a felony. Instead, GLBT political activism increasingly pushed for domestic partner benefits, for the right to serve in the military, and, later on, for the right to marry. These new focuses manufactured the GLBT person as a domesticated, monogamous, upstanding, patriotic citizen far removed not only from child-abusing trailer park sex parties and man-boy-loving artists, but from poor African American women like Ronda Williams. This focus intensified, rather than abated, after the year 2000 when the "marriage rush" to California, Massachusetts, and other states legalizing the institution made same-sex couples in black tuxedos or white wedding dresses the leitmotif of mainstream GLBT culture and politics. Turning to futures on the altar chased away the specter of the pervert, the pedophile, and the prostitute that haunted queer people in the 1980s.

The point of this brief historical inquiry into the relationship between GLBT political movements and privatization is not to say that activists should drop their concern for workplace rights or relationship recognition and come out swinging to defend child abusers and people who knowingly spread HIV. Instead, it has aimed to recover what was lost in turning a blind eye to the sex panics of the 1980s. Indeed, the denigration of Ronda Williams as an AIDS whore, the uproar over imagined interlocking sex rings, and the ridicule of Kathleen Morris as a means to avoid atoning for the Jordan controversy reveal how class and race discrimination, homophobia, and antifeminism worked together to manufacture the austere politics and economies of the 1980s. This dilemma—of whether to remain attentive to public dilemmas like Williams's and Morris's, or whether to turn to the private marriage bedroom as the sole domain of GLBT politics—would continue to trouble activists over the coming decades.

Notes

This chapter would not have been possible without the research assistance of Danielle Kasprzak, Joel Kinder, and Stewart Van Cleve. Each of their undergraduate research projects, and endless hours spent in regional history archives, not only provided the "data" for the project, but shaped its intellectual and theoretical contributions. In particular, Danielle Kasprzak's commitment to the Oral History Project since its inception deeply influenced all of our writing. Her spatial approach to lesbian feminism and women's political, cultural, and sexual networks in the 1970s inspires the second snapshot of this essay. In addition, we would like to thank Larry Knopp, Jennifer L. Pierce, and Kevin P. Murphy for their editorial support and guidance during this process. We would also like to thank the Tretter Collection and Social Welfare History Archive at the University of Minnesota, and the Minnesota Historical Society.

1 "Minnesota Lumber History," http://www.mnhs.org/places/sites/fhc/logging.html (accessed 05/06, 2007).

2 Ibid.

3 J. C Ryan, Lorayne Sielaff, and St. Louis County Historical Society, *Under the Tarpaper* (Duluth: St. Louis County Historical Society, 1985). Subsequent references are given in the text.

4 John Zitur, Greg Scherer, Mark Scherer, and Scherer Brothers Lumber Company, *In*

Their Own Words: Lumberjacks and Their Stories—In the Camps (Minneapolis: Scherer Brothers Lumber Co., 1988), 13.

5 "Williams Is Doomed to Gallows," *St. Paul Pioneer Press,* May 20, 1906.

6 "Insanity Is His Defense," *St. Paul Pioneer Press,* May 18, 1906.

7 In two samplings of police records from 1906–8 and 1917–19 in Hennepin County, there was not a single arrest for sodomy.

8 "Insanity Is His Defense," *St. Paul Pioneer Press,* May 18, 1906.

9 "Botched Hanging Was Minnesota's Last Execution," *Star Tribune,* December 26, 1988, 5B.

10 Ibid.

11 David L. Rosheim, *The Other Minneapolis, or the Rise and Fall of the Gateway, the Old Minneapolis Skid Row* (Maquoketa, Iowa: Andromeda Press, 1978), i–x.

12 Ibid., 49.

13 Minneapolis Department of Police, *Bertillon System Record No.1: From Jan. 4, 1907 to Dec. 19, 1907* (Minneapolis: Cerber Bros., 1906), record no. 232. For a detailed analysis of the policing of homosexuality in the gateway district, see Stewart Van Cleve, "Homohemia: The Lost Gay Ghettos of Minneapolis," unpublished manuscript (2009).

14 Minneapolis Department of Police, *Bertillon System Record No. 1,* record no. 3559.

15 Ibid., record no. 3565.

16 Ibid., record no. 321, 3/13/1908.

17 Rosheim, *The Other Minneapolis,* 75 and 95.

18 Paula C. Baker, *The Moral Frameworks of Public Life: Gender, Politics, and the State in Rural New York, 1870–1930* (New York: Oxford University Press, 1991).

19 Ibid.

20 F. A. Schaffnit, letter from the rector of the Wartburg, Minneapolis, September 1, 1931, 1.

21 Ibid., 2–3.

22 *Articles of the Incorporation of the Lutheran Hospice and Benevolent Association of Minneapolis, MN* (April 13, 1925), 1.

23 J. B. Rochat to Mr. Woodworth, "Letter in Support of the Wartburg," Minneapolis, December 30, 1931.

24 Schaffnit, letter from the rector of the Wartburg, 1.

25 B. E. Bergesen, "Letter from the President of the N.L.C.A. Pastoral Conference to B. H. Woodworth in the Chamber of Commerce," Minneapolis, January 13, 1932, 1.

26 "Wartburg Newsletter," Minneapolis, January 1933, back page.

27 The United Way files at the University of Minnesota Social Welfare History Archives contain hundreds of letters between the United Way and the Wartburg. For more than ten years the Wartburg would ask for money from the community chest and be denied.

28 The Social Welfare History Archives at the university and United Way documents suggest over and over that the Wartburg offered a redundant service because it housed out-of-work men, and the goal was not to put them in a family but to get them back to work.

29 For examples of this process, see the first section of this chapter. For a detailed analysis of the contradiction between the imaginings of a universal nuclear family and the needs of labor, see Roderick A. Ferguson, *Aberrations in Black: Toward a Queer of Color Critique* (Minneapolis: University of Minnesota Press, 2004.)

30 Margot Canaday, *The Straight State: Sexuality and Citizenship in Twentieth-Century America* (Princeton, N.J.: Princeton University Press, 2009).

31 Allan M. Brandt, *No Magic Bullet: A Social History of Venereal Disease in the United States since 1880* (New York: Oxford University Press, 1985), 5.

32 R. R. Sullivan, "Minnesota Venereal Disease Control Program in Connection with Military Maneuvers," *Journal of Social Hygiene* 26:8 (1940): 372.

33 Ibid., 373.

34 Brandt, *No Magic Bullet.*

35 Canaday, *The Straight State.*

36 Chris, personal interview, November 11, 2004.

37 Lynda, personal interview, January 8, 2004.

38 Gary, personal interview, January 10, 2004.

39 Grace Kyungwon Hong, *The Ruptures of American Capital: Women of Color Feminism and the Culture of Immigrant Labor* (Minneapolis: University of Minnesota Press, 2006), 33.

40 Lynda Clark, personal interview, January 8, 2004.

41 Ted, personal interview, December 20, 2005.

42 Bruce Brockway, "Meeting/March/Vigil Draws 1200," *Positively Gay* 1:3, July 1979, 1.

43 Tim Campbell, "Thank You, Barbara," *Positively Gay* 1:4, August 1, 1979, 1+.

44 Jim Schroeder, "Special Task Force Forms to Solve String of Gay Murders," *Equal Time,* October 29, 1986.

45 "Police Raid Minneapolis Bath," *Positively Gay* 1:4, August 1, 1979, 2.

46 Bruce Brockway and Thom Higgins, "Deputy Mayor Raids Gay Bath," *Positively Gay* 1:4, August 1, 1979, 1.

47 Bruce Brockway, "Jury Acquits Houle in Taylor Murder," *GLC Voice,* March 1980, 1+.

48 Steve Compton, "Unsolved Indian Murders Focus of Human Rights Conference," *The Alley—The Phillips Community Newspaper* 11:1, January 1987, 1+.

49 Ibid., 1.

50 Julie Gravelle and Kevin Diaz, "Transient Found Slain Had Tested Positive for AIDS," *Star Tribune,* September 24, 1986, 1B+.

51 Bruce Brockway and Alan Strombaugh, "Benscotter Murder Case Detailed," *Positively Gay* 1:3, July 1979, 1.

52 Dennis J. McGrath and Kevin Diaz, "Lingering Fear Spurs Search for Links in 15 Unsolved Murders," *Star Tribune,* October 22, 1986, 1A+.

53 Ibid.

54 Tim Campbell, "Summer of Police Hostility Sparks New Activism," *GLC Voice,* October 1984, 1+.

55 Tim Campbell, "New 'Public Sex' Laws Pushed by Spear and Friends as 'Sodomy Repeal,'" *GLC Voice,* February 16, 1987, 1.

56 Lewis Cope, "WCCO Documentary on alleged gay prostitute receives divided reviews," *Star Tribune,* March 21, 1986, B03.

57 We have changed the name of the woman in question to minimize further public scrutiny.

58 "When an AIDS Carrier Becomes a Public Menace," *Star Tribune,* April 6, 1986, 28A.

59 Lewis Cope, "Male Prostitute with AIDS Virus Had 1,000 Sex Partners in Cities," *Star Tribune,* March 27, 1986, A01.

60 Dan Oberdorfer, "Court Hears Arguments on Suits in Sex Cases," *Star Tribune,* May 14, 1986, 1B.

61 Kay Miller, "I Still Believe the Children," *Star Tribune,* September 6, 1987, 06SM+.

62 Ibid.

63 Paul Levy, "Project Hopes to Set Guidelines for Dealing with Child Molesters," *Star Tribune,* October 26, 1986, 01B+.

64 Kay Miller, "Sex Abuse Case Was a Long Time in the Making; the Kids Raised the Curtain," *Star Tribune,* May 19, 1991, 01E+.

65 Dan Oberdorfer and Jim Adams, "Unhealed: The Scott County Families," *Star Tribune,* November 15, 1987, 01A+.

66 Miller, "Sex Abuse Case Was a Long Time in the Making."

67 "Curbing HIV// Don't Treat Virus Carriers like Crooks," *Star Tribune,* May 7, 1994, 26A.

68 Tim Campbell, "Carlson–Alexander Connection Exposed," *GLC Voice,* October 16, 1989, 1.

69 Ibid.

4. THE MYTH OF THE GREAT WHITE NORTH

CLAIMING QUEER PEOPLE OF COLOR HISTORIES IN THE TWIN CITIES (A ROUNDTABLE DISCUSSION)

Charlotte Karem Albrecht, Brandon Lacy Campos, and Jessica Giusti

This chapter is based on a roundtable discussion that took place in the community room at Brandon's apartment building on Saturday, March 31, 2007. This diverges from other chapters in *Queer Twin Cities* in several ways worth noting. First, most chapters focus on historical processes and individual histories, but we address the politics of being queer and "of color" in the Twin Cities today. Much of the oral historical evidence that shapes this book is drawn from interviews with older queer people, but our group consisted of relatively younger residents who were eager to engage in a dialogue around the current realities of being a queer person of color. This conversation emerged from a need to insert ourselves into the historical narrative of the Twin Cities while simultaneously resisting the dominant representations of the queer community. Our focus on the present was a way to write ourselves into future tellings of what the queer Twin Cities looked like during the first decade of the twenty-first century.

Second, this chapter is presented as an edited transcript in order to emphasize the voices of people working in the community. (We recorded the entire conversation; it was transcribed by Andrea Nordick and Kandace Creel Falcón.) With minimal edits, a transcript of the roundtable offers the reader the rawest possible picture of the discussion, clearly articulating on its own terms the critical issues present in the Twin Cities' queer-of-color communities. Throughout the roundtable, the participants made incisive critiques of the structures of power within their lives and described how they employ theories of organizing, response, and resistance. We feel that the participants respond directly to the crucial question of GLBT history and futures, allowing for a thorough engagement without editorializing from the "authors" of this chapter.

Developing a protocol for the roundtable was complex, as it caused us to have tough conversations about our own social locations and privileges, as well as about our end goals for the project. The project was first envisioned by Twin Cities GLBT Oral History Project cofounders Kevin Murphy and Jason Ruiz, who asked Jessica and Charlotte if they would like to organize the roundtable well before that meeting on Lake Street. We recognized that in order for this process to be legitimate the conversation (and this chapter) had to be rooted in the voices of individuals working in diverse communities in the Twin Cities—and who identify with these communities themselves. We began by questioning the framework of the roundtable, including the following questions: Who would we ask to attend the roundtable? How would we facilitate the roundtable? Who would design the questions? As three queers who identified differently in terms of race, what would our individual roles be?

In addition to these practical questions, we wanted to acknowledge that the occasion to participate in the Twin Cities GLBT Oral History Project and to create this occasion for queers of color to discuss their experiences living and organizing here came by way of Charlotte and Jessica's enrollment in the University of Minnesota's Feminist Studies Program. We recognized that scholars have a long history of extracting, co-opting, and appropriating knowledge from communities of color. Although this chapter cannot undo this history, we knew throughout its planning that it needed to be of value to the communities involved in its creation. Ultimately, our goal is for this transcript to work in the hands of other organizers. When Jessica and Charlotte were getting this project started, they hoped to work with someone who was more deeply rooted in activist work and queer communities of color than they were at the time. Brandon, a committed activist and visionary poet who was well known in overlapping networks of Twin Cities social-justice communities, emerged as the perfect collaborator. Charlotte had met Brandon through a mutual activist friend (realizing that they had met a few years earlier at a conference); she introduced him to Jessica when he expressed interest in the idea for a roundtable. Once on board, Brandon worked to envision, design, and facilitate the discussion.

After our preliminary conversations, we held three open meetings at

Brandon's apartment that were widely advertised and open to any queer-of-color-identified individual in the Twin Cities. Our goals for these pre-roundtable meetings were to generate interest and, more important, input in the roundtable. The attendees were invited to join us through word of mouth, as well as through academic and community listservs to which we had posted notices. We described the OHP to those in attendance, brainstormed ideas for how to attract a diverse group of discussants, and worked to develop questions that would address their concerns as members of communities of color in Minneapolis and St. Paul. These sessions were powerful beginnings to what would become a very passionate and important conversation between activists with distinct but similar goals.

Our personal investment in creating such a conversation was further complicated by our individual relationships to whiteness. Brandon is multiracial and has long been involved with communities of color in the Twin Cities. At the time, both Jessica and Charlotte identified as white and were graduate students who were not active in local activist circles. But they brought a complicated relationship to whiteness to this project. Although Jessica has identified as white her entire life, Charlotte was struggling to understand her own racial identity as someone who is of Lebanese origin but was raised to think of herself as white. Charlotte now identifies as a light-skinned, mixed-heritage Arab American, but at the time she saw her whiteness as complicating her relationship to a project for queer activists of color. Like Jessica, she wanted to be sure that her white privilege would not disrupt the participants' abilities to speak openly about their experiences.

We decided that Jessica and Charlotte would be present in the planning meetings but would not be in the room for the actual roundtable discussion. We made this decision because we felt that having white-identified people present during the discussion would alter the conversation in the ways that Jessica and Charlotte feared. In addition to Brandon, Jason Ruiz, who had been involved with the OHP since its inception and active in organizing the roundtable, would also participate in the discussion. Brandon and Jason co-facilitated the roundtable, but strove to intervene in that capacity as little as possible. As is clear from the conversation, the people in the group were socially and professionally interconnected. Some met for the first time, but some were old friends. Some worked together as colleagues and some were just acquaintances. This is not an inconsequential detail, but speaks to how organizing works in the Twin Cities, where the queer community of color is relatively small and relies on such connections.

This chapter is the product of multiple voices—and not just the ones listed as authors. We hope that this chapter will not only speak to the academy but also offer a way to speak back to (but never for) the communities to which the participants belong. Of course, the eight voices represented here cannot begin to speak for all of those marginalized or excluded by dominant modes of queer history. We hope that this chapter will instead be a catalyst for further discussions regarding the roles that people of color play (and have historically played) in broader queer history.

Roundtable Participants

Gilbert Achay was born and raised on O'ahu, Hawai'i. His personal transitions from being a member of a majority to minority group, coming out, and as the first person from his family to attend college ultimately shape his future commitments. His work with urban youth and public health initiatives derives from a concern about the educational and health disparities that impact low-income communities, immigrants, and refugees.

Brandon Lacy Campos is a thirty-one-year-old, HIV-positive, queer, and multiracial (Afro-Puerto Rican, black, white, Ojibwe) poet, organizer, journalist, playwright, and writer. Lacy was born in Duluth, Minnesota, and currently lives in New York City, where he is a Fellow and Democratizing Elections Program Director with the Liberty Tree Foundation for the Democratic Revolution and the staff grant writer for Camp Heartland. Brandon's work in queer communities and with youth is rooted in a belief that a new world is possible and will be shaped by queer people of color and young people.

Elliot James, twenty-four, was born and raised in the Bronx and moved to Minnesota in 2000 to attend Carleton College. After working in the St. Paul public schools as an AmeriCorps volunteer, he entered the University of Minnesota as a PhD student in African history. His graduate research explores the interrelationships among environment, representation, everyday practice, and subjectivity in South Africa. He intends to write his dissertation about public transportation in Cape Town.

Andrea Jenkins, who grew up as a child of the 1960s, is a longtime community activist concerned with social justice for all people. A published poet and writer, she works as a senior policy aide for the city of

Minneapolis. Andrea holds a BS in Human Services and Communications from Metropolitan State University and an MS in Community Economic Development from Southern New Hampshire University.

Nicole J. Kubista, thirty-one, is a queer Korean adoptee living with her partner, cat, and dog in St. Paul. She advocates for low-income people and for social change in the criminal justice system as a public defender in Ramsey County. Nikki also serves on the St. Paul Human Rights Commission and as a board member of the Minnesota affiliate of the National Asian Pacific American Bar Association.

Kelly Lewis, twenty-three, came to Minnesota in 2002 to attend Carleton College by way of Lafayette, Louisiana. She has since transferred to the University of Minnesota–Twin Cities, where she is finishing her undergraduate degree in political science. Her passions include cooking, politics, golf, and working toward social justice in her community.

Kevin Lanier Moore, twenty-nine, was born and raised in Cleveland, Ohio. He moved to the Twin Cities for a job as an HIV prevention worker on December 1, 2004—World AIDS Day. Kevin is a spoken-word artist, writer, actor, and activist who began HIV prevention work in 2001 and began the first Centers for Disease Control–funded initiative for Young African American Men Who Have Sex with Men (YMSM) in Ohio, as well as redeveloping the Stopping AIDS Is My Mission (SAMM) intervention for youth aged thirteen to twenty-four. He currently coordinates the Health Education Program for Pillsbury United Communities, which includes the "Brother Circle" biweekly men's brunch and rapid HIV testing.

Jason Ruiz, born in 1976, moved to the Twin Cities from East Chicago, Indiana, in 1997 to attend the University of Minnesota. As an editor of *Queer Twin Cities,* his bio appears at the end of this book.

The Discussion

BRANDON: The first question for discussion is: Does naming pose barriers to us in forming communities and fostering support for each other? How do terms like "LGBT," "queer," "person of color," "activist," and "organizer" complicate the community?

GILBERT: A lot of these terms—"LGBT," "queer," "activist," "organizer"—were formed by members of the GLBT community who are white, just as the issues that are determined to be GLBT are formed by white people, so

I don't necessarily identify with a lot of these terms. I also don't identify with the debate over GLBT versus LGBT. I think that was some debate that was trying to focus on diversity but it doesn't focus on ethnic diversity, cultural diversity, or religious diversity. They were just focusing on who had more power—gays or lesbians. That is emblematic of where the GLBT movement is today. So, does this complicate us forming community? Yeah, I think so.

BRANDON: When I think about this, what also comes to mind are the labels that we use for ourselves, particularly in communities of color, which often don't get translated into the rest of the community, like "same-gender loving," "two spirit," "*joto*" and "*pato*." A lot of men in Latin America who fuck men don't think of themselves as "queer" and that translates here. I know a lot of guys from the Latino community who love to be with men but would never identify themselves as "queer" or with a relationship to the queer community. Because that happens, artificial barriers are set up for us, so that if we want to be part of the LGBT community we have to adopt a certain identity, and this immediately inhibits our relationships with other folks, particularly with other queer people of color who may not come from that specific identity formation pattern or for whom it's not a primary identity. I know a lot of men who are, like, "I love men, I sleep with men, but that's not how I focus my identity—that's not the focal point of how I look at the world." And often they see folks who are queer identified as dangers to the community for all kind of reasons. So I do think we have to make choices that oftentimes white LGBT people don't have to make. That's frustrating and limits our ability to work effectively with the folks in our community that I want to work with.

NIKKI: I'm really struggling with this question in a lot of ways because, although I believe identities are hugely important—they are shorthand for finding each other, they are the beginning of the conversation—they are not necessarily the *full* conversation. I would hate to say that they are *all* bad, because you go to a new town and are gay and you look for specific things, coffeehouses and newspapers, as a way of initially making that connection. But in terms of organizing or about how things work in the world, then they start to hamper us. The one example I can think of is when I was sitting on a panel a long time ago that was all queer Asians. The guy next to me essentially said, "You're not Asian, you don't speak an Asian language, you didn't grow up Asian!" I was, like, "But I *am* Asian. I didn't grow up the same way you did, but I am Asian." Essentially, we were just fighting with each other about something that was strongly felt by both of us, but ridiculous at the same time. It's an important conversation to have, but at the same time it kept us from really talking. We were just trying to figure out if we should be in the same category, and that's a problem.

ELLIOT: In terms of my identity, it really came out of college. I think going to college, in an environment where people used words like "GLBT" and "people of color," gave me the language to express what I was feeling. In that sense, it was very formative for my development in terms of using the language. In terms of my history, these terms were extremely useful when I came out.

JASON: At the same time that I recognize the problems with identity categories, I see how they can be extremely useful. It's complicated for me because I also consider Chicano and Latino to be identity categories that should be treated with some suspicion, especially because of the homophobia in those communities. I was at a University of Minnesota Chicano Studies Department meeting a couple of years ago that was supposed to build a partnership between the Chicano community and the academy. This long-term activist who was a student in Chicano studies in the seventies was there. He identified me at this meeting and said, "Who is this faggot? He doesn't belong in a Chicano Studies Department!" He shouted me down in the meeting because he saw me as queer. At the same time, I find it hard to identify with the mainstream gay/lesbian community in the Twin Cities. Like when you open up the free magazine, it doesn't include a space for me. So I see that calling myself queer and calling myself Chicano each puts me out on a limb because each community articulates that there is not a space for me in certain ways.

ELLIOT: I try not to organize my communities based on language. Sometimes it happens in the sense of, these are my community of color people or these are my gay community people. Sometimes the people around me could be categorized as queer people of color. Whether we would call ourselves queer people of color is another story. So there is always that connection as well, feeling what's comfortable. At the same time, I think my identity was probably solidified when I left college and went back to

New York and worked in a same-sex loving community at the Gay Men's Health Crisis. That's where I had this shift in knowing the limitations of categories.

KEVIN: I agree. I think a lot of these terms are very academic. If you're in academia, people understand terms such as "queer," "GLBT," "activist," "organizer." If you're going to actually work with community members, these terms are not going to be meaningful. I'm not going to organize a group of people who don't identify at all with these terms and use these terms. For the most part, the people who I work with who identify as G or L or B or T don't use these terms. I have strong reservations. "Activist," "organizer"—those are the terms I use for myself, but I won't use them in the presence of other people because I think it puts me at a different place than it puts them and that's anticommunity building for me.

BRANDON: I think part of my personal narrative is, like Nikki said, that using the terms to identify with a community is helpful. Coming out as queer first, and then building and identifying a community of support, helped me to become comfortable with my identity as queer. I did that first and I had to stack identities. So, first I did that because I grew up with my white mother outside of real POC [people of color] communities. Then, when I was comfortable with being queer, I was able to engage in my racial background and I could be, like, "I have a lot of work to do here." After that I could start demanding a space in both. That was a process where, for me, the identities became important to me in terms of labels, but then later they became inhibitors. Now that I've become secure with myself in this community, I want to be able to live how I want to live in both communities, and at that point these labels start to break down. That's where the language around *who* we are and how we are becomes very difficult and complicated because that's the point where identity becomes a barrier and not a community builder—particularly in Minnesota, in the Twin Cities, where there is such a strict separation between how communities of color see themselves and organize themselves. Especially when I came out in the mid nineties, there was no Latin Night at the Saloon [gay bar popular with a younger crowd]. You were lucky if you saw three black people at the Saloon; you didn't see any Asians. For me, if you wanted to see queer Latinos, you had to go to salsa bars, and that's where you found community. You know, you had to go to community to find community and see how people were organizing themselves and there just weren't any spaces where you could be who you wanted to be, all of who you wanted to be. And our history is really clear. Like where would black churches be without sissies? You know they just would not be there! No choir, no preacher! The history is there but it is made invisible by our own communities. It's not that we don't belong, but that the way we have belonged has been dictated by other people.

KEVIN: Yeah, right, and we kind of settle for it, we kind of subscribe to it. A lot of times we talk a lot of S-H-I-T against it; however, we don't really take the proper steps to identify it for ourselves. Personally, in Cleveland and here, I've never felt a part of any queer or GLBT community. That is because, for the most part, there is kind of a profile, there are certain things that we tend to do, certain places we tend to hang out, certain clothes we tend to wear, certain ways we tend to talk, and I've never been the status quo gay man—African American, Caucasian, or whatever. So it's been really, really hard for me to find people that I feel like a personal connection with because there are so many people out there—it's like they have taken this gift they have been given of being queer or GLBT and they have kind of dropped the ball.

JASON: What you're describing is really interesting. I have conducted other interviews with older people—mostly white people, but some people of color—who describe this same feeling that you're describing, especially back in the day. They're talking about feeling alone and the difficulty of making community for themselves or finding other people like them. I think the question for you and the rest of the group is: How have you found other people and how do you form community?

KELLY: Well, going into some of these labels, I feel like some of them can coexist better than others. Just this morning I spoke to my grandmother and I was "granddaughter." I wasn't queer, I wasn't an activist, I wasn't an organizer—I was granddaughter. I feel like, as people of color in the queer community, it is a life in transition, so to speak. It's who you are today—are you a person of color, are you LGBT, are you a family member, and where do you want to be? What is your priority? I guess I look at it as a double-edged sword. Some would look at it and be, like, Wow we have the ability to do that within ourselves and come out sane at the end of the day. It's an art and it's sad that it exists and you have to do that, but that's where we are. For the sake of my grandmother, I will continue to be granddaughter today and for as long as she shall live.

GILBERT: I love what you just said, though, because I would say that when I am with gay people, mostly white gay people, it's my ethnicity that comes to the fore. Actually, even when I'm with other people of color that's what is involved more than anything else. Also, my class upbringing. I think a lot of people feel that it is very middle-class in the gay community here, and white. I am not white and I was not raised middle-class, so already I feel a sense of deep distance from the gay community and queer community. I know a lot of people here and there is a sense of mutual understanding that I cannot get no matter how hard I try with white, middle-class gay people. I just haven't been able to find that whatsoever.

KEVIN: It seems like in Minnesota, even when you're not thinking about your race, they [white, middle-class gay people] are. They always seem to find a way to remind you that you are the color that you are or their perception of whatever color you are. But yeah, I agree with you totally and it's kind of unfortunate, but the most community I feel all day is when I step into the office—when I see Gilbert, my outreach worker, or other folks of color there, who share the same thoughts, goals, passions, as far as what we want from the community collectively. There are a lot of times when I feel more of a sense of community with the average heterosexual community, based on certain music that I like, or places that I hang, or things that get my attention, things that I enjoy. It's not that I am turning my back on the same-gender-loving people of Minnesota, it's just that I have yet to find a significant number of them who are on the same thing that I'm on.

NIKKI: I'm having a hard time with the question of where you find community that Jason just asked, because I feel like I used to know the answer to that but now that I've left school, I don't spend a lot of time at the bars anymore, I have friends but I don't necessarily see them as often as I used to . . . I don't know any more about community. I would hate to say, like Kevin, that my community is at work because I see them every day and you can kind of whittle out the people you like and the people you don't like and they know who you are. That just feels sick to me. I don't work in a community activism organization, I work for the public defender's office. I definitely do what I see as socially just work, but it's just not the same kind of work. That question really freaks me out, actually, because if you asked me ten years ago, I could tell you exactly what community was, what it meant, and how it felt. I'm going to think about that one because that makes me feel uneasy.

ELLIOT: In terms of Kelly's comment about these different identifications she has, I feel like that's how I built half my communities, based on these different identities and how they come together. When I think of community, I think of my friends, I think of my family, and I think of people who I work around. At the same time, that kind of divides as well. I mean, I have certain friends here and certain friends there. It's just all a big ball of communities that correspond to not only my identities, but also my interests. It's just very complicated in that sense. So, if I wanted to build a community around something, it would have to be around an issue that a lot of people identify with, and that's how I basically operate. And I'm not certain that community would overlap with others.

JASON: For me, the question of community is sort of a trick question because part of the Oral History Project, or the perception of it, is that what we are defining here is "the community." Maybe that would be a goal of a different project—this is the community, this is where we find it historically. But the more I listen to older people tell me their stories, the more I realize this is not new. We asked the same question about what it was like to be in the gay community in the 1960s and their answer is often: "What community? It was me and my circle of friends or maybe some people that I knew off the street, or this bar, or this café, or these house parties that would happen clandestinely." So it's interesting to me how you talk about community because that's also some historical answer that we've been getting a lot. And maybe in our generation, which is roughly similar in this room, we imagine a time when there was community, like the sixties and seventies. It's a false sense of nostalgia, as if there must have been a community once. But what people have asked me consistently in the interviews that I've done is, What community? There isn't this imagined community that was there.

BRANDON: I just want to be clear that I went through that process I was, like, "Yeah! I'm gay! The gays are my community!" And then, "I'm mixed!

So the mixed community is my community," which is *real* dramatic. Then I went through my Afro-Latino phase and I moved to Puerto Rico and was like, "Yeah! This is my community!" I was on this constant journey, and was thinking, when I get there, it's going to be joyous and musicals happening spontaneously! But now I'm really clear about my community, I have no ambiguity about it. I think the clincher for me was that I always thought community was linked to geography. For example, I would not leave Powderhorn Park; it took a giant step for me to cross Lake Street and come over here to the Phillips neighborhood. But at this point, my community is built around people who have shared values, and race and sexual orientation play a role in that, but often they are not primary. So, like, there are people in this room that are in my community, but I have people all across the country that are just as much of my community as the people I get to see every day. It's based on shared values. So, at that level, when I decided to make community based on the people that loved and supported me and I got to support them in the way that I wanted to, then geography and race and gender and class became less important. It means that those people are engaging themselves around their privilege and around their oppression in a way that allows you to build community across those dynamics. It doesn't mean that we don't have conflict sometimes. But my choices to be who I am are not called into question at a fundamental level. I might be challenged on the way I move through the world, but it's not about defending who I am around the identity choices I made for myself. That's something really powerful for me. But I had to go through the process of searching and coming to terms with myself. That's an ongoing process that just doesn't end. I think I could not have had the relationships and community that I have now if I hadn't gone through all the drama to get there. I hope those that follow us are spared that journey. Part of that also is to model what community looks like because it's also about a lack of knowing our history, a lack of knowing our stories, a lack of knowing those people over fifty who have done the do and fought the fight and probably have some wisdom that they could have shared. But we don't know who they are, we don't know where they are, and that is part of my interest in the queer POC part of the Oral History Project—I want to know who they are.

KEVIN: I second that. It really sucks how Minnesota doesn't have a history of community in the GLBT of color class. Cleveland is a very conservative city in a lot of ways. However, it was about 50 percent easier to get people rallied around certain issues that were very important to the African American community or communities of color—say, HIV, social justice, equality, whatever. It was easier for me to rally the troops there, for some reason. You would probably be in more danger walking down the street rallying. However, up here in a place where it is really, really comfortable to do it, it's kind of like no one wants to. At least in the African American community, it's like we are all still in the closet even though this is a very comfortable environment for people to come out and do gay things and be all the gay you want to be. And I think back to Cleveland and how hard it was for me to get to the point where I was coming out to close friends or let a few people here and there know. It was just so challenging to do that, but I was met with open arms for the most part. A lot of that had to do with—again going back to how "gay" looks, feels, smells, or sounds—a lot of that had to do with me being a palatable gay person. I could be in any environment and be totally comfortable with being who I am sexually and making the choices that I make in my career or my friends. But outside of that, it's made me a little more uncomfortable. Not to say that I'm any less proud of who I am, but it really sickens me that it has to be the subject of every conversation up here.

JASON: That brings me to a question I have about what it's like to be a queer person of color *here*. That is, one thing that I keep hearing you guys describing is the sort of invisibility versus visibility in the local context. Something that drives me nuts is, what does that do to the perception of what it means to be a Minnesotan? To me, I sometimes feel erased in the stereotype of what a Minnesotan is. I got a phone call from a prospective student in my department who was from New York and kept saying, "I went there on your recruitment weekend and everyone is white! I'm a person of color and I'm not sure if I can go to a place where everyone is white. I've never seen so many white people before. How do you have a community for yourself when everyone is white?" I said, "You know what? Stop. How are you helping? You are also rendering people of color who are here invisible. Maybe you weren't looking hard enough, because I have formed for myself a kinship network of friends who are not white." So I guess the question is, How do you all deal with the perception of what it means to be a Minnesotan?

GILBERT: I have a question, though: Don't you think that maybe her response was based on the fact that—I was a student at the University of Minnesota—it *is* largely white, it's a white school? There aren't many people of color in graduate school.

JASON: She was talking about the Twin Cities. The thing is that if you come to my department, which is about 40 percent students of color and say that everyone is white, what would that do to my presence there? Yes, at the University of Minnesota, students of color are underrepresented, and in the state, people of color are underrepresented, especially in positions of power. But I was there, several of us here went to the university together, we were there, so to come to the University of Minnesota and say that it's all white, what does that do to those of us who were there?

GILBERT: Well, I was there and I felt like it was all white. I really did. I remember several years ago when there were two gay heads of the Minnesota Students Association [MSA, the undergraduate student government of the University of Minnesota] and their biggest platform was getting gay people into straight fraternities. That was not an issue that was really important to me—I was just thinking about how I was going to pay my bills and tuition. I was so thrown off by that, I felt like that was representative of what my experience was like at the university, where you have queer people who are supposed to be advocating for you, but they're not addressing all of the concerns and issues that are more important.

BRANDON: Again, I want to support what Jason is saying. Take the MSA, for example; we have a former president sitting right here who is a queer woman of color. Also, we are here regardless. I think there are two things. One is the way we feel here, and I think that is very valid. I grew up here, and especially if you grew up here and had the privilege of having access to good education, you often find yourself isolated. I went to a high school that was 50 percent African American, but in my magnet program, it was 10 percent. There are ways in which we have to identify and build community for ourselves, but also I think we're not invisible. We were made invisible, but we're here. I get really frustrated when people assume that I don't have a history here or that I'm not connected here. I like to tell people that members of my family were cofounders of the city of Duluth.

My history here, as part of my personal narrative, goes back a long, long way. My history here as a person of color is deeply rooted to the significant peoples of color who have lived in the Twin Cities, at least in the last forty years. So, we're here, the community is here, but often I feel, at least from what I hear of the people who move here, is that the community is so hard to break into on multiple levels. That is a Minnesota cultural phenomenon that, as a person who lives here, I never have had to engage with. But to move here and not have any of that base of knowledge, it's really ridiculous. I can't imagine going to the University of Minnesota as an undergraduate and not being from Minnesota and trying to find community and walking into the Queer Student Cultural Center, where there is this unspoken rule that there can only be one person of color present at a time. Realizing that tokenism is how things operate here. You get to be "The" whatever. There is a special category and you get to be "The."

KELLY: In planning for the Alphabet Soup Conference I attended a meeting, and that was my first meeting as a University of Minnesota undergraduate. I was just sitting there and I introduced myself and they said, "Well, I think you should be on the committee." At first I was honored and then I was, like, "Well, hold up, wait a minute." Then I never went back. In the moment, I kind of wanted to appease everyone and say, "Sure, I'll plan, and Margaret Cho will come, and all these people, and it will be dandy." But that's not something I saw myself doing or where I felt comfortable, and I didn't return.

ELLIOT: When I moved to the Twin Cities, I went to Northfield, so that was my first experience in southern Minnesota. I don't know if I feel like I was rendered invisible by the language here we're speaking about. At the same time, my experience was to the contrary. I was at a predominantly white school, it wasn't predominantly Minnesotan, so that was probably a distinction, in a very small town in the state. I felt like, in terms of scales, I was rendered invisible in that sense. But I was able to find a community and this is where community was very helpful. It was not only in black students, it was also with gay students, and then that got a little problematic because I learned that a lot of black students were not the most queer-friendly people, at least in the particular organization that I was involved with. But then I was the only person of color in the queer organization. Luckily, I had people come in and I was better able to foster a community and an identity. Then I left. I decided that I needed to explore that side of my identity a lot more, so I moved to New York City and I was able to see myself more in the story of Northfield. But Northfield has changed in terms of immigration, thank God, with other people of color moving in and colleges recruiting more students of color. It got to be a better place. It's still not the same as the Twin Cities. I would come up to the Twin Cities as an escape from Northfield. So I saw Minnesota as being a lot larger than just the Twin Cities or southern Minnesota. I saw them as being together and also kind of created by the relationships I formed.

NIKKI: As I was listening to folks, just being here is helpful in ways that you can't put your finger on. I live in the Midway, and I couldn't imagine saying that Minnesota is filled with white people. I mean, I'm not crazy—it is. But you can make conscious choices and find hosts of communities of people. For example, my neighbor Phyllis loves Jesus in a way that I think might be unhealthy, but we live together in a community. We shoveled her yard and she watched our dog. There are a lot of people of color who live in the Cities, who are normal people, who are doing their own thing and I get that frustration of Minnesota being so white. But you have to be a little more conscious of how you want to live or where you want to live, and maybe if you live in Bloomington—I don't know how to get there, but I imagine it's filled with white people—you can do that, but at least in the Cities you can make conscious choices and efforts to live in communities of people who are [of color]. You might not completely agree with them, but there is just something about them that is not white. That might be a Minnesotan thing. Like, being here, I can tell you right now that going to the University of Minnesota feels highly isolating, and you sit in giant classes with highly vocal white students who think it's really fun to make these kind of arguments that are essentially offensive to your very core. They are just kind of having fun, learning about the way the world works and testing out their intellectual abilities. And you're sitting there thinking, "I will get up, I will do something violent." Now that I bought a house in a place where I thought there were people of color and also gay people, it's very odd that there are just gay people floating around. I don't know who they are, they're just "the gays." I've never seen them out and about, but they have their OutFront signs and their gay things. My neighbors are, like, "You look like Jackie Chan." And I'm, like, "I don't look like Jackie Chan!" They were kids and I was, like, "Well, you guys look like the Ying

Yang Twins." So, you know, part of it is that you have to be ready to be a little bit more thick-skinned, but it's, like, Hey, I'm willing to make a commitment to this time and space.

KEVIN: Right, you have to learn to love them, learn to live with them, to get along with them. I think I've been pretty good at weeding through those. But I can see why she said that. A lot of people who are from my old city, and a lot of other cities around the country that I know, all say the same thing when they first found out that I moved up here: "Oh, there are black people up there?" And I'm, like, "Yeah, there is a nice chunk of them in the Twin Cities. Most of them are transplants, but there are a lot of black people." But I mean, everything that is stereotypical about communities of color—and I see that in droves up here, just tons and tons of people who represent that. But when I turn around to look for people who do represent the quiet intelligence or that are vocal and are actually doing things with the movement, I feel like we're just this really small and outnumbered force. It gets kind of sickening. So again, to go back to that whole thing of feeling torn between two worlds and not knowing where you belong, that happens to me constantly.

JASON: Kevin is describing this feeling of being torn between two worlds, so I would like to tease that out a little more, if people have personal stories or reflections upon having these kinds of multiple identities we're all navigating. It reminds me of what Kelly also said about being something to your grandmother that is different from being in other communities that you are in. I can relate to that definitely too because I'm also trying to carve out a place for myself in these different worlds. So, did anyone else want to speak to that?

ANDREA: When Kevin made that statement, I immediately thought about the 104-year-old book by W. E. B. Du Bois called *The Souls of Black Folk*. He was the first person to verbalize this. In the history of humanity, many people have felt that way, but Du Bois talked about it in the context of Africans living in America and how African Americans have always had to live this dual existence, one in the black world and one in the broader society, which we could call the white world, if we wanted to. And certainly, as an African American, I experience that dichotomy, but also I think even in the so-called LGBT community, I, as an African American transgender woman, actually feel that duality within this context of this community, that "supposedly" I am a part of. And so I am always feeling like an outsider or somehow trying to make my way into the context of being on parity or an equal level with other members of my "community." And that gets exacerbated in the larger community as well, but you would like to think that it would be more comfortable within the community that you call home, and that's not always the case.

BRANDON: For me, a lot of the writing that I do and the work that I do is about living at the intersection of these different identities and trying to make sense of them. I think a lot of us carry around experiences where we exist in multiple worlds. We're in the queer community living inside a world that is straight, we're people of color living inside a world that is white. And my familial relationships growing up, my mom's family is predominantly white and I was one of the only faces of color in that space. And so I spent a lot of personal time just trying to get in and doing that journey home and wounding myself a lot on that journey. Because my original thought was to get in, I had to try to make myself like the other, not realizing until I had done a lot of damage on top of the damage that the world already gives to you, that the world I am trying to get into is not a world that I actually want to be part of. So the journey for me led back out. You brought up an interesting statement, Andrea, that we spend a lot of our time trying to be "equal to." A really brilliant man I know named Ricardo Levins Morales always asks the question, "Equal to what? To what are you trying to be equal when the systems in which we live are inherently flawed?" We are told that we need to strive for this other journey and lots of us are trying to change the world as we journey. For me, it's become really important that we make this world into a different place where equal is no longer a question, but it's a question of justice, and the world is reimagined in a whole different way. And that's really scary work because when you live at the cross section of borders, you get to be a visionary and you get to imagine worlds that other people haven't had the chance to imagine, but then you also get to engage with the fear of how you actually make that happen when the world is what it is. So I've found now, not historically, that to live at the border is a place of power, because when you live at the border, you realize that the borders are artificial and were created for us and around us and we're trying to fit into them. I think that is one of the unique and powerful things about being queer people of color, being multiracial people, being multigendered people, you get to live in those places. The key part becomes, again going back to the discussion that we had earlier, finding that community that is going to support you and your healing, so the system itself doesn't break you down.

ANDREA: I think that is very well said, Brandon, in that there is a beauty and a privilege even of being able to live in multiple worlds and multiple identities, if you will, that the majority of people don't share, and don't have the opportunity to even envision that world. But it gets challenging and frustrating at the same time. Life itself is beautiful, but we are on a constant death path. Within that beauty, each day that we live, we are dying. And so to live in those worlds is a bit of a paradox because, yes, it's beautiful to be able to say, you know, I've walked in wingtips and heels and have been able to navigate both. But I can't diminish the pain that sometimes you experience with that. And the point that I initially tried to bring out was that you do have some expectations that it might be painful in the broader community, but you also have that expectation in your own community that you don't have to be an educator and an activist to stand up, to be a part of what is supposedly your community.

GILBERT: I think what Brandon said a few minutes ago was really interesting, because I come from a place, Hawai'i, which is incredibly multiethnic in so many ways. And I came here to a place where the "emerging communities," the communities of color, are immigrants and from refugee communities. It was very different because I didn't have any sense of ethnic identity before I moved here. Everybody else was just like me. Being mixed was the norm, but coming over here, it's completely different and it's really tough to find yourself. I never thought of myself as Asian before I moved here, but that's because I wasn't Asian there. I was Filipino, I was Hawaiian, I was Puerto Rican, whatever, and that's what was most important. Over here, all of a sudden I became Asian or mixed and then, what did that mean for me? I started to try to search for those communities and then found that those communities themselves weren't necessarily as open as I thought they would be. Being told by other gay Asians that you're not Asian because you're not fully Asian, you know, that's very disheartening for me. But those are the types of reactions where I have to constantly navigate multiple identities. You know, not seeing myself reflected in the people that have power in the gay community, not seeing people who look like me holding those powers. That's basically where I'm at, but despite all of those frustrations, I think that it's an amazing opportunity. I am here, and I've been given the chance to work with multiple communities and try to address some of their issues. And I think part of it is because I was able to come from a place where the model was different. Communities of color did have power. I'm able to think of a place where, hey, this is possible, communities of color here can have the capacity to have power. I think we do have that opportunity, and right now the people here at this table are some of the leaders in making this happen, and that's exciting. At home in Hawai'i, you're in the long line of other people who are trying to make those changes. And they're so much farther along. But I'm able to do that in Minnesota.

KELLY: On the question of social change and dualities, I would like to bring up a situation that happened to me last week, where I had to question being black and being gay. I was denied entry into a bar/club and it wasn't a particularly fancy place but the guy just said, "You're not getting in." And it hit me like a brick. After my exchange with him, I completely fell apart. In that moment I had to ask myself, "OK, who am I? What does he see?" Because, as I saw the people in line it was just like, wow, my jeans aren't tattered. I'm not wearing sandals. It's Minnesota, you know, we're in April. I've still got shoes on, I look fairly appropriate, I look better than that, you know? I felt confident about that, and then I started questioning, What do I look like? And so, I'm speaking to my antithesis here, who's this tall, large, heterosexual, white man. I'm looking at him and saying, "But sir, but sir, but sir," and these people are passing and passing and he's shakin' his head "no." I said, "Well, is there someone else I can speak with?" And someone else comes and he looks at me and says, "Well, ma'am we reserve the right to refuse service to anyone for any reason at any time" and I was done, I had had it. I said I have just been handed something by someone so far up that I can't even—I just wanted to put it down on paper how intelligent I was and hand it to them. It was like I needed my papers to have my voice feel valid, in a way. And they weren't hearing it. And the question of duality—I was wondering, is it because I'm black or is it because I don't look like the other women coming into this club? I'm not in heels, the fact that I look kind of androgynous, OK. This is my style, this is what I like. But it's not what they let in, and I said, "Well, what's appropriate to get in here?" And he says, "I don't know, upscale." And I said, "Sir, what is upscale?" And he said, "Not you!" And so I left the establishment. I wanted to slash his tires. I wanted to—this anger inside of me that I could not even verbalize at that time, a mess downtown, just walkin' around and watching all these people going in and out of bars and no one really understanding, you know, what's the psyche of this. But that's the position I feel like we're at—this question of why. Is it my skin color or is it my sexuality? Can they see through that? Am I that transparent in a way that they can smell the gay on you? Is it my locks 'cause they're not tied back and pretty and I'm not wearing stilettos, you know? I don't get it.

BRANDON: What I think is telling is actually at the end of the day, it's not about you or what you were doing or what you weren't doing, it was all about them and, unfortunately, the way the system is set up is that it becomes about us. Like, you went there and you were the fierce Kelly that we all know, the beautiful woman that I see. And it was about them and their perception and what they wanted when they decided what is beautiful. But we end up internalizing that shit even if just for that minute when you're, like, "I'm about to break down." It's in that moment when we've been taught that the judgment that is laid on us by others is the judgment that we should have for ourselves and that we should try to fit ourselves into that.

KELLY: And believe for the rest of that week, I was on point. Every day I was good, I was feeling good, looking good, fresh and clean. I was looking *upscale.*

JASON: Well, I think this conversation is very interesting and very telling because Andrea brought up Du Bois and double consciousness and Brandon spoke to the power of living in a borderland with a double consciousness, but there are also the perils of the double consciousness. But add queer to that and then what happens? It's sort of these moments that we're talking about. I went on a road trip with my boyfriend—I was living in DC at the time—and we went down to Charleston and it's like everywhere we went I felt like people were staring at me. And there aren't a lot of Latinos in Charleston, so after a few days of this I'm finally, like, this is driving me nuts, why is everyone staring at me? Is this a queer thing or is this an of color thing? And my boyfriend was just, like, "Honey, it's a queer of color thing." You know, like, it was bold. I was operating at bold and I had both stacked against me in that moment.

GILBERT: You know what's so amazing about that? I've been out for about eight years now and I'm at a point where, I hate to sound trite, but I like being gay and I like being a person of color and I'll stick it in people's faces. You know, it's like, I'm a queer person of color and if you don't like it, then too bad because it's better! I feel like this is so empowering to be put in this position. I know that there was a time when it was so challenging to me, and I know that a lot of people are currently experiencing that as well. But I feel like I've moved past that. When I was doing HIV prevention work, I was able to meet a bunch of gay Asians who didn't identify as Asian, but I think it was really empowering for them to see that somebody like me could be out and visible because they asked me about those kind of questions—"How do I do it?" And I was, like, "You know, it's not easy, but I've done it for a while now and I'm used to it." That's one of the great things about being in this place and time in Minnesota. I think that if I were in San Francisco I'd be a dime a dozen, I really would. In Hawai'i a dime a dozen as well. So, over here, personally, it feels good to be able to affect change by example.

BRANDON: That's a perfect segue to the next question: Who are our mentors? How do we identify people as our mentors? And where have you found the people that mentor you? And also I think the question is, When have you found yourself as a mentor, particularly when you're least expecting it?

ANDREA: You mentioned leading by example, and as you guys know, I'm African American, transgender, six feet two inches tall, and I like to wear heels, and so you know, I'm visible. I mean, some queer people can move through the world without necessarily having that identity be visible unless they choose to make it so. But for me, my shit is pretty much on the table every day, as soon as I walk out the door. And I've come to embrace it as an empowering opportunity to teach people and to provide that role model, if you will, of being in the world and being effective and being engaged, while maintaining my authenticity to myself and to people I care about. It's kind of a cool thing, and I don't know how else to describe it. I mean, it does open you up to those constant stares at times, but I've tried to reprogram that to myself—that people are admiring me because I'm unique and beautiful and that's why they're staring. And I don't think that's necessarily a cop-out. I don't always think that's always the case, because I know there are a multiple number of reasons, but for me, that's how I process it.

NIKKI: For myself, and I was telling Kelly this earlier today, living in multiple worlds for me meant that I wanted to be prepared so that I wouldn't be vulnerable and so, I know this is sort of a gay syndrome, but I wanted to be the best little girl ever. I mean, I was smart, and I did what I needed to do, and then I went to college, and I did some things in college, and I went to law school. I made this conscious choice of wanting to be a lawyer because I wanted people to stop second-guessing what I was saying. I say the same things, you know, but when I said it and was just an undergraduate or some whatever, you know, it didn't seem to mean as much as when I say I went to the university Law School and so that should mean something more. And, I get that that's not about changing systems because it's not, because it's completely about working within systems, and there's a whole host of problems that go with it. But living in two worlds for me means that I just don't want to be vulnerable and I don't want to have to work harder than I already work to go out, to get out my door and live the life I live, be happy and safe, and so I felt like I wanted to build a little armor around myself. So that's what I did, and I'm not convinced it's the best idea—I mean, it works for me, but, I think, it's not about dreaming about a world that's bigger or better in lots of ways because it is so invested in really evil and insidious systems of oppressing people. It's what I do right now, but I don't think it's an answer. I'm trying to decide if I would change what I have done to be the person that I am today, and I don't necessarily think that I would, but at the same time, I'm not sure it was the best answer. It's like you're constantly thinking about "how can I make this world better" and "how much damage have I done to this world" because, like Andrea said, "we're living and dying at the same time," you're building and destroying at the same time. I hope I even out in the end and hit net zero, and maybe even be positive, but I'll aim for zero at this point and see if we can keep working.

KEVIN: I was going to say, like, "hitting zero" is a lot better than just "destroy, destroy, destroy." There's nothing we can do about what we might have done in the past or how we've influenced or haven't influenced things. However, what's clear now is that you probably can see where some things were a little marred, so, you know, trust that same thing's gonna come around again. So, in a sense, people like us, everyone who's here around this table, we still carry this very large and significant portion of the energies and the spirit of our ancestors. The ones that did affect change, the ones who did, maybe if it wasn't getting on some bus in Alabama and refusing to give up your seat, it was making sure that these three or four kids that you knew, who were going to an all-white school on the other side of town, got there and got there safe. That's activism. Teaching your kids now that it's OK to do your homework before you hit the PlayStation or "Aqua Team Hungerforce"—that's revolutionary! You understand what I'm saying? So, in so many ways, we all are doing some really, really good revolutionary work. The trouble comes when others don't recognize it. But here in Minnesota as far as mentorship, Andrea is one of my mentors, little does she know it. And I have been my own mentor at times, and I'm still working on that because I want to be my one and only—but, hey, baby steps.

ELLIOT: Yeah, I would say that I'm my own mentor as well. I can't think of any mentors. In terms of being protective, I think I've always been callous. Like, I consider myself a callous individual. I don't let others look into me. Maybe it was because I was a victim of sexual abuse, because I left home, and I just decided to be independent and do things on my own, that I've never seen, that I've never had a mentor. I already have this distrust for people who are "my superiors." So, in terms of that, I think a lot of people have viewed me as a mentor because of my callousness at the same time. And seeing things not affect me; me just keeping my cool. I don't know if that's a positive or a negative thing. Like, I don't really think of my life history as being bad or good, but it has been the past that has shaped what I have been doing. It's probably the reason that I'm in academia, which is a stressful environment, but it really doesn't phase me, 'cause I just have my own kind of way of going as well. So, like, being a mentor, being a part of community, is all very difficult for me, but at the same time I do pursue interest in the sense that, I don't know, I just like to see change happen. I also think of myself as kind of a mom in terms of wanting to make sure that people are OK.

BRANDON: Well, personally, I think that we have a distressing lack of mentorship that happens in our communities in lots of different ways. I know, for myself, I went through my own period of "I am my own superhero" for lots of reasons, like the kind of stuff that you bring up about past abuse and lack of trust. So I tried to rely on myself, to guide myself. My story was that I was too hurt, flawed, and in pain to do, to guide myself to where I needed to be. And sort of the catalyst to what happened to me was that I ended up going to chemical dependency treatment a couple of years ago. And at that point I realized two things: one is I can't be my own superhero, and the other thing is that I also had really amazing mentors in my life. And not just in the traditional sense. Like, I have some people who I view and they're older folks in the community and they have lots of wisdom and history, like Beth Zemsky and Susan Raffo, and some other people who I've worked really closely with and that have this amazing political knowledge and have walked such a path. You know, I can go to them and say, "I have this idea, I have this energy, I have this thought, I have this passion," and they're able to build me up even while providing critical feedback. But I also have folks that I consider my peer mentors, like Jason, Nikki, and Coya and people who I've grown with and that know me when I can't always know myself. Or that are able to see things with me that I might not be able to see for all those things that are blocked out when you look at yourself in the mirror. And because so many of our elders are hidden, particularly in communities of color, that haven't had the privilege to be out in the world in the way that I would have liked them to have been able to be out, I feel like I have to look to the people that are my age, that are my community, that I build community with to say, "You know what? I believe I'm a super, wonderful, magnificent person, but I also believe I'm crazy. And I also believe, I always have, that I'm learning what I need to do, and then, therefore, I need you to help me with that and then try to model that back when people step to me." And I think that it's really key that we all are wounded people that are walking this world and are walking our paths, and we often see it as being alone, but we're not really.

JASON: Something that Gilbert said actually connects to mentorship for me, about moving here and being suddenly a bigger fish, and if you lived in San Francisco you'd be one of the throngs of gay Asian males. I also grew up in a predominantly Latino environment and there, I was one of many, and then I moved here, especially being out and queer, and I was one of very few. Being in academia, I've gone through my own bouts of tokenization; you know, being asked to serve on committees, being asked to represent who I am, or large groups of people I don't know, based on my own personal identity. But one of the questions I have is, being one of fewer here, can that lead to a coalitional politics that's not possible elsewhere? We have to form coalitions, because I can't lead, or be part of a mass movement of gay Chicanos here. Because it would be a small little army, so I need friends and allies of other communities to march with me. So, if you'll allow me to segue, I ask that because it also has to do with my own form of mentorship. When I moved here in '97, I was this undergrad who didn't really have political experience, and two of my mentors are in the room—Nikki and Brandon—who I really looked up to in undergrad and still do. But on paper, we have very little in common, you know? In terms of race, class, gender, and sexuality, like, the three of us and our other little gaggle of friends are very different, and to me, that's coalitional politics. That would not have been available to me if I was one of 270 queer Latinos like I might've been at the University of Texas or at UCLA.

GILBERT: What's the motivation to do that if you're like everybody else? Over here, we have to work to get something; we all do. I feel like it's kind of tied to multiple identities. I have a lot of mentors for different reasons and I have a friend who was a mentor to me—he is a white guy, a really close friend. He was very instrumental in helping me come out. He had done it years before I did, so it was very helpful. But then I had to recognize that I also disagreed with him on many other issues as well. For example, he had a difficult time recognizing that there are special issues in queer communities of color that he completely minimized—how I felt it was slightly different coming out as a person of color. He did not see that as an issue; he thought that we were all coming out the same way, and so I had to recognize that I have other people in the community who are Asian who are my mentors, especially in the public health field. And yet I have to kind of convince them about the needs of the GLBT people who are Asian because they don't see it at all. They kind of minimize it or are embarrassed by it, for the most part. And so, my coalition building is pieced by different people, for different needs. I always thought about "Is there a way to get all those people in the same room?" I think there would be lots of Jerry Springer–like fights breaking out, but I think it's helpful when I'm always there, I'm a constant presence with Asians, Latinos, or with gay people, and trying to change what everybody thinks of people from those groups.

ELLIOT: Yeah, I totally agree with this idea of coalition and also the idea that coalitions are also strategic in the sense that you can use a particular coalition for particular purposes. And I think I do that as well, with, not necessarily having mentors, but I think the coalitions that are built in the Twin Cities have been extremely instrumental in just having a social environment, being around people who care about political issues, etcetera. And I think that's how I form my communities as well.

NIKKI: I think one of the things that comes with being smaller as a group of people is that you can get sort of starstruck with being the token—that everybody wants to hear what you have to say and that it's sort of important enough for them to listen but not act on, but still they are people who want to invite you to these things. I think to truly do coalition building, and to truly move forward, at some point, you have to shed some of that self-importance. Our titles aren't that important. And some of our organizations are good today, but they may not always be good in the future, and it's really sort of a recommitment to us as opposed to the things that others have sort of bestowed upon us. You know, we talked, also, about the negative things, but when we want to do coalition work, sometimes it *is* Jerry Springer work because we all kind of bring that in, and we all have our little piece of the pie. And we're big fish in Minnesota because there just aren't a lot of us, and yet it can be detrimental to us to move it and to do what we need to do to see each other's agendas. My thought, in answer to your question, is that it's a lot less about me, and trying to figure out, what is our "us"; it's hard to describe who "us" is. It's problematic on all sorts of levels, but to get there, at least I know that I have to be able to walk in and try to acknowledge my own baggage and leave it at the door. I can't always do that, but I will try.

KELLY: I guess, going off of what you just said, that's an issue on a much larger scale within other communities, not just this one. I know that, whatever community we choose to say this is, but hearing that black people don't want to vote for Barack Obama because he's Kenyan and he's not "African American." And I mean, you brought up the Willie Lynch syndrome and pitting people against each other based on these very, very minute differences and it's like . . .

ANDREA: Well, that's not even a difference, you know, he is African American. He's Kenyan and he lives in America, so he is African American. So, it's a really way-out concept that I can't even fathom.

KELLY: Exactly, and this coalition that we're talking about, even at this level, it's hard to build within larger communities because people are constantly saying that "Gosh, he doesn't promote my agenda!" And sometimes I think you have to prioritize your agenda and say, "Well, OK, let's not be idealistic for one minute" and let's just say in politics—and as a Rastafarian I say, "politricks"—you gotta say, "All right, well, what are my beliefs and what do I want to represent?" And if this person can promote my agenda as best he can, or from my options, then . . .

KEVIN: How far will I go to promote my own agenda? How far will I go to get that person into office? We're talking about fighting ignorance, and ignorance is a very strong mofo [motherfucker] and it's been around for hundreds and thousands of years, so I agree with you totally. That's the mistake we make the most. And not being open to the fact that there are different opinions and that my agenda isn't always the most important thing. My agenda is not going to keep somebody's lights on or food in their belly, but if you're the type of human who doesn't care about others, if you are only just selfish—which again is one of those things that we've been taught to do since we were little, "Don't let your friend play with that," or "Keep that for yourself," whatever—then you'll never get to the point in which you'll grow. You'll never get to the point of saying, "I need you in order to make this work over here." That's when you start to actually see some results and get happy.

ANDREA: I think it's so cool that you ended on that last comment because, you know, I just want to encourage us around this table as queer activists of color. I think the biggest challenge we're facing is that I don't really see a lot of work being done organizing within the queer community. I mean, literally, I feel like, and maybe it does go back to personal politics, but I feel like I struggle constantly in my identity as being trans, as being bisexual, as being African American within the LGBT community. And that just shouldn't have to happen. There's enough issues and work that we have to do as a queer community outside of that community to effect change that we shouldn't have to struggle within this community. And so, that's a frontier that we're not, as a broad-based, coalition-based queer community, doing enough work around, making sure that we can get to some level, common playing field in terms of respecting the members of our communities.

GILBERT: I think that as queer people of color, if there was a stage of coalition building, we're sort of at the beginnings of it. I think it's very difficult to address all of the issues, especially when the leadership is so thin. And so what I've been thinking, my goal is to help build the leadership, like with gay Asians, for example. I have to try to build that leadership, so that it's not just one, or two, or three people, it's more people who can address these issues. I struggled with that every day when I first started doing this kind of work. I thought that I had to do all of it. And now, I'm trying to focus on other things like, again, building that leadership. I want to contribute to that as opposed to just doing a little work here and there.

JASON: I think that call and challenge is a beautiful place to end this conversation.

Note

We are indebted to several individuals and organizations for making this project a success. The Twin Cities GLBT Oral History Project had the vision to begin collecting oral histories in the first place and to realize the need for a roundtable discussion focused on queer of color activism. Kevin Murphy was especially adamant in voicing this need and in supporting us through the process. Several people offered valuable advice during the process of putting together the roundtable, including Dennis Anderson, Kale Fajardo, Max Gries, Juliana Pegues, Anh Pham, Anne Phibbs, and Susan Raffo. Kandace Creel Falcón and Andrea Nordick provided quick and accurate transcription services. Jason Ruiz was a fabulous editor, collaborator, and friend. Finally, we want to thank that Powderhorn Park community of Minneapolis, where so many of the roundtable participants live, work, and play, and—of course!—the roundtable participants.

5. A SINGLE QUEER VOICE WITH POLYPHONIC OVERTONES ELISE MATTHESEN AND THE POLITICS OF SUBJECTIVITY IN THE TWIN CITIES

Mark Soderstrom

The world is full of surprises, and . . . I couldn't possibly invent such wild and complex human beings and options as seem to spring up naturally . . .

. . . even though I know that bisexuality is not half homo and half hetero . . . I've slipped into language supporting dualistic thinking instead of . . . challenging . . . the dualism itself. Sure, the division is . . . as real as any other social construct. . . . Whether that's a tool used to build or a weapon used to divide depends on what we're doing, and how we're defining . . . Us and Them at the moment.

—ELISE MATTHESEN, "What's So Funny about Bisexual Separatism?"[1]

We each create our own history, but we do so in a cultural context not of our choosing. This is the essence of what is called subjectivity. While dominant populations might understand themselves as self-made, nondominant populations are more likely to understand themselves as complex products of their own will in negotiation with their environment. In other words, a queer woman forms her subjectivity in and despite both heteronormative and homonormative culture; the subjectivity of a queer "farm kid" may negotiate one set of prejudices about sexuality on the farm and another set about rural life from queer people in the city. A close reading of one person's self-narrative and subjectivity may provide an effective way to examine issues of intersectionality—that is, how influences from multiple communities may interact to create that person's subjectivity, and how identifications with different communities may intersect in (and through) the life of the individual. For example, a person might be a white, middle-class American—and may also be both bisexual and a farm kid. By investigating one individual's subjectivity for the many constituencies that shape her self-understanding, we may also challenge the myth of the heroic individual who creates herself ex nihilo, and craft a more accurate portrayal that recognizes how we are all products of our larger contexts.

I first met Elise Matthesen in 1984 when we were both musical performers at the Minnesota Renaissance Festival. Through the years we kept in touch through music circles and a shared social network. When I went to my first bisexual conference, I found that not only was Elise there, she was one of the organizers. When I became involved in the Twin Cities GLBT Oral History Project there was no question that I would interview her. That initial interview that began in the early evening and didn't end until after midnight has since blossomed into a series of interviews and recorded conversations (as well as e-mails, IM chat sessions, shared archival material, open access to weblogs and online journals, and even the odd occasion of singing together again). This dialogue has all formed the source base for this article. Elise's willingness to tell her many stories and examine their interconnections allowed us to explore together the intersectionality of bisexuality, queerness, and life in the Upper Midwest. Although the peculiarities of Elise's life story brought me back to spend days in the process of listening and talking, all of our life stories share the same structure of being made and spoken in the intersections of many communities. What follows, then, is particular to one Midwestern bisexual activist, but the larger shape of it is common to the experience of all of us.

Elise Matthesen, née Krueger, was born in 1960, in a small town in Wisconsin. As a child she attended a conservative sectarian Lutheran parochial one-room school that was also part of her church. As an adolescent she refused her parents' request to go to a parochial high school out of town, and instead attended the local public high school. There she learned about the Kinsey scale and identified herself to herself as bisexual. She graduated high school and moved to Minneapolis in 1977 to major in mathematics at the University of Minnesota. She found the urban university environment jarring, but participated in activities such as community access television network ETC, Everyone's Television Channel. Elise dropped out of the university in 1981, the same year that she married a man, a union she acquiesced to because she didn't believe that other people like her—that is, bisexuals—existed. She also began performing at the Shakopee-based Minnesota Renaissance Festival. Elise left her marriage after "one year, one month, and six days, but who's counting."[2] Her economic and social circumstances were difficult, but she found refuge from her sense of isolation within the lesbian community. She became active in various women's communities in the Twin Cities area, and began to expand her political activism and involvement in GLBT issues. She has been a keynote speaker at various national and international conventions, cofounded the local bisexual organizations Biwimmin Welcome and BECAUSE, wrote the FAQ for the alt.polyamory site, wrote for the Twin Cities GLBT magazines *Lavender* and *GAZE,* and has become a figure of some prominence in several communities, among them the bisexual community.

This précis might be a way of summarizing Elise's life—but it tells us only how the world might define Elise. Such a story is too simple to capture anything about how Elise sees herself, or how she interacts and negotiates with the world. It certainly does not provide any detail about how her bisexual identity might intersect with her rural Midwestern identity, much less any of the other affiliations she might have. We must take a closer look at Elise Matthesen's narrative in order to perceive the finer-grained detail of her individual subjectivity, the way she negotiates her life within different communities.

Elise's narrative also provides an important challenge to the traditional gay/lesbian coming-out narrative—that is, a homosexual rural youth is misunderstood and unhappy, moves to the city, discovers that she is neither alone nor unworthy, and achieves acceptance by joining the larger lesbian community. The coming-out story is one of progress, emphasizing the elements of suffering, epiphany, and transformation.[3] It posits an essential self that is suffering because of denial; that self is then recognized at the moment of epiphany, and is made whole by the unifying transformation of coming out, of ending the fragmentation brought about by denial and self-repression. In Elise's narrative, by contrast, the open and contested nature of bisexuality creates a subjectivity that is also open and contested, encompassing many intersecting issues without privileging any single standpoint. Consider her remarks on bisexuality:

> If bisexuals are people who are attracted to both genders, then I am not a bisexual. I have deep reservations about any system for classifying sexual preference that requires definitions of both the desirer and the desiree in a binary, pick-ONE, model of gender as a basis for identifying sexual orientation or affectional preference.[4]

Above all, the traditional coming-out narrative presumes the ability, and desire, to join the (or at least a) mainstream—and presumes that the deviation from the "norm" is limited to sexuality and that that oppression/struggle is the only, or central, struggle in its subjects' experience/lives. By aligning experience along one single axis of identity and oppression, the traditional coming-out narrative elides vital other aspects of subjectivity. Sexual orientation is not always a singular oppression from which all the other aspects of identity resolve into a coherent unity. Rather, for many people, it is one aspect of subjectivity that intersects with many other aspects of many other identities, which together mutually inform each other (and sometimes contest each other). In Elise's case, her presentation does not privilege a sexual self as the only key to understanding her identity. Thus, although she adopts the term "coming out," that process has a different impact in her self-telling and self-making as a bisexual. Similarly, her presentation and activist writings link multiple oppressions to multiple identities, and she emphasizes commonalities between many oppressions, among them sexual, regional, and class oppression. Coming out does not provide closure in Elise's narrative; rather, it is another act (one of many) that continues processes of self-creation and performance.

Whether as a genre-literature fan dealing with mainstream literary disdain, a woman in patriarchy, a bisexual person dealing with mainstream heterosexual culture (and the orthodoxies of gay/lesbian culture), a Midwesterner dealing with coastal arrogance, a farm kid dealing with urban assumptions, a hearing-impaired person dealing with ableist structures, or as any of a number of other aspects of her identity, Elise finds and/or creates communities to support her. Elise's personality, sexuality, and activism are all expressed within a complex web of intersecting communities and identities. Her own construction of her self and identity rejects easy answers that would embrace a unified binary ideology (i.e., male/female or hetero/homo) in favor of a vision of multiplicity, shifting fluid identities, and variation. Her self-narrative is developed in tension between solidarity and individuation, and reveals a savvy navigation of the inadequacies of any one movement or group to encompass the variety of its constituents.

Elise performs identities that stand in the center of a multiplicity of communities and that function as intersection points between those communities. It is in this role as both center and intersection that she acts as a nexus point where communities come together—and, in the act of intersecting, create new communities and opportunities for activism and growth. In the same way that she herself participates in a number of overlapping peripheral communities, many of the specific constituencies of those groups are geographically located in the Twin Cities. In this way, Elise gives a portrait of one individual, and one location, that encompass multiple intersecting liminal communities and identities.

Elise resists current trends toward normativity in gay and lesbian politics, in part through these networks of associations that enable her to live a life outside the mainstream that is intellectually, materially, politically, socially, and perhaps spiritually fulfilling. This diversity of associations enables Elise to construct a subjectivity that is not tied to a single identity category; instead, her personality, sexuality, and activism are all expressed within a complex web of multiple communities, all queered to the mainstream—all, in ways, marginal. As many of these groups revolve around aspects of acting, costume, writing, performance, and music, I am terming the kind of identity construction that Elise engages in as "performative liminality." This is enacted in community ritual, writing, and music. It offers a space for critique, enables her style of activism, and empowers her preferred form of organization. Elise positions herself outside dominant American consumerist culture, even when she perceives elements of that culture among already-minority groups such as the gay and lesbian community, and this outsider status shapes her commitments, self-identity, activism, and politics:

> [Y]ou've got just as many people in the lesbian community or anywhere else that are—I could say I don't mean this as badly as it sounds but I don't think it's possible to say that with a straight face—who are mindless consumers. And, you know, a lot of people are mindless consumers. They seem to like it. I would run a-freakin' from it, but you know, there really were a lot of women in the lesbian community who wanted their parents' lives with the genders of their partners switched. . . . And that's okay. But really not what I wanted. I felt like an odd duck. I was an odd duck . . . in the lesbian community. . . . [which] is one of the reasons why when I would do some of the activist stuff . . . I didn't build assimilationist organizations [laugh], if you know what I mean.[5]

Elise's powerful emotional ties to liminal community networks of social support, and her performance of transgression as a part of her self and her self-conception, enable her to create a meaningful self-narrative that can instantiate her identity as nonnormative by providing a space that enables her to envision herself outside a narrative of assimilation. Shared communal rituals of parody and critique enable Elise to draw meaning for herself that is not generated by the dominant symbol system of consumerist mass society. In addition to providing the psychic space for re-visioning a self apart from dominant social expectations, for Elise liminal performance communities provide the actual social and material connections that enable her daily life and self-creation, through networks of shared affection, affiliation, critique, literature, music, recreation, resources, stories, and work. As one example, consider the intricate emotional and material ties that Elise has among the community of authors and organizers within science fiction and fantasy (SF/F) fandom. The Twin Cities have long been a site where many groups of SF/F fans and authors interact in such venues as conventions, festivals, bookstores, writers' groups, and house parties.[6] Elise herself has numerous friends in the community, has been and is romantically involved with members of the community, has had stories published in Fantasy anthologies, sells her jewelry at SF/F conventions, speaks and makes social and business connections at conventions, and has just published a chapbook of stories that were all inspired by pieces of her jewelry (and were written by well-known SF/F authors).

A closer look at how Elise discovered, participates in, and identifies with some of her liminal communities will give a better sense of how she sustains herself, imaginatively, socially, and materially, outside a system that privileges assimilation.

Many of the intersecting communities that support Elise involve literature (reading and production), music, and performance. One of the spaces where all of these intersect is in the filk music of SF/F fandom. Filk (the word itself is a parody of the term folk) is parody music written by amateurs for performance at gatherings of science fiction fans. Filk draws its melodies and themes from sources in mainline society and cleverly reinterprets and spoofs those themes in terms of its own community's issues, ideologies, sources, and so on, effectively mocking and critiquing dominant mainstream society (whether such critique is intentional or not). An example of filk would be this verse (sung to the tune of "A Bicycle Built for Two"):

> Daisy, Daisy, won't you come out and play?
> Bring your boyfriend, he won't get in the way.
> I'm getting a lot of practice

At *coitus interactus.*
I seem to be
Quite naturally
A bisexual built for two.[7]

In essence, and like other outsider cultural traditions such as labor music (from which filk draws directly), camp, remixing, and slash, filk queers mainstream society. It depends on it, draws from it, reacts to it, and engages it, but always sets itself at an oblique angle to it, an ironic distance that reinforces its self-aware nature. Elise is a composer and performer of filk music, and there is a way in which the queering that filk performs on the norm provides an ideal metaphor for Elise's own self-narrative and presentation.

Elise links her own musical styles and performance to the music that her father performed in her childhood. He sang in her community and church, writing and performing parody musical pieces; Elise describes her father as writing filk music even though he didn't know what filk music was.[8] She also mentions that her father, she feels, really wanted a son to be a minister and raised her that way—thereby imparting skills that Elise now uses in delivering speeches. In fact, she ties her broader sense of comfort in nonmainstream communities to the early childhood training she experienced in her family's church, emphasizing its separate nature ("peculiar," in the Deuteronomy sense). Although the church may be peripheral to the dominant society, her family's position inside the church is as one of the core families in that community.[9] This dynamic is often the case for Elise in her other communities as well. Elise often centers herself in her various liminal communities and is skilled at performing the roles of community founder, coordinator, or nexus point—all roles that convey deep insider status.

Early in her first interview Elise lays out the liminal position of her former church by narrating its history of withdrawal to the religious margins:

> It's a very fundamentalist Lutheran church. And it's a very small one. . . . But you know how churches keep breaking off from each other in the Lutherans? There'll be like a clump of them and some of them will say, oh, well the rest of you guys are too liberal. You're all going to hell. We're going to make a church that's right. Okay, so, the Lutheran church, and a clump breaks off and becomes the Missouri Synod. Then a few years later some people in the

> Missouri Synod look around and say, you guys are too liberal, you're all going to hell. And they break off and they become the Wisconsin Synod. My bunch broke off from the Wisconsin Synod because they were too liberal and they were all going to hell! And as far as I know, nobody has broken off from my bunch yet. 'Cuz I guess they're not too liberal.[10]

Elise draws a direct parallel between the lessons her father instilled in her about creating a small separate church and her own skills at building communities. Her mixed reaction to any political or cultural doctrine that she encounters also comes from her direct experiences with doctrine as a child: on the one hand, she learned to suspect doctrine as a divisive and dangerous force; on the other hand, she often emphasizes that a person should take doctrine (principles) seriously and be willing to sacrifice for them, either by creating a new separate church or community or by leaving that church and community as a matter of principle. She recounts her own process of leaving the church as one of doctrinal disagreement about issues of gender and sexuality.[11]

Having separated herself from her separatist church, Elise continues to draw on her childhood experiences: as she entered radical sex politics, she brought her past with her. The lessons learned in childhood she connects to her practice as a radical sex activist in her adult life:

> The stuff I learned that I agree with and think was good stuff—I don't see myself as ever having turned away from that. My religious practice has changed a lot. My communities changed a lot. The people in it and what they do changed a lot . . . But I really do see that I was taught to, I was taught to learn things. I do that! I was taught by my folks, tell the truth and be honest. . . . There was a lot about bearing witness and that you have a duty not to be silent when your silence is permitting or condoning or being complicit in a sin. . . . Because it was very much—in a way it was kind of a separatist church. . . . My view of Jesus and the disciples . . . is pretty radical and pretty queer.[12]

For Elise, church is not a site of assimilation, but a base of social resistance.

After Elise had left the university, the Minnesota Renaissance Festival became an important community in her life and activism. This provides a good illustration of the way that liminal communities intersect.

The Festival itself is a collection of disparate communities: many people spend their lives year-round traveling around the United States at various festivals and fairs, and make their entire livelihood on that circuit. This would include craftspeople as well as sought-after performers; Penn and Teller and the Flying Karamazov Brothers spent their early careers performing at Renaissance Festivals, including the one in Minnesota. Other people work at the Minnesota Festival for free; they are there to enjoy the carnivalesque atmosphere. A third community, the paid local professionals (performers, crafters, and musicians like Elise), only work their local Festival but earn a portion of their livelihood from it. While the traveling segment often lives on the Festival site for the entire run, locals like Elise form an intense but perennially temporary community that lives on-site for the weekends through the course of the run.

For Elise, the space of the Festival provided room to reconceive her life in a context outside the events in the rest of her life—where she was struggling financially and getting divorced between her first season working at the Festival and her second season. "Being out there performing the weekends of the Festival was wonderful and grueling in a good sort of a way and different from the stuff I had to deal with during the week when I was living in one room . . . and trying to figure out where the fuck I wanted my life to go."[13] She came into the Festival as a street performer, singing with a partner she knew from community-access television, and drawing performance ideas from her background performing a clown character/storyteller for her mother's library. Her time at the Festival gave Elise support as her life changed and she developed into a performer and a bisexual activist.

The Renaissance Festival was a nexus point that connected Elise to a variety of other significant communities. There is a somewhat more complex narrative that Elise tells about her entrance into the Festival—the long version versus the shorthand version—which demonstrates very clearly how Elise's communities intersect and how entrée into one such community would lead her into others. Instead of progressing from liminality into the mainstream via a mechanism of assimilation, Elise's life blooms as she encounters more of the interlocking web of queered communities that she lives in and through:

> So science-fiction fandom, definitely, I came to from the Renaissance Festival as well because it was at Wendy Ward's house [Wendy is a St. Paul musician,

> crafter, and artist, and provided a social center for a large number of local artists and musicians] that I met this guy who came to one of her parties. I think he probably came to the Dickens Christmas Tea . . . [Wendy] said, "Oh, you are really into science fiction, you should talk to this guy" [named Eric, who] . . . said, "Oh, well, you like science fiction, I really think you should come to Minicon" [a Minneapolis science-fiction convention; at her first Minicon, Elise moderated a panel on Heinlein and sex]. . . . I got into fandom because I talked to Eric at Wendy Ward's Victorian Christmas Tea, and I went to Wendy Ward's Victorian Christmas Tea because I met Wendy when I worked at the Festival, and I went to the Festival because Jane, my singing partner, said, "You should come perform with me out at Festival." . . . So Jane got me into the Festival and I met Jane because I worked on a comedy television show . . . in the beginning days of cable—community-access programming. . . . We did the comedy show for something called ETC: Everybody's Television Channel. . . . And Jane was in radio, when I met her she was in WMMR at the University.

This is one thread of many that can be traced through Elise's narrative and self-construction. The commonalities that link many of her communities to each other are their nonmainstream aspects, often their involvement in performance (theatrical or musical). They are havens where participants can reimagine themselves through masquerade or other sartorial experimentation (science-fiction/fantasy conventions, Renaissance Festivals, pagan ritual, leather, drag, etc.).

From the Renaissance Festival grew a collaborative partnership that would be integral to the rest of Elise's life and activism: she met Victor Raymond, a fellow sex activist. Together they founded and coproduced a fanzine—a self-published journal distributed in person or through the mail—about bisexuality and science-fiction/fantasy literature called *Politically Incorrect: The zine your lover warned you about*. The founding of this zine, and the longer-term activism and community building that sprang from that early collaboration, demonstrate the possibilities of cross-pollination, progress, and support that Elise's communities provide through their multiple intersections:

> Also, it was in a tent, in the campground, of Ren Fest that *Politically Incorrect* started, which was a fanzine for, as we said, "bisexuals and our friends and if you can't find yourself in either category that's just too damn bad." *Politically*

> *Incorrect* grew out of science-fiction fandom, the Festival, and bisexuals getting uppity. And the way it started was I was sitting in my tent one day on the hill. . . . And this guy comes up and plops down in the door of my tent and says, "Hi, I hear you're a bisexual, so am I, we've gotta talk, my name is Victor Raymond." That's how I met Victor.

Upon meeting Victor and discovering their common interests, Elise describes producing a zine as "the natural thing to do." In this way, Elise's experience shows how cultural styles of communication influenced the development of her approach to bisexual activism and even her conception of herself as an activist, performer, and fan. As she and Victor produced *PI,* Elise recalls that they used the two sets of lenses: genre literature, "which was outcast," and queer sexuality. *PI* would alternatively use one set to examine the other and then both sets at the same time to examine something else. For Elise these two lenses are linked.

Although *PI* itself was short-lived, it brought Elise and Victor into contact with many other bisexual activists. According to Elise, the energy generated by this journal significantly contributed to the development of a long-lasting Twin Cities–founded Midwestern bisexual organization and conference, BECAUSE, which was organized in part as a result of polarizing pressures from the larger gay/lesbian community that often treated bisexuals as immature at best, traitors at worst.

Another sexually liminal community that Elise participates in is the polyamorous community, which she initially encountered chiefly online during the early days of the Internet. Elise distinguishes between live and virtual communities, and is careful to recognize that being polyamorous and being part of the polyamorous community are not the same thing:

> Polyamory means "loving more than one." This love may be sexual, emotional, spiritual, or any combination thereof, according to the desires and agreements of the individuals involved. . . . "Polyamorous" is also used as a descriptive term by people who are open to more than one relationship, even if they are not currently involved in more than one.[14]

Elise discovered the newsgroup for her online polyamorous community early on, "back when there were only a few newsgroups and so people who were online would get a list in the morning if there had been any new ones made in the last week or so. . . ." In that virtual realm, she began to consider and discuss her polyamorous identity. For a while, that part of her life remained largely online: as Elise puts it, her polyamorous community lived in a box in her attic—the computer that she bought and her primary partner maintained. This online dialogue framed a significant aspect of Elise's self-conception as polyamorous. Her sexual subjectivity, therefore, in part developed in negotiation with others as part of the formation of an electronically mediated community. She recalls that the online polyamory groups were a community that included a significant number of people that she already knew from her involvement in SF/F fandom: "When I say mostly, it's . . . 30 percent people I already knew through fandom or could place—friends of friends. And the others just turned out to be feeling like that to me anyhow."[15]

Elise suggests how the online community interacts with other communities when she discusses how many polyamorous people she knew from elsewhere "in real life," including local people who, when they had realized who she was and that they knew each other, would invite her out to talk about polyamory issues in person over coffee.[16] The online community space allowed for conversations that might not have occurred outside the virtual realm. Thus, even among people she knew locally, it was through online interaction that she discovered aspects of their queerness, such as polyamory.

As Elise discusses the links among her diverse communities, such as polyamory, bisexual activism, pagan groups, science-fiction fandom, and leather, she sums it up as: "It all connects. It's hilarious how it all connects, actually. It's almost something I don't see. A fish trying to describe water."[17]

In describing her later phases of activism, Elise explicitly recognizes that her presentations and performances have drawn on the resources learned from her involvement in diverse liminal communities. She credits much of her ease with presenting keynotes at conferences to her performing experience on television and at the Renaissance Festival and other places; she also acknowledges the "mind and heart work" of performing and coordinating rituals in the pagan community, and the experience in coordination and communication that she gained through fandom.[18] Liminal communities gave Elise the opportunity to create a self outside the mainstream and the tools with which to build that self and other communities, and furnished necessary interpersonal networks.

Elise's self-narrative also shows a subjectivity that develops in tension with larger and more mainstream communities. This is certainly the case

Elise Matthesen in her living room in 1995. This photograph was featured on the front page of the Minnesota Women's Press *11, no. 20 (December 26, 1995–January 9, 1996) in a story about women in online communities. Photograph by Linda Cullen Weiley; courtesy of Linda Cullen Weiley.*

when she discusses her relation, as a bisexual activist, with the larger and more dominant gay and lesbian communities.[19] Elise draws from and has participated in larger Twin Cities gay and lesbian institutions: the Amazon Bookstore (a Minneapolis feminist bookstore), A Brother's Touch (a Minneapolis gay male bookstore), and the local Take Back the Night organization and marches, among others. However, she also frames her narrative within a discourse of exclusion. Her description of her relationship with the larger lesbian communities in Minneapolis is one of participation and yet marginalization, along lines of class, gender presentation, and especially sexuality. It is a fraught issue in which Elise expresses respect and a commitment to defend the women's community and yet describes and condemns aspects of its exclusionary practices against her and other bisexual women.

Elise often demonstrates her distrust of and exclusion from larger communities by renaming. A large part of her narrative and self-presentation centers on her relationship to a community that she characterizes as the "women's-which-means-lesbian-but-if-you're-not-don't-talk-about-it-and-we'll-still-let-you-in-community."[20] Another example is her filk-ish use of the word *wee-moon* to parody a specific part of the lesbian community: "there were all these alternate spellings: women, wimmen, wimmin, wymyn. . . . And I got all snarky with it, probably because the same people who were all wymyn-solidarity at me were also real skeptical of biwimmin, pushing us away. . . . I see my use of it as within a tradition of feminist self-satire."[21] The pressure Elise felt to organize as bisexual and to strongly identify as bisexual was in part a result of her perception that those communities tried to erase bisexual identity in general and to force her to identify as either straight or lesbian in particular.

Elise began going to feminist coffeehouses with her university roommates, and began going regularly in the spring of 1982 after her divorce.[22] She describes finding refuge in the lesbian community after the end of her marriage. She began to go to A Woman's Coffee House on Groveland Street and Nicollet Avenue in Minneapolis[23] and lived in an apartment on Twenty-sixth Street and Aldrich Avenue (which she characterized as being a place where 30 percent of the Minneapolis lesbian community had lived before). She characterizes the feminist communities she encountered and joined as a set of overlapping circles:

> The Amazon Bookstore days and the women's coffeehouse days were separated in time by a little bit. But I knew a lot of people from the women's coffeehouse days that I saw in Amazon later. A big overlap of people. The same community, really. I usually say community as plural because it's a Venn diagram and there's overlapping ones. But in that particular sense in that particular time, there was kind of a big community. It was the hugest circle of the Venn diagram.[24]

Elise was also involved in the recovery community, in which she witnessed a great deal of community building through basic social and physical interaction. In particular, Adult Children of Alcoholics (ACA) provided tools that allowed women to examine their lives in terms that included but transcended the persona and engaged the larger political realm:

> And a lot of them were not just about the effects of alcoholism on a family. A lot of people were in there dealing with effects of patriarchal upbringing. And effects of really basic misogynistic upbringing. And those things all could be addressed in the same place because ACA had a framework for

> dealing with what happened and dealing with what you want your life to be now. . . . [A]lmost all of the connecting and organizing I knew about at that point happened around 12-step stuff. . . . So I kinda think the big political and community stuff of . . . maybe 1980 to the late '80s, a lot of it centered on recovery stuff.[25]

Another cohort that overlapped with Amazon and ACA was the bar circle. Elise went to a women's bar, Foxy's, on West Seventh Street in St. Paul. The Coffee House was housed in the basement of a prominent Protestant church. As Anne Enke demonstrates, this physical space shaped the psychic and social space of the Coffee House, skewing it toward a middle-class respectability, propriety, and sobriety, which at once provided legitimacy and security, but also limited the behaviors (including the sexual expression) of its denizens.[26] Foxy's space had fewer of these imperatives. Elise discusses Foxy's, along with the Coffee House circle, contrasting the approaches of the different communities:

> Foxy's was, you know, different from going to the women's coffeehouse. The women's coffeehouse was very organic and it was also . . . definitely a politically correct place. And the bar was not. You don't wear leathers in a women's coffeehouse. Or, if you did, be prepared to get some shit for it. You could wear leather to the bar. You could shoot pool at the bar. . . .
>
> It was very exciting going to Foxy's. I think one of the things that was useful of the bars versus the coffeehouse was people would cop to desire a lot more in the bar. People in the coffeehouse . . . were looking to connect up with somebody. That would be really good. And then they could move in. But at the bar it was like, wow, I just want to watch all these women. I just need to be here in this room with all these women and I just need to see them. And I need to go, "ooh." Because my spirit needs that. My body needs some stuff too; we'll get to that [laugh]. But not that I got to it very often or much during those years. But at least the bar was a place where you felt like you could be that. There were more rules, more unwritten rules at the women's coffeehouse.

A different circle that Elise mentions is Dianic Wicca, which hosted rituals on major pagan holidays in the same space as the Woman's Coffee House:

> You pretty much had to know about the community to find out where it was going to be and when. But if you could find it, you could come. . . . [T]he people that did those rituals tended to be of two types. Pagan first and lesbian second. Or, lesbian first and pagan second. And they did not always see eye to eye on how to do things, but managed to get it together for the group, for the open community rituals . . . A lot of overlap between that and the 12-step because the 12-step thing about a god of our understanding, well, mostly goddess.[27]

Yet another community within the Venn diagram that Elise describes was one that she characterizes as having had significant overlap with the coffeehouse, and to a lesser extent with recovery, and even to some extent with the pagans: the Take Back the Night community, which focused on politics and activism—organizing workshops and rallies:

> Take Back the Night was very lively because it was overtly political. And it was a lot of workshop and rally. You know, big stuff. Trying to stop violence against women, violence against women and children. And so there were a lot of people doing a lot of work. There was also a certain amount of sexual orientation . . . community work going on in Take Back the Night as part of it.[28]

In a few particular ways, Elise did not feel entirely comfortable with the women's communities she encountered, even initially. For one thing, although Elise was hardly the only rural, working-class person in the women's communities, she felt marginalized nonetheless among a largely urban community in which she encountered ignorance of rural life. She explicitly draws a parallel between her previous experiences at the university, which she decries as unwilling to recognize the needs of working-class or farm kids, and the unexamined class biases of the women's community. This may stem from Elise's experiences in the Coffee House community, which, according to Enke, was shaped in part by its conformity to "white, middle-class cultural imperatives," despite its egalitarian commitments and intentions. The community's evolved practices often demonstrated little conscious regard for the concerns of its own rural or working-class (or nonwhite) members.[29] Particularly as someone who did not aspire to middle-class status, Elise felt unwelcome in that way. Also as a working-class person who presented as femme, Elise felt that the community's de facto "dress code"—short hair, work shirt, jeans, and work boots—was, aside from being another example of unmarked class privilege,[30] enforced in such a way that the community "turned their flannel backs on me en masse."[31]

She also describes an initial tension that was much more personal, rooted in the power dynamics of her own family:

> My parents met . . . when my mother was the director of a play and my father was the leading man. Which will tell you something about power and authority in my family and why I actually have a difficult time taking male figures of authority seriously. 'Cause to me—yeah, I understand the world we live in and all that and I am not arguing with the analysis of patriarchy—but somewhere in my head women are the powerful ones. So when I get involved with people it was a lot scarier to be involved with women. . . . they're the big bad ass. If they are not happy with you your life will not work.[32]

Elise's earliest outreach to women's communities therefore also had to navigate her own sense of women as threatening, and illustrates why for her the stakes were so high with regard to feeling accepted.

Elise remarks that at the time she became involved with the lesbian-feminist community, it was during an exciting time of change: "A lot of women's stuff springing up. A lot . . . already there, but a lot of stuff springing up."[33] And even though she was shy at that time and often "wasn't there to say boo to anybody,"[34] she herself describes the experience of "hang[ing] out and at least be[ing] in *some* kind of place that welcomed womyn who loved womyn" as much-needed "rain in the desert."[35] Her feelings toward those communities continue to be strongly protective: "I get cranky when I talk about it, but if anybody else ripped into it, I would go and defend it! [Laughs] I could be cranky about it because it's partly mine. Nobody gets to bash on it but me."[36] Even so, her experience of that community was not one of unalloyed acceptance; in addition to the class/rural/presentation issues, she felt a growing sense of her bisexual identity being unwelcome:

> [T]here was a lot of attitude against bis (personal ads saying "NO BISEXUALS" were the norm, for one thing, and everybody seemed to think bisexuality had better be a phase and you'd better get over it damn quick and "move up" into being a proper lesbian) in the community.[37]

In that way, Elise's narrative characterizes her relationship to the women's communities not as one of complete self-liberation, but as one of enforced self-denial that is reminiscent of her descriptions of what one didn't talk about in her church. She describes the support group she attended as a "lesbian support group that was mostly 'If you're bisexual, don't mention it because we're allegedly a lesbian support group.'"[38] The same institutions that provided support and a place for development and expression would also, in Elise's perception, act to discipline deviance and enforce conformity.

Elise describes as particularly intense the pressure she felt from the lesbian community to "drop bi" and identify as lesbian. She recalls that among many lesbians in her experience "bisexual" was an illegitimate category of self-identification for women. She argues that this pressure was directed entirely toward bisexual women, as (according to her) the lesbian community did not really believe in the existence of bisexual men.[39]

Even a liminal narrative still relies on the construction of others. There are times in Elise's rhetoric and self-conception that she posits a local lesbian movement that is stronger, more unified, more focused on mainstreaming, and more powerful than perhaps it was in the hindsight of the larger political context. However, from Elise's perspective as a bisexual woman attending the Woman's Coffee House and working at the Amazon Bookstore, that perception was her social reality. And, as Enke has shown, that section of the local movement was indeed influenced by middle-class aspirations, and by the time Elise encountered it in the early 1980s, it was also becoming more focused on sexual identity (i.e., lesbian identity) as the defining aspect of the movement. Thus the early 1980s were, in the words of a Chicago activist but applicable to the Twin Cities as well, "a bad time to be a bisexual."[40]

Bad, indeed. Marjorie Garber documents that the exclusion of bisexuality as a legitimate identity category has been a part of the creation of gay/lesbian as stable identity structures that parallel ethnic identity labels.[41] Elise's experience is not unique, nor is it safely in the past as an artifact of a previous era. As Christian Klesse points out:

> Within lesbian and gay politics bisexuality has always been perceived as rather problematic. Although early gay liberationism attacked rigid gender and sexual categorization as an expression of heterosexism . . . to consciously claim a bisexual identity was not well perceived. . . . The historical emergence

> and growing influence of political lesbianism within (lesbian) feminism created a situation in which this kind of criticism has been particularly pronounced, if directed against women."[42]

Amazon Bookstore was another community institution in which Elise felt pressure to adopt a more acceptable identity. When recounting her time working at Amazon, Elise describes feeling pressured to identify as "a lesbian who makes exceptions."[43] The idea of identifying that way is a modern coming-out frame in which, as Garber, Robyn Ochs, and Amber Ault all argue, bisexual women are persuaded to identify as lesbians because it is the same-sex-attraction side of bisexuality that is repressed. The construction of exceptions shows that the lesbian community perceived bisexuality as a two-sided choice, one hetero, one homo—in other words, that bisexuals had one lesbian side and one straight side. Therefore, the correct choice to move forward politically was to identify exclusively with one's lesbian side, that is, the more repressed identity, for the purposes of advancing society.[44]

Elise initially agreed to identify as an "exceptional lesbian" for purposes of solidarity; however, within a week she decided that such a move was "stupid,"[45] and she returned to identifying as a bisexual. Elise's writing about the issue argues that bisexuality (despite the root word for "two") is not dualistic but rather embraces a multiplicity of perspectives, identities, and behaviors. In her rejection of the "lesbian who makes exceptions" label, Elise resists the ideology of "one oppression per customer."[46] Ault examines the influence on bisexual women's self-labeling within the lesbian community and shows that Elise's experience is not at all uncommon. Many bisexual women in Ault's study report significant pressure to cover up their bisexuality in order to function in the larger lesbian communities. Like Elise, many of these women enthusiastically embrace the word *queer* as a more inclusive term.[47] It is interesting to note that in this context Elise's multiplicity-oriented rhetoric of bisexuality was formulated, at least in part, in antithesis to the normalizing binary pressure exerted by the larger lesbian community.

Even as Elise describes a dynamic tension with the larger lesbian community in her self-narrative, she also stresses a contemporaneously developing ideological affinity with gay men and a sense of gay camp sensibilities. At the same time that she was separating from her husband and discovering the women's communities, Elise also found *The Faggots and*

Their Friends between Revolutions, a 1977 book that delineated a politics of gay liberation and sexual revolution.[48] Elise describes the influence that that book, and the larger movement it represented, had on her while she was entering into women's communities in which she felt politically and personally isolated:

> this was something which, while I didn't agree with everything in it, sounded at least vaguely like where some of my politics were coming from. And the lesbian community . . . was not close to me politically on stuff about sexuality and stuff about sex and politics. And so there are two quotes from here that are—I lived on those quotes for years while in the frozen tundra of not having anybody around in the women's community who understood what the fuck I was talking about.[49]

Elise links her own politics to the radical and antiassimilationist positions of such groups as the Radical Faeries (whom she also relates to as fellow rural queers). The sensibilities and identities that Elise staked out were heavily influenced by gay male culture in a number of ways, including her femme sensibility and a gay male camp sensibility. She claims for herself the status of a femme who is not afraid to act butch because "as a true femme she knows how good it looks on her." Elise triangulates a gender identity in which her position is rejected simultaneously by her Amazon Bookstore colleagues as too female because her femme presentation adhered to traditional gender performance and too male since the camp spin she put on that performance was rooted in gay male culture. Her ironic confusion of identity categories is foregrounded in her framing of her narrative when she retells her joke that in her last life she was a "good little drag queen who said, 'Please, God, next time I wanna be a blonde with tits!'"[50]

Elise's collaboration with Victor Raymond and their writing on bisexual issues led them to the event that spawned BECAUSE, the local organization and conference for bisexuals. Again, this happened in direct relation to the larger gay/lesbian community; Elise places the date at 1990 or 1991. The Gay Lesbian Community Action Council brought together a panel of local bisexuals that included Elise and Victor, and it was through that meeting (according to Elise) that the idea for BECAUSE was born:

> Victor and I got together on that, and then we met a bunch of coconspirators at a famous in-service that Gay Lesbian Community Action Council

> had. They had an in-service on bisexuality. Because they . . . had bisexuals in the mission statement and it was pointed out that they . . . had a lot of unexamined bi-phobia floating around the community and in the office too because you open the door and it gets in there. . . . So they invited all their board members and their people . . . and everybody. And a bunch of known bisexuals to sit on a panel. And on the panel, it was me, it was Victor, there was Gary Lingen, pretty sure Gary was there. There was Rob Yeager . . . [and] Joe Duca, who did the bisexual needs assessment at the university in the late '80s, early '90s.[51]

Elise traces the birth of BECAUSE to this event, as she and her fellow panel members decided that they were more interesting than the audience and ought to have their own organization and conference (along the lines of the kind of conventions that they were involved in working on for SF/F fandom):

> At the break, at the intermission of the in-service was when all of us on the panel went out in the hallway and said, goddamn it, we need a bisexual conference! And that's when we decided to make BECAUSE. Because we had so much fun being on a panel with each other, we're like, man, let's ditch these guys and just hang out! [laughter] You know? There's tons more of us, I know there's more of us. Okay, we gotta have a conference, damn it. All right, you're right. So then we had an organizing meeting at the University of Minnesota. . . . So, that came out of the GLCAC in-service.[52]

Elise narrates early discussions about whether or not to adopt the word *bisexual*. Despite its problems (implicitly reinforcing dualistic thinking), she suggests that the tension with the larger homosexual community prompted the choice. *Bisexual* is the right word for Elise, in large part because "it makes gatekeepers nervous":

> The right people to make nervous were the people who had laid out an entire . . . intellectual chart of exactly how sexuality works. Because, you know, . . . generally the odds are I'm in one of the categories they'd missed. No matter who is making the chart. . . . Also, sometimes gatekeepers are absolutely the right people to bug. People who say, "Well, this is the lesbian community. Here's what you have to do to get into it. If you're not in it, you're in the straight community." . . . Gatekeepers to the straight community too who really want to think of, you're either straight or you're gay. And if you're

> gay you're sinful and fallen. . . . They have a lot in common . . . [with] the gatekeepers in the lesbian community. Well, you're either lesbian or you're straight. And if you're straight you are sinful and fallen and patriarchal and all that shit. Mean, nasty, ugly stuff. Oh, [the word *bisexual*] made the purists really nervous. I like making purists nervous.[53]

Here again Elise stresses her in-betweenness, in that she points out that she never fit within the clean categories of the community "gatekeepers." It is interesting that Elise frames her experience with lesbian/women's community politics through the lens of her childhood in sectarian religion. Her parallels of lesbians and fundamentalists as similar from a bisexual perspective is not hers alone: Amber Ault demonstrates that while bisexuality indeed draws the ire of gay and lesbian activists, it also draws the strongest condemnation from the Christian Right, as the Traditional Values Coalition labels bisexuality the "ultimate perversion," even beyond homosexuality.[54]

Instead of leaving home and overcoming, as in a traditional coming-out narrative, Elise frames her experiences as a process of finding what she left at home in the communities that she moved to. On the one hand, she finds the rigidity and dogma of her childhood in the alternative communities; on the other hand, the tools she learned from her childhood are also valuable in motivating her and enabling her to build (what she sees as) new and more liberatory communities and organizations. Elise's subjectivity has been deeply shaped by her positive and negative encounters with the larger and more dominant gay and lesbian communities, and her narrative shows both the pressures to assimilate and the motivations to oppose assimilation. While the gay and lesbian communities have increased their visibility, the pressures on bisexuals leave them as the "often . . . vigorously suppressed" letter of GLBT.[55]

Whenever anyone asks for Elise's biography, she emphasizes that she is a "lifelong Midwesterner in the Upper Midwest of the U.S.," pointing out that she has only lived in Minnesota and Wisconsin.[56] On the one hand, it seems ironic to emphasize Elise's self-constructed liminality and to suggest that she rhetorically places herself squarely at the heart of a Midwestern community and its traditions; however, in Elise's framing, the Midwest (especially the working-class, rural Upper Midwest that she identifies with) is itself portrayed as a liminal community in terms of dominant national ideologies. She posits that Midwestern working-class, rural identity is often overlooked by coastal activists who don't see that the Midwest has its own traditions of activism and reform. Elise's rhetoric metonymically links the opposition to normalizing pressures on bisexuals (whether from heterosexual mainstream society or gay/lesbian binary society) with what she sees as Midwestern resistance to coastal arrogance. Whether she is describing herself as an "uppity" bisexual resisting pressures from gays and lesbians to "grow up" and choose one gender or the other, or as a proud, lifelong Midwesterner who has never lived in the East or the West and developed her queerness in the heartland, her rhetoric maps bisexuality as resistance to binary normality and Midwesternness as resistance to bicoastal imperialism.

Elise chooses to open her first interview with a declamation on her Midwestern identity and roots. The emphasis that she puts on Upper Midwestern identity marks her position as outside what she sees as the dominant coastal siting of the gay and lesbian (and even bisexual) movements. Her insistence on being seen by others as Midwestern creates a statement of oppositionality:

> When I go other places . . . I would say that I was a lifelong Midwesterner in the Upper Midwest of the U.S. Born and bred and never lived anywhere else, because that's always been really important. Especially . . . if I was giving a keynote somewhere, or doing something at a Pride parade or a gathering or whatever. Because I think there's really particular history in the Midwest, and especially in the Upper Midwest, and especially in the Twin Cities and the larger whole state of Minnesota that a lot of people not from here don't understand. And . . . it's really, really important in shaping how . . . we do things here. . . . here really matters.[57]

Elise also describes how coastal activists assume that she came out and acquired her theoretical understanding of bisexuality while living on the coast, or else assume that she wants to move to the coasts and just hasn't yet. In typical filk fashion, she has responded by writing a song titled "California Dickheads" (sung to the tune of "California Dreaming"). In her poem "Just Because," which she read at the International Conference Celebrating Bisexuality in New York City on the twenty-fifth anniversary of Stonewall,[58] Elise disparages a perceived coastal ignorance of Midwestern issues, and even geography. The poem was written in response to Midwestern organizers' frustration with the interference of more dominant coastal-based organizations in Midwestern activities; it focuses on an incident when coastal leaders of bisexual organizations were seen to be imposing their agenda on Midwestern activists from the top down. She read from her poem:

> . . . musta been a bad week on the east crust
> and likewise on the west
> . . . let's go tell some midwestern hicks
> how to run their liberation
> gawd knows they'll never get it on their own
> you got to put on a conference
> they called and told us
> . . . meanwhile
> we're having our lives
> putting on a small but intense conference of our own
> . . . and building our own communities
> we have our own agendas
> we grow em in between the rows of corn
> fetch em up from the lake with the bluegills
> hang em along the roofline with the icicles
> to catch the light
> when the sun comes up over the prairie. . . .[59]

This is a good example of Elise constructing a Midwestern identity in opposition to what she perceives as the dominant identity. Elise connects her Midwestern background to her embrace of a type of populist politics of participation. Asked whether citizenship, as opposed to consumerism, is a Midwestern value, she replies:

> Oh, yeah, I really think so. Definitely Minnesota, the Dakotas, Wisconsin because, I mean, all the grange stuff here, all the history. It's people generally banding together to say, "Hey this thing isn't working right." Or "Hey, that deal is stacked. We gotta do something about this." Or sometimes it's people making a farmers' co-op for not so much "that deal is stacked" reasons, although that's in there too, but "we need to buy a lot of this. Let's get together and make the purchase jointly. We need to do this." So there's a whole lot of stuff is made by people. Organizations are made by people. Institutions are made by people. . . . people that talk about the individualist

thing in the Midwest really don't get what the history of farmers' co-ops and granges stuff is here. Because it is about individuals banding together. And you have to have both at once.[60]

Again, far from transcending, leaving, or abandoning her rural upbringing, Elise carries it with her. She still proudly announces that she is from farm stock and grew up in a farming town. These roots are fundamental building blocks of how she sees herself in the world and they are tied closely to how she views herself as a Midwesterner. Her descriptions of the Midwest have a strong rural association (and her rural identity also has a strong working-class component). Even as Elise cites Midwestern history, she foregrounds its rural elements: Ignatius Donnelly, the Grange, the co-op movement, agricultural settlement, and so on. She sees her own activism as a product (and in the tradition) of left-wing working-class prairie populism. This tradition, she suggests, has been largely marginalized and ignored even among otherwise progressive people. She ties this to what she perceives as a history among liberal reformers of overlooking the region, and the working class generally.

Elise takes great care to defend the complexity of rural life and community, and often challenges stereotypes of rural communities as monolithically intolerant. In an article in which she is interviewed for the Twin Cities GLBT magazine *Lavender,* Elise explicitly addresses and parallels urban antirural ignorance and stereotypes with antigay stereotypes. In a companion piece, she also suggests that the urban homosexual community makes assumptions about rural queer life: in particular, it assumes its own cultural and moral superiority, and the superiority and greater tolerance of the city.[61] In the *Lavender* interview, Elise defends her rural roots, stating that while rural people may not be "the most tolerant of people," they also "are . . . not likely to judge someone based on one issue." She sees the rural tradition of cooperation as a source of tolerance, and stresses the interdependence of farm life as a cultural attribute. In her portrayal of the more nuanced rural perspective, being queer is not as significant a moral failure as "getting the garden in late."[62]

Elise is especially careful to emphasize climate and geography as influences in the Midwestern populist tradition. She traces her style of finding grounds for cooperation to living in a place where this is necessitated by weather, and characterizes Midwestern solidarity and community as a cultural product of the climate, Nordic heritage, and rural roots.[63]

In an article on polyamory, Elise ties her rhetoric about the climate and geography of the Upper Midwest into her political activism. She parallels herself, as a polyamorous woman, to the prairie that no one person or tribe can own but that many can share. She then describes the jealousy that comes from the desire for sole ownership as a blizzard or sleet storm:

> Having experienced jealousy . . . I know it is painful, like being outdoors during a sleet storm, feeling little needles of freezing doubt pierce my skin and my heart. . . . Terror is cold, like prairie cold. . . . I said, "No one owns me, but these are the tribes that range over me," and I felt like I was speaking in the first person prairie. . . . My people came to the prairie recently; they learned some things from the people who were here before them. These lessons are more urgent now, but they are the same lessons. The land cannot be owned.[64]

Often Elise's consistent positioning of herself as a product of her region and heritage plays with ethnic and regional characteristics and stereotypes. In an aside as she reads a speech during one of the interviews done for this essay, she suggests that conscious misunderstanding is a "tactic amongst my people."[65] She often deliberately calls attention to her use of idiomatic Scandinavian-influenced Upper Midwestern language.[66] At times she has functioned as a sort of Midwestern cultural booster to people from other regions. When describing the tour that Elise gave him of the landmark Minneapolis Norwegian store Ingebretsen's, for example, native Arizonan and current New Yorker Patrick Nielsen Hayden said: "We have been to Ingebretson's [*sic*] with Elise Matthesen, which is something like visiting the Grey Havens with Legolas."[67] This interaction also points to the intricacy in which Elise's liminal communities intersect rhetorically: as a member of the fandom community that Elise inhabits, Nielsen Hayden uses Tolkienian references to describe his experience, much in the way that Elise occasionally employs that frame when characterizing the Upper Midwest to SF/F fans as "the Shire."[68]

It bears mentioning that Elise's rhetoric often narrowly defines Midwestern identity as based in the (largely ethnically Scandinavian, or, as she calls it, "Scandesotan") farm experience.[69] She often tweaks the types popularized by Garrison Keillor, but at times her descriptions partake of the homogeneous perspective that lies behind Keillor's characterizations. Elise's depiction of the Midwest may partly play into the trope of the nostalgic narrative of a white urban migrant who can speak of her rural childhood with fond longing from the comforts of an urban home on a bus line providing access to medical care or college classes, on the one hand, and an Asian grocery or Uncle Hugo's Bookstore, on the other. Nonetheless, Elise, rather than leaving behind her rural, Midwest, working-class, unfashionable upbringing, proudly carries it with her and uses it to fashion the foundation of her personal, sexual, and political identity.

Aside from the traditional coming-out narrative, another standard way of interpreting Elise's narrative would be through the religious frame of her own childhood: a young, upright-but-willful girl leaves her home in the virtuous rural countryside and moves to the city for her education, where she falls in among liberals and other bad influences. Her pride leads her to question the wisdom of her church, which she leaves, ultimately sliding into sin and sexual depravity and away from the true faith and righteousness.

Neither the progress nor the perversion tale does justice to Elise's narrative, nor does either capture her own framing of her subjectivity. The standard narratives of coming out as gay or falling into sin are both story structures that furnish resolution: they are both ends in themselves that provide a modernist sense of closure and completion of an identity. In Elise Matthesen's words, coming out as bisexual does not answer questions or close conversations—instead, it provokes and necessitates them. Thus, her narrative does not become whole. It remains fragmentary and divided, a continuing exploration rather than a completed journey. Instead of progressing from the marginal to the conventional, Elise lives in the intersection of many communities, each helping to form and inform the others, and each remaining apart from the dominant mainstream. While this sets the background for her subjectivity's relation to the dominant social system, her subjectivity is neither assimilationist nor mere inversion. Rather, Elise's tale is postmodern: a tale of many tales, without teleology or convenient closure. It is a tale that stresses multiplicity, fragmentation, irony, and indeterminacy. However, even as her tale resists reduction to a single standpoint or community, her life is enriched, not impoverished, by the multiplicity of her liminal communities.

Nan Alamilla Boyd argues that the way oral histories are often collected can constrict the shape and categories of LGBT identities.[70] Limiting LGBT, or QQIA (Queer, Questioning, Intersex, Asexual), for that matter, to the one axis of sexual orientation erases and elides many other queer identities and aspects of the lives of queer people. Even along that one axis, identities such as bisexuality and trans identities have been variously treated as traitors, regarded with suspicion, or at best offered an uneasy coexistence. The result of that process is that the community is losing access to understanding vital aspects of its own history and constituencies. It does not have to be this way, however. Oral history can instead be used to enlarge the scope of subjectivity within the queer community. By embracing intersectionality, by understanding the ways in which queer people's subjectivity can vary fluidly within a complex matrix of intersecting social hierarchies and identities, we gain a much more nuanced and accurate picture of who we are and how we live. Elise Matthesen's story is one example of this—by appreciating the way that she creates herself in alliance with, in negotiation with, or in opposition to various other communities, we can see the way that her subjectivity operates. Although not all of us are as politically involved in as many overlapping communities as she is, all our subjectivities are the complex products of many social circles and forces. It behooves us all to apprehend how this works.

Notes

1 Elise Matthesen, "What's So Funny about Bisexual Separatism?" (keynote speech presented at the International Conference Celebrating Bisexuality, also referred to as Third International Bisexual Conference, New York City, June 25, 1994), 2–3.

2 Elise Matthesen, interview by Mark Soderstrom, digital recording, Minneapolis, July 29, 2005. As a stylistic note, ellipses in interview quotations represent only elisions made by the author, not pauses made by the interview subject.

3 Ken Plummer, *Telling Sexual Stories: Power, Change and Social Worlds* (London: Routledge, 1995), as cited by Merl Storr, "Postmodern Bisexuality," *Sexualities* 2, no. 3 (1999): 312.

4 Elise Matthesen,"Female-to-Elf?" (keynote speech presented at the Eighth Annual BECAUSE conference, St. Paul, April 2000), 8. Speech available online at http://groups. google.com/group/alt.polyamory/msg/37032e158dbefc85?hl=en.

5 Matthesen, interview, July 29, 2005.

6 Historically, Minnesota, and particularly the Twin Cities, has had active science fiction/fantasy organizations since 1935, which have included such genre luminaries as Clifford D. Simak, Poul Anderson, and Gordon R. Dickson. Notable contemporary fandom organizers in the Twin Cities SF/F community include David Dyer-Bennett and

Fred Levy-Haskell; notable contemporary authors include Patricia Wrede, John M. Ford, Pamela Dean, and Lois McMaster Bujold. For more on the history of fandom in Minnesota, see Lloyd Biggle Jr., Dave Innes, Steve Innes, Ted Reynold, Doug Rice, and Candace Massey, "From the Wilds of Minnesota, an Account of Fandom in Minnesota," as quoted on "Minnesota Day," compiled by Joyce Scrivener, *views,* Minnesota Society for Interest in Science Fiction and Fantasy (MISFITS), 1999: http://www.misfit.org/views/jscrivner20000215.htm.

7 Nate Bucklin, "A Bisexual Built for Two," as quoted by Elise Matthesen, interview by Mark Soderstrom, digital recording, Minneapolis, August 11, 2006.

8 Elise Matthesen, interview by Mark Soderstrom, digital recording, Minneapolis, August 11, 2006.

9 Matthesen, interview, July 29, 2005.

10 Ibid.

11 Ibid.

12 Elise Matthesen, interview with Mark Soderstrom, digital recording, Minneapolis, December 22, 2005.

13 Matthesen, interview, August 11, 2006.

14 Elise Matthesen, "alt.polyamory Frequently Asked Questions (FAQ)," September 9, 1997: http://www.faqs.org/faqs/polyamory/faq/.

15 Matthesen, interview, August 11, 2006.

16 Ibid.

17 Matthesen, interview, July 29, 2005.

18 Ibid.

19 Her relationship with the larger lesbian communities in Minneapolis is a particularly important factor in her self-construction and narrative, as is shown by its repetition in different interviews in which aspects of this relationship are repeated, sometimes in identical rhetorical formulations (interviews, July 29, 2005; December 22, 2005; August 11, 2006).

20 Matthesen, interview, July 29, 2005.

21 Elise Matthesen, instant message to author, June 14, 2008.

22 Matthesen, interview, July 29, 2005.

23 Elise Matthesen, e-mail message to author, July 22, 2007.

24 Matthesen, interview, July 29, 2005.

25 Ibid.

26 Anne Enke, "Smuggling Sex through the Gates: Race, Sexuality, and the Politics of Space in Second Wave Feminism," *American Quarterly* 55, no. 4 (December 2003).

27 Matthesen, interview, July 29, 2005.

28 Ibid.

29 Enke, "Smuggling Sex through the Gates," 647, 657, 658.

30 As Enke notes in ibid., 647.

31 Matthesen, "Female-to-Elf?" 3.

32 Matthesen, interview, August 11, 2006.

33 Matthesen, interview, July 29, 2005.

34 Ibid.

35 Matthesen, e-mail, July 22, 2007.

36 Matthesen, interview, July 29, 2005.

37 Matthesen, e-mail, July 22, 2007.

38 Matthesen, interview, July 29, 2005.

39 Matthesen, "Female-to-Elf?" 8.

40 Kathleen Thompson, as quoted by Anne Enke, *Finding the Movement: Sexuality, Contested Space, and Feminist Activism* (Chapel Hill, N.C.: Duke University Press, 2007), 82.

41 Marjorie Garber, *Vice Versa: Bisexuality and the Eroticism of Everyday Life* (New York: Simon and Schuster, 1995).

42 Christian Klesse, "Bisexual Women, Nonmonogamy, and Differentialist Anti-Promiscuity Discourses," *Sexualities* 8, no. 4 (2005): 455.

43 Matthesen, interview, 29 July 2005; Matthesen, interview, 22 December 2005.

44 Garber, *Vice Versa;* Robyn Ochs, "What's in a Name? Why Women Embrace or Resist Bisexual Identity," in *Becoming Visible: Counseling Bisexuals across the Lifespan,* ed. B. A. Firestein (New York: Columbia University Press, 2007); Amber Ault, "Ambiguous Identity in an Unambiguous Sex/Gender Structure: The Case of Bisexual Women (1996)," in *Bisexuality: A Critical Reader,* ed. Merl Storr (New York: Routledge, 1999).

45 Matthesen, interview, July 29, 2005.

46 Victor Raymond, as quoted by Elise Matthesen, interview by Mark Soderstrom, digital recording, Minneapolis, August 11, 2006.

47 Ault, "Ambiguous Identity," 177–78.

48 Larry Mitchell, *The Faggots and Their Friends between Revolutions* (Ithaca, N.Y.: Cadmus Books, 1977).

49 Matthesen, interview, December 22, 2005.

50 Matthesen, "Female to Elf?" 3.

51 Matthesen, interview, July 29, 2005.

52 Ibid.

53 Matthesen, interview, December 22, 2005.

54 Ault, "Ambiguous Identity," 171.

55 Robert Mills, "History at Large: Queer Is Here? Lesbian, Gay, Bisexual, and Transgender Histories and Public Culture," *History Workshop* 62 (autumn 2006): 258.

56 Matthesen, interview, July 29, 2005.

57 Ibid.

58 Also referred to as the Third International Bisexual Conference, or 3icb. See "A Brief Trip thru Bisexual NY's History," New York Area Bisexual Network, http://www.nyabn.org/Pages/WhoWeR/OurHistory.html.

59 Matthesen, interview, August 11, 2006.

60 Matthesen, interview, December 22, 2005.

61 Elise Matthesen, "Letter to a Relative Who Is Moving to Minneapolis," *Lavender* (November 21, 1997): 30.

62 Aaron Lichtov, "Out in the Sticks: Growing up queer in rural America," *Lavender* (November 21, 1997): 28.

63 Matthesen, interview, July 29, 2005.

64 Elise Matthesen, "First Person Prairie: Reflections on Jealousy," *Flood Tide* 5, no. 3 (spring 1994): 1–2.

65 Matthesen, interview, August 11, 2006.

66 Ibid.

67 Patrick Nielsen Hayden, comment, December 12, 2004, at 11:24 p.m., on Teresa Nielsen Hayden's post, "So that's why . . . ," *Making Light* blog, http://nielsenhayden.com/makinglight/archives/ 005917.html#70524.

68 Matthesen, interview, December 22, 2005.

69 Elise Matthesen, "A Rant," *Honour Your Inner Magpie,* LiveJournal post, April 28, 2008, http://elisem.livejournal.com/1248186.html?page=2.

70 Nan Alamilla Boyd, "Who Is the Subject? Queer Theory Meets Oral History," *Journal of the History of Sexuality* 17, no. 2 (May 2008).

6. TWO-SPIRITS ORGANIZING INDIGENOUS TWO-SPIRIT IDENTITY IN THE TWIN CITIES REGION

Megan L. MacDonald

GLBTTwo-Spirit (GLBT2SP) indigenous people began organizing in the late 1980s in the Twin Cities region in an amazingly active way. While unclear if they perceived themselves as part of a more U.S. national, or transnational, GLBT movement, indigenous GLBT organizers in the Twin Cities region certainly embedded themselves at the centers of indigenous politics and community building on an intertribal level. They founded groups that became powerful cross-country networks for intertribal GLBTTwo-Spirit connection, conversation, and support. These networks are of particular importance because, while Minnesota is home to many bands of primarily Anishinaabe and Dakota people, the Twin Cities themselves are an urban magnet for indigenous individuals from across the United States, Canada, and, increasingly, Mexico. A predecessor of the Twin Cities indigenous GLBTTwo-Spirit activism is found on the west coast of the United States. The Gay American Indians (GAI) organization had been well established, emerging in 1975, and was already a loud voice in indigenous GLBTTwo-Spirit social community construction and larger Native political issues facing its community members (particularly fishing rights, land and water rights).[1] Around 1987–88, the Twin Cities was proving incredibly fertile in GLBTTwo-Spirit organizing, with the advent of groups such as the Indigenous Peoples Task Force (formerly the Indigenous AIDS Task Force) and American Indian Gays and Lesbians (AIGL), both in 1987.

This chapter discusses the activism and organizing in and around the Twin Cities of GLBTTwo-Spirit indigenous people. It contextualizes this organizing within the larger scope of indigenous activism and positions the activists as playing a pivotal role for the sustenance of GLBTTwo-

Spirit community and well-being. This chapter also discusses Twin Cities organizing as a microcosm of the larger, intertribal, pan-U.S. national Two-Spirit movements taking place over the course of the last twenty years.

If all this organizing was happening, on what were the two-spirit movements founded? In the early 1990s, the term "two-spirit" evolved out of an international–intertribal conference of Native and non-Native gay men and lesbians in Canada, many of whom traveled from Minnesota. The intention of two-spirit was to provide indigenous people with active language with which to encompass American Indian queers, but also to serve as a replacement for the outdated term "berdache."[2] Two-spirit, as both a name and an ideology, developed out of a long history of co-optation, power, and colonization. In many ways, two-spirit gives the power of naming back to indigenous people by emphasizing the spiritual space (which stems from indigenous ways of knowing) within sexualities that Western society considers purely physical in origin. Beth Brant, a Mohawk lesbian, finds satisfaction in the term "two-spirit," stating that she will "not make distinctions between sexuality and spirituality."[3] She continues: "our sexuality has been colonized, sterilized, whitewashed . . . what the dominant culture has never been able to comprehend is that spirit/sex/prayer/flesh/religion/natural is who I am as a Two-Spirit."[4] Brant also indicates that when Native people fight over who or what is "more traditional," we are in fact participating in our own colonization by "linking arms with the ones who would just as soon see us dead. Homophobia has *no* justification within our Nations."[5] By definition, the term encompasses a wide variety of sexual preference and partnership or nonpartnership, as well as "gender bending, gender blending, and gender changing."[6] Two-spirit challenges the dichotomous categories of male and female at their core. It was not intended to "mark a new category of gender" but was intended to bridge indigenous conceptualizations of "gender diversity and sexualities with those of Western cultures."[7]

A significant part of connecting indigenous activism and queer activism for Native people is maintained through the reclamation and usage of indigenous language. As well, the sustenance of multiple gender roles in indigenous communities is ultimately dependent on the preservation of indigenous languages. For example, in his book *"You're So Fat!": Exploring Ojibwe Discourse,* Roger Spielmann explores linguistic concepts as the root of cultural differences. He indicates that "ojibwe is, in a very real sense, a non-sexist language."[8] The equality of men with women is indicated, for him, by the lack of "specification of gender in the pronominal system. Whether one is referring to a man or a woman can only be determined by the context of what is being said."[9] As Diné scholar Wesley Thomas notes, "in Native North America, there were and still are cultures in which more than two gender categories are marked," and in many cases the language accommodates for reference to bodies that encompass multiple genders and sexualities.[10] Language becomes a marker of two-spirit identity, knowing the words by which to call oneself, creating one's own gender markers and categories, roles, and responsibilities. Two-spirit, by definition, is about both sexual partnership or expression and gendering roles within both indigenous and Western societies. Like the term "queer," two-spirit may or may not include both gendered and sexual behaviors. Interestingly enough, much of the discussion of homosexuality among American Indians is constructed under the rubric of a third gender role—or, for some indigenous nations, even fourth and fifth gender roles—a role that was accepted in oral history as well as in practice.[11] The third-gender space, beyond that of male and female, was a combining of the social attributes of the two, creating a two-spirit who encompasses actions traditionally constructed as male or female, or the spirits of both male and female.[12] When looking at tribally based definitions of two-spirit and third-gender space, one goes far beyond simply male and female, reaching into gender variability that flexes to meet the person embodying the tribal language used. Native scholar Bea Medicine offers words of caution to those attempting to generalize a third-gender role in Native societies:

> Translating the word *two-spirits* into some languages could lead to misunderstanding that could have adverse effects on the person using the term. One should be cautious and careful to contextualize gender terms and how they are used in Native communities. *Spirit* is an extremely variable term, and in some Native languages connotes sacredness.[13]

The Two Spirit Press Room, a media-network group based in Minneapolis, issued a phenomenal community briefing handbook in August 2005 that provided a welcome beginning list of how two-spirits call themselves in their respective languages. By no means is the list comprehensive, nor does it cover all gender roles in any given tribal language. But it does offer a linguistic foundation, a history for contemporary indigenous people to begin conceptualizing and using languages to speak about themselves, thus revitalizing and rebuilding indigenous ways of knowing. The list from Two Spirit Press Room includes *okitcitakwe* (Ojibwe), *sipiniq* (Inupiaq), *aijahnhuk* (Aleut), *winktah* (Dakota), *aranu:tiq* (Yupik), *he'eman* (Cheyenne), *alyha* (Mohave), and *lhamana* (Zuni) as alternatives to two-spirit.[14] These are just a few ways of calling people who behave in ways close to two-spirit, or outside of traditional gender roles. In these languages, there exist many other ways of calling two-spirits in all of their social and gendered roles. Two Spirit Press Room serves as a "GLBT Indigenous Media and cultural literacy project," is housed in Minneapolis, and is one of the more recent organizing efforts of indigenous queer people initiated by Minneapolis activist Richard LaFortune, also called Anguksuar (*Yupik*), and community organizer Debra Williams (Ojibwe).[15] 2SPR, as they refer to themselves, is aimed at networking indigenous GLBT journalism, finding a lack of coverage in both the national media and the Native news networks about issues affecting indigenous queers.

Problematically, the term "two-spirit" is like that of the Euro-American "queer." It encompasses any person who is not "straight," that is, those who partner with the opposite sex or embrace the gender role society has constructed for their respective sex. I cannot offer a resolution for how to avoid the generalizations that accompany two-spirit as a label, other than to listen to those who use the word and the community context in which it is being referenced. We stand at an important intersection in history in which we begin to interrogate the very terms our people created for themselves. In this way, indigenous communities can move away from the generalizations of colonization and move toward reclaiming gender systems and roles within their own nations. Wesley Thomas and Sue-Ellen Jacobs write of the number of indigenous two-spirits who do not use that term at home on the reservations, citing homophobia as an import of colonization as the rationale. For them, the issue lies within European homophobic understandings of sexual roles, which "focused on sexual behavior rather than the intricate roles Two-Spirit people played" in their societies.[16] Yet, a history of the term as it coalesced within indigenous communities in Minnesota can help provide perspective on how two-spirit has operated in the struggle for self-definition against the faces of colonization and homophobia.

Conceptualization of what it means to be two-spirit places the queer body in the space between daily life and spirituality, allowing for recognition of a spiritual, as well as social, sanction of alternate sexualities and gender roles imparted in teachings from elders, parents, and grandparents on how to live as a two-spirit person. In Minneapolis, Anguksuar (Richard LaFortune) referenced the Tenth Annual Gathering as "an expression of culture, not sexual identity or gender politics. . . . It's a place to heal and a chance to see the community grow," thus leaving out a conversation about a gendered/sexualized orientation for the organization of community. Participant Kathleen Riley adds that "this gathering allows us to come together and nurture our spirituality and our sexuality, but our sexuality doesn't get the same kind of public emphasis as it would at Pride [festivals]."[17]

In 1991, the *Minneapolis Star Tribune* ran an article on local GLBT people who are also racially diverse, and who illustrate challenges in balancing their cultural community and their sexual identity. Although this conversation is not unique to Minneapolis, the article quoted below does present a certain sense of openness about one's indigenous sexuality that is negotiated constantly, particularly in the urban environment of the Twin Cities:

> For Joyce, keeping the sacred, spiritual traditions of her native Ojibway tribe is essential to maintaining a sense of balance in her life.
>
> So is acknowledging that she is a lesbian.
>
> . . . homophobia within the American Indian community kept her from making peace with those two parts of her identity. Maintaining the duality and secrecy of her life was a constant struggle. . . .
>
> Some Indians said that, before boarding schools and white missionaries erased many traditional tribal belief, "two-spirit" people . . . held places of honor in native cultures.
>
> Now, some American Indian gays and lesbians contend, European biases have replaced those old traditions.[18]

Joyce's concerns in many ways represent the issues that the Twin Cities GLBTTwo-Spirit organizers are facing on the intertribal level. She speaks of homophobia in indigenous communities, the idea that indigenous queers do not fit in with mainstream GLBT society, of past and current aggressions of colonization, and of the progress in reclaiming indigenous ways of knowing about bodies that operate outside a male–female dichotomous gender system. Anguksuar notes that "hundreds of tribes in this hemisphere, still speaking many hundreds of languages, have always acknowledged the contributions of GLBT people, long before the appearance of

Europeans here in our ancient domains."[19] In light of Joyce's and Anguksuar's comments, two-spirit organizing in the Twin Cities region of Minnesota represents an important example of indigenous people's ongoing struggle against U.S. colonization. As the following pages will show, their activism illuminates how being and enacting two-spirit touches on a number of issues at the heart of decolonization movements and the everyday lived reality of American Indian people.

In the face of colonization and urbanization, the Twin Cities gave birth to an annual event designed to bring together international indigenous GLBTTwo-Spirits for community building, socializing, connecting, learning, and spirituality. The first-ever Two-Spirit International Gathering (The Basket and the Bow) happened in 1988, hosted by the two-spirit community in Minnesota. The Basket and the Bow found its name when organizers referenced one indigenous tradition in which children were presented with both a basket and a bow when they were young. Social gendering was established based on which tool they chose to use; female social rules for the basket choosers, male social rules for the bow choosers. Events were covered for the public by the Minneapolis publication *Equal Time,* which reported that "A spirit of hope, shared sorrow and dreams, and gentle good humor permeated 'The Basket and the Bow,' the first-ever gathering of American Indian gays and lesbians, held in Minneapolis June 18 and 19 at the American Indian Center and the Gay 90's, a gay bar in Minneapolis. The conference was sponsored by American Indian Gays and Lesbians, a Twin Cities–based group."[20] A number of indigenous attendees were called upon to describe their Gathering experiences:

> BEVERLY LITTLE THUNDER: I've never seen a whole roomful of gay and lesbian natives before. It's wonderful.
>
> BETH BRANT: I was at a pow-wow last year and someone said, "aren't we the prettiest people in the world?" I said yes, and part of that is because we are lesbian and gay.
>
> LEE STAPLES: We were at a family gathering and my nieces and nephews started calling my lover "Auntie." I took offense. I told them, "I'm the Auntie."
>
> BETSY REVARD: Coming out is a constant process. We do it everyday. In a political community, dealing with hostility is very wearing. The times I've wanted to throw up my hands and walk away are numerous. But I can't because I want to work for Indian people.[21]

Indigenous voices from the Basket and the Bow gathering indicate the difficult challenges facing GLBTTwo-Spirit indigenous people in their lives. As well, the voices normalize a sexuality-based social role that might not otherwise negotiate a normal familial position. The best example is Lee Staples's comment about who plays the Auntie better, or perhaps a jealousy over who embraces the role of Auntie more. All of the comments captured a sense of celebration for a two-spirit social role returning to traditional communities. Betsy Revard (Osage) also noted "that she has an 'easier time' dealing with homophobia in the straight community than with racism in the mainstream gay and lesbian movement."[22] These issues, including naming, politics, working for our communities, racism, dancing, and community, and simply finding others who share your identity, are not unique to indigenous queer people, but they do give some indication of the fundamental foundations behind organizing indigenous GLBTTwo-Spirit gatherings in Minnesota.

For the eight years following the Basket and the Bow in Minneapolis, a variety of two-spirit groups across the country hosted a yearly gathering around Labor Day. Organizers noted that "during the next several years, as the Gathering was hosted by communities in Winnipeg, Seattle, Vancouver, Arizona, Kansas and Nova Scotia, the Gathering plainly served as a powerful organizing tool for people who have faced extraordinary social and cultural obstacles in developing and sustaining communities and personal support."[23] At the ten-year mark, it was suggested that the Gathering should return to Minneapolis. In 1997, the Tenth Annual Gathering was organized by a contingent of indigenous, largely volunteer, staff. The advertisement in an indigenous newspaper read as follows:

> The 10th Annual International Two Spirit Gathering, August 28–31, 1997, Onamia, MN
>
> The Minnesota Gay Lesbian Bisexual Transgender "Two Spirit" Community welcomes all Two Spirit Gay Lesbian Bisexual Transgender Indigenous people, their partners and families to this chemically free, accessible event. This event is specifically for the Native Gay Lesbian Bisexual Transgender Community and friends and is not an educational forum to learn more about indigenous GLBT people. The international Two Spirit Gathering has been a time for Native GLBT people to get together to share information, relax, support each other, and share our cultural and spiritual traditions.
>
> We are excited to be celebrating the tenth anniversary of the gathering with old and new friends. The site we have chosen is located near Onamia,

The poster announcing the Tenth Annual International Two Spirit Gathering, 1997. Artist: George Littlechild. Courtesy of the Tretter Collection, Special Collections and Rare Books, University of Minnesota Libraries.

MN, about 2 hours from Minneapolis/St. Paul. Some of the activities scheduled are talking circles, sweat lodge, Giveaway, the No Talent show, pow-wow, and daily beading sessions for those last minute giveaway contributions.

Some new ideas being hatched for this event are:

A forum to discuss forming a national activist organization to share ideas.

Workshops to share knowledge of healing traditions[24]

Unique to two-spirit gatherings is the idea that the mainstream gay community is, in fact, excluded. Indigenous gatherings such as powwows or stomp dances have a long history of attracting non-Native spectators interested in indigenous culture.[25] One of the initiatives local organizers decided was vital to the success of the two-spirit community was to have a "closed" gathering. This marks the gatherings as distinctly different from mass public queer gatherings such as pride festivals or parades. An interview with Minneapolis organizers Sharon Day and Anguksuar, in the Minneapolis biweekly GLBT magazine *Lavender,* elaborates on the fundamentals of limiting public access to the two-spirit gathering, and the interviewer aptly points out that "Those looking for a spiritual one-night adventure to write up in their journals may want to cross the Two Spirit Gathering off their list."[26] The interview continues:

> Organizers of Native gatherings are experienced in the way non-Native people invite themselves. Sharon Day, a local Native community and Ojibwe tribal member, says, "We've been getting some calls about the Gathering. People say, 'I'd really like to go,' and it turns out they're not Native people. So we explain that is really is a gathering for Native people. It's really not a forum for non-Native people to learn about Native people."[27]

Day goes on to recommend that non-Native people interested in indigenous culture have plenty of forums with which to invest their time, such as housing and land-use concerns, health care, employment and education of indigenous youth, or substance-abuse programs. As well, the protection of indigenous spirituality from co-optation is a big issue in indigenous communities:

> According to Anguksuar (Richard LaFortune), a Yupik Eskimo who lives in Minneapolis, "we see sweetgrass, cedar and sage, all sorts of things that are specifically Native spirituality, and a lot of people do make a tidy income on it. A lot of local businesses profit from it." Part of the damage done, Day says, is "creating an impression that spiritual experience can be purchased." The double standard on marketing spirituality is also apparent: dream catcher earrings are available at 10 different handy locations, but there is nowhere to purchase a souvenir consecrated host.[28]

Particularly annoying is the arrogance that accompanies the appropriation. Vine Deloria Jr. notes, "The non-Indian appropriator conveys the message that Indians are indeed a conquered people and that there is nothing that Indians possess, *absolutely nothing*—pipes, dances, land, water, feathers, drums, even prayers—that non-Indians cannot take whenever and wherever they wish. . . . A sizable number of people have come to American Indians, seeking to join tribal religious practices or take from the tribal traditions those things they find most attractive."[29]

Indeed, the marketing of spiritual items is a particularly sensitive topic:

> Until 1978, we were not allowed to practice our spirituality, so before that it was underground. Now, there is a proliferation of marketing of Indian spiritual items. Day says, "I used to make dream catchers, like when a baby was born or something like that. I stopped doing them because I was in a little gas station and saw a rack of dream catcher earrings." Day still makes dream catchers occasionally, but says, "I only make them if they are meaningful to the person."[30]

The co-optation of Native spiritual practices does not stop at dream catchers, medicine men/women, or "seekers," but in fact branches into the queer identity. A good number of New Agers perpetuate the universal, queer-loving Indian because it reinforces the universal ideal Indian. Indeed, many "two-spirit" Web sites and organizations have arisen across the country, run by non-Native New Agers. Two-spirit societies, whether linked with queer people or not, are arising as part of shamanistic New Age societies as well. Those who do attend the Gathering are there for a variety of reasons. Deb Williams (Ojibwe), longtime two-spirit organizer, notes: "Different people come to the Gathering for different reasons. . . . Some come for spiritual reasons; others come for social reasons; for others, it's their first time being around other Native two spirit people."[31] As such, a community of safety and cultural nurturing is established through the Gatherings. Nick Metcalf, who also led the Twin Cities–based group Men of Color, was a newcomer to organizing two-spirit gatherings when the tenth annual one came around and he became cochair.

According to Metcalf, learning about yourself from an Indian perspective, rather than relying on what mainstream gay culture may dictate, can help correct much of the sexual disjointedness many two-spirit men experience: "There's an attitude within the larger gay community that says 'I can't be a Native man and gay because the community doesn't leave room for us to celebrate our cultural identity.' . . . I hope to learn more about my Indian side and my gay side from some of the other men from the Rosebud tribe who will be at the gathering."[32]

During the Tenth Annual Gathering, in 1997, Minneapolis indigenous two-spirits who collectively organized spoke out about how indigenous people historically circumvented some governmental restriction on language and spirituality. They collectively noted: "Through renewed relationship with our Elders and Medicine People, we have been unusually fortunate in recovering information that had been taken 'underground' for preservation and protection. These teachings are the keystone for a cultural renaissance that has made it possible for Native 2 Spirits to once again gain recognition and support of individuals, families and institutions in our communities."[33] It was those elders who could provide leadership and mentoring in the ways before boarding schools, before language destruction, and loss of social roles for those who do not conform to the European models of masculinity and femininity, and many of the Twin Cities organizers recognized that they had to seek out those elders for knowledge about GLBTTwo-Spirit words and roles they were missing. The Twin Cities activists noted: "In many areas of the continent, [indigenous GLBTTwo-Spirit people] are becoming included and acknowledged in our communities. This is not to say that we do not continue to face very serious problems; these same problems have profound impact across the country, which is why these opportunities to gather and exchange information carry such significance."[34]

The organizers of the Twin Cities two-spirit networks, including Sharon Day and Anguksuar, realized that such networks are key to dismantling colonial attitudes and influences in indigenous communities. Frantz Fanon argues that decolonization is necessary and the realization of freedom involves the overturning of the colonial structure.[35] Such challenges to the colonial structure are fundamental for indigenous persons in the United States, where they are not treated as sovereign nations by the federal government and they are mythologized and created as a national mascot by society at large. This places indigenous Twin Cities organizers directly in the center of a national indigenous effort to dismantle the colonial establishment in North America. Wahpetunwan Dakota scholar Angela Cavendar Wilson, from the Upper Sioux Reservation in southwestern Minnesota, notes, "Decolonization in its farthest extension moves us beyond mere survival and becomes a means of restoring health and prosperity to our people by returning to traditions and ways of life that have been systematically suppressed."[36]

In 1987, the group American Indian Gays and Lesbians (AIGL) in Minneapolis opened its doors to the public.[37] The organized group itself only lasted a few years, but the work it began was soon picked up by subsequent GLBTTwo-Spirit groups that formed. The activism is largely part of an amazing cohort of indigenous GLBT folk who, at one point or another, found themselves living in the Twin Cities. Some remain in the Twin Cities, continuing work to build and sustain GLBT indigenous community. Others have gone home to their communities or on to other projects, continuing to give back to indigenous people. Building off the large indigenous population found in Minneapolis and St. Paul, indigenous GLBT organizers saw a variety of needs—particularly, but not exclusively, for GLBT indigenous people in the community—and employed personal skills, degrees, talents, and community ties to meet those needs successfully over the last twenty years. The organizing of a GLBTTwo-Spirit collective serves many purposes, not the least of which is to provide GLBTTwo-Spirit Natives with a culture-based network for knowledge and experience sharing, and community outreach. GLBTTwo-Spirit people face many challenges that the mainstream queer community also faces, but often need the indigenous cultural component in the support communities. For example, Nick Metcalf (Lakota), Minneapolis organizer of gatherings and two-spirit community member, participated in a unique interview for *Lavender* magazine on the changing face of GLBT parenting. Faced with a challenge as a gay man of wanting to raise a family, his pregnant sister could not care for her son and asked Nick to help. The challenges facing Nick are those that many GLBT parents can share:

> Nick's son, Sonny, came to him in April of last year [1999]. His full name in Lakota is Hoksicila Cante Ma Yuha, which means "child of my heart." Nick says his life has changed "in every way I can think of" since his son's arrival. Among the changes, Nick says, has been losing connections with his child-free gay friends, who seem to have vanished. Nick finds support instead from other GLBT parents, his church, and his partner Terry.
>
> Nick and his sister have agreed that she and Sonny's biological father will have open visitation rights. As Sonny grows up, Nick anticipates that Sonny

> will be angry and confused while coming to terms with his biological mother's decision not to raise him herself. Nick plans to tell Sonny that "he was my son from day one, and what his mother did for him, she did out of love."
>
> In the meantime, Nick is concentrating on the basics: feeding, naptime, and changing diapers. Nick is HIV-positive, so maintaining his own health is another high priority. "I think about that every day," Nick says. "I want to be here for Sonny as he grows up."[38]

So, while Nick's story, in many ways, is not so different from his non-Native counterparts, his Lakota self is at the center of his life. AIGL cofounder Lee Staples observes:

> We are the missing part in our Gay and Lesbian organizations. It has been difficult to fit in with White organizations; many times there has not been much there for us. But we can fit in with our community on a spiritual level. I went to the San Francisco Gay Pride parade last summer but didn't find anything there to nurture Indian people beyond what we have in our community.[39]

Lee Staples (Ojibwe) indicates that indigenous GLBTTwo-Spirit people thrive when all aspects of their identity are nurtured. The imperative need for cultural community connections, as well as communities emphasizing sexuality identity, is inherent in the definitions of two-spirit and played out daily by indigenous GLBTTwo-Spirit people. In a way, this is what sets indigenous GLBTTwo-Spirit people apart from their mainstream queer counterparts. "What I'm finding out in my recovery is that I have another identity within the community which is different from the one I had," Staples remarked in an interview. "It's a spiritual identity; and I'm finding that our Gay and Lesbian spirituality, to be two-spirited, is considered a gift in our culture." Staples's position on his own sexuality and spirituality fits into a larger conversation by academics who situate two-spiritedness in a socioreligious conversation utilizing an intertribal lens. It is often argued that an understanding of two-spirit implies an interconnectedness of the religious/spiritual basis of the concept, the social and economic roles of the two-spirit person, and how one may socially develop into the two-spirit role:

> What I'm trying to do is to find out what that means in terms of culture and as a people. There's a purpose for why we're born two-spirited and the Creator

> wants us to use that purpose for our people. We're the missing piece within the Circle—we can connect with others in that lace in the Circle where we've been missing. . . . Part of that process is looking at the alcohol abuse we have in our community—that's not a way of respecting our bodies. Once we ask the question, "what was the Creator's will in creating us?", then we can begin to use our gifts to help us take our rightful place in our community."[40]

Staples's connections of identity to community building and community to revitalization are fundamental in the reacceptance of two-spirit people back into their nations. The realization of the interconnectedness of all beings within the circle of life, as referenced by Staples, is a way that all two-spirit people complete themselves and their communities. In 1990, Richard LaFortune (Anguksuar) and Lee Staples served on a sixteen-member Governor's Task Force on Lesbian and Gay Minnesotans, trying to reiterate these connections as fundamental to building a safe indigenous GLBTTwo-Spirit community within Minnesota's indigenous nations. As part of this task force, a wide range of issues affecting GLBT Minnesotans were examined. Richard and Lee examined a very specific aspect of indigenous GLBT life in Minnesota as well, presenting information regarding issues specific to Native American lesbians and gay men. Lee Staples and Anguksuar, one of the founders of a national organization for gay and lesbian Native Americans and a task force member, spoke about the positive role of gay and lesbian people within the traditional understandings of many Native peoples, and how this has been lost owing to the impact of Western Europeans. Staples also highlighted some of the special needs of this group, and indicated the poor response from many human service programs.

The Governor's Task Force introduced indigenous GLBTTwo-Spirit issues to the greater public, including that of inadequate AIDS education in Native communities, the challenge of social- and human-service programs to negotiate needs of indigenous GLBT people, and general colonial attitudes regarding GLBT indigenous people, particularly in rural areas of the state. Part of the issue that Lee and Richard introduced to the larger audience included the navigation of a social system different from that of the dominant culture. When programs are run by the state, often they conform to a mainstream conception of what it means to be gay or lesbian, and fail to consider the ramifications of colonization or the alternative knowledge systems that indigenous people live under. Such programs can then be seen as rejecting or responding poorly to the needs of gay and lesbian indigenous people.

In their news release about the Tenth Annual Two-Spirit Gathering in Minnesota, the organizers again made it a point to reference the struggle of colonization challenging indigenous people every day. This is a particular concern for those indigenous folks in the Twin Cities, as many of them are away from their community homes and living in an urban environment. The organizers stated: "Although most Aboriginal cultures in this continent recognize, respect and include 2 Spirit people in their traditional social constructions that incorporate multiple-gender distinctions, colonization nearly wiped out the teachings that explain and support the presence and participation of 2 Spirits in our communities." The rebuilding of these teachings was a necessity, primarily because the loss of these teachings resulted in "Native 2 Spirits, our families and communities . . . experienc[ing] disastrous consequences, resulting in disproportionately high levels of chemical dependency, violence, suicide, discrimination—and in the last 16 years, HIV infection." Because indigenous GLBTTwo-Spirits often found little or no support in their respective Native communities, "nor in a racist and bar-oriented gay society, Natives have had few other options to affirm our identity and history," as both indigenous people and GLBTTwo-Spirit people.[41]

Within the urban environment, indigenous community members are often subjected to non-Native perceptions of their lifestyles and cultures. Urban indigenous community building and two-spirit activism often coincide for both community outreach and non-Native education on indigenous cultures. One example is the Maynidoowhdak Odena Housing Cooperative in Minneapolis for indigenous families living with HIV/AIDS, administered by the Indigenous Peoples Task Force.[42] Maynidoowhdak Odena promotes community healing and a supportive environment for those indigenous people living away from their tribal communities. Although neither of these urban community enclaves is targeted specifically at GLBTTwo-Spirit Natives, they do provide services and space for two-spirits. Indeed, urban indigenous community building remains a vital part of urban Natives' struggle against colonization.

Through her involvement in task forces and indigenous initiatives at the state level, Sharon Day, the young queer Ojibwe woman mentioned earlier, helped form the Minneapolis American Indian AIDS Task Force. Founded in South Minneapolis, the task force later expanded beyond assisting those with HIV/AIDS and AIDS education, and now calls itself the Indigenous Peoples Task Force. Day, the founder and current executive director of the task force, was awarded a Pride Award in 2006 by *Lavender* magazine.[43] Her interview includes conversation about the cultural foundation for her task force's initiative: "When we were growing up, my father instilled in us the responsibilities of our clan, the Wahbahzhezhi, or wood marten. . . . We are the clan responsible for taking care of the people. So, my entire adult life has been devoted to fulfilling my clan responsibility."[44] As such, the task force provides health-based programs for the Twin Cities indigenous community, involving education for Two-Spirit people. Other components of its programs include a fourteen-unit housing complex for people living with HIV/AIDS and their families, the aforementioned Maynidoowhdak Odena; peer education programs for youth about STDs and HIV/AIDS; and counseling, testing, and substance-abuse education programs, among other education initiatives. Day, who is also a local actress and singer, has played an important role in local indigenous GLBTTwo-Spirit activism, helping to found and maintain years of two-spirit gatherings.

An amazing hub for indigenous queer activism is present in the Twin Cities region. It shapes gay and Native urban identities and is inextricably connected to the strong indigenous communities and political movements that have shaped Native life in Minneapolis and St. Paul. One cannot separate out the GLBT Two-Spirit activism from indigenous organizing. In many ways, both feed off the needs of the indigenous community and the members of that community. In a letter from the Two-Spirit community in Minneapolis, upon planning the Tenth Annual Two-Spirit Gathering, the committee notes a history across the nation of GLBTTwo-Spirit community planning activities, and the lack of a centralized network for GLBTTwo-Spirit Natives who are often disconnected, for one reason or another, from their indigenous communities.

A missing connection between GLBTTwo-Spirit organizing and indigenous activism and outreach throughout much of the 1970s and 1980s in the Twin Cities needed to be bridged before two-spirit activists could strengthen their voices. Native organizers in the Twin Cities region began talking and meeting informally during 1986–87 to discuss the need for an organization that would meet the cultural and social needs of two-spirit Natives. Although similar efforts in organizing had begun some ten years earlier on the West Coast, no comparable community organizing had happened in the Upper Midwest, home to one of the larger urban populations of Natives in the country and the heart of significant international indigenous organizing. Coincidentally, the 1987 March on Washington for Lesbian and Gay Rights brought together Native folks from different parts of the country, and discussions about an ambitious organizing mechanism resulted in the birth of the first gathering—called The Basket and the Bow. This inaugural gathering was hosted by the community in Minnesota in 1988 and supported in part with two thousand dollars in surplus funds from the March on Washington organizing committee on the basis of the Native organizers' successful histories.[45] The Basket and the Bow, then, demonstrated the new ways of thought, identity, and action that can emerge when marginalized people explore their lives, cultures, and oppressions in common to create new voices for themselves in their struggle for self-determination.

Epilogue

Twenty years later, in August 2008, the Minnesota and the Twin Cities two-spirit community again had become host to the international gathering when it met in Sandstone, Minnesota, over Labor Day weekend. A weekend of teaching, bonding, camping, cooking, beading and crafting, dancing and drumming nurtured the community of two-spirit bodies from all over the United States. Again largely a volunteer project, fund-raising and collections began early for the planning of the gathering. The gathering served as a safe location for indigenous queer people to come together as a collective community and renew their sense of common spirituality, sexuality, and personhood. The negotiations and affirmations of indigenous GLBTTwo-Spirit people happening at the Twentieth Annual Gathering reinforced the reacceptance of Native queers into their communities, while continuing to fight the effects of colonization that generate homophobia in our indigenous communities. The Twentieth Annual Gathering opened with a "traditional Ojibwe Water Ceremony . . . observed before numerous well wishes, proclamations, congratulations and welcomes that were conveyed from Minneapolis City Hall by the City Council and Mayor RT Ryback; in a joint letter from both chambers of the Minnesota Legislature, officials extended an invitation for Native participants to call upon the state for any assistance needed during their stay in Minnesota; and US Democratic presidential candidate Barack Obama

The poster announcing the Twentieth Annual International Two Spirit Gathering, 2008. Artist: Hulleah Tsinhnahjinnie. Courtesy of the Tretter Collection, Special Collections and Rare Books, University of Minnesota Libraries.

sent a surprise greeting that caused a favorable reaction among participants."[46] While the gathering marked many highlights from the past two decades of two-spirit activism, it also pointed to future struggles. Native youth suicide, HIV/AIDS transmission and treatment among two-spirits, and the partnership of LGBT foundations and their relationship to indigenous communities continue to be needed points of activism for two-spirit indigenous communities.

Notes

1 Sabine Lang, "Various Kinds of Two-Spirit People," in Sue-Ellen Jacobs, Wesley Thomas, and Sabine Lang, eds., *Two-Spirit People: Native American Gender Identity, Sexuality, and Spirituality* (Urbana: University of Illinois Press, 1997), 110.

2 For a detailed history of the French word *berdache* used to reference indigenous people, see Jacobs, Thomas, and Lang, *Two-Spirit People.*

3 Beth Brant, *Writing as Witness* (Toronto: Women's Press, 1994), 55.

4 Ibid., 60.

5 Ibid.; emphasis in the original.

6 Jacobs, Thomas, and Lang, *Two-Spirit People,* xiii and 1.

7 Wesley Thomas and Sue-Ellen Jacobs, "'. . . And We Are Still Here': From Berdache to Two-Spirit People," *American Indian Culture and Research Journal* 23, no. 2 (1999): 91.

8 Roger Spielmann, *'You're So Fat!': Exploring Ojibwe Discourse* (Toronto: University of Toronto Press, 1998), 45.

9 Ibid.

10 Thomas and Jacobs, "'. . . And We Are Still Here,'" 96.

11 Will Roscoe, "Strange Craft, Strange History, Strange Folks: Cultural Amnesia and the Case for Lesbian and Gay Studies," *American Anthropologist* 97, no. 3 (September 1995): 448.

12 Will Roscoe, "We'Wha and Klah: The American Indian Berdache as Artist and Priest," *American Indian Quarterly* (spring 1998): 127.

13 Bea Medicine, "Changing Native American Roles in an Urban Context *and* Changing Native American Sex Roles in an Urban Context," in Bea Medicine and Sue-Ellen Jacobs, eds., *Learning to Be an Anthropologist and Remaining "Native": Selected Writings* (Urbana: University of Illinois Press, 2001), 147–48.

14 Richard LaFortune and Debra Williams, *Two Spirit: Native Media and Community Briefing* (Minneapolis: Two Spirit Press Room, August 2005), cover.

15 Richard LaFortune (Anguksuar), Campaign Director, 2SPR Native Media and Community Briefing, August 2005.

16 Thomas and Jacobs, "'. . . And We Are Still Here,'" 98.

17 Mark Kasel, "Sacred Land, Sacred People: Tenth International Two Spirit Gathering," *Lavender* 3, no. 58 (August 15, 1997): 12.

18 Suzanne Kelly, "Gays Seek Niche in Minority Communities: Balancing Racial and Sexual Identities Can Be Difficult," *Minneapolis Star Tribune,* September 9, 1991.

19 Two Spirit Press Room Web site, "Int'l GLBT Native Press Archive" http://home.earthlink.net/~lafor002/id9.html.

20 Cynthia Scott, "The Basket and the Bow: A 'First' for Gay/Lesbian American Indians," *Equal Time: A Non-profit community newspaper for gay men and lesbians,* issue 163, July 6, 1988.

21 Ibid.

22 Ibid.

23 Richard LaFortune, Sharon Day, and Two-Spirit Gathering Organizing Committee, "Request to the St. Paul Companies for funding on behalf of the 10th Annual gathering"; history and background of the two-spirit community in Minneapolis letter; Two-Spirit Collection, Anguksuar Archive, Tretter Collection, University of Minnesota Special Collections.

24 *Indian Country Today,* August 11–18, 1997.

25 For further reading on non-Native spectatorship, see Eva Marie Garroutte, *Real Indians: Identity and the Survival of Native America* (Berkeley: University of California Press, 2003), and Philip Deloria, *Playing Indian* (New Haven: Yale University Press, 1998).

26 Elise Matthesen, "Indian in a Past Life, or Spiritual Tourist?" *Lavender* 3, no. 58 (August 15, 1997): 13.

27 Ibid.

28 Ibid.

29 Vine Deloria Jr., *For This Land: Writings on Religion in America* (New York: Routledge, 1999), 227 and 269.

30 Matthesen, "Indian in a Past Life, or Spiritual Tourist?" 13.

31 Kasel, "Sacred Land, Sacred People," 12.

32 Ibid.

33 LaFortune, Day, and Two-Spirit Gathering Organizing Committee, "Request to the St. Paul Companies for funding on behalf of the 10th Annual gathering."

34 Ibid.

35 Frantz Fanon, *The Wretched of the Earth* (New York: Grove Press, 1963).

36 Angela Cavendar Wilson, "Reclaiming Our Humanity: Decolonization and the Recovery of Indigenous Knowledge," in Devon Abbott Mihesuah and Angela Cavendar Wilson, eds., *Indigenizing the Academy: Transforming Scholarship and Empowering Communities* (Lincoln: University of Nebraska Press, 2004).

37 Mark Kasel, "American Indian Gays and Lesbians Open New Office with New Future," *Twin Cities Gaze: Newspaper for the Gay/Lesbian Community,* no. 133, January 1991.

38 Abigail Garner, "The Changing Face of Parenting: GLBT Minnesotans Raising Kids," *Lavender* 5, no. 123 (February 11–24, 2000): 41.

39 Kasel, "American Indian Gays and Lesbians Open New Office," 8.

40 Ibid.

41 LaFortune, Day, and Two-Spirit Gathering Organizing Committee, "Request to the St. Paul Companies for funding on behalf of the 10th Annual gathering."

42 For more information on the Indigenous Peoples Task Force and its programs, see http://www.indigenouspeoplestf.org/.

43 Michael Davis, "Pride Award: Sharon Day," *Lavender* 12, no. 288 (June 9–22, 2006).

44 Ibid.

45 LaFortune, Day, and Two-Spirit Gathering Organizing Committee, "Request to the St. Paul Companies for Funding on Behalf of the 10th Annual Gathering."

46 Richard LaFortune, Two Spirit Press Room release: http://home.earthlink.net/~lafor002/id16.html.

7. SKIRTING BOUNDARIES QUEER BAR CULTURES IN THE POSTWAR TWIN CITIES

Amy M. Tyson

I knew there were queer bars in cities like New York—I'd been to one—but I never dreamed a place like that could exist in St. Paul.

—Ricardo J. Brown, *The Evening Crowd at Kirmser's: A Gay Life in the 1940s*

On February 27, 1955, Cedric Adams, a Minneapolis news columnist, alerted his readers to "a social danger in our midst."[1] The social danger was what Adams called the "homosexual problem," which "a father right here in Minneapolis" brought to his attention by means of a letter. Adams included the letter in full in his Sunday *Tribune* column so that he could help "point a finger at the condition" that was supposedly threatening Minneapolis youth.[2] Through the letter we learn that the father had always considered his "a typical American family," with two boys in college and a daughter in high school.[3] The family's youngest son, to whom the father assigned the pseudonym "Jack," is the subject of the letter. At twenty years old, Jack first alarmed his parents when he "dropped his girl friend as well as his former school and church friends" and "began an association with a strange group of fellows." Because Jack's college studies had also been suffering, the father initially suspected that he "had joined a group of dope addicts." A private investigator hired by the father proved otherwise: Jack "had fallen in with a large group of homosexuals frequenting several Minneapolis public bars and so-called supper clubs." Even more alarming, "most of the clubs were operating almost exclusively for homosexuals with just a sprinkling of on-lookers present" and police officers were present "in two of the bars during one of his [the investigator's] visits."

According to the letter, Jack was confronted with the findings and agreed to consult with a psychiatrist, who, subscribing to the then dominant conception of homosexuality as a psychological disorder, assured the family that Jack's "upbringing had been normal and that . . . he had simply fallen in with the wrong group." Because Jack apparently "had not been an active homosexual" and was "ashamed of his venture," he was successfully restored to his family as a "normal" heterosexual. On behalf of other endangered Minneapolis youth, the father wrote to Cedric Adams in hopes that Adams could use the influence of his newspaper column: "Here is a force as deadly in its operation as anything in the world. Something should be done. Can't you spearhead the drive with publicity at least?" Adams obliged, proud to do his part to alert his readers to this "shocking but vital issue."[4]

Regardless of Jack's ostensible "rescue," it is clear from the column that bars were central to his social foray into homosexuality. Jack's case clearly illustrates the important function of bars as social gathering places for those who sought same-sex companionship, regardless of whether those patrons identified as queer, or gay, or if they had been sexually "active" with other men.[5] In this chapter I examine how queer bar patrons in the Twin Cities used, interpreted, and defined these public spaces, paying special attention to the ways in which categories of class and race organized the tentative forging of community.

Following another lead offered by the exchange about "Jack" in the *Tribune,* I argue that, to an unexpected degree, Minneapolis police tolerated queer bars and their queer clientele. This tolerance runs counter to historical accounts of other metropolitan regions in the period that emphasize police harassment of queer bars. In the Twin Cities, law enforcement tended to quietly accommodate these spaces as long as the patrons performed gender identities according to normative standards. However, as this chapter will show, nonnormative gender performance, whether on the stage or in the street, clearly tested the limits of Minnesotans' "tolerance."

"Can't Close Bars Because of Deviates"

The *Tribune* exchange about "Jack" was in no way exceptional; throughout the 1950s, newspapers and magazines across the United States ran stories exposing the supposed menace of homosexuality and its subversive underground cultures. Such stories must be viewed in their postwar and Cold War contexts. World War II was a watershed event in the history of sexuality, as it provided new and extended opportunities for individuals to distance themselves from the confines of their previous social contexts (i.e., small towns or tightly knit urban communities), to confront their own and other people's sexualities within these new contexts.[6] Individuals interested in same-sex relationships and nonnormative gender performance found others like themselves and contributed to the proliferation of queer public spaces—including bars and cabarets—that had previously existed primarily in large cities and port towns.[7] In response to the expansion and increasing visibility of queer public culture, local governments stepped up attempts to police "homosexuals" in order to "maintain public order" and the American press constructed homosexuals as dangerous outsiders who threatened national security and family values.[8]

While the moral posturing of Cedric Adams's column exemplifies this reactionary Cold War response to homosexual visibility, a published response to one of his columns suggests that Twin Cities authorities were less harshly condemnatory than might be expected. The day after Adams ran the concerned father's letter, Minneapolis Police Chief Thomas R. Jones commented (in a newspaper story titled "Can't Close Bars Because of Deviates") that "[b]ars patronized principally by sex deviates cannot be closed simply because of their patrons" and that "no arrests could be made, nor could the bars involved be closed, unless actual violations of law were detected." Jones also told the reporter that "the mere presence of suspected sex deviate[s] in a bar is no violation of any law."[9]

Chief Jones's assertion stands in marked contrast to dominant accounts of urban queer life in the 1950s—and may surprise those who lived through the bar raids and sexual witch hunts that took place elsewhere in the nation, most notably in New York, Miami, Philadelphia, Washington, D.C., and San Francisco.[10] In the early 1950s, the District of Columbia saw around a thousand arrests each year that were related to policing homosexuality, while in Philadelphia "misdemeanor charges averaged one hundred per month."[11] Similarly, a 1951 *Chicago Tribune* article reports that fifty-eight men were arrested after police raided "Cyrano's Tavern, 8 E. Division St., a reputed hangout for homosexuals," and were charged with "being inmates of a disorderly house"—a common charge levied at establishments that were allegedly morally disruptive to a community owing to the presence of illegal gambling, prostitution, or other "vices."[12] Typical of newspaper accounts of the time, the *Chicago Tribune* listed the names and addresses of some of those who were arrested.[13] Likewise, historian

John Howard offers examples of oppressive policing in the postwar South, including one report of the arrest of thirty-eight Birmingham, Alabama, men "on charges of disorderly conduct and visiting a disorderly house," which was followed by the "listing of the arrestees' names and addresses in a local daily newspaper."[14]

Chief Jones's comments suggest that police forces in the Twin Cities did not aggressively police queer bars in the postwar years to the extent that they did elsewhere in the country. Individual accounts support this general impression. For example, Gloria Olson, a visitor to several queer bars in the postwar years, reports that while police would sometimes appear to "case the place," outright harassment was rare. Jean-Nickolaus Tretter notes that raids of queer bars did not occur frequently until the closing of the gay bathhouses in the 1980s. Tretter claims that from the 1950s onward, many Minneapolis "gay bars" were Mafia-controlled and that police were paid off: "We've been a little bit more lucky in Minnesota than a lot of other places. During the 1950s we didn't have the witch-hunts. We had a number of gay bars. They weren't stormed and closed by the police."[15] Donna Mellem, who moved to Minneapolis in the early 1950s, echoed this claim. When asked about the frequency of police raids, Mellem emphatically stated: "No, no not in my time, never. No. No. They [the cops] were paid off, bought off. Along with the liquor license, there was the payoff to the cops and they'll leave you alone."[16] Even if police were relatively less repressive in the Twin Cities region, however, they proved far from tolerant of individuals and acts that flouted heteronormative models of respectability.[17]

Class and the Limits of Community in Twin Cities Queer Bars

Police were not the only ones to enforce models of respectability. Queer bar patrons also brought with them notions about what constituted proper behavior in the bars. While proper behavior sometimes meant maintaining anonymity or "playing straight" (so as to not attract unwanted attention), cultures at Twin Cities queer bars were organized along class lines, and as such, patrons were often at odds as to what would be counted as a respectable performance of one's class, race, or gender. In this sense, community at the bars had its limits.

During the World War II years, Minneapolis and St. Paul had only a handful of bars that might be considered queer public spaces. These included Kirmser's in St. Paul, and the Viking Room and the Persian Palms in Minneapolis. In his memoir, Brown carefully noted the class distinctions operative within two of these queer spaces (he makes no mention of the Persian Palms). Recalling his life in St. Paul in 1945–46 (after being dishonorably discharged from the army because of his homosexuality), Brown reflected on the "evening crowd" at Kirmser's, a place he describes as a "workingman's bar, straight in the daytime and queer at night" that "had no particular decor and . . . made no pretensions to style."[18] Named after the surname of its owners, a German heterosexual married couple who prepared and served the bar's modest menu of food and liquor, Kirmser's was located at 382 Wabasha. According to Brown, in sober appreciation for the patronage of her regular customers, Mrs. Kirmser would sometimes "shoosh" her evening regulars when their "conversations got a little loud or a little careless" when a stranger would come in off the street, unsuspecting that the bar's evening clientele was queer. Kirmser's regulars appreciated the owners' "willing participation in the ruse that kept all of us safe" and having a public space where they could somewhat let their guard down.[19]

Gloria Olson, who was born in 1928 in Pepin, Wisconsin, remembered going to Kirmser's in 1944, dressed in moccasins, navy dungarees, and her "dad's white shirts." At only sixteen years of age, but with a fake ID, she guessed that she "probably looked like a baby faced boy" and wondered how the bar rationalized serving her. Olson mentioned that she "had to be real careful because they had raids all the time"—particularly during election seasons.[20] Curiously, Brown, who was much more of a regular at Kirmser's than Olson appears to have been, did not mention any police raids in his memoir, suggesting either that Brown left them out deliberately or that perhaps Olson's recollections of bar life, some fifty years later, may have been colored by her subsequent understanding of the larger history of the time. That these accounts contradict each other points to the challenges of using oral histories to reconstruct a "truthful" account of the past; often memories conflict with what might be otherwise known as fact. This should not diminish the value of the narrative, but rather should prompt us to consider how and why history is both remembered and misremembered.[21]

According to Brown's account, Kirmser's had little competition from other bars for the patronage of this particular "evening crowd." A major reason for this was geography. The Viking Room, a bar located in the

Radisson Hotel, for example, was located about ten miles away in downtown Minneapolis. This distance would have seemed a world away for many St. Paulites prior to the completion of the interstate highway that more easily linked the Twin Cities (for those who had automobiles) in the late 1960s. More important, the Viking Room catered to a "mixture of affluent queers and straights"—a class of folks that Brown's crowd at Kirmser's found to be "too elegant and too expensive, almost intimidating; waiters wore black pants, black ties, short white jackets, and they expected big tips."[22]

Allan H. Spear's foreword to Brown's memoir aptly notes how one's class status significantly affected how individuals experienced bar life:

> Middle- and upper-class men had more space to expand their closets. In New York, by the 1920s, they had their own apartments, clubs, and social networks. Ricardo Brown and his friends, on the other hand, were distinctly and self-consciously working class. Most of them lived with their parents into their twenties and thirties and even beyond. Few owned automobiles. Kirmser's was their only free space, the only place where they could escape the restrictions of their lives.[23]

Thus, one's class identification affected one's social *and* geographic mobility.

Although Kirmser's may have been a "free space" for its patrons, this freedom appears to have been almost exclusively reserved for whites. For example, Brown recalls an African American man who came into Kirmser's a few times. The "crowd" seems to have tolerated his presence at the bar, but the memoir suggests that they resented him for what they interpreted as pretentious behavior. Brown reports that the man walked "into Kirmser's like he owned the place" and that "[t]here was something aloof, almost snotty, about him."[24] Brown even perceived something "haughty" in the way the man cleaned his glasses (ibid.). The regulars were "a little irritated" when they found out that the man was a "waiter on the Great Northern" Railroad (101); though considered a good job for an African American at the time, it did not seem to give him license to treat them with (what they perceived) as "contempt" (100). While the man's race made him immediately suspect to these white St. Paulites, his mannerisms (both gendered and classed) further marked him as an outsider and the bar's regulars were not eager to accept into their "evening crowd" this well-dressed black man in tailored French cuffs (ibid.). Ultimately, what drew the most ire from the Kirmser's regulars was this man's apparent inability to appropriately conform to the bar's established white, working-class culture.

The more upscale Viking Room was also a predominately white space. Although he had never been to the Viking Room during the 1940s, Minneapolis-raised and Ivy League–educated lawyer Richard W. Bosard relayed what others had told him about the Viking Room in his oral history.[25] In particular, he reported that the spatial configuration of the bar itself "was very helpful" to gay men because "the Radisson had a rule that no women could sit at the bar." Explaining this organization of space, Bosard noted that "there was a Minneapolis ordinance passed at the request of the hotels who did not want the single women or prostitutes (whatever you want to call) preying on men at their bar. Women had to be seated at the tables. . . . [T]here were only men at the bar, not that they were all gay but, I was told that was a place for picking people up like they do today."[26] Interestingly, a measure intended to combat heterosexual vice held beneficial but unintended consequences for men who were interested in sex with other men.[27] Gay men used the ordinance to their advantage and converted a white, male homosocial space into a white, male homosexual one.

It is important to note that the Viking Room was not an exclusively homosexual space; both Brown and Bosard note that the Viking Room attracted a mixed clientele. In many Twin Cities bars during the decade following World War II this generally would continue to be the case. As Bosard noted, "A gay bar in those days was not [what] it is today, it was a regular bar to which some gay people went."[28] In this manner, the Viking Room was likely akin to upscale New York bars such as in the Astor Hotel where gay men "had to be 'subtle' so that the straight men all around them—including the occasional strangers who unwittingly sat down on the gay side of the bar—would not realize that they were surrounded by 'queers.'"[29]

Although both Spear and Brown suggested that Kirmser's and the Radisson's Viking Room were the only two queer bars in the Cities during the 1940s, Bosard had heard through the grapevine that "during or before the Second World War" the Persian Palms Tavern, which stood at 109–111 Washington Avenue South in Minneapolis, had "a small bar behind the main room which some gay people went to."[30] If Bosard's sources were correct, then a 1945 interior photograph of the Persian Palms Tavern

According to Ricardo Brown, the Viking Room at the Radisson Hotel in Minneapolis (pictured here in 1936) catered to a "mixture of affluent queers and straights" in the postwar period. Photograph by Norton & Peel; courtesy of the Minnesota Historical Society.

further suggests that this space catered to Minneapolis's working-class crowd (even if even this photograph does not depict the "small bar behind the main room"). Although the servicemen are in uniform, several individuals, including the older men in the center of the photograph, are casually dressed (with their sleeves rolled up, for example), suggesting that this was not a posh club with a dress code requiring a jacket and tie for men. Likewise, trash and cigarettes litter the floor, setting a very different tone than the Radisson's crisp elegance. Finally, the signs posted above the bar address a money-conscious clientele, noting that the prices of the liquor included federal tax—a gesture that might have seemed gauche to Radisson regulars.

Advertisements for the Persian Palms bolster Bosard's suggestion that the bar attracted a queer crowd. For example, in December 1949, the Persian Palms heralded "a thrill-packed floor show extravaganza featuring female impersonators" performing in the "sensational 'Gay Time' Revue."[31]

This photograph from 1948 shows the alley entrance to the Persian Palms Tavern, which stood at 109–111 Washington Avenue South in Minneapolis. This was likely the entrance that patrons used when they visited, in Richard W. Bosard's words, the "small bar behind the main room which some gay people went to." Courtesy of the Minnesota Historical Society.

Clues from this interior photograph of the Persian Palms Tavern suggest that the bar served a working-class crowd. Photograph by Minneapolis Star Journal; *courtesy of the Minnesota Historical Society.*

The use of the word *gay* here is significant: by the time this advertisement was placed, *gay* had become firmly associated with homosexuality in the popular American vernacular.[32]

Oral history narrators recalled a number of bars in the Twin Cities in the years following World War II, including the Dugout, Schieks, the Dome, the Music Box, the Ritz Hotel's Panther Room, Frolick's, Herb's Bar, the Little Dandy Bar, the Hippopotamus, the Happy Hour, the Holland, the 19 Bar, the Drum, the Townhouse, the Hurdle Bar, "and the third floor of Harry's (one of the best restaurants in town)."[33] The 19 Bar (which remains open in the Loring Park neighborhood as of this writing in 2009), and the now long-defunct Dugout (which stood at 206 Third Street South),[34] however, were the first to cater more exclusively to a queer clientele, rather than to be surreptitiously adopted. The Dugout, in fact, was the first bar that might be considered "exclusively gay" in the Twin Cities. Bosard appreciated that Dugout proprietors sought out a queer clientele by actively soliciting their patronage from the neighboring Herb's Bar—a "mixed bar" of straights and queers:

> [The Dugout] was a large workingman's bar. The sort of place where men would stop in after work and order their boilermaker. After about six o'clock the business died out entirely. They were having their lights turned off because they couldn't pay their bills. At that time they had a gay organist. During one of his breaks, Ebe, the son of the Danish owner of the bar came over to Herb's Bar, a mixed bar. Ebe came in with the help of his organist, went around and started buying drinks for everybody. Then, Ebe would say, "Come on over to my bar, come on over to my bar." How Herb ever allowed that, I don't know. Except, later on, Herb wanted to become just a jazz bar and not have any gay people in it so, maybe he welcomed that idea.[35]

After one such solicitation, Bosard went over to the Dugout and ordered a gin and tonic, but the "bartender had no idea what [he] was talking about so [he] changed his order and ordered something else." Here, Bosard's initial drink order betrayed his more middle-class tastes (as opposed to a more working-class "boilermaker"). Bosard recalled, however, that the next time he went into the bar

> The guy next to me ordered a gin and tonic. I turned to the guy and told him they didn't know what that was here. Ebe came up to me and patted my hand

> and said, "Oh, yes we do. I heard you order it the other night and I found out what it was and now we have it." That was kind of the attitude there. Every night Ebe was at the door and he would shake hands with everybody who went out and say, "Thank you for coming. Come again." That was very unusual for bars in Minneapolis; not only did [the Dugout] put . . . up with you, they were courting your business and actually made you feel comfortable.[36]

The Dugout's financial straits led its owners to see a business opportunity in wooing queer customers from Herb's Bar, some of whom, like Bosard and "the guy next to [him]," had more middle-class tastes than the Dugout's previous clientele. To keep newfound customers satisfied, the bar's owner adjusted the drink menu to accommodate their tastes.As customers shifted their business to the Dugout, we can see how "queer bars" were not static spaces, as Herb's Bar—an adopted queer space—lost favor with its queer clientele (and, as Bosard suggests, likely without protest from Herb).

As with other bars mentioned here, the Dugout's clientele was neither exclusively queer nor exclusively male. Gloria Olson, who had gone to Kirmser's as a teenager during the mid-1940s, also patronized the Dugout during the 1950s. She recalls the bar's gender division and the "mixed" crowd of straights and queers that Bosard also mentioned:

> The men kind of used the front bar and, then, the back bar was where they had the dance floor and they had a woman playing the organ . . . that was where the women went. You'd very seldom see a guy back there. Then, they served food in there, too, so they had booths in the front. Some straight people would come in the front. Nobody ever bothered anybody in the back. They just thought they were a bunch of softball players playing ball . . . a bunch of ball players going there after ball games. Nobody thought anything of it.[37]

Olson described a practice of tolerance that helped the owners of the Dugout to stay financially solvent, which also provided its queer clientele opportunities to socialize publicly with members of the same sex.

According to Olson, other business entrepreneurs (she names "the Syndicate"—i.e., the Mafia—and "Jewish men") tried to get "the crowd" who patronized places like the Dugout to patronize their own establishments. However, she asserts that many couldn't "get a gay bar off the

The Dugout Café and Bar, shown here in a photograph from 1942, was located at 206 Third Street South in Minneapolis. It was one of the first bars in the Twin Cities to deliberately court queer patrons for their business. Photograph by Minneapolis Star Journal; *courtesy of the Minnesota Historical Society.*

ground" with much success because of a more general climate of heterosexism in these other spaces—a climate that stood in stark contrast to the atmosphere in places such as the Dugout: "[These other places] didn't work because the people didn't like some of the clientele that would still come in there. They'd hassle the gay people. They didn't *bash* them like they do now, but they used to hassle them a lot, and put them down, and make fun of them, and stuff."[38] Thus, even while some business owners may have wanted to capitalize on the burgeoning queer client base, gay men and women chose which public spaces they would adopt and adapt. In particular, they avoided bars with a pervasive climate of heterosexism, even in spite of an owner's efforts to court their business.

Even in bars claimed as queer, there was sometimes violence among patrons. For example, Donna Mellem recalls having received "a royal pounding" from a "big bad diesel dyke" and her "equally as big buddy" in the alley outside of the 19 Bar—the Loring Park bar that was founded in 1952 and was gay-owned by partners Everett Stoltz and George Koch. This traumatic experience profoundly shaped Mellem's sense of safety at the 19 Bar and she never returned as a patron there.[39] But she did return as a patron of the Dugout because the space because gave her "the feeling [she] wasn't alone" and that "[t]here were people like [her] out there" with regard to her sexual attraction to other women.

Even so, Mellem, who identified as respectably middle-class, often felt excluded from the working-class culture at the Dugout: "I could never be one of them. I never felt that I was one of them. I never wanted to be, in that sense, think, or act like they did. I wanted to maintain respect and kindness. I never really fit into the gay life." Although Mellem valued the Dugout, she also "was ashamed of some of the types of people that [she] was observing there." In her final estimation, she did not feel that there was really meaningful "community" for her among the largely working-class Dugout regulars, but she went there because "it was just a place to go to let hair down."

Reflecting on his experience at the Happy Hour, a Minneapolis queer bar that opened in 1957 at Fourth and Hennepin, Charles betrayed a similar ambivalence about gay community. Even from his inaugural visit to the Happy Hour in the early 1960s, Charles remembers seeing "what appeared to [him] to be drunks hanging out in this dark bar." Having been newly resigned to the fact that being gay "was not a phase," the image of the bar's clientele frightened the seventeen-year-old Charles:

> I looked around and thought, is this how I'm going to end up? And I said, "No. This is not how you're going to end up." But that's what I saw—these are my people. You know? You look both ways before you go in. This was in the 60s, '61, '62. And walked in here and it shocked me. I knew they were gays, homosexuals. And I guess I was one, but I didn't want to end up like that. And over the many years that I went to the Happy Hour, I rarely if ever met somebody to have sex—well, maybe five or six in, what, seven or eight years.

As was the case for Mellem, Charles expressed ambivalence about the kind of gay "community" proffered in working-class bars. On the one hand, he felt that because of a shared sexual orientation, the men at the Happy Hour were his "people"; on the other hand, the upwardly mobile Charles (who would later attend college and seminary) didn't want his life to be "like the people sitting around the bar at the Happy Hour."[40]

The personal narratives consulted for this chapter suggest that boundaries surrounding categories of race (as we see with Brown) and class (as we see with Brown, Bosard, and Mellem) led to internal policing of queer bars with regard to insider/outsider status in the burgeoning, if tenuous, sense of "community" forged in these spaces. Even so, the heterogeneous sets of queer bar patrons did seem to understand that, despite significant differences, there was also common ground. As Brown wrote about the "first black man to come into Kirmser's"—despite the crowd's finding him "obnoxious," "black or white, he belonged to the lodge. He was as queer as any of us; he was 'one of the boys.'"[41]

Being "one of the boys" (or girls) meant more than just a shared sexual attraction to members of one's own sex. Regardless of whether they identified as "gay" or "queer" at the time, patrons of Twin Cities queer bars during this era were profoundly shaped by the climate of heterosexism, a reality that they shared across lines of race, class, or gender. They had reason to fear that should someone expose their sexual proclivities to their families, coworkers, or bosses (also known as "dropping a dime" in the era's hard-boiled parlance), they might lose their jobs or be ostracized from their families or other social networks. Their sense of personal risk was very real, and many queer bar patrons took pains to perform appropriately heteronormative behavior, which, in the Twin Cities, was key to avoiding run-ins with the law. As we will see in the next section, it was in the breaching of this performance that one could get into trouble.

Social and Legal Sanctions in Public Space: The Spectacle of Cross-dressing

In 1949, a Minneapolis supper club called Curly's entered into a six-month contract with the Miami-based entourage of female impersonators, the Jewel Box Revue. The Jewel Box Revue was known throughout the nightclub circuit for its elaborate costumes, large production numbers, and repertoire of songs sung by the performers themselves alongside a band of musicians. Even though the Revue had "been attracting capacity business throughout its run," Curly's elected to "terminate the engagement of the '*Jewel Box Revue*' . . . at the expiration of its . . . contract, Jan. 13 [1950]" at the request of local police.[42] The December 9, 1949, issue of the Minneapolis *Morning Tribune* explains that Police Chief Thomas R. Jones said that although there had been "no complaints about the contents of the show itself . . . there were complaints about some undesirable people frequenting the café since the show opened." Jones explained that both "policewomen and members of the morals squad" had reviewed the show and "found no obscenity."[43] Thus "there were no legal grounds on which the show could be closed." Nonetheless, the "department asked Curly's to cooperate" and noted that it planned to investigate another impersonator show at the Persian Palms, even though it had received no complaints about it.[44] Notably, the pending closing of the Jewel Box show received national attention in *Variety,* the country's premiere entertainment periodical.[45]

As *Variety* put it, this termination was part of a "crackdown on Femme Impersonator Spots" in the Twin Cities. Indeed, just a month before, on November 8, 1949, St. Paul police closed a female impersonator show at a bar called the Drum and the Radisson's Flame Room in Minneapolis "banished" singer Paula Drake for merely singing "a song about a female impersonator at a rehearsal."[46] This series of "crackdowns" led to a ban on such shows for five years, until February 1955 when the Minneapolis nightclub the Gay 90's (which in the 1950s was known for its "steak dinners and strip-show theater")[47] brought the Jewel Box Revue back to the region.

Variety reported that police may have lifted the "ban on switch shows" as a goodwill gesture to the local nightclub businesses that were in the midst of "one of the lowest ebbs in all loop history"; the Jewel Box Revue, so they hoped, would "liven it up."[48] It did. But in an unfortunate case of déjà vu, the Gay 90's ended the Revue's engagement to avoid "a disorderly conduct charge," this time after just five weeks at the venue.[49] Again, as in 1949, the "*Revue* did big business . . . [and] other clubs welcomed the crowds it attracted," but police saw the Revue as a magnet for what was perceived as effeminate social deviants, specifically, two men who were arrested for "walking about downtown in feminine attire."[50] Neither man had "any connection with the show" but claimed to have come to Minneapolis for the sole purpose of joining the troupe. Like the incident in 1949, "[a]fter giving the show the onceover, the police morals squad had reported it contained nothing obscene or immoral and was unobjectionable."[51] What the police objected to was that the Revue had attracted the two men who were arrested for "parad[ing] in drag" on the streets of downtown Minneapolis.[52]

That onstage female impersonation lent itself to moral scrutiny in the 1950s is not surprising, but neither was such scrutiny unique to the postwar period. Professional impersonators had been defending themselves from accusations of offstage effeminacy ever since they became part of the national popular culture on the vaudeville stages at the turn of the century.[53] Increasingly, vaudeville impersonators attained a cultural legitimacy in the theater world and effectively dissociated themselves from the female impersonators who performed in disreputable venues such as the honky-tonk and who mingled, in drag, with their (primarily male) audiences, hustling drinks and sexual favors.[54] However, when vaudeville ended in the mid-1930s, so did this clear boundary between the moral and immoral female impersonator, as both the honky-tonk impersonators and the vaudevillian impersonators sought employment in the newly booming nightclub industry. As a result, all female impersonator acts were again subject to moral censure.

Those acts that harked back to the legitimacy of the vaudeville acts (i.e., those that insisted on a separation between the audience and the stage illusion) could still hold a cultural legitimacy and social decency, as *Variety*'s 1935 review of Cleveland's Torch Club "femme impersonator" floor show illustrates: "Seven are in the troupe, all wearing gowns and making appearances on a small stage leading to floor. . . . Nothing risqué or particularly objectionable about opening performances. All of them play straight, keeping a vaudeville stage illusion. Besides freak attraction, Torch Club has a good cuisine."[55] Although such shows were certainly not considered highbrow entertainment, the writer legitimates a mainstream interest in the show not only because the show harked back to the legitimacy of vaudeville, but also because at its worst it was merely a "freak show"—a mainstay of American popular culture where spectators were encouraged to gawk at the humans on display, but where there was no confusion between the identities of those on display and those doing the watching.

Other female impersonator acts clearly did not keep up the stage illusion. Again in 1935, in St. Paul this time, *Variety* reported: "Following complaints to police, four femme impersonators doing a nightly 'Dance of the Fairies' at the Stables, local nitery, were shagged back to Chicago by John

Law. Boys did their dance and then circulated about the tables to dance with the male customers and act as 'hostesses.' Cops objected specifically to the latter practice."[56] The cops might not have objected to the act had the "boys" kept their performance to the Stables's stage. But when the performers moved their dance off the stage and into the audience, the cops were quick to act to make sure that no one in the Stables would be sexually unbridled by these Chicago outsiders.

When the Jewel Box Revue appeared at Minneapolis's Gay 90's in 1955, the troupe maintained the boundaries between stage and audience. Its producers, Danny Brown and Doc Benner, took pains to ensure that the Revue be seen as "true art, and not the burlesque it had come to be" in many venues.[57] One of the ways to attain that status of "true art" was to ensure that the Revue's illusionists did not enter into the real world like the "fairy" dancers in 1935, or the hapless lads in frocks who Minneapolis police arrested in 1955 precisely because they crossed the boundary dividing acceptable cross-gender performance onstage and disruptive cross-gender performance on the street. Where social and legal boundaries were concerned, it was important that female impersonators not break "the fourth wall" and allow the world of the stage and the house to collapse into each other.[58] If the boundary was maintained, such shows could potentially offer a safe space for some audience members to reckon with same-sex desire because, while homosexuals could not overtly express same-sex desires without facing social sanction, onstage, female impersonators could publicly express desires for men when they impersonated women.

The uproar surrounding cross-dressing in the Twin Cities in the postwar years complicates our understanding about how heteronormativity was policed in urban centers. Although oral history narrators do not speak of repressive policing in Minneapolis and St. Paul at midcentury, this should not suggest that the urge to police and control social boundaries related to nonheteronormative performances was absent. On the contrary, the archival and oral historical sources examined in this essay suggest that these boundaries were strictly policed, so that even while the postwar period did provide for more open public spaces where queer individuals might gather and socialize, there was still little room for those who challenged the gendered norms of the North Star State.

Sources suggest that nonnormative gender performance was less severely penalized in St. Paul than in its twin city. Of all the narrators consulted for this essay, Gloria Olson most clearly paints a picture of this

Minneapolis "cracked down" on female impersonators during the postwar period, but by the 1960s even the risqué female impersonator Lee Leonard regularly performed at the Gay 90's bar at 408 Hennepin Avenue in Minneapolis, as this photograph of the bar's marquee taken in 1964 illustrates. Photograph by Norton & Peel; courtesy of the Minnesota Historical Society.

difference, claiming that "in Minneapolis, they had different laws than they did in St. Paul."[59] Here, Olson's memory is only partially correct; Minneapolis had an anti-cross-dressing ordinance on the books since 1877,[60] whereas St. Paul's city ordinance dating from 1891 prohibited people from publicly wearing "clothes not belonging to their sex."[61] Nonetheless, it is possible that the anti-cross-dressing laws were more strictly enforced in Minneapolis than they were in St. Paul. In Minneapolis, Olson recalled, "If you were a female and you didn't have three articles of women's clothes on, you could be arrested for male impersonation." Olson, who preferred to dress in masculine attire, recalled that she and others felt more freedom to dress as they wished in St. Paul. In particular, she recalled how the Little Dandy Bar in St. Paul employed a "morphadite" [*sic*] bartender named Mitzy who was "real big and . . . looked like man."[62] When Mitzy "went to Minneapolis, she had to be dressed like a male. So, she'd comb her hair back and have to wear men's clothes over there or she'd be arrested."[63] By contrast, Olson notes, "In St. Paul she could get by with being dressed like a woman."[64]

This distinction between Minneapolis's and St. Paul's enforcement of sumptuary laws did not impact the vast majority of homosexual men and women who patronized queer bars in the Twin Cities in the postwar period. Most patrons did not risk the social stigma of performing counter to gendered norms that could mark them as "queer."Regulars at queer bars in this era generally preferred a certain anonymity even within the bars, as indicated by the practice of sharing first names or nicknames only, even among those they considered their friends.[65] Likewise, at this time, the overwhelming majority of queer bar patrons in the Twin Cities likely had no interest in cross-dressing, much less in female impersonation. Ricardo Brown's memoir, for example, describes how he did not feel comfortable as an audience member watching a drag show in a "seedy" New York nightclub in 1945. The show, in Brown's estimation, "made a mockery of everything I'd been told was masculine," and not in a way that he found particularly liberating: "When the bus pulled into the St. Paul Greyhound depot a few days later, I realized how good it was to be back in Minnesota."[66]

Quietly Accommodating Queer Bars

I want to conclude by addressing why Minneapolis and St. Paul were more accommodating to queer bars than other major cities in the postwar period. First, I believe that this accommodation relates to Minnesota's public image in the 1950s as being vice-free—an image that many Minnesotans may have had a vested interest in upholding. This vice-free image was newly won in the postwar period; during the 1920s and early 1930s, St. Paul was a notorious hangout for organized crime and high-profile gangsters such as John Dillinger, "Babyface" Nelson, and the Ma Barker Gang. In the early decades of the twentieth century, St. Paul's police department had made a deal with gangsters and the Mafia that the police would not pursue the outlaws so long as they abided by St. Paul's laws—and so long as Mafia- and gangster-owned businesses paid off the cops.[67] By 1935, two years after the end of Prohibition, the agreement had crumbled after a wiretap on phones at the St. Paul Police Department led to prosecution of a number of St. Paul's finest. At the end of the investigation, "[t]hirteen members of the Police Department were suspended or fired for corrupt activities [and] Police Chief Michael J. Culligan was forced to resign."[68] "Under a new administration," notes the St. Paul Police Historical Society, "the Saint Paul Police Department began to rebuild its image,"[69] which no doubt included distancing itself from its previous practices of accepting bribes from Mafia-controlled businesses. This context might explain why our interviews suggest a Mafia presence and payoffs in Minneapolis, but not St. Paul, in the postwar years.

By the early part of the 1950s, Minnesota Governor Luther Youngdahl boasted to Senator Kefauver's Special Committee on Organized Crime in Interstate Commerce that, under his leadership, Minnesota at large—not merely St. Paul—had successfully rid itself of vice.[70] Although far from a wholly accurate claim, this no doubt bolstered Minnesota's national public image as a vice-free state. Writing in his July 19, 1951, column "Roaming in the Gloaming" for the *Lake Wilson Pilot,* a local paper in southern Minnesota, columnist Bob Forrest suggested just this when he complimented the excellent job that the city of St. Paul had done in cleaning up its act:

> This so-called anti-crime wave in Minnesota did not start with Gov. Youngdahl as many admirers assert. A couple of decades ago the city of St. Paul was just about as tough as they made 'em. They had everything they shouldn't have and a lot of it. Crime ran rampant. The city fairly reeked with vice. It was the refuge for criminals. The big mobs moved in. . . . There was no waving of flags, no drums beat. Just the minds of an awakened citizenry, and what a wonderful job they did. From being a cesspool of vice they changed it to one of the cleanest cities in the United States.[71]

Likewise, Jack Lait and Lee Mortimer's best-selling *U.S.A. Confidential,* a 1952 sensation that detailed crime and vice in states throughout the nation, noted Minnesota's wholesome public image. [72] In a section of their book titled "Carry Me Back to Old Minnesota," they claimed: "Minnesota has long been thought of as the habitation of peaceful, home-loving Svenskas whose only vices were Saturday night binges on 100-proof aquavit and a yen for their neighbors' wives, mostly gaunt Anna Christies."[73] But Lait and Mortimer's purpose was not to praise and good-heartedly tease Minnesota. Their aim was to point out the blemishes on Minnesota's seemingly perfect complexion. Given Minnesota's public face, they confessed that such a project would take "imagination—or deep digging."[74]

Given their mission, it is not surprising that Lait and Mortimer did not extend the kind of compliments for Minnesota that Forrest did in his "Roaming in the Gloaming" column; in their six pages of "confidential lowdown, from gutter to statehouse," they enlisted both their imaginations and their dirt-digging shovels to compile a litany of current Minnesota-based crime and vice-related activity. In so doing, however, they reserved just two lines to comment on the homosexual presence in Minneapolis: "Sexual deviates patronize Curley's [*sic*] in the Loop, as Minneapolis' business district is called. Here are gay shows with entertainers working in drag."[75] Of note, Lait and Mortimer only offered this one mention of an establishment that "sexual deviates" patronized—suggesting that this pair of investigative journalists lacked imagination, interest, or the right "dirt-digging" shovels. Perhaps it was all three.

Likely, Lait and Mortimer were unable to imagine queer bars as being anything other than obviously and readably queer (i.e., the presence of female impersonators), whereas, as Bosard's words remind us, "a gay bar in those days was not [what] it is today, it was a regular bar to which some gay people went."[76] As such, the "gay bar" of the 1950s was a space that was mostly invisible and unreadable to outsiders; as addressed earlier, this was an invisibility that both social and legal sanctions enforced. But I would venture that this invisibility was desired because it allowed Minnesotans to perpetuate the wholesome public image of their state. Thus, perhaps Minneapolis "cracked down" on female impersonators throughout the 1950s because such a spectacle could tarnish that image, while St. Paul did not target female impersonators in the same manner because such efforts would not have been worth the negative attention. After all, Minneapolis gained national attention in *Variety* when it conducted its "crackdowns." To maintain the vice-free appearance that Youngdahl and others seemed to cultivate for their state, local authorities may have vigilantly swept the issue of how to regard queer bars in their urban centers under the rug. As mentioned earlier, the "concerned father" letter makes it clear that police were aware of at least some of these queer spaces, but their mission was not to shut down the bars but to serve as an occasional surveillance mechanism that would demand that queer bar patrons readily perform heteronormativity: "Nothing to see here, folks—just some peaceful, home-loving Svenskas." In short, if a city or state was trying to cultivate an image of being "vice-free," it would not likely elicit the efforts of its police force to stamp out the pockets of the *invisible* "vice."

Although the urge to protect Minnesota's public image may tell part of the story, another nuance to the question of the relative dearth of police intervention in Minnesota queer life may lie in state's burgeoning liberalism during the postwar period. As Jennifer Delton details in *Making Minnesota Liberal: Civil Rights and the Transformation of the Democratic Party,* following World War II, Minnesota was at the vanguard of civil rights and antiracism rhetoric and reform, a position that Hubert H. Humphrey's liberal Democrats pushed forward (which, in turn, lent national relevance to Minnesota's Democratic-Farmer-Labor Party and offered issue-based cohesion to the tenuous DFL alliance).[77] Of course, it would be far from accurate to intimate that Humphrey's brand of civil rights reform included any consideration for homosexuals; in a letter dated June 9, 1965, and addressed to the Mattachine Society's Franklin Kameny, Humphrey made it clear that "neither the Federal Executive Orders on fair employment nor the Civil Rights Act which constitute the authority for the program on non-discrimination are relevant to the problems of homosexuals."[78] Nonetheless, it is clear that some Minnesotans would have taken issue with Humphrey's position on this issue even as early as the 1950s.

Indeed, in 1951, Donald Webster Cory's (pseudonym of Edward Sagarin) *The Homosexual in America: A Subjective Approach* argued for the "remarkable similarity between the problems facing the homosexual and those facing national and ethnic minorities in society," advancing the notion that homosexuals were a protectable minority that deserved society's compassion.[79] From a series of letters published in the March 5, 1955, edition of the Minneapolis *Star*—letters sent in response to the "concerned father" letter that began this chapter—it is clear that some Minnesotans, at least, were embracing precisely this line of thinking. According to Cedric Adams, these letters represented one portion of "one of the greatest mail responses This Corner has had in several months." In order "to give the homosexuals their chance," Adams submitted excerpts of five such letters—all of which took a civil rights approach to "the homosexual problem" against which Adams had warned. The first letter asks: "Why did you pick on one minority for a scathing attack? Why not work toward a happy integration of all men into a society we can be proud of rather than striking at minorities on senseless grounds and forcing them underground?" In a similar manner, the second letter proclaims: "If they prefer to be with people of their own sex, why not leave them alone? I am really sincere when I say that I think both you and the Minneapolis father made a vicious attack on an innocent minority of our society. And you class them with thieves, dope addicts, and other social misfits. You would have done better to study the situation before you attacked." Another letter writer drew even closer ties to Cory's thesis, suggesting that newspaper readers examine it for themselves:

> All we ask is to be understood and left alone. I have two suggestions for you and others similarly concerned. Read the book, "The Homosexual in America" by Donald Webster Cory or a magazine called "One," published in Los Angeles. Before the citizens in this area lose their minds worrying about their children becoming homosexuals, let them read the above material and do a little serious thinking. I don't mean to imply that homosexuality is not a problem, but I do say the problem will not be solved by closing the places we frequent or by sending us off to mental institutions or a workhouse or a prison.[80]

These excerpts, though poignant, are far from radical positions. Rather, they exhibit precisely the rhetoric of liberal pluralism that Minnesotans increasingly espoused with regard to antiracism and civil rights during this same era. The Cedric Adams letters open the possibility that some Minnesotans were extending their brand of liberal pluralism beyond the arena of race and into that of sexuality: "Why not work toward a happy integration of all men into a society we can be proud of rather than striking at minorities on senseless grounds. . . ." With this operating logic, the question of what to do about the bars that so horrified the "concerned father" in 1955 were moot.

Oral historical evidence suggests that many queer men and women valued the bars precisely because, in Mellem's words, they offered a place "to let hair down," even if any sense of a gay and lesbian "community" did not necessarily cut across race and class lines. This letting down of one's hair meant more than merely relaxing; it meant the rare and cherished opportunity to be somewhat less guarded about one's sexuality in a public place. Without a doubt, patrons enjoyed a certain freedom in these spaces, even if that freedom was limited by social and legal codes for how individuals were to behave if they wished to stay out of trouble. “Freedom” as such hung like choke chains around the necks of those who patronized queer bars in the Twin Cities during this era, as they skirted the boundaries of both heteronormative performance and queer expression.

Examining the Twin Cities bars in the postwar period not only adds new stories to the historical record but raises new questions for *old* case studies by highlighting how quieter forms of policing gender norms shaped the lives of queer bar patrons no less than the more dramatic scenes unfolding with police raids. In the postwar period, patrons at Twin Cities queer bars did not experience the police raids that were found elsewhere in the nation, even though we find legal and social sanctions to encourage heteronormative appearances and queer invisibility. But while the case studies presented here demonstrate ways in which the Twin Cities' methods of accommodating and policing were exceptional, we should not lose sight of the broader connections across geography. If patrons crossed the boundaries rather than skirted them, queer individuals could face dangerous consequences, including arrest, loss of job, or violence. Those threats were real. In that sense, the Twin Cities were not exceptional.

Notes

For their assistance in locating sources or refining ideas, thanks to Emily Callaci, Kim Clarke, Robert Frame, Michael David Franklin, Devorah Heitner, Debbie Miller, Margo Miller, Shannon Munstenteiger, Brent Nunn, Mary Rizzo, Kathy Robbins, and the University of Minnesota Press's outside peer reviewer, Anne Enke. For their thoughtful editorial comments and ready encouragement, thanks to editors Kevin P. Murphy and Jason Ruiz.

1 Cedric Adams, “In This Corner, with Cedric Adams,” Minneapolis Sunday *Tribune*, February 27, 1955, 13.

2 Ibid.

3 The quotes in this paragraph and in the following paragraph are all taken from the reprinted letter, featured in ibid.

4 Adams's words here. Although Adams offered this column as a cautionary tale to his readers, no doubt some of his readers received the details with some excitement, and were eager to learn the whereabouts of these public spaces that catered to a “large

group of homosexuals" so that they themselves could participate in this emerging postwar queer bar culture.

5 In describing certain bars as "queer," I am attempting to portray the spaces as accommodating a broad clientele whose identities, sexual desires, or practices did not conform to heteronormative (and occasionally gendernormative) formations. (Notably, such "queer bar patrons" did not necessarily identify as gay, queer, lesbian, bisexual, or homosexual.) Likewise, as this essay will make clear, in the postwar period, a "queer bar" was not a static space, as its clientele might abandon a once-frequented space in favor of another.

6 See especially Allan Bérubé, *Coming Out under Fire: The History of Gay Men and Women in World War II* (New York: Free Press, 1990).

7 See, for example, George Chauncey, *Gay New York: Gender, Urban Culture, and the Making of the Gay Male World, 1890–1940* (New York: Basic Books, 1994).

8 To take just a couple of examples from the press, see "Perverts Called Government Peril," *New York Times,* April 19, 1950, 25; and "Police Decide Sex Deviate Killed Missing Boy Scout," *Chicago Daily Tribune (1872–1963),* August 11, 1955; ProQuest Historical Newspapers, Chicago Tribune (1849–1985), 7. For an extensive account of the federal government's role in persecuting homosexuals during the Cold War, see David K. Johnson, *The Lavender Scare: The Cold War Persecution of Gays and Lesbians in the Federal Government* (Chicago: University of Chicago Press, 2004). Chauncey has noted that homosexuals "were depicted in ways that drew on patterns of demonization that had become familiar and habitual through their widespread use to demonize Jews as well as communists." Depicted as "cosmopolitan outsiders," homosexual men and women were considered threatening both to national security and to the nation's moral fiber, as many believed that a homosexual's "loyalties" could only be to a "community of people like themselves" (George Chauncey, *Why Marriage? The History Shaping Today's Debate over Gay Equality* [New York: Basic Books, 2004], 19).

9 Incidentally, the *Star* reported on the same page that the Minneapolis morals squad had recently raided a bar and arrested a seventy-three-year-old Elks Club bartender who was "charged with selling liquor without a license." In this latter case, the bartender had transgressed clearly demarcated legal boundaries, thus permitting the police to act. See "Police Raid Club on Liquor Charges," Minneapolis *Star,* February 28, 1955, 29.

10 For an extensive case study of San Francisco during this period, see Nan Alamilla Boyd, *Wide Open Town: A History of Queer San Francisco* (Berkeley and Los Angeles: University of California Press, 2003). The national mood was certainly not sympathetic to those who engaged in homosexual activities. (Neither were those who engaged in such acts necessarily ready to develop their identities or politics around

their same-sex attractions, as suggested by oral historical evidence gathered by the Twin Cities GLBT Oral History Project.) During this period, homosexuals were stereotyped as threatening the very core of the nation. Those who worked for the U.S. government were considered "security risks" because it was assumed that exposure of their private actions could easily put them "under the threat of blackmail"—making them ideal informants for the Communists (John Fisher, "Morals-Purge Aids Rehired, House Is Told," *Chicago Daily Tribune (1972–1963),* April 20, 1950; ProQuest Historical Newspapers, Chicago Tribune (1849–1985), 8. In 1953, to show his intolerance for these "perverts," President Eisenhower signed an executive order that expelled gay men and lesbians from federal jobs. See especially Johnson, *The Lavender Scare,* 119–46. John D'Emilio and Estelle B. Freedman note that such demonstrations of state and national intolerance for homosexuals "encouraged local police forces across the country to harass them with impunity" (John D'Emilio and Estelle B. Freedman, *Intimate Matters: A History of Sexuality in America* [Chicago: University of Chicago Press, 1998], 295).

11 D'Emilio and Freedman, *Intimate Matters,* 295.

12 "Vice Charges Filed against 58 in Bar Raid," *Chicago Daily Tribune (1872–1963),* December 31, 1951; ProQuest Historical Newspapers, Chicago Tribune (1849–1986), B7.

13 It is important to note that the Twin Cities were midsized cities in the 1950s. Although urban renewal and suburban flight would contribute to their population decline in subsequent decades, in 1950 Minneapolis alone had a population of 521,718. If St. Paul is added to the mix, the Twin Cities population was more than 830,000 persons at midcentury, collectively surpassing San Francisco's population by more than fifty thousand. See http://www.demographia.com/db-city1970sloss.htm, accessed April 28, 2008. Lest we think this manner of policing bars to be a big-city phenomenon—with the more cosmopolitan cities calling on their police forces to stage bar raids and to engage in wide-scale homosexual entrapment—we need only look to the case of Boise, Idaho, with its population of 34,393 in 1950, to see that police harassment of suspected homosexuals was not specific to the larger, and more cosmopolitan, coastal cities. In 1955–56, Boise made national headlines for its efforts to rid the city of homosexuals, efforts that resulted in the arrests of sixteen men suspected of having sex with teenage boys and the questioning of more than 1,500 suspected homosexuals and local community members. See John Gerassi, *The Boys of Boise: Furor, Vice, and Folly in an American City,* with a new forward by Peter Boag (Seattle: University of Washington Press, 2001). With regard to police raids on bars, the Twin Cities would seem to have more in common with another midsized industrial city—Buffalo, New York—as detailed in Elizabeth Kennedy and Madeline Davis's ethnohistorical study of Buffalo's working-class lesbian communities at midcentury. Contrasting the experience of those

who took part in queer bar life in the 1950s in cities such as New York City, Miami, or Washington, D.C., in Buffalo, Kennedy and Davis note that "[i]n the 1950s there were even fewer raids on lesbian and gay bars than in the 1940s," most likely because Buffalo's police were receiving payoffs from bar owners, many of whom were Mafia-controlled (Elizabeth Lapovsky Kennedy and Madeline D. Davis, *Boots of Leather, Slippers of Gold: The History of a Lesbian Community* [New York: Routledge, 1993], 75). Oral history narrators who reflected on queer bars in the Twin Cities during this same period made similar claims about the Mafia, as we shall see.

14 John Howard, "Place and Movement in Gay American History: A Case from the Post–World War II South," in *Creating a Place for Ourselves: Lesbian, Gay, and Bisexual Community Histories,* ed. Brett Beemyn (New York and London: Routledge, 1997), 217.

15 Jean-Nickolaus Tretter, interview by Scott Paulsen on November 29, 1993. Interview transcript, *Twin Cities Gay and Lesbian Community Oral History Project,* Minnesota Historical Society, 9.

16 Donna Mellem, interview by Mary Weiland on January 30, 1997, interview transcript, *Lesbian Elders Oral History Project Interviews,* Minnesota Historical Society, 18.

17 For example, Ricardo Brown recalls that his friend Red Larson, who was discovered having consensual sex in a car with another man, was arrested, jailed, and outed by the local press. In response to this event, Brown found himself praying "in earnest, not for Red Larson, exactly, but for myself. I thanked God that I hadn't been caught and publicly exposed as a queer, that my name had never gotten into the papers" (Brown, *The Evening Crowd at Kirmser's,* 132). Notably, Larson was not arrested as part of a bar raid; he was arrested for "cornholing a guy in the back seat of his dad's car" and was charged with "indecent exposure" (ibid., 131).

18 Brown, *The Evening Crowd at Kirmser's,* 4.

19 Ibid., 7.

20 Gloria Olson, interview by Mary Weiland on January 22, 1997, interview transcript, *Lesbian Elders Oral History Project Interviews,* Minnesota Historical Society, 6.

21 For more on this subject, see Alessandro Portelli, *The Death of Luigi Trastulli and Other Stories: Form and Meaning in Oral History* (Albany: State University of New York Press, 1991).

22 Brown, *The Evening Crowd at Kirmser's,* 8.

23 Allan H. Spear, in ibid., xiv.

24 Brown, *The Evening Crowd at Kirmser's,* 100. Subsequent references are given in the text.

25 Richard W. Bosard, interview by Scott Paulsen on October 31, 1993, interview transcript, *Twin Cities Gay and Lesbian Community Oral History Project,* Minnesota Historical Society.

26 Ibid., 6–7.

27 Kennedy and Davis, in *Boots of Leather, Slippers of Gold,* note that through World War II, "several cities, including Chicago, passed laws prohibiting women's entrance into bars in an attempt to limit the spread of venereal disease" (31).

28 Bosard, *Twin Cities Gay and Lesbian Community Oral History Project,* 5. Although I do not elaborate on it in this chapter, Gloria Olson makes note of going to predominately black bars and that "They weren't necessarily gay bars, they were just a bar where lesbians would go and black people didn't bother." She notes that "house parties would be mixed [race]" as well (Olson, *Lesbian Elders Oral History Project Interviews,* 13). Although information I have found on mixed-race bars is scant (limited to Olson's brief recollections), it seems to echo Allen Drexel's work on Chicago during this same time period, in which he argues that "the black press, and black communities in general, demonstrated considerably greater openness" (Allen Drexel, "Before Paris Burned: Race, Class, and Male Homosexuality on the Chicago South Side, 1935–1960," in Beemyn, *Creating a Place for Ourselves,* 139). Even so, it is important to remember that the black population was a much smaller percentage of the Twin Cities' overall population than they were in Chicago's during this period; although the numbers climbed significantly in the decades that followed, in 1950 there were only roughly fourteen thousand blacks in the entire state of Minnesota. See David Vassar Taylor, "The Blacks," in *They Chose Minnesota: A Survey of the State's Ethnic Groups,* ed. June D. Holmquist (St. Paul: Minnesota Historical Society Press, 1981), 84.

29 George Chauncey, "The Policed," in Beemyn, *Creating a Place for Ourselves,* 21.

30 Bosard, *Twin Cities Gay and Lesbian Community Oral History Project,* 6.

31 The Minneapolis *Star,* December 3, 1949, 35.

32 The *Oxford English Dictionary* traces the first uses of *gay* as a reference to homosexuals to the 1920s (in the literature of Gertrude Stein and Noël Coward), although it was not until the 1940s that the word was more decisively being used as such, in a wider sense. As in the 1920s, in 1941, the word was still somewhat coded; according to G. Legman's 1941 entry in the volume *Sex Variants II, gay* was an "adjective used almost exclusively by homosexuals to denote homosexuality, sexual attractiveness, promiscuity or lack of restraint, in a person, place, or part" (*Oxford English Dictionary Online,* March 2008).

33 Bosard, *Twin Cities Gay and Lesbian Community Oral History Project,* 6.

34 The "Chronology of Gay and Lesbian Life in Hennepin County" that accompanies Timothy Trent Blade's article "'Sodom on the Mississippi': The Homosexual Presence Shown in the Media," in *Hennepin History* (Minneapolis: Hennepin History Society, 1993), 23 and 28, gives the Dugout's location as 206 South Third Avenue. The chronology also reports the Dugout's opening as being in 1953. Contradicting this is the

Minneapolis Star Journal photograph of the Dugout, which notes the bar's location as 206 South Third Street (a difference of a couple blocks from the Hennepin History chronology); also, the photograph is dated 2/18/1942, which suggests that the bar was open sooner than the date given in Blade's article. An interesting detail in Blade's article is that "[w]hen the Dugout was torn down in 1959, its loyal customers bought bricks as souvenirs" (23).

35 Bosard, *Twin Cities Gay and Lesbian Community Oral History Project,* 9. Gloria Olson cites "Honey Herrold" as owning the Dugout in addition to other bars (Olson, *Lesbian Elders Oral History Project Interviews,* 7).

36 Bosard, *Twin Cities Gay and Lesbian Community Oral History Project,* 9.

37 Olson, *Lesbian Elders Oral History Project Interviews,* 16.

38 Ibid., 16–17; emphasis in the original.

39 Ibid., 16.

40 Charles, interview by Jason Ruiz and Ann McKenzie on January 25, 2004, interview transcript (by Danielle Kasprzak), *Twin Cities GLBT Oral History Project,* University of Minnesota, 17.

41 Brown, *The Evening Crowd at Kirmser's,* 101.

42 "Minneapolis Cracks Down on Femme Impersonator Spots," *Variety,* December 14, 1949, 51.

43 Ibid. With regard to the content of the Jewel Box Revue shows, it is important to note that in the 1950s some members of the Revue used double entendres in their songs to open up the possibility for queer or sexualized readings, but audience members would have to read between the lines. For example, in "The Spinach Song," a Revue impersonator sang the lines: "I didn't like it the first time/But I was so young you see/But I've smartened up and I've gotten wise/Now I've got enough for two dozen guys/I didn't like it the first time/But oh how it grew on me." The ambiguity of songs such as this allowed the audience members to be in control of otherwise dangerous encounters because only they could ultimately decide on the song's meaning. "The Spinach Song," for one, offered a full gamut of possible interpretations: from affirming a growing affinity for marijuana, for sex, or simply for greens. Quoted in Don Paulson and Roger Simpson, *An Evening at the Garden of Allah: A Gay Cabaret* (New York: Columbia University Press, 1996), 81.

44 Will Jones, "Impersonators to Leave Curly's," Minneapolis *Morning Tribune,* December 9, 1949, 29.

45 "Minneapolis Cracks Down on Femme Impersonator Spots," *Variety,* December 14, 1949, 51.

46 Will Jones, "Paula's Gone," Minneapolis *Morning Tribune,* December 9, 1949, 29.

47 Blade, "'Sodom on the Mississippi,'" 23.

48 "Mpls. Lifts Ban on Switch Shows," *Variety,* February 2, 1955, 64.

49 "Mpls. Cops Padlock Switch Show after 2 Parade in 'Drag,'" *Variety,* March 2, 1955, 57, 59.

50 Ibid. Incidentally, the 1955 closing of the Jewel Box Revue show occurred just days after the publication of the Cedric Adams column that began this chapter, and Chief Jones's response saying that the police could not "close bars because of deviates." It is possible that the police pressured the Gay 90's to shut down the Jewel Box Revue as an effort to show Minnesotans that Minneapolis cops were not entirely soft on "deviates" after all.

51 Ibid.

52 If the Revue's cross-dressing at any time left the realm of the stage, its legitimacy would be immediately called into question. But so long as the show was kept both onstage and within the range of the dominant culture's standards of morality, its cross-dressing as women would not in and of itself result in an automatic charge of indecency. In order to maintain the publicly safe space for both the performers and the audience, the Jewel Box Revue was mindful to keep the show within the acceptable boundaries, physical and otherwise.

53 See Thomas Arthur Bolze, "Female Impersonation in the United States, 1900–1970," PhD dissertation, State University of New York at Buffalo, 1994, 60.

54 See Chauncey's *Gay New York* for how this was a common practice in the first half of the twentieth century.

55 "Torch Club," *Variety,* August 21, 1935, Club Reviews.

56 "Femmers Chased," *Variety,* March 20, 1935, 47.

57 Undated Souvenir Program, Billy Rose Theatre Collection, file folder "Clippings—Jewel Box Revue," New York Public Library for the Performing Arts.

58 There are two exceptions to this. One was the emcee, who provided an acceptable link between those worlds. The other is recalled by Revue impersonator Jerry Ross: "We always had a ballerina on the show. When I was on the show, our ballerina was Kenny Richard. He was billed as 'Our male toe dancer, a ballerina supreme. She'll tiptoe into your hearts, dance on your table and tiptoe into your glasses.' Kenny was near-sighted and once at Sofie's Cat and the Fiddle Club in Cincinnati, Kenny danced right on the tables. There were no footlights on the stage and the tables were on the same level as the stage. I don't know how she did it; she'd make a turn and be on a table and not even realize it" (quoted in Paulson and Simpson, *An Evening at the Garden of Allah,* 87).

59 Olson, *Lesbian Elders Oral History Project Interviews,* 18.

60 William Eskridge, *Gaylaw: Challenging the Apartheid of the Closet* (Cambridge: Harvard University Press, 1997), 339.

61 This St. Paul city ordinance was repealed in 2003 when the "City Council unanimously agreed to strike the ban from Chapter 280 of the city's legislative code." See Robert Ingrassia, "Antiquated Ban on Cross-dressing Lifted," *St. Paul Pioneer Press,* December 24, 2003, B2. See also Robert Ingrassia, "Old Law Getting a Dressing Down: St. Paul's 1890s Ban on Cross-dressing Is Called Outdated and Discriminatory," *St. Paul Pioneer Press,* November 26, 2003, A1. Councilman Chris Coleman sponsored the repeal on behalf of the queer advocacy group OutFront Minnesota. See "St. Paul abolishes cross-dressing ordinance," OutFront Minnesota, www.outfront.org/library/legal/crossdress, accessed July 8, 2009. Although the city council voted unanimously for repeal, the Minnesota Family Council, a conservative public policy organization, "did not favor the repeal." See Robert Barnett, "St. Paul repeals cross-dressing ban," Minnesota Family Council, www.mfc.org, accessed July 8, 2009.

62 Olson, *Lesbian Elders Oral History Project Interviews,* 7.

63 Ibid., 18.

64 Ibid.

65 On the use of nicknames in particular, see Brown, *The Evening Crowd at Kirmser's,* 24.

66 Ibid., 20.

67 See Paul Maccabee, *John Dillinger Slept Here: A Crooks' Tour of Crime and Corruption in St. Paul, 1920–1936* (St. Paul: Minnesota Historical Society Press, 1995).

68 *In the Beginning-6* by the St. Paul Police Historical Society, http://www.spphs.com/history/2000/beginning6.php, accessed July 9, 2009.

69 Ibid.

70 Jack Lait and Lee Mortimer, *U.S.A. Confidential* (New York: Crown Publishers, 1952), 115.

71 Bob Forrest, "Roaming in the Gloaming: Things Material and Immaterial," *Lake Wilson Pilot* (July 19, 1951): www2.whidbey.net/forrest/pub/web/roam51b.html, accessed July 15, 2009.

72 It is important to note that some *U.S.A. Confidential* readers likely used the book as a guidebook if they sought places that were amenable to "vice."

73 Lait and Mortimer, *U.S.A. Confidential,* 115.

74 Ibid.

75 Ibid., 116. Likely, Lait and Mortimer's "research" on this particular topic took place in 1949, when the Jewel Box Revue had its contract at this establishment. They also mention the Persian Palms, but not in relation to a queer clientele. They do write, however, that the Persian Palms and a few other bars "cater to the lowest winos and the blowziest hags" (116).

76 Bosard, *Twin Cities Gay and Lesbian Community Oral History Project*, 5.

77 Jennifer A. Delton, *Making Minnesota Liberal: Civil Rights and the Transformation of the Democratic Party* (Minneapolis: University of Minnesota Press, 2002).

78 "Letter from Hubert Humphrey, Vice President of the United States," correspondence from *The Kameny Papers*, an online archive: www.kamenypapers.org/correspondence.htm, accessed July 15, 2009.

79 From the dust jacket on the second printing (by 1956 the book was already on its sixth printing). See Donald Webster Cory, *The Homosexual in America: A Subjective Approach* (New York: Greenberg, 1951).

80 Cedric Adams, "In This Corner with Cedric Adams," Minneapolis *Star*, March 4, 1955, 48.

8. SEX AND THE CITIES REEVALUATING 1980S FEMINIST POLITICS IN MINNEAPOLIS AND ST. PAUL

Pamela Butler

I am interested in examining the concept of "queer" in order to think about how we might construct a new political identity that is truly liberating, transformative, and inclusive of all those who stand on the outside of the dominant constructed norm of state-sanctioned white middle- and upper-class heterosexuality.

—Cathy J. Cohen, "Punks, Bulldaggers, and Welfare Queens: The Radical Potential of Queer Politics?"

The prostitute symbolized poor and working-class communities' potential threat to gender stability and sexual normativity.

—Roderick Ferguson, *Aberrations in Black: Toward a Queer of Color Critique*

In 1989, a woman who identified herself as "A Former Dancer" wrote a letter to the editor of *City Pages,* the popular Minneapolis weekly paper. She was responding to *City Pages*' "exposé" of Solid Gold, a new downtown club that marketed topless dancing, "boxing bimbos," oil and hot-cream wrestling, and other "adult" entertainment to business travelers and middle-class men, women, and heterosexual couples. According to the *City Pages* article, Solid Gold's self-conscious claim to "classiness" was limited to its expensive decor, and undermined by its clientele—one need only look as far as the "fat, sweat-drenched men" in "polyester stretch slacks" to see that the supposedly "classy" club was really just as sleazy as any other topless dancing establishment in the Twin Cities. In her letter, A Former Dancer highlights these passages, describes the *City Pages* article as classist, arrogant, sneering, superior, and flip, and admonishes its author, Meleah Maynard, for setting herself up as a "poor little suburban girl out slumming to see what 'bad women' do for a living." Comparing sex work to other forms of feminized service labor ("I didn't exactly like the work, but I wouldn't have been any happier flipping burgers, or being a cocktail waitress anywhere else"), A Former Dancer demands that Maynard and *City Pages* readers recognize labor in sex industries *as* labor. "Honey, I've worked in some scary places," she scoffs. "Your icky-poo disdain for Solid Gold is misplaced."

Making visible the conditions of sex work, A Former Dancer inserts herself into an ongoing conversation about feminism and sexuality that has consistently marginalized the women and men whose bodies and labor make pornography and other sex industries possible. In fact, while a kind of middle-class voyeurism does pervade Maynard's article, she largely ignores the "bad women" working at Solid Gold, focusing instead on the club's male managers and clientele. This erasure of the *work* in sex work is typical of hegemonic feminist debates about gender, sex, and pornographic cultures in the 1980s—debates that garnered national media attention at the time, and continue to shape academic and popular conversations about feminism and sexuality. The established narrative of these feminist "sex wars"—a story that continues to be told and retold in college classrooms and in mainstream media—produces and reproduces a framework upon which any discussion of feminism and pornography in the United States implicitly rests.

This chapter revisits the feminist antipornography movements of 1980s Minneapolis in part to argue for approaches to feminism and sexuality that are more complex than can be accounted for by the simplistic discourses surrounding the "sex wars"—approaches that can, for instance, understand and make use of the insights that A Former Dancer and other commercial sex workers have to offer. Looking closely at the cultures that produced the feminist antiporn movement in Minneapolis—the politics of women's space, the social and legal contexts for public and commercial sex, and recent histories of gay and lesbian activism in the Twin Cities—this chapter seeks to complicate the established narratives of the feminist "sex wars" in ways that highlight the importance of race, space, and labor to feminist and queer political activism. By foregrounding issues of labor and the politics of space, and the ways in which they are intimately tied up with race and political economy, I hope to use the lessons learned from the feminist antiporn movement to promote a queer politics of sex that is, in Cathy Cohen's words, "truly liberating, transformative, and inclusive of all those who stand on the outside of the dominant constructed norm of state-sanctioned white middle- and upper-class heterosexuality."[1]

After a brief summary of the feminist "sex wars," my analysis begins by describing the social and legal contexts for public and commercial sexual cultures in Minneapolis, and for local activism (feminist and otherwise) that fought against public sex, commercial sex, and the porn industry. This section focuses in particular on the development of the Minneapolis Antipornography Civil Rights Ordinance of 1983–84, and is followed by an examination of the local lesbian/feminist spaces out of which the feminist antipornography movement grew. By focusing on the particulars of the Minneapolis case and the lesbian/feminist cultures that produced it, this section works to challenge or complicate some of the stories that are commonly told about antipornography feminism and the "sex wars." At the same time, my reading of these spaces and cultures reveals the ways in which they produced and relied upon a kind of middle-class "respectability" that was both sexually restrictive and racially exclusive. Examining the 1982 Gay Pride parade and the activities of the Committee to Close Solid Gold, the chapter then shows how these lesbian/feminist claims to "respectability" were central to (1) conflicts between lesbian/feminist and gay male activists and organizations, and (2) an understanding of sex-work-as-victimization that further erased the insights and needs of sex workers from local antipornography feminist politics. This chapter revisits and reframes the battles over feminism, sexuality, and pornography in the Twin Cities in order to illuminate the ways in which race and political economy shape feminist and queer activism, and to ask what lessons we might take from the Minneapolis case into current and future coalitional work. Ultimately, I read 1980s Minneapolis antipornography feminist activism, its social and political context, and the cultures that produced it, through the lenses of race, space, and labor, in order to argue for a politics of sex that can build diverse and effective coalitions for antiracist feminist and queer activism.

Beyond the "Sex Wars": Antiporn Feminism, Anti-Antiporn Feminism, and the Minneapolis Ordinance

The scripts that guide popular and academic conversations about the feminist sex wars are well rehearsed. The story often begins as one of strange bedfellows, where radical feminists in the United States are said to have collaborated with a newly powerful Christian Right in drafting and campaigning for antipornography legislation. (These two seemingly incompatible groups, we are told, were unified not only by a strongly held belief that pornography posed a great threat to women and to the sexual health of American society, but also by a shared politics of white, middle-class sexual priggishness.) Feminist antipornography activism in the 1980s grew out of radical and lesbian-feminist sexual politics that explored the possibilities of egalitarian sex between women, and that sometimes also attempted to regulate sexual practices, desires, and identities that involved power exchange (S/M) and/or gender difference (butch/femme).[2] According to the dominant story of the sex wars, the feminist antipornography movement's myopic focus on pornography and sexual practices as the root cause of women's oppression—and campaigns for legislation that entrusted the state with the regulation of pornographic materials—led to a dramatic and seemingly intractable rift between antipornography feminists on one side, and "sex-positive" and anticensorship feminists on the other.

In popular media, the sex wars are even more oversimplified, to the point that "sex-positive" and anticensorship feminisms fall out of the story altogether. In the 2005 documentary *Inside Deep Throat,* for instance—a love letter to the "golden age" of porno chic—Harvard law professor and *Penthouse* columnist Alan Dershowitz claims that "the worst censors in the country" during the 1980s "were the feminists."[3] In an antifeminist maneuver common to popular media representations, "the feminists" are depicted here through a simplistic caricature of antipornography feminism that stands in for the multiple and diverse feminist movements of the 1980s. This familiar dismissal glosses over the complexity of antipornography feminist activism and politics. Moreover, the equation of "the feminists" with a partial, simplistic characterization of antipornography feminism erases the work of a wide range of feminists in the United States—including civil libertarians, porn stars, and academics, among others—who campaigned and spoke out *against* antipornography legislation in the 1980s. Instead, anti-antipornography feminists of all stripes are lumped in with and overshadowed by First Amendment activists like Dershowitz. Lost in this erasure are the many feminist critiques of First Amendment and civil libertarian defenses of pornography, and feminist calls for radical theories of sex that can challenge both (1) the regulation of sexually explicit materials and (2) the heteropatriarchal cultures and institutions that shape those materials.[4]

We can tell a different story about the feminist sex wars by paying more careful attention to the Minneapolis Antipornography Civil Rights Ordinance, and to local feminist antiporn organizing in the 1980s. As the first U.S. city to pass a (doomed) antipornography civil rights ordinance, Minneapolis was and is central to feminist debates about the production, consumption, and regulation of pornography. At the same time, however, specific histories of feminism and politics in the Twin Cities mean that Minneapolis is also a unique site of convergence between particular formations of sex, race, space, and capital. Missing from both popular and academic feminist conversations about the sex wars are (1) the ways in which feminist and antifeminist debates about sexuality and pornography are also about race; (2) a consideration of how the politics of urban space and "development" shape political discourses about pornography; and (3) commercial sex workers, such as A Former Dancer, on whose lives and labor pornography and other sex industries depend. Because the Minneapolis story subverts or challenges many of the historical narratives that have come to dominate the ways in which feminists and leftists in the United States think and talk about antipornography feminism, we can use it as a way to reframe 1980s feminist activism and debates about sexuality. By focusing on how antipornography feminism operated in Minneapolis, and on the radical and lesbian-feminist politics out of which it emerged, this chapter asks what these histories can tell us about how feminisms operate in relation to space, race, labor, and queer political organizing. For instance, while established ways of remembering the feminist sex wars leave no space for the experiences and critiques of A Former Dancer, examining the history and context of Minneapolis antipornography feminism can open up a different point of entry that enables us to understand the politics of labor in debates about feminism and sexuality. Part of reframing the sex wars in this manner, then, is beginning with—and returning to—A Former Dancer and other commercial sex workers whose bodies, labor, and lives have been at once central to, and marginalized by, debates about sexuality and public space in Minneapolis and beyond.

The battle over pornography in Minneapolis began nearly a decade before the infamous Antipornography Civil Rights Ordinance was drafted, when Ferris and Edward Alexander (the Alexander brothers, who would soon own more than a dozen "adult" businesses in the area) bought the Rialto Theatre at 735 East Lake Street in Minneapolis.[5] The Rialto Theatre and Bookstore soon became a hub for commercial hetero- and homosex, drawing patrons, workers, and pimps from across the city, and transforming the surrounding neighborhood. It also became a popular site for cruising among gay men, and would be one of several bookstores consistently targeted in a police crackdown on public sexual cultures throughout the late 1970s and 1980s. Residents of the working-class and poor areas surrounding the Rialto increasingly reported harassment on the streets and, according to a 1980 study by the Minnesota Crime Prevention Center, "adult entertainment establishments" contributed to the existing cycle of decline in the Central and Powderhorn neighborhoods.[6] Although the complex relationship between socioeconomic class, property values, segregation, and public and commercial sex is impossible to pin down in causal terms, the Rialto was generally blamed by residents and local media for the increase in crime, and the decrease in property values, in the area surrounding East Lake Street.[7]

After the 1973 Supreme Court ruling in *Miller v. California,* obscenity laws became somewhat more difficult to apply than they had been in previous years.[8] Unable to simply ban adult businesses and their wares, local governments across the country began to use zoning laws in an attempt to confine pornography sales to nonresidential areas. In 1977, under pressure from Minneapolis residents and organizations such as Neighborhood Fight Back, the Minneapolis City Council enacted a zoning ordinance that outlawed the operation of adult bookstores and theaters within five hundred feet of churches, schools, or residential areas. According to Brest and Vandenberg, these restrictions would have forced nearly all of the Alexander brothers' eleven businesses to shut down or move.[9] When Ferris Alexander filed suit in federal court, a federal district judge, and later the court of appeals, found that the Minneapolis zoning ordinance was an unconstitutional violation of the First Amendment. In 1983, after the appeals court ruling ultimately struck down the zoning ordinance, Minneapolis witnessed an explosion of local grassroots and government resistance to the adult entertainment and pornography industries. Residents of the largely working-class Central and Powderhorn neighborhoods formed a Neighborhood Pornography Task Force that began organizing direct action against the Alexanders' businesses, as well as pressuring local policy makers to regulate pornography and public and commercial sex in the area. After the task force took city officials and local news media on a guided "tour" of the Rialto Theatre, the city attorney's office was persuaded to begin work on a revised zoning ordinance.

Meanwhile, the national feminist antipornography movement that had begun in the early 1970s was being institutionalized, as particular feminist theories of violence and gender oppression entered academic and policy conversations. Partly in response to the rise of "porno chic" and the mainstreaming of the hard-core feature film in the 1970s, feminists had begun to ask what effects pornography had on women and on society in general. Drawing upon certain elements of radical feminist and lesbian-feminist thought, activists formed antipornography organizations across the country in response to the sudden increase in sexually explicit imagery in mainstream, middle-class culture. The antipornography feminist movement that emerged was loosely organized around two basic claims: (1) that pornography was degrading to women, and (2) that it was complicit in—and possibly a direct cause of—male violence against women, both in its production (where labor practices were notoriously exploitative for women in the industry) and in its consumption (where, activists argued, pornographic images eroticized and reinforced patriarchal violences). In simplified terms, the antipornography feminist view on sexuality became one characterized by *danger:* that is, sexuality in a male-dominated society involves danger because sexual practices produce, reproduce, and perpetuate the problems of male domination of, and violence against, women.[10] Although pornography was the central support for this argument, some antiporn feminist groups also pointed to BDSM practices, commercial sex work, and queer female butch/femme formations as evidence that sexuality was a realm where women face very real physical and psychic dangers.[11]

Antipornography feminism was closely tied to radical feminist movements, including lesbian and lesbian-separatist feminisms. Liberal feminist organizations, regardless of their members' personal or political views on porn, were typically more concerned with protecting freedom of speech and the sanctity of the First Amendment, and thus wary of any approach to cultural production that might be used to support censorship as a tactic for political liberation.[12] Yet there were a number feminists and feminist organizations with decidedly radical politics who challenged antipornography feminism. Activists and organizations calling themselves "sex-positive" or "pro-sex" (including feminist scholars, feminist pornographers, anticensorship feminists, and "radical perverts" who wished to defend the sexual practices that antiporn feminisms sometimes characterized as oppressive or collusive) responded to antipornography feminism's emphasis on danger by instead highlighting the *pleasures* of the sexual realm. These feminists were interested in exploring—theoretically and practically—how sex could be liberating for women. They argued that the exchange of pleasure between consenting partners could be a site of political meaning and resistance, and they opposed political and social attempts to regulate sexual desires, practices, or expression.

Clearly, we can recognize that sex is both of these things—that sex and sexuality involve both danger *and* pleasure—and most feminist scholars and activists involved in these debates at the time acknowledged as much. Although both antipornography and anti-antipornography feminisms are typically understood as dogmatic and politically homogeneous, there were actually significant disagreements within them. Antipornography feminists, for instance, debated the wisdom of entrusting the regulation of sexuality to a patriarchal state. "Sex-positive" feminists disagreed about a number of issues as well, such as where children's sex and sexuality fit into a politics of radical perversion. And both groups were quite diverse in their membership: both included sex workers and prostitutes' rights advocates, radical lesbians and queer women, and large numbers of women of color and working-class women relative to mainstream liberal feminist movements (although, as Hollibough and Moraga note, the visible leadership of the national antipornography feminist movement was almost entirely white and middle-class).[13] In the early 1980s, however, amid a revolution in economic and moral conservatism that produced multiple policy-based "sex panics," significant pressure developed for feminists in the United States to choose sides—pleasure versus danger—in what became known as the feminist "Sex Wars."[14] In the late 1960s, mainstream women's liberation politics had emphasized both a defense of women's right to pleasure (for instance, in calls for education about the clitoris and female orgasm) *and* legal protection from sexual violence and loss of reproductive freedom. With the increasing prominence of lesbian feminism in the 1970s, many feminists similarly emphasized both women's right to sexual pleasure with women *and* their right to legal protection from the violences of racism, heterosexism, and homophobia. It was not until the early 1980s that the pleasure/danger binary came to so dominate feminist discussions of sexuality in the United States.[15]

In the fall of 1983, Catharine MacKinnon, a feminist scholar and law professor at the University of Minnesota, asked the university to host author and activist Andrea Dworkin for a semester-long visiting appointment. MacKinnon and Dworkin, both prominent in the national antipornography feminist movement, developed and co-taught an interdepartmental course on pornography that enrolled fifty-five students from across the university. The class studied feminist and political theory, and examined primary texts that included field trips to adult bookstores and "live sex shows" in the Twin Cities, as well as pornographic films, magazines, and novels—mainstream examples such as *Playboy* and *Deep Throat,* as well as exceptionally violent texts like *Raped Bitch Wife* and *Slave Auction.* According to Brest and Vandenberg, students were intensely affected by the experience: they were upset and disturbed by the materials, and some were inspired to reexamine their own sexual relationships, or to relive long-suppressed memories of sexual abuse. Ultimately, "the shared educational and emotional experience created a community with strong antipornography views and a sense of mission," and many of the students would later campaign in support of the Antipornography Civil Rights Ordinance.[16]

When University of Minnesota professor of philosophy and women's studies Naomi Scheman joined the Neighborhood Pornography Task Force for a brainstorming session, she suggested that the group invite MacKinnon and Dworkin to assist with their campaign. The task force subsequently asked MacKinnon and Dworkin to testify before the city's Zoning and Planning Committee in support of the new zoning ordinance designed to confine adult businesses to nonresidential areas. The two women attended the committee's hearings, but when they spoke, their testimony argued *against* zoning ordinances in general, challenging the notion that such policies were an effective or appropriate tactic for fighting pornography. To regulate porn through zoning, they argued, is to accept the notion that pornography must exist somewhere, and that the role of public policy is simply to keep it in its proper, nonresidential, place. As an alternative to the zoning approach, MacKinnon suggested that the city expand its existing ordinance against sex discrimination to establish the production and sale of pornography as a violation of women's civil rights. The goal of such an expansion would not be to regulate pornography, but to eliminate it altogether. Previous legislation that attempted to regulate sexually explicit material had typically done so based on the assumption that such material was sexually immoral; MacKinnon's approach claimed instead that pornography was a form of patriarchal violence that oppressed women and denied them their civil rights. Built around the civil rights paradigm of the Warren Court era, this redefinition frames antipornography legislation not as a reduction in civil liberties but as a move away from the moral politics of "obscenity" and toward the distributive justice and rights-based models of the 1960s.

Republican city council member Charlee Hoyt was so impressed by Dworkin and MacKinnon's testimony that she asked them to author the proposed ordinance, and the city attorney's office subsequently contracted the two women as consultants. They were charged with the task of expanding the city's existing antidiscrimination policy to (1) define pornography as a violation of women's civil rights and (2) allow anyone harmed by pornography to sue its producers and distributors for damages in civil court. Another unique aspect of the ordinance was its definition of pornography: rather than approaching pornography as obscenity, defined by its sexual explicitness, the ordinance built a definition of pornography around radical feminist theories of gender, sex, power, and violence. The final draft of the ordinance thus defined pornography as "the sexually explicit subordination of women, graphically depicted, whether in pictures or words." To be actionable, such materials would have to include one of nine themes or characteristics, such as "women are presented as sexual objects who experience sexual pleasure in being raped," or "women are presented as sexual objects tied up or cut up or mutilated or bruised or physically hurt."[17]

Public hearings on the ordinance were scheduled for December 1983. Dworkin, MacKinnon, and supporters of the ordinance recruited witnesses whose testimony could illustrate the claim that pornography harms women. Therapists, researchers, social workers, and numerous survivors of sexual abuse lined up one after the next to testify to the grave injuries caused by porn. Experts showed examples of violent and degrading pornographic texts, and survivors described their experiences in harrowing detail. Dworkin and MacKinnon had designed the hearings to build a legislative record that demonstrated "how pornography adversely affects women and is part of women's socially subordinate status," and few witnesses deviated from this narrative.[18] When speakers did raise questions about the constitutionality or enforceability of the proposed policy, they were met with boos and jeers from the audience of witnesses and supporters.[19] Absent from the hearings were local groups that had already publicly opposed the ordinance; no one represented the local pornography industry, civil libertarian organizations, or the Christian Right, all of which had previously spoken out against the proposed law.[20] According to their attorney, Randall Tigue, the Alexander brothers were unthreatened

Taking the "guerilla theater" to the streets: as the language of this flyer from 1984 suggests, the local group Organizing Against Pornography used a no-holds-barred approach to draw supporters to demonstrations against leisure establishments that sold sex, like the Chicago–Lake Theatre and Bookstore in Minneapolis. Courtesy of the Minnesota Historical Society.

by the ordinance: "I'd get a temporary injunction against its enforcement that would ripen into a permanent injunction, the ordinance would be declared unconstitutional, the city would give me a bundle of money, and it would be over with."[21] Matthew Stark, director of the Minnesota Civil Liberties Union, boycotted the hearings because, in his words, "MacKinnon and Dworkin stacked the audience day after day, not to listen, but to engage in guerilla theatre."[22]

The Antipornography Civil Rights Ordinance passed with a vote of 7–6 from the Minneapolis City Council. Minneapolis Mayor Donald Fraser vetoed the ordinance, which was subsequently rewritten and again approved by the city council, at which point Fraser vetoed it a second time in 1984. Meanwhile, the city of Indianapolis—where the antipornography movement was led not by radical feminists and grassroots neighborhood organizations but by a conservative mayor and city council—hired MacKinnon and Dworkin to draft an antipornography ordinance modeled on Minneapolis's. After the Indianapolis mayor signed that city's ordinance into law, the policy was struck down as unconstitutional, a decision affirmed by the U.S. Supreme Court in 1986.

The Minneapolis ordinance garnered national attention, in mainstream news media as well as in academic, activist, and policy conversations, and antipornography ordinances became a central conflict in the feminist sexuality debates.[23] "Sex-positive" and anti-antipornography feminists worked "to counter anti-porn accounts of 'pornography' as a unified (patriarchal) discourse with a singular (misogynistic) impact," arguing instead that the category "pornography" encompasses a wide range of sexually explicit materials whose meanings are multiple, layered, and highly contextual.[24] In light of the Minneapolis and Indianapolis ordinances, "sex-positive" feminists connected antipornography activism to a long history of repressive, women-led "purity" campaigns in the United States, and critiqued both the ordinances' definition of pornography and the impossibility of applying and enforcing such policies.[25] The definition of pornography on which the ordinances were built, they argued, was not only vague—it included such undefined phrases as "postures of sexual submission" and "whores by nature"—but also not significantly different from the definitions produced by traditional obscenity laws; that is, the wording and examples allowed space for the ordinances to be applied not only to materials that were sexually explicit *and* violent *and* sexist, but also to *any* sexually explicit material. Of the nine characteristics and themes that made sexually explicit materials actionable under the proposed ordinances, only four included the intersection of violence, sexism, and sexual explicitness. Others, such as "being penetrated by objects" and being "tied up," were not specifically violent or sexist, and could in fact be part of sexually explicit representations that feminists find politically useful. Sexually explicit speech, feminist critics of the ordinances argued, serves positive social functions for women, and regulation of that speech is more likely to impede than to advance feminist political goals.[26]

Sex, Race, Private Space: Feminism and Sexuality in Minneapolis

The conversations in which the Minneapolis ordinance has been invoked—in mainstream news media, in feminist debates about sexuality, and in policy studies focused on its constitutionality—have emphasized certain elements of the Minneapolis case and obscured others. Specifically, as the Minneapolis case has been wedged into the discursive framework of the feminist sex wars, or into debates about pornography and constitutional law, the focus has almost always been on the ordinance itself. Even in detailed histories of the ordinance, its creation, and its aftermath in Minneapolis and across the United States, little attention has been paid to the specific social, cultural, and political context of Minneapolis as the original site of such policy making. We might ask, however, what elements of the Minneapolis case might not fit neatly into the discourses of either constitutional legal studies or the pleasure/danger binary that dominates feminist debates about sexuality. And, on conversational ground as well trod as that of the "sex wars," what new lessons can possibly be learned? By focusing on the particulars of the Minneapolis case and the lesbian/feminist cultures that produced it, this chapter works to challenge or complicate some of the stories that are commonly told about antipornography feminism and the feminist "sex wars": the notion that antiporn feminisms are simply "sex-negative"; the claim that antiporn feminist organizations in the 1980s collaborated with the newly powerful Christian Right; and the overall erasure of the labor and laboring bodies that make pornography and sex industries possible.

We might begin by considering the particular spaces in which the Minneapolis feminist antipornography campaign began and grew, beyond the classroom, the courtroom, and city hall. Multiple factors related to space, race, and class shaped the radical and lesbian-feminist circles out of which the feminist antiporn movement was built. In the Twin Cities, "women's spaces" such as A Women's Coffee House, the Lesbian Resource Center, and the Amazon Bookstore were central to the creation of lesbian and feminist activist cultures, as sites of protest against the gendered exclusions of public space, and as meeting grounds for lesbian and feminist political work, including the antipornography movement.[27] Among "sex-positive" feminists and gay male observers, radical and lesbian feminisms in the 1980s were often depicted as overly earnest, dowdy, and "sex-negative"—not an unreasonable characterization if based on some of the simplistic discourses that were part of the antiporn movement's political strategy. If we pay attention, however, to the day-to-day operations of lesbian/feminist spaces in the Twin Cities, and the ways in which women experienced them, we get a picture far more complex than can be described by discourses of "sex-negativity." Anne Enke's 2003 study of A Woman's Coffee House, for instance, describes the vexed politics of female nudity and sexuality at the Coffee House's all-women dances. Debates about shirtless dancing arose in the mid-1970s, and according to Enke, "some women at the Coffee House embraced the sensuality of seeing women's bodies, and the rare feeling of hot air, sweat, and occasional touches on their own bare skin in a semi-public space" (653). Others, however, felt that bare breasts must be de-eroticized in order to distance feminist nudity from the heteropatriarchal objectification of women's bodies, or that shirtless dancing was inappropriate altogether in the church basement where the Coffee House operated. Similarly, although women certainly met lovers and sexual partners at the Coffee House, the politics of "cruising" was, like shirtless dancing, a subject of debate among feminists who frequented women's spaces. Enke juxtaposes one interviewee's disavowal of cruising practices ("[the Coffee House] was not a cruising space. Sexuality was absent there.") with another's fond memories of them ("if it was *anything*, it was a *cruising space*!" . . . "*sexuality* was the *whole* reason for it" [654, 655]). Clearly, far from being monolithically or simply sex-negative, these were spaces where sex and power were thought through and wrestled with, where feminist sexualities were explored, debated, constructed, and deconstructed in theory and in practice. Such debates are a window into the ways in which the pleasure/danger framework of the sex wars is inadequate for understanding feminism and sexuality in the 1970s–1980s United States, and in the Twin Cities in particular. Foregrounding these contestations and contradictions allows us to get at a more productive understanding of how these 1970s–1980s radical and lesbian feminisms approached sexuality than the pleasure/danger binary allows. That is, radical and lesbian-feminist cultures in the Twin Cities worked to theorize the political meanings of sexual desires and practices in the context of both the supposed safety of "women's space" and the supposed danger of a broader patriarchal and heteronormative culture. And participants enjoyed themselves doing it.

This is not to say that women's spaces in the Twin Cities were utopian, or that they existed outside of sociopolitical hierarchies in the United

States. In fact, Enke details the ways in which these intentionally democratic and inclusive women's spaces also enacted class- and race-based exclusions that produced and reproduced white, middle-class privilege within radical and lesbian/feminist communities in the Twin Cities. For instance, debates about what sexual behavior was appropriate at A Woman's Coffee House were shaped by the fact that the Coffee House was hosted by Minneapolis's progressive, predominately white, middle-class Plymouth Congregational Church. In order to have and retain access to the church's basement social hall, Enke describes how the Coffee House established itself as "respectable" according to dominant white, middle-class progressive Christian standards. The word *lesbian*, for instance, was never used in promotional materials, or in communication with church leadership, in spite of the fact that a majority of women who attended Coffee House dances, workshops, and political events were lesbian-identified (643). And the space of the church conferred a kind of (white) racialized, (middle-)classed legitimacy upon the women who attended the Coffee House, many of whom were more accustomed to the smaller, run-down spaces in which lesbian and feminist collectives were typically housed. A Coffee House founder described the Lesbian Resource Center, for instance, as "a very depressing place, couches with springs coming out, it just had a terrible feeling to it. It was dark. You really felt like a pervert going there" (645). In contrast, the church allowed the Coffee House—a "nice," "bright," "first-rate" space for female homosocial and homoerotic social and political gatherings—to distance itself from sexual deviance, commercial sex, public sexual cultures, and the spaces associated with them (ibid.). The church basement thus reinforced the long-standing connection between respectability and "nice" places, and between whiteness and property, while simultaneously confirming the long-standing association of places that *aren't* "nice" with deviance, vice, homosexuality, and interracial and commercial sex (649). If the respectability of the Coffee House indicated a physical and discursive distance from the places typically associated with stigmatized sexualities, then its white, middle-class, semiprivate space signaled a parallel distance from nonwhite, working-class, and/or public spaces like the Rialto Theatre. In other words, the (white-racialized, middle-class, private, respectable) lesbian/feminist sexual cultures of the Coffee House were defined *against* the (nonwhite-racialized, working-class, public, deviant) cultures of pornography and public sex in the Twin Cities. The Coffee House, and the radical and lesbian-feminist cultures it enabled, thus depended for their existence on modes of privilege that reinforced racialized systems of sexual respectability. In spite of the Coffee House's racially diverse membership and consciously antiracist politics and activism, these spatial hierarchies shored up the power structures that maintained white privilege within feminist movements, and circumscribed the visibility and influence of women of color within radical and lesbian feminisms (658).

Clearly, the radical and lesbian-feminist cultures out of which the Minneapolis antipornography movement emerged defined and understood sexuality in complex ways that exceeded the stereotype of such cultures as simply "sex-negative." How can we account, then, for the apparent contradiction between those complex approaches to sex and power and the sometimes didactic "danger" narratives of the feminist antipornography movement? Why, for instance, is there no space for A Former Dancer within this iteration of queer feminism? While antipornography feminism is often imagined as a white, middle-class women's movement, antipornography organizing in Minneapolis was in fact remarkably diverse in terms of both race and class. Antipornography feminist groups collaborated with working-class and largely nonwhite neighborhood organizations, and working-class white women and women of color were well represented both in radical and lesbian feminisms and in the antipornography movement.[28] Politically, radical and lesbian feminisms worked hard to consciously challenge racial, sexual, and class hierarchies. Lesbian and queer feminisms would thus have had common interests with multiple and diverse groups and movements invested in making Minneapolis safe for nonnormative sexualities. Such common interests, however, may have been obscured by lesbian/feminist communities' investments in systems of cultural capital and privilege that demand and reinforce claims to (white, middle-class) sexual respectability. Enke's analysis of whiteness and spatial privilege helps us to foreground questions of race and class that have too often been elided or obscured by the sex wars'—and by hegemonic feminism's —singular focus on gender and sexuality.

Questions of Coalition: Gay and Lesbian Activism in the 1980s Twin Cities

In addition to the charge of "sex negativity," antipornography feminism has often been accused of collaborating with the burgeoning moral and economic conservatisms that gained power in the United States during the

1970s and 1980s. Along with attempts to regulate and/or censor obscenity, right-wing organizations and policy makers became involved throughout the 1980s and 1990s in sex panics regarding issues such as child sexuality, arts funding, reproductive control, sex education, and legal protections for gay men and lesbians. And certainly feminist campaigns against pornography had some goals in common with the right-wing war against smut. MacKinnon and Dworkin praised some aspects of Ronald Reagan's controversial 1986 Meese Commission Report on Pornography, which used dubious science to establish a supposed causal connection between pornography and violence, and called for the strict regulation of all sorts of sexually explicit materials (and, according to some reports, very nearly included dildos and vibrators in its long list of obscene items).[29] "Today could be a turning point in women's rights," MacKinnon told a press conference after the Meese Commission's Final Report was released. "Women actually succeeded in convincing a national governmental body of a truth that women have long known: pornography harms women and children."[30] Moreover, in Indianapolis, the MacKinnon and Dworkin–authored antipornography ordinance was promoted by a conservative Republican mayor and sponsored by a city council member who had been an activist in Phyllis Schlafly's Stop ERA movement.[31] Mostly, however, antipornography feminist collusion with the moral Right was rare, strategic, and largely tacit. As Dworkin put it, "I think it's been terrifically distorted. There hasn't been any institutional support from the right wing, no money, no political support and no intervention in litigation. On the other hand, when Jerry Falwell starts saying there's real harm in pornography, then that is valuable to me."[32] In Minneapolis, where the antipornography movement was built around radical and lesbian-feminist principles, there was substantial conflict, not cooperation, between antiporn organizations and the Christian Right. Some "right-wing, pro-censorship people" had attempted to join the local antipornography feminist groups forming in the late 1970s, but were rejected by the groups' members.[33] Later, right-wing Christian organizations in Minneapolis would publicly denounce the antipornography ordinance because of its association with radical and lesbian-feminist politics. The story of the alleged alliance between radical feminists and the Right has become an indispensable part of dominant narratives about antiporn feminism, and while its rendering is often simplistic, overstated, and/or antifeminist, it's not entirely untrue. A larger problem, however, with this persistent focus on feminists being "in bed" with the New Right is that it displaces other productive questions about

Bundled-up antipornography demonstrators gather outside the Rialto Theatre at 735 East Lake Street in Minneapolis at night in the winter of 1983–84. Photograph by Jane Larson; courtesy of the Minnesota Historical Society.

coalitional politics that the feminist antipornography movement in Minneapolis might raise. For instance, how did antipornography activism shape relations between lesbian/feminist and gay male activist organizations? And how did the feminist antipornography movement interact with the workers laboring in the porn and sex industries the movement was fighting?

For one thing, the feminist antipornography movement exacerbated tensions between lesbian and gay male activists in the Twin Cities. As radical and lesbian feminisms were flourishing in the Twin Cities, Minneapolis was witnessing a violent crackdown on public sexual cultures that disproportionately affected poor people, trans people, people of color, and commercial sex workers. In the years between 1979 and 1986, Minneapolis saw a wave of police repression and arrests for crimes of indecent exposure and "lewd and lascivious behavior." The fifteen adult bookstores in Minneapolis—the same bookstores that antipornography feminist organizations were working to shut down—were a central site for these arrests.

Thus, while some gay men were supportive of or active in the feminist antipornography movement, antiporn feminism was largely viewed by gay male activists in the Twin Cities as complicit in the state regulation of public sex and gay male sexualities. Feminist demonstrations and calls for the closing of the Rialto and other pornography retailers—most of which were also home to gay male, interracial, and other queer sexual cultures—overlapped with vice squad raids and arrests in those same establishments. Hence, for many gay men, feminist antipornography activism seemed to dovetail neatly with the increased state regulation of queer, public, and commercial sex in Minneapolis.

Conflicts between lesbian feminists and gay male activists in the Twin Cities arose in the mid-1970s, and came to public light when residents organized to combat Anita Bryant's antihomosexual "Save Our Children"

By the mid-1980s, the neighborhood surrounding the Rialto Theatre was experiencing plummeting property values, swelling crime rates, and mounting poverty. Social scientists, neighborhood groups, and antipornography feminist activists largely attributed such developments to the presence of the porn theater and bookstore. This view of the Rialto demonstration in 1983–84 shows the number of demonstrators willing to brave the Minnesota cold to "stop porn." Photograph by Jane Larson; courtesy of the Minnesota Historical Society.

This mangled life-size doll of a woman covered in blood and dumped at a side entrance of the Rialto Theatre reveals the intensity of the demonstrators' conviction that pornography is violence against women. Photograph by Jane Larson; courtesy of the Minnesota Historical Society.

Antipornography demonstrators march in line under the Rialto Theatre's marquee. Photograph by Jane Larson; courtesy of the Minnesota Historical Society.

campaign. Many lesbian feminists critiqued the misogyny and sexism that underlay the anti-Anita activism, suggesting that "the gay male vitriol at her was not examined very carefully in terms of gender."[34] Furthermore, in 1978, the Target City Coalition, which had initially formed to prepare Minneapolis for Bryant's campaign, decided to focus its gay rights activism exclusively on "enemies of the *gay male* community." Tensions between lesbian and gay male activists in the Twin Cities intensified as adult bookstores became targets for both police vice squads and antipornography feminist demonstrations. In 1980, the *Gay and Lesbian Community Voice (GLC Voice)* reported that police representatives had assured local antipornography feminists that they were working to get enough arrests to shut down the shops. There was thus a sense among many gay men that antipornography feminist activists (and radical and lesbian feminists in general) supported or were partly responsible for the escalation in police harassment at the bookstores. On the contrary, the local Women Against Pornography (WAP) organization had publicly denounced the raids, explaining that the police crackdown was not useful for their cause because its target was sexual minorities, not pornography.[35] Antipornography feminism in Minneapolis, at least in 1980, was rooted more in a radical politics of dissident sexuality than in the kind of prudery with which it would come to be associated. For the Minneapolis chapter of WAP, the goal was to eradicate not only violent and misogynist pornography, but also the "sexually restricting atmosphere that produces it." According to one WAP representative, "religious puritanism and antisexuality go hand in hand with violent pornography." In her analysis of the bookstore conflicts, Susan Carleton, a University of Minnesota graduate student writing for the *Voice,* thus concluded that "a close examination of WAP's priorities and those of the police reveals that they are really not the same at all."[36]

Nevertheless, simultaneous attacks from both antipornography feminists and the state led many gay male defenders of the bookstores to grow increasingly caustic about lesbian feminism and lesbians in general. By 1982, the *Voice* was publishing articles that accused antiporn groups of being "puppets" of local government, and using sensational headlines such as "Gay versus Lesbian."[37] In the same year, tensions between gay male and lesbian activists came to a head with the division of the annual Pride festivities. In what became known as the Big Split, "the gender equity issue, which had been smoldering since 1974, finally erupted."[38] In 1981, the Gay Pride Committee had renamed the event Gay *and Lesbian*

Pride Week. In 1982, however, the all-male Pride Committee voted narrowly to remove the word *lesbian* from the event title and all related publicity and paraphernalia. According to the committee, lesbians had failed to participate in planning Pride events. Lesbians countered that they *had* been helping out, but in jobs that were invisible and unrecognized, doing background and legwork rather than occupying visible leadership positions.[39] In response to the committee's decision, a group of women organized a separate lesbian Pride event at Powderhorn Park and called for a boycott of the Gay Pride celebration. Some Gay Pride organizers were content to see the women go: "As far as I'm concerned, if lesbians want to have a lesbian pride week, let them have their own . . . let them organize themselves."[40] But other committee members expressed concern about dividing ranks in the face of an increasingly powerful conservative movement: "We need the unity or the right-wingers are going to strike down everything we do."[41] In these calls for a united front, however, there was often a nostalgic longing for notions of gayness uncomplicated by feminism, and an underlying assumption that such an alliance would again organize under the umbrella identity "gay." "Back in the early 70s," one Gay Pride organizer lamented, "we were all gay." Another activist likened the phrase "gay and lesbian" to saying "animals and horses"—lesbian was simply a subgroup of gay.

In a 2004 retrospective, activist Koreen Phelps looked back at the Big Split of 1982, remarking, "It didn't happen everywhere. For some reason, it happened very strongly here."[42] Why, then, *was* Minneapolis a site of this rift? The dramatic divisions of 1982 were certainly due in part to unexamined sexism, misogyny, and antifeminism among gay male activists, and to many gay men's distrust of the lesbian-feminist politics that informed the antipornography movement. But tensions were also deepened by lesbian and lesbian-feminist claims to sexual "respectability" in the context of local racial, class, and sexual politics. According to one organizer of the 1982 lesbian Pride boycott, "All gay issues are not lesbian issues. I'm sick of defending faggots, child sex, bathhouse arrests and pornography." Here again, "respectable" (white-racialized, middle-class, private) lesbian/feminist sexualities in the Twin Cities are explicitly defined in opposition to the "deviant" (nonwhite-racialized, working-class, public) cultures of public sex. This repeated disavowal of public and marginalized sexual cultures reinforces the link between lesbian/feminist activism in the Twin Cities and racial and class privileges that depended on and reproduced racialized systems of private property and sexual respectability.

The Big Split was well publicized. *Equal Time,* a local gay newspaper, devoted an entire issue to the problems, and the story dominated gay and mainstream press coverage of the 1982 Pride events. Less widely recognized were the ways in which there was political resistance to the split, and conscious attempts among some gay men and lesbians to work together before, during, and after '82 Pride. Some gay men, for instance, were actively critiquing gay male sexism and working to articulate shared politics with the women's movement. In 1980, when Twin Cities residents traveled to Chicago to march in support of the Equal Rights Amendment, the story made the front page of the *Voice.* The story's gay male author described how the experience of marching in Chicago had instilled in him a "greater sense of pride and confidence in the gay rights movement and our natural ally—the women's movement."[43] While tensions remained after the Big Split—particularly surrounding antipornography activism—such coalitional politics laid the groundwork for a newly reunited Gay and Lesbian Pride Week in 1983, and for cooperative work between lesbians and gay men in response to the growing HIV/AIDS crisis. Ten years later, when the Twin Cities Lesbian Avengers organized the first Pride Week Dyke March, future city council member Gary Schiff would stand in support, holding a sign that read, "Cocksuckers for Muffdivers."[44]

The story of the Big Split, then, is one of both failure and success in terms of political coalition work between gay male and lesbian activists, and is built in part upon the same racialized, classed politics of sexual respectability and deviance that so significantly shaped Minneapolis antipornography feminism. As the decade unfolded, gay male activists would find themselves facing their own big split: having both to advocate for safe, public sexual expression in response to increased police harassment and to embody their own politics of sexual respectability in response to growing panics about HIV/AIDS and child sexuality in Minnesota.[45] Throughout the 1980s, lesbian and gay rights discourses in the Twin Cities would increasingly find common ground in their insistence on sexual "respectability" and in their parallel framings of homosex as a domestic, private, adult matter. Critical to this framing was the articulation of a distance between respectable gay and lesbian sexuality and the "faggots, child sex, bathhouse arrests, and pornography" associated with less respectable, public, and/or commercial sexualities. Indeed, when Gay and Lesbian Pride reunited in 1983, some gay men and lesbians took issue with the year's theme—"taking it to the streets"—because it "emphasized the hustling aspect of our culture."[46]

The 1970s and 1980s were a period in which gay and lesbian movements struggled to articulate a politics that was antiracist and anti-imperialist, but that also defined the uniqueness of gay and lesbian experiences and identities as a basis for civil rights activism. Following Enke's analysis of lesbian/feminist investments in white spatial privilege, we can see here the ways in which—no matter how carefully gay and lesbian activist movements worked to articulate and enact antiracist politics—gay and lesbian identity and rights-based social movements depended on and reinforced the spatial and economic privileges of whiteness. Thus the failure to effectively articulate a queer politics that can account for racial formations as well as gender and sexuality is not a simple matter of absence or exclusion, but of deeply embedded discourses and practices that rely on systems of white and middle-class privilege to define gay and lesbian identity and community. As demands that public spaces be made safe for diverse genders and sexualities gave way to calls for the right to privacy, they took with them a site of possibility for a queer politics attentive to the links among race, class, gender, and sexuality. The persistent focus on how some goals of antipornography feminism may have overlapped with the Christian and moral Right draws attention away from this overall domestication and rightward shift of gay and lesbian political activism in the Twin Cities, as well as the ways in which the racialized politics of respectability that emerged intersected with conservative economic and moral agendas for "cleaning up" city parks and low-income neighborhoods. A careful analysis of radical, lesbian, and antipornography feminisms' claims to sexual respectability in the 1980s Twin Cities reveals processes and logics through which—despite explicitly antiracist politics and intentions—identity-based gay, lesbian, feminist, and/or queer activism may in fact depend on and reinforce existing racial and class hierarchies.

The Work in Sex Work: The Committee to Close Solid Gold

As the domestication of queer sex required a disavowal of public and marginalized sexual cultures and practices, commercial sex workers became further alienated from the gay and lesbian rights movements. While local gay activism in the 1970s and early 1980s sometimes critiqued the stigmatization and material conditions of male homo-sex work as part of a battle against police harassment and violence, gay politics had no more space for A Former Dancer or other female hetero-sex workers than local feminist organizations did. Sex workers, and the labor of commercial sex, are clearly central to pornography and other sex industries, but are also largely absent both from the debates of the feminist sex wars and from historical memory of those debates. Nationally, "sex-positive" feminisms often articulated complex understandings of sex workers' agency, but, in their attempts to counter antipornography feminist representations of sex workers as unwitting victims of patriarchy and false consciousness, they tended to gloss over the actual conditions of labor in sex industries. Because antipornography feminisms saw sex work as one of countless examples of heteromasculine exploitation of women and women's bodies, antipornography feminist rhetoric typically presented multiple and diverse types of sex work as universally exploitative, and more or less interchangeable. In her letter to the editor, A Former Dancer intervenes in both sides of the sex wars, simultaneously naming the material conditions of sex work and writing back against this logic of commensurability: "If you really cared about me," she admonishes, "or really wanted to fight porn, you'd go into some of those windowless dens on Lake Street and shed some light." On one hand, by locating the real problems of porn in those "windowless dens on Lake Street," A Former Dancer sets up male, trans, and nonhetero sex work—and the spaces in which they take place—as dangerous and suspect relative to commercial topless dancing. But she also calls attention to the differences between different types of sex work, and makes a claim for sex work as a feminist labor issue. In response to all the attention that antipornography feminists and local media paid to Solid Gold, she demands, "Why don't you investigate the conditions in our society that make this sort of thing acceptable? Why don't you investigate the difficulty that single, high-school educated women have in making enough money to support themselves?"[47]

Even before its opening night in 1989, the Solid Gold nightclub had been targeted for protests by Organizing Against Pornography (OAP). As the Pornography Resource Center, OAP had been critical to the feminist campaign for Minneapolis's Antipornography Civil Rights Ordinance. After the ordinance was overturned, the group continued its educational and direct-action work, presenting slide shows at community meetings and in college classrooms, and campaigning to shut down local "adult" businesses. Their direct-action campaigns mainly focused on establishments like the Rialto and the Chicago–Lake bookstores that sold pornographic materials and offered "live sex shows." On the surface, Solid Gold seemed like just another topless dancing club in downtown Minneapolis. As one of several similar establishments owned by the Florida-based Dollhouse chain, however, Solid Gold's marketing strategy worked to set it apart from the smaller, older clubs already in the city, and to establish it as an "*upscale* gentlemen's club." Local media took note. Feature articles about the club appeared in the *St. Paul Pioneer Press Dispatch, Skyway News, City Pages,* and the *Twin Cities Reader.*[48] The Minneapolis *Star-Tribune* ran a cover story on Solid Gold in its *Variety* lifestyles section, and received at least thirty-five angry letters in response.[49] This extensive mainstream press coverage focused heavily on Solid Gold's niche marketing strategy surrounding "classiness," describing in great detail the club's lavish decor and expensive drink menu. With sensational pun-laden headlines like "Turning Flesh to Gold," "Softcore Is Golden," and "All That's Solid Gold Isn't Glitter," the articles emphasized how the "upscale" club was hoping to attract businessmen visiting the Cities for events at the newly built Convention Center. According to Solid Gold's general manager, Minneapolis was an attractive place in which to begin the chain's northern expansion because it was "on the brink of being a world-class convention city."[50] The club's manager and multiple newspaper articles cited both the Convention Center and the new Minnesota Timberwolves NBA franchise as evidence of the tourist economies that were expected to emerge in the city. In this manner, Solid Gold from its inception was tied up with a complex network of capitalist, grassroots, and feminist attempts to "clean up" the city of Minneapolis.

OAP targeted Solid Gold for a number of reasons, not least of all because it was such a popular focus of mainstream media attention.[51] But OAP's Close the Solid Gold Committee (CSGC) also expressed concern over the club's promotion and sexualization of violence against and between women. A letter from the CSGC to Minneapolis City Council members described the club's "sensual athletics" (boxing and wrestling) as "men paying to batter women or to watch women batter each other."[52] Mainstream press coverage, however, emphasized how much the women enjoyed the boxing and wrestling matches, which are described as "slightly less convincing than pro wrestling."[53] These are common ways of representing female sex workers in the United States: antiporn feminisms often construct sex workers as unwitting victims of, and/or colluders with, heteropatriarchal violence, and mainstream media prefer to see them as free-floating agents who—and this is emphasized again and again in newspaper articles about Solid Gold—enjoy their work. In this manner, while the CSGC invoked sex workers in its activist rhetoric, it did so in a way that used the *figure* of the sex worker to support its political agenda, without allowing the perspectives or concerns of *actual* sex workers to shape that agenda.

Antipornography feminist activists also targeted Solid Gold because they felt a need to challenge the club's claim to be "upscale." Unlike existing working-class topless dancing clubs and peep shows in the Twin Cities, Solid Gold worked to market itself as safe for women patrons. The club's cover charge was always waived for women accompanied by paying men, regular Ladies' Nights featured all-male dancers and performers, and heterosexual couples were often spotted in the audience for boxing and wrestling matches. The *City Pages* exposé with which this chapter began speculates that "maybe the real move that's afoot is not to eradicate pornography, but to gentrify it. Give it a little *class*."[54] Feminist criticism of Solid Gold—including the *City Pages* article and CSGC activism—thus attempted to discredit the club by proving just how *not* classy it was. The *City Pages* article did so with "icky-poo disdain," describing patrons' sweaty sleaziness in graphic, classist detail. For the CSGC, undermining the club's claim on "classy" meant exposing how it was no different from the city's existing (smaller, shabbier) topless clubs, or from other kinds of sex work like "pornography, prostitution, and peep shows."[55] In its letter to city council members, the CSGC uses the figure of the victimized dancer to create a logic of equivalency among all kinds of commercial sex work, from foxy boxing to street prostitution. Both popular media and antipornography feminism are working here to pull back Solid Gold's middle-class or "upscale" veneer and expose the seedy sex club underneath. Meanwhile, the club's attempts to class up the sex industry resulted in questionable hiring practices with regard to class and race. Dancers and waitresses at Solid Gold were prized for their "wholesome," middle-class appearance and demeanor, and newspaper articles about the club emphasized the "all-American" (white) blondeness of the women working there. When it came time for the general manager to pose for a photograph with some of the dancers, he was particular about being pictured with "the right girls," rather than "the dogs."[56] According to some local dancers employed by Solid Gold, the work was in fact safer and more comfortable than most topless and nude performance jobs in the area. Those better conditions, however, were only available to dancers who could embody the club's racialized standards of feminine "classiness." "It's dangerous, because they're trying to sell it as something classy," said one member of the CSGC.[57] With slogans like "Sexual Exploitation of women is never classy," the Close the Solid Gold Committee—like the club itself—opted to defend the boundaries of middle-class respectability rather than interrogate "classy" as a racialized category that regulates both femininity and female sexuality.[58]

Both local media and antipornography feminists took a level of interest in Solid Gold's female workers that was unprecedented in their previous approaches to local pornography and sex industries. Not surprisingly, newspaper articles often discussed the workers as part of their sensational descriptions of the club's services, and antipornography feminist materials used the figure of the victimized sex worker in predictable ways. But the ways in which the workers were represented by both the media and CSGC also reflect anxieties about race and labor in Minneapolis in the 1980s. Both media descriptions of the club and CSGC materials took great care to explain the different job categories for Solid Gold's dancers. First, there was the "A-Team" of "syndicated entertainers" who were paid individually negotiated salaries, and most of whom traveled around the country performing at different Dollhouse-owned clubs. Then there were the local dancers: "independent contractors" paid five to ten dollars per song, plus tips.[59] Newspaper coverage consistently depicted the A-Team performers as coddled, overpaid jet-setters, describing how much fun and how little work their jobs seemed to be. The local dancers, on the other hand, were represented as victims of this imported labor, economically exploited and denied the chance to work the club's cushier, more lucrative jobs. One *St. Paul Pioneer Press Dispatch* article, for instance, describes a friendly, hardworking twenty-eight-year-old mother of three, with "a figure any mother would envy," who was excluded from the A-Team.[60] This image—of hardworking locals besieged and displaced by outsiders who are getting something for nothing—is reproduced clearly in CSGC descriptions of the club's labor practices, and it mirrors racialized and sensationalized conversations about welfare and work that dominated Twin Cities news media and public policy throughout the 1980s and 1990s. A kind of public hysteria emerged around the notion that masses of poor black migrants from Chicago and Detroit were moving to Minneapolis to take advantage of its generous public assistance programs. These new residents, it was feared, would settle in the Central and Phillips neighborhoods, bringing down property values and overloading public resources.[61]

These ways of depicting Solid Gold's labor practices—including the contradiction between idealizing the imported dancers' wholesome blonde appeal, on the one hand, and suggesting that they are taking jobs from hardworking locals, on the other—point to the bizarre and complex web of anxieties about race, sex, and urban space that plagued Minneapolis in the 1980s and 1990s.

The Close the Solid Gold Committee included "survivors of the sex industry," but those actually working in sex industries seem to have been excluded from local debates about feminism, pornography, and the state in the 1980s. Evidence of their investment in those debates is limited to archival traces such as A Former Dancer's letter to the editor, or occasional quotations in newspaper articles about Solid Gold. In New York and San Francisco, sex workers and prostitutes' rights organizations like COYOTE (Call Off Your Old Tired Ethics) cooperated with anti-antipornography feminists and worked to carve out a place for the needs and concerns of sex workers in "sex-positive" feminist organizing. This consideration is evident in national anti-antiporn feminists' complex assessment of the give-and-take between agency and victimization in sex work. In their critique of feminist antipornography legislation, for instance, Feminist Anticensorship Task Force (FACT) activists Lisa Duggan, Nan Hunter, and Carole Vance explain that "women do not become pornography models because society is egalitarian and they exercise a 'free choice,' but neither do they 'choose' this work because they have lost all power for deliberate, volitional behavior."[62] In the Twin Cities, however, radical and lesbian feminisms were deeply invested in racialized notions of sexual respectability that could only make sense of sex workers as exploited victims. Moreover, the terms of the debate about pornography in Minneapolis were tightly organized around questions of urban space and civil libertarian conceptions of free speech. The only local public feminist opposition to the antipornography ordinance thus came from civil libertarian activist

Feminist graffiti on the pedestrian enclosure of the upper deck of the Washington Avenue bridge on the University of Minnesota campus. This undated photograph, probably taken in 1983 or 1984, shows lesbian-feminist activism's opposition to pornography and nuclear weaponry. Incidentally, much as many socioeconomically depressed neighborhoods were "cleaned up" in the 1990s, so too was this footbridge in 1997, when then–university president Mark Yudof had it renovated and repainted in the school colors of maroon and gold as part of a campus beautification campaign. Courtesy of the Minnesota Historical Society.

organizations, whose politics seemed even less concerned with sex work and labor than antipornography feminisms'.

Throughout the 1980s and 1990s, attacks on public sexual cultures, adult bookstores, and city parks would contribute to urban gentrification and the loss of affordable property and housing in the Twin Cities. Religious and economic conservative ideologies came together to support a moral "cleanup" that bolstered capitalist expansion and the privatization of public resources, opening up spaces for urban "redevelopment" in Minneapolis and St. Paul.[63] Ironically, as property in the Cities became less affordable because of the "cleanup" enabled in part by antipornography feminist activism, lesbian and feminist businesses and organizations became less and less able to access private space.

Conclusion

I began this chapter with a quotation from Cathy Cohen's 1997 essay calling for a vision of queer politics that encompasses all sorts of positions outside of dominant sexual norms—including "punks, bulldaggers, and welfare queens"—as the basis for transformative coalition work. Rather than reinforcing a simple hetero/not-hetero binary, Cohen suggests that the category *queer* has unrealized radical potential for creating political coalitions across established racial and sexual identity categories. The exclusion of questions of race, space, and labor from local debates about feminism, pornography, and sexuality may have made such a broadly conceived queer politics difficult to imagine for Twin Cities radical and lesbian feminisms in the 1970s and 1980s. Yet an examination of the complexity of radical and lesbian feminisms in the Twin Cities, and antipornography feminism in Minneapolis, also challenges popular characterizations of those movements. Exceeding the pleasure/danger binary of the "sex wars" narrative, the sexual politics of antipornography feminists and feminisms in Minneapolis included both stereotypical middle-class prudery *and* radical sexual politics that aligned the fight against misogynist pornography with struggles against multiple forms of gender and sexual regulation.

When Ferris Alexander died in 2003, *City Pages* ran a two-page feature about his legacy as a First Amendment crusader, titled "The Porn Warrior at Rest." When Andrea Dworkin died two years later, the paper's coverage of her passing was limited to a two-sentence post on its online arts blog. When popular historical memory about the Minneapolis porn debates is so partial, so dismissive, and so clearly colored by the sense that antipornography feminism simply "lost" the sex wars, it seems especially important to seek out new points of entry into those debates, and to think carefully about what lessons we want to take from them. For one thing, the history of antipornography feminism in Minneapolis helps us to identify how the conservative and neoliberal movements that emerged in the 1970s and 1980s impacted queer and feminist identities and political activism. Furthermore, an examination of that history—its successes and its failures—yields important lessons about queer political coalition building; that is, an analysis of the feminist sex wars and the Minneapolis antipornography movement can help us to think through the ways in which race, class, labor, and sexuality operate in relation to one another, and to space and place, to shape the possibilities and pitfalls of transformative queer political coalition. Perhaps such work can be one small step in shifting conceptions of "queer" to include *all* those who, in Cathy Cohen's words, "stand on the outside of the dominant constructed norm of state-sanctioned white middle- and upper-class heterosexuality," and to build creative coalitions that can make race, space, and labor central to a radical politics of sex.[64]

Notes

1 Cathy Cohen, "Punks, Bulldaggers, and Welfare Queens: The Radical Potential of Queer Politics?" *GLQ* 3 (1997): 441.

2 See Robin Ruth Linden, Darlene R. Pagano, Diana E. H. Russell, and Susan Leigh Star, eds., *Against Sadomasochism: A Radical Feminist Analysis* (East Palo Alto, Calif.: Frog in the Well, 1982). For critiques of antipornography feminist claims about queer female sexualities, including butch/femme and BDSM practices, see Amber Hollibaugh and Cherríe Moraga, "What We're Rollin' around in Bed With: Sexual Silences in Feminism," in *Powers of Desire: The Politics of Sexuality,* ed. Ann Snitow (New York: Monthly Review Press, 1983), 394–405; Pat Califia, "Anti-Anti-Porn," *off our backs,* October 1980, 25; Joan Nestle, "The Fem Question," in *Pleasure and Danger: Exploring Female Sexuality,* ed. Carole Vance (Boston: Routledge and Kegan Paul, 1984), 232–41; Gayle Rubin, "The Leather Menace," in *Coming to Power,* ed. Samois (Boston: Alyson, 1982), 192–227; Paula Webster, "Pornography and Pleasure," and Pat Califia, "Feminism and Sadomasochism," *Heresies* 12:2 (1981): 48–51, 30–34; Scott Tucker, "Gender, Fucking, and Utopia: An Essay in Response to John Stoltenberg's Refusing to Be a Man," *Social Text* 27 (1991): 3–34.

3 Fenton Bailey and Randy Barbato, directors, *Inside Deep Throat,* 2005.

4 See Gayle Rubin, "Thinking Sex: Notes for a Radical Theory of the Politics of Sexuality," in Vance, *Pleasure and Danger,* 267–319; Hollibaugh and Moraga, "What We're Rollin' around in Bed With"; Nan D. Hunter, Lisa Duggan, and Carole S. Vance, "False Promises: Feminist Antipornography Legislation in the U.S.," in *Women against Censorship,* ed. Varda Burstyn (Vancouver: Douglas and McIntyre, 1985), 130–51; Alice Echols, "The Taming of the Id: Feminist Sexual Politics, 1968–83," in Vance, *Pleasure and Danger,* 50–72; Audre Lorde, "Uses of the Erotic: The Erotic as Power," in *Sister, Outsider: Essays and Speeches* (New York: Crossing Press, 1984), 53–59; Amber Hollibaugh, "Desire for the Future: Radical Hope in Passion and Pleasure," in Vance, *Pleasure and Danger,* 401–10.

5 This chronology of the antiporn movement and the Antipornography Civil Rights

Ordinance is greatly informed by Paul Brest and Anne Vandenberg, "Politics, Feminism, and the Constitution: The Antipornography Movement in Minneapolis," *Stanford Law Review* 39:3: 607–61; Catharine MacKinnon and Andrea Dworkin, *In Harm's Way: The Pornography Civil Rights Hearings* (Cambridge: Harvard University Press, 1997); Lisa Duggan and Nan D. Hunter, *Sex Wars: Sexual Dissent and Political Culture* (New York: Routledge, 1995); the Organizing Against Pornography archives housed at the Minnesota Historical Society; and research notes from Danielle Kasprzak.

6 Marlys McPherson and Glenn Silloway, *An Analysis of the Relationship between Adult Entertainment Establishments, Crime, and Housing Values* (Minneapolis: Minnesota Crime Prevention Center, 1980).

7 This simplistic correlation between property values, segregation, and racialized leisure cultures is part of a long history of troubling discourses surrounding race, class, and residential and recreational uses of public space. See Samuel Delaney, *Times Square Red, Times Square Blue* (New York: New York University Press, 2001); Alison Isenberg, *Downtown America: A History of the Place and the People Who Made It* (Chicago: University of Chicago Press, 2005); Matthew D. Lassiter, *The Silent Majority: Suburban Politics in the Sunbelt South* (Princeton, N.J.: Princeton University Press, 2005); Bryant Simon, *Boardwalk of Dreams: Atlantic City and the Fate of Urban America* (New York: Oxford University Press, 2004); Thomas J. Sugrue, *The Origins of the Urban Crisis: Race and Inequality in Postwar Detroit* (Princeton, N.J.: Princeton University Press, 2005).

8 *Miller v. California,* 413 U.S. 15 (1973). The case established a definition for "obscenity" that overturned *Memoirs v. Massachusetts*'s definition of obscenity as materials that were "utterly without redeeming social value." *Miller* upheld prior rulings that obscenity was not protected by the First Amendment, and established the "Miller Test" for determining what constituted obscene material. Although the creation of the Miller Test technically made obscenity prosecutions easier (by imposing "community standards" and shifting the responsibility for regulation of sexually explicit materials to local governments), strict procedural requirements have made civil and criminal actions costly and time-consuming. According to Brest and Vandenberg, "Existing obscenity legislation has just not proved an effective response to the adult entertainment industry" (Brest and Vandenberg, "Politics, Feminism, and the Constitution," 610).

9 Brest and Vandenberg, "Politics, Feminism, and the Constitution," 610.

10 See Laura Lederer, ed., *Take Back the Night: Women on Pornography* (New York: William Morrow, 1980); Andrea Dworkin, *Pornography: Men Possessing Women* (London: Women's Press, 1981).

11 See Dworkin, *Pornography;* Lederer, *Take Back the Night;* Robin Morgan, "Theory

and Practice: Pornography and Rape," in Lederer, *Take Back the Night,* 134–40; Diana Russell, "On Pornography," *Chrysalis* 4 (1977): 11–15.

12 Brest and Vandenberg, "Politics, Feminism, and the Constitution." Supporters of the ordinances emphasized that they did not advocate or enable censorship. See Andrea Dworkin, "For Men, Freedom of Speech; For Women, Silence Please," in Lederer, *Take Back the Night;* Patricia Gruben, "Feminists and Censorship: The Girls Are at It Again," *Centerfold* (February–March 1979): 86–90. Feminist and civil libertarian opponents of the ordinances, however, argued that they either amounted to de facto censorship or laid the groundwork for future state censorship. See Lisa Duggan, "Censorship in the Name of Feminism," in Duggan and Hunter, *Sex Wars,* 30–42; Jeanne Cordova and Kerry Lobel, "Feminists and the Right—Merging over Porn?" *Lesbian Tide* (May–June 1980): 17.

13 Hollibaugh and Moraga, "What We're Rollin' around in Bed With."

14 For a discussion of the "sex panics" of the 1980s, and their relationship to the culture wars and to antipornography feminism, see Lisa Duggan, "Sex Panics," in Duggan and Hunter, *Sex Wars,* 74–79.

15 It's important to note that, even at the time, feminist scholars and activists were critiquing dogmatic oversimplifications perpetrated by *both* sides of the "war." A 1984 special issue of the feminist journal *Signs,* for example, described the debates as not only overly simplistic, but ahistorical: antipornography feminisms tended to view patriarchal dominance as a monolithic institution that had never changed or been challenged, while sex-positive feminist discourses often understood sexual repression as a monolithic force that had similarly never changed or been challenged. See *Signs* 10:1 (1984): 102–5. And a number of feminist scholars also pointed out the white-centered nature of these debates. See Rubin, "The Leather Menace"; B. Ruby Rich, "Review Essay: Feminism and Sexuality in the 1980s," *Feminist Studies* 12 (1986): 525–61; Cherríe Moraga, "Played between White Hands: A Response to the Barnard Sexuality Conference Coverage," *off our backs* (July 1982).

16 Brest and Vandenberg, "Politics, Feminism, and the Constitution," 614.

17 The ordinance also notes that "The use of men, children, or transsexuals in the place of women is also pornography for purposes of this law," and that "Any man or transsexual who alleges injury by pornography in the way women are injured by it shall also have a cause of action."

18 City of Minneapolis consulting contract, quoted in Brest and Vandenberg, "Politics, Feminism, and the Constitution," 628.

19 Ibid., 629.

20 Joe Kimball, "Head of State MCLU Asks Fraser to Veto Pornography Law," *Minneapolis Star Tribune,* January 2, 1984, 1.

21 Brest and Vandenberg, "Politics, Feminism, and the Constitution," 632.

22 Donald A. Downs, *The New Politics of Pornography* (Chicago: University of Chicago Press, 1989), 83.

23 Lisa Duggan, "Introduction," in Duggan and Hunter, *Sex Wars,* 6. See also Kate Ellis, *Caught Looking: Feminism, Pornography, and Censorship* (New York: Caught Looking Incorporated, 1986).

24 Duggan, "Introduction," 7.

25 Hunter, Duggan, and Vance, "False Promises."

26 Ibid.. See also Cordova and Lobel, "Feminists and the Right"; Nadine Strossen, *Defending Pornography: Free Speech, Sex, and the Fight for Women's Rights* (New York: New York University Press, 1994).

27 Anne Enke, "Smuggling Sex through the Gates: Race, Sexuality, and the Politics of Space in Second Wave Feminism," *American Quarterly* 55:4 (2003): 635–67. Subsequent references are given in the text.

28 As Hollibaugh and Moraga note, however, the visible leadership of the feminist antipornography "single-issue movement" was almost entirely white and middle-class (Hollibaugh and Moraga, "What We're Rollin' around in Bed With," 405). For a critique of the feminist antipornography movement's exclusion of poor, third-world, and lesbian women, see Susan Chute, "Backroom with the Feminist Heroes: Conference for Women Against Pornography, New York City, 1979," *Sinister Wisdom* 15 (1980): 2–4; Rich, "Review Essay"; and Moraga, "Played between White Hands."

29 Pat Califia, "The Obscene, Disgusting, and Vile Meese Commission Report," in *Public Sex: The Culture of Radical Sex* (San Francisco: Cleis Press, 1994), 42–53.

30 John Leo, "Pornography: The Feminist Dilemma," *Time,* July 21, 1986; http://www.time.com/time/magazine/article/0,9171,961806,00.html.

31 Duggan, "Censorship in the Name of Feminism," 34.

32 Judy Klemesrud, "Joining Hands in the Fight against Pornography," *New York Times,* August 26, 1985, B7.

33 Susan Carleton, "Tug-o-War over Bookstore," *GLC Voice,* December 1980, 1.

34 Dylan Hicks, "Pride: How the Twin Cities Pride Fest Helped Turn Minneapolis into the San Francisco of the Wheat Belt," *City Pages,* June 23, 2004; http://www.citypages.com/2004-06-23/news/pride/1.

35 Carleton, "Tug-o-War over Bookstore," 1.

36 Ibid.

37 Tim Campbell, "Officials Backing Puppet 'Neighborhood Groups' in Fight with Bookstores," *GLC Voice,* April 5, 1982, 1.

38 Jean-Nickolaus Tretter, "20 Years of Twin Cities Pride," pamphlet (1992), Tretter Manuscripts: GLBT Pride/Twin Cities, University of Minnesota Libraries, Tretter Collection, Special Collections and Rare Books.

39 Jil, "Pride Group Snubs Lesbians; Boycott Called," *Equal Time,* June 2, 1982, 13.

40 Ibid.

41 Ibid.

42 Hicks, "Pride," 6.

43 Philip Willkie, "75,000 March for ERA in Chicago," *GLC Voice,* May 1980, 1.

44 Hicks, "Pride," 7.

45 See chapter 3 in this volume.

46 Tretter, "20 Years of Twin Cities Pride."

47 "Solid Gold, Round Six," *City Pages,* May 1989.

48 See David Brauer, "Getting 'Em Coming and Going," *Twin Cities Reader,* March 8–14, 1989, 2–3; Dan Hauser, "Opponents Join Forces against Solid Gold," *Skyway News,* June 6, 1989, 1, 4; David Hawley, "Turning Flesh to Gold," *St. Paul Pioneer Press Dispatch,* March 12, 1989; Meleah Maynard, "Softcore Is Golden," *City Pages,* March 1989.

49 "For Dancer, All That's Solid Gold Isn't Glitter," *Minneapolis Star Tribune,* April 3, 1989, 1E; Lou Gelfand, "Article on Solid Gold Nightclub Draws Complaints," *Minneapolis Star Tribune,* April 9, 1989, 31A.

50 Hawley, "Turning Flesh to Gold."

51 Hauser, "Opponents Join Forces agaoinst Solid Gold," 4.

52 Close the Solid Gold Committee, correspondence, May 5, 1989, box 2; Organizing Against Pornography, Organizational Records, Minnesota Historical Society.

53 "For Dancer, All That's Solid Gold Isn't Glitter," *Minneapolis Star Tribune,* April 3, 1989, 1E.

54 Maynard, "Softcore Is Golden."

55 Close the Solid Gold Committee, correspondence, May 5, 1989, box 2

56 Hawley "Turning Flesh to Gold."

57 Hauser, "Opponents Join Forces against Solid Gold," 4.

58 In a move that reflects antiqueer hysteria about children and sexuality in Minnesota in the mid- to late 1980s, the Close the Solid Gold Committee also argued that the club posed a threat to children, because "the sex industry traffics in minors." To support this claim, it called attention to a seventeen-year-old dancer at the club (the minimum legal age for topless dancing was eighteen). Months earlier, two working-class nude bars in St. Paul had been shut down after their owner was convicted of hiring a thirteen-year-old dancer, but the committee didn't mention those incidents in its materials.

59 In 1990, dancers and entertainers at Solid Gold would file a class-action lawsuit against Solid Gold, alleging violations of state labor and minimum wage laws (*Minneapolis Star Tribune,* "Club Dancers Can Sue as Class," April 4, 1991, 7B).

60 Hawley, "Turning Flesh to Gold."

61 For a discussion of the ways in which gay and lesbian identities have been mobilized in the service of gentrification, see chapter 9 in this volume.

62 Hunter, Duggan, and Vance, "False Promises."

63 Doug Grow, "War on Porn May Be More Political Than You Think," Minneapolis *Star-Tribune,* February 3, 1995, 3B. See also Tim Campbell, "City Forfeits $1 Mil near Bookstore," *GLC Voice,* December 1980, 1, 3.

64 Cohen, "Punks, Bulldaggers, and Welfare Queens," 441.

9. THE GAY LAND RUSH RACE, GENDER, AND SEXUALITY IN THE LIFE OF POST-WELFARE MINNEAPOLIS

Ryan Patrick Murphy

In a deluge of freezing rain on an October night in 2005, I hurry into a cocktail party in a storefront in the Stevens Square neighborhood of inner-city Minneapolis. A hip young woman in a fashion-forward geometric pattern dress and go-go boots immediately approaches me as a potential customer—a young white man in a group of other fashionably dressed young men. As she reaches out to shake my hand I am distracted by the splendor of the scene before me. Richly textured granite countertop samples, austere stainless steel appliances, gleaming chrome plumbing fixtures, and snaking lighting tracks surround a credenza filled with freshly cut flowers and European wine varietals. Digital renderings on the walls showcase condominium units ranging from a $160,000 700-square-foot first-floor studio with a view of the parking lot to a $450,000 two-bedroom with a formal dining room and skyline veranda.

As the young agent begins her presentation while pouring me a glass of wine, I watch the driving rain pummel the rainbow-flag banner over the doorway heralding "Lavender Night," and "welcoming the Gay, Lesbian, Bisexual, and Transgender Community" to the new project and the neighborhood. Immediately past the banner, three men huddle under the eaves of a liquor store. Their rain-soaked hair, clothing, and shoes mark them as more likely living on the street than in the loft complex next door. Homelessness disproportionately affects Stevens Square and adjacent neighborhoods at the intersection of racism and poverty, neighborhoods where 70 percent of residents are people of color, where 50 percent of people live below the poverty line, and where residents are twice as likely to be poor than the average Minneapolitan.[1] My attention returns to the go-go boots-wearing agent as she points past the huddling men to the structure rising

Lifting a softening condo market with GLBT community: the Eat Street Flats sales team spruced up their usual half-page biweekly advertisement in Lavender *magazine with martini glasses and cocktail olives as they recruited the dollars of "lavender" buyers. From* Lavender *(October 14, 2005): 14.*

from the ruins of an abandoned gas station across the street. She notes that the new condominiums will be "a perfect match for the design- and trend-conscious gay market," providing a win-win opportunity for the gay community, the neighborhood, and the developer, as "gays are great owners, and really add value to the buildings and to the neighborhood."[2]

This chapter examines how the politics of race, gender, and sexuality participate in the life of neighborhoods like Stevens Square, where lifestyles of plenty in luxury condominiums tower over streetscapes of poverty. In particular, I take up events like "Lavender Night" to explain how my sexual identity as a gay man—the assumed nature of my buying, living, eating, working, and social and sexual networking habits—becomes a "value add" on the urban landscape. I argue that the value add of "GLBT community" drives a "Gay Land Rush" that has become an increasingly prevalent solution to the crisis of racialized and gendered poverty intensifying with the demise of the welfare state.[3] To do this I analyze how sexual understandings of the causes of poverty—child rearing outside of marriage, lack of sexual self-restraint, and the failure to commit to monogamy and domesticity, among others—justify new public policy initiatives that redistribute wealth and power upward and out of poor urban neighborhoods. I then examine how other sexual narratives—in this case, about a GLBT community linking its identity to boutiques, banks, and BMWs—have become a primary means to revitalize these same neighborhoods. I conclude by briefly exploring horizons of queer politics based on building new alliances that interrupt the sexual justifications for an increasingly regressive local and national policy agenda.

This chapter departs from a variety of other work in GLBT urban studies in that it refuses to offer a single, coherent story of gay and lesbian urban history. Studies of gay and lesbian city living—notably Manuel Castells's foundational work on San Francisco's Castro district[4]—often document the experiences of "moral refugees," making economically stagnating cities "beautiful and alive" in their own plight to escape antigay violence and discrimination.[5] Although GLBT enclaves have been essential to the physical, emotional, and economic survival of many queer people, the community histories documenting them often deploy incomplete and problematic understandings of the relationship between the GLBT community and the economy. In such narratives, GLBT community is imagined as a space external to capitalism. Queer neighborhoods and populations are cast as suffering exploitation or as pure and innocent sites of resistance against this exploitation. This chapter instead argues that

GLBT community—the social networks, cultural institutions, commercial establishments, and romantic and sexual practices of people whose sexual affinities or gender presentations depart from heteronormative expectations—is one of many sexual narratives that supplement and reinforce the capitalist system.[6] Stories told about sexuality in the city—the sexual urban legends running a gamut of topics from "welfare babies" of women of color to white gay men in boutiques—have played a critical role in producing the regressive and exploitative political and economic policy shifts of the last thirty years. I trace this relationship not to cast the gay community as a colonizing force of "urban pioneers" or to render poor people of color dispossessed victims, but because a more precise understanding of the relationship between sexuality and the economy will be necessary to build a more effective GLBT political movement and more equitable public policy.

Serving a "Certain Customer": A Gay Land Rush at the Turn of the Millennium

"Lavender Night" was a star in a constellation of marketing events and media representations linking GLBT community and identity to urban real estate in Minneapolis after the turn of the millennium. Stock-market declines amid a bursting "dot-com bubble" propelled investment professionals and individual speculators to move financial assets into real estate. By 2003, Twin Cities home prices ballooned in the most robust real-estate market since the 1970s, and in perhaps the largest urban condominium boom in the region's history.[7] The sudden proliferation of high-density, high-end condos in a metropolitan area long famous for its sprawling, sleepy, and modest landscapes led the *Star Tribune,* the Twin Cities' leading daily, to launch a multipart series titled "The New Land Rush" in the spring of 2005.[8]

Yet, for all the millenarian hype surrounding the New Land Rush, gradually rising interest rates and a seemingly unending stream of new construction fueled growing fears of overbuilding. Investors, developers, and builders scrambled to identify new market niches to distinguish individual projects in a crowded market. The consumption and domestic practices of the GLBT community were increasingly leveraged to provide such a niche market, launching a "Gay Land Rush" to save the stagnating New Land Rush. The formula of "Lavender Night"—transforming real-estate markets with GLBT cultural practices and social networks—became the mainstay of this new phenomenon. For example, a riverfront condominium project in downtown Minneapolis hosted "Queen for a Day," where attendees were shown the Joan Crawford–themed gay cult film *Mommie Dearest* after a pitch from the developer.[9] Equally campy was the "Condo Queen," the marketing alias of a prominent local real-estate agent. Although her billboard and bus bench advertisements were not specifically aimed at gay men, her tiara and magic wand reference presumed alliances between gay men and elite women: gay male adoration of eccentric, sassy, independent, financially successful older women, gay male bonding with "fag hags" around the trope of the queen, and alliances between gay men and women professionals in the real-estate, fashion, and financial services industries.

Few were as closely linked to the emerging Gay Land Rush as the real-estate agents serving GLBT clients and institutions. For example, Ann Leviton has spent her twenty-year career in Minnesota working as both a real-estate agent and an affordable housing advocate. Although she actively supports a comprehensive regional strategy to provide low-cost housing, her role as a prominent lesbian businesswoman, and her campy and humorous advertising in local GLBT weekly *Lavender* as "The Real Estate Fairy," land her calls from motivated sellers working to cash in on appreciating values associated with the Gay Land Rush. "Straight people will call me and let me know their house is for sale, because they know I serve a certain person," she notes as she reflects on her marketing presence in the gay press.[10]

Ann describes why gay and straight clients are interested in this GLBT "value add" in the Twin Cities:

> An interesting geographic phenomenon of the gay community is the turning around of North Minneapolis's Camden neighborhood. And it was primarily the gay men who did this. They love the character of the bungalows. I have heard time and again that it is the impact of the gay investment in those neighborhoods that has had the greatest impact on turning them around. As a result, Camden has had some of the highest levels of appreciation in Minneapolis.[11]

Camden is just twenty blocks north of the Jordan and Hawthorne neighborhoods of North Minneapolis, where the region's largest African American population lives in several of the poorest census tracts in the state. But through the domestic and consumptive practices of gay men—"loving bungalows" and "investing" in neighborhoods—Camden becomes an island, spatially and temporally isolated from the shrinking supply of affordable housing, the high unemployment rate, and the termination of welfare programs significantly impacting Jordan and Hawthorne. Through its assumed ability to foster these islands of appreciating value, the Gay Land Rush was emerging among homeowners, the media, and the real-estate industry as a remedy for the economic and social anxieties of life in post-welfare Minneapolis.

Accumulation by Dispossession in Minneapolis

To begin to understand how a set of sexual identities and practices could be offered as a solution to the crisis of urban poverty in the Twin Cities, dominant understandings of the relationship among race, gender, culture, and poverty must be explored. At first glance, the economic anxieties of home sellers and the real-estate industry seem unfounded, as the Twin Cities economy has long been far healthier than its large Midwestern neighbors suffering amid the rapid disappearance of high-wage, heavily unionized employment in the manufacturing sector. The regional economy is particularly diverse, mixing a burgeoning service sector with financial services, real estate, agribusiness, and light manufacturing.[12] The Twin Cities had the highest overall education rate of any major U.S. city by 1990, and its poverty rate was half of the national average.[13] Unemployment had decreased to a staggeringly low 3.5 percent by 1988, and remained well below 5 percent for the remainder of the millennium.[14]

Despite the robust economy, entrenched racist practices of exclusion prevented many Minnesotans from enjoying the region's wealth. By 1990, while poverty had decreased to unprecedented lows, the African American poverty rate nearly doubled the national average. And, as the years passed, African American poverty was exacerbated rather than mitigated by the increasing wealth of the region. Whereas 27 percent of Twin Cities African Americans were living in poverty in 1980, the number jumped to 47 percent by 1990, when an African American child was eight times as likely as a white child to live below the poverty line.[15] By 1995, the number of census tracts in the central cities with concentrated poverty had tripled in ten short years. The trend did not just affect African American Twin Citians. Although as a whole the most educated metropolitan area in the United States, the education rate for Latinos lagged behind thirty-nine others. Increasing poverty and crime, and the disappearance of jobs in the lowest-income central city neighborhoods, intensified the process of segregation. During the 1980s, the white population of the city of Minneapolis dropped by 25 percent, while the African American population increased by 61 percent, and the Southeast Asian population rose 248 percent.[16]

The striking disparities of wealth, education, and housing along racial lines in the Twin Cities by the year 2000 are evidence of what scholars term "accumulation by dispossession." Although scholars often define "dispossession" as a particular occurrence in the transition from Feudalism to capitalism—stripping peasants of their land and forcing them to work for wages—others have argued that dispossession is an *ongoing process* required for the capitalist system to flourish, confiscating land, labor, and money from poor and working populations, and placing them in the hands of the elite.[17] In addition, rather than understanding dispossession as a mere economic phenomenon, Gillian Hart and others have insisted that dispossession happens in a broad spectrum of social relations, especially in relation to gender, race, and sexuality.[18] Accumulation by dispossession is a critically important concept for analyzing urban poverty in the Twin Cities because it reminds us that racialized and gendered poverty are manufactured every day. Rather than a naturally existing condition of neighborhoods where people of color live, or an uncontestable "legacy of slavery," accumulation by dispossession depends on legislative innovations, legal decisions, lending practices, marketing strategies, policing, and political organizing that extract resources from poor people of color and their neighborhoods.

Perpetuating Accumulation by Dispossession with Public Policy

Accumulation by dispossession along racial lines is perhaps nowhere more visible or contentious than in the history of home ownership. A number of scholars have noted that the suburban tract home was perhaps "the most important generator of wealth in American history." Racial covenants restricting the suburbs to whites only, "redlining" practices in which banks refused homeownership loans in neighborhoods of color, and vigilante violence blocking neighborhood integration worked in concert to deny people of color access to the generational wealth and economic stability of residential property ownership.[19] Skyrocketing housing costs owing to gentrification of low-income Twin Cities neighborhoods, and a wave of regressive housing policy reforms, exacerbated this history of dispossession at the turn of the millennium.

But instead of exposing the troubled historical intersection of housing policy and racism, public debate in response to expanding racialized poverty in Minneapolis sensationalized one of its consequences: crime. The murder rate doubled in just two years after 1993, with a person murdered in Minneapolis nearly every day during the summer of 1995. Half the killings were in gang-related violence disproportionately affecting young men of color.[20] *Fortune* magazine's widely publicized ranking of Minneapolis 188th out of two hundred metropolitan areas for safety perpetuated the racialized fear of public space.[21] Violent crime gained national attention after Mark Koscielski, a white firearms activist with ties to the police department and owner of a gun shop in the largely African American and American Indian Phillips neighborhood, began selling T-shirts in 1995 with the slogan "Murderapolis: City of Wakes." The shirts were a play on the city's motto, "Minneapolis: City of Lakes," and became the centerpiece of a less-than-flattering *New York Times* cover story labeling the city "not your father's Minneapolis" as it documented an expanding population of color in the urban core.[22] Koscielski's racialization and hyperbolization of the crime wave reinforced the activism of his genteel and elite counterparts. In April 1997, the CEOs of three of Minnesota's largest employers, Honeywell, Allina Health Care, and First Bank, met with governor Arne Carlson and threatened to relocate unless drastic steps were taken to arrest the upsurge in violence.[23]

Although the crime wave and the racialized economic practices in which it was embedded were certainly not a trend unique to the Twin Cities, Minnesota's political tradition—often cast as progressive, populist, and enlightened—spawned a troubling set of public policy responses. Despite its liberal facade and explicit rejection of the harsh anti-welfare reforms of the Reagan, Bush, and Clinton administrations, Minnesota politics largely reinforced, rather than challenged, accumulation by dispossession. Liberal politicians frequently used the crime controversy to make white, liberal generosity and benevolence—rather than intensifying practices of dispossession—the center of pubic consideration of the intersection of race and poverty. Elected officials argued that poor people were moving to Minnesota to take advantage of generous welfare benefits. "We have a lot of people coming here who don't share the kind of ethic we expect in Minnesota," Minneapolis's Mayor Sharon Sayles-Belton, a centrist African

American Democrat, argued in 1996.[24] Centrist, white Republican Governor Arne Carlson drew upon Sayles-Belton's logic to argue that trimming Minnesota's welfare system, and restricting the flow of low-income people of color from out of state, must be a primary element of effective crime fighting in Minneapolis.[25] By the mid-1990s, accusations of welfare fraud—the heavily racialized and gendered centerpieces of the national attack on the welfare state—were becoming the primary means for Minnesota liberal politicians to exempt themselves from culpability in the crisis of racialized poverty in their home state.

Two significant mid-1990s public policy initiatives consolidated the attack on welfare as a response to the "Murderapolis" hysteria. First, Democratic leaders in the legislature amended the state's welfare laws to ban all benefits to new arrivals for thirty days, and to cap benefits at the level of the previous state of residence for the first eleven months in Minnesota. The legislative initiative served to complicate migration for African Americans and other poor people fleeing deindustrialization in Illinois, Ohio, Michigan, and other states with stagnating economies.[26] Second, the Metropolitan Livable Communities Act of 1995 (LCA) comprehensively reformed affordable housing policy in the Twin Cities. Although the LCA mandated increases in the *absolute* availability of affordable housing, guaranteeing construction of lower-priced rentals across the metropolitan area, it failed to mandate increases in *relative* availability, omitting requirements that affordable housing supply keep pace with the region's rapid population growth. These and other weaknesses allowed the LCA to label 68 percent of housing in the region as "affordable" despite skyrocketing housing costs, and to set benchmarks that were actually *below* the number of affordable housing units already existing in two-thirds of municipalities. The LCA in fact guaranteed a 13 percent *decrease* in availability of affordable housing by 2010 if population growth projections proved accurate. An act heralded to make the Twin Cites more "livable" would certainly do so for white, middle- and upper-income Twin Citians, but would simultaneously perpetuate accumulation by dispossession, reducing the supply of housing for those at the bottom of the income spectrum.[27]

Sexuality as a Basis for Dispossession

While legislative responses to increasing poverty and violence in the Twin Cities transformed *economic* policies to make life more difficult for poor people and people of color, public policy continued to operate on the assumption that poverty was a *sexual* problem. Local antipoverty activism frequently echoed Senator Daniel Patrick Moynihan's infamous 1965 report *The Negro Family: The Case for National Action.* Such analysis blamed families deviating from heterosexual norms—in particular those with absent fathers, matriarchal structures, child bearing at a young age, and frequent unemployment—for being poverty-producing "tangles of pathology."[28] 1990s Minnesota liberal reformers, while contesting efforts to dismantle the welfare state, pursued policies that referenced and reinforced Moynihan's social science, though doing so while replacing Moynihan's familiar "culture of poverty" argument with a new focus on "concentrated" poverty. Former Minnesota State Representative and University of Minnesota Law Professor Myron Orfield defines the terms of this debate about concentrated poverty in his Brookings Institution–published text *Metropolitics:*

> The residential concentration of poverty creates social repercussions far greater than the sum of its parts. Physical separation from jobs and *middle-class role models* and dependence on a *dysfunctional welfare system* reinforce social isolation and weaken work skills. Poor individuals living in concentrated poverty are far more likely to become pregnant as teenagers, drop out of high school, and remain jobless than young people living in socioeconomically mixed neighborhoods.[29]

As a scholar, activist, and politician, Orfield was among the most innovative, committed, and effective defenders of Minnesota antipoverty programs, providing prolific research to a coalition of urban, regional, and state government officials to bolster public housing, health care, and welfare programs in the 1990s. Yet the sexual undertones in Orfield's focus on "concentration" expose long-standing liberal and conservative tendencies to make the cultural and reproductive practices of middle-class white families, rather than ending accumulation by dispossession, the solution to urban poverty.[30] The centrality of sexuality in government understandings of the causes of and remedies for poverty are evident as Orfield continues:

> An "oppositional culture" emerges that appears to reject many closely held middle-class mores. Poor young men and women, without connections to outside opportunity or hope for a better life, engage in self-reinforcing, promiscuous sex in search of affection or status. Single parentage in poor neighborhoods is part of conforming to peer group expectations. At first, the

> infant represents a focus of love, identity, and purpose in an otherwise bleak setting; later, the child becomes another burden in a life overwhelmed by hopelessness.[31]

In this passage, pathologized social and biological reproduction practices justify state efforts to intervene in poor people's lives.

By the mid-1990s, this state's focus on sexuality spawned a new generation of public policy aiming to relocate poor people of color out of the lowest-income neighborhoods and into whiter and wealthier parts of the city.[32] Such efforts to "deconcentrate poverty" propelled Minneapolis's history of racial segregation into national headlines. In the landmark 1995 case *Hollman v. Cisneros,* the NAACP successfully sued the Metropolitan Council, the City of Minneapolis, the Minneapolis Public Housing Authority, and the Minneapolis Community Development Agency. The NAACP proved that these institutions had worked to "concentrate" people of color in the city's poorest census tracts with the fewest economic opportunities. Yet, rather than simply demand the improvement of infrastructure, landscape architecture, access to services, and employment opportunities in the most impoverished areas, the legal consent decree settling the *Hollman* case mandated the demolition of one thousand units of public housing, the reconstruction of this housing in wealthier neighborhoods, and transportation subsidies to allow low-income people of color to live in communities outside areas of urban poverty.[33] The consensus that emerged around *Hollman* assumed that relocating public housing residents away from family, friends, neighbors, lovers, and the neighborhoods they grew up in would be the primary element in solving the problem of urban poverty.

Mobilizing against the Sexual Politics of Dispossession

Women of color blamed for the dispossession to which they are subjected mobilized against these policies, demanding a diversity of housing options for people on welfare, people of color, and those unwilling or unable to subscribe to white, middle-class family norms. Angel Buechner, an African American welfare rights activist in Minneapolis, argues that cultural analyses of poverty, and related "deconcentration" efforts, justify accumulation by dispossession: "Now they are trying to get the working folks back in the city because they say the city needs to be revived, and needs more taxes. But it's like moving the Africans back to Africa. I'm saying, 'Yes, massah, shove me on down South!'"[34] Angel challenges this process by organizing low-income women, many of whom are American Indian, African American, Latina, and Southeast Asian, via the Twin Cities Welfare Rights Committee. The activists fuse legislative lobbying, community education, performance art, and direct-action protest, explicitly challenging attacks on women of color and their friends and families with concrete political and economic demands on the state. Central to Angel's activism is her explicit rejection of efforts to "deconcentrate" poverty, arguing that such a policy leaves those on housing assistance isolated in unwelcoming suburban communities:

> I know people who are leaving the city, but not by choice. They are giving suburban housing to people who have been on the (Section 8) waiting list for a long time. People are moving because "Hey, I need somewhere to go" and this is affordable and I'm moving. So you're in the burbs, you're poor, you don't have a car, and you're stuck because no bus runs there. People who have been out in the suburbs want to be back in the city, but the programs are trying to keep all lower income folks out in the suburbs.

With low-income people pushed into suburbia, Angel argues that city neighborhoods are then able to become fashionable consumption districts for the elite. Angel has watched the Phillips neighborhood corner of Chicago and Lake Street, a longtime hub of commerce catering to lower-income people of color, transformed to attract white tourists and condo dwellers:

> Chicago and Lake has always been the four corners where you can catch a bus, but now they built this transit stop down the street, which is housed by nothing but cops. So they're saying, "This is the way to clean up Lake Street." Because now the Sheraton is there, and there's this Global Marketplace. And I just want to ask, is all that geared toward corporate, white America? It isn't there to be convenient for us black folks or for us people of color.

Angel's comments expose the contentious and contradictory nature of efforts to transform the city. The Midtown Global Marketplace to which Angel refers is by no means an exclusively elite redevelopment project. The Marketplace is growing inside a long-abandoned Sears department store, and hosts a multiplicity of "small business incubator" public–private partnerships aimed explicitly at first-time business owners who are people of color. In addition, 81 percent of 220 units of both rental and ownership

The Midtown Global Market is in a former Sears department store on the corner of Lake Street and Chicago Avenue in south Minneapolis. A minimalist steel and glass transit interchange and a fortress-like Sheraton hotel and restaurant shield the redevelopment area from the local streetscape. Photograph by Ryan Patrick Murphy, July 2009.

housing above the Marketplace are affordable to those living at or above 60 percent of the community median income.[35] Yet, with a wealth of new business opportunities for an extremely diverse neighborhood, opportunities that never existed inside an abandoned warehouse, came an upscale hotel and a redesigned transit facility and shopping center that are heavily policed to help assuage racialized fears of crime by affluent potential shoppers.[36] Angel argues that for many unable to access even the affordable spaces inside the Marketplace, the landscape reinforces a culturalized and sexualized debate about poverty in the city, positing a sanitized, fortified redevelopment project against the existing landscape of low-income people in the city. Such tensions are particularly evident at Chicago–Lake Liquors, a gritty storefront lying kitty-corner to the towering Marketplace. Angel insists:

> Chicago–Lake is the spot. That's where everybody goes. It does not matter if you're black, white, Mexican—everybody goes to Chicago–Lake Liquor. I think the way they will make Chicago–Lake Liquor work (with the redevel-

> opment) is to make it a wine and spritzer store—you know, [laughs] little, geared towards the white people. "Oh yeah, you can go over here and get all your wine and cheese and all that."[37]

Via the notion of "spritzers," her humorous term for expensive wines, cordials, and aperitifs for white people, Angel argues that adding value to the neighborhood hinges upon the removal of the cultural practices and social spaces of low-income people and people of color, and replacing them with the profitable lifestyles of wealthier, whiter populations. At the very moment that the sexual practices of women and youth of color were becoming grounds for their removal from the city after *Hollman v. Cisneros,* the social and sexual practices of the GLBT community—particularly those onstage at "Lavender Night" and other real-estate industry events—were emerging as useful new tools to perpetuate this process.

A New Tool for Urban Renewal: GLBT Lifestyles

By the early 1990s, mainstream media outlets and political and cultural pundits were beginning to document and publicize what they argued was an important new force in revitalizing central city neighborhoods struggling with decades of entrenched poverty: the GLBT community. In the fall of 1994, the *Star Tribune* devoted the cover of its Metro Section to exposing the role that gays had played in "turning around" Loring Park, the leafy span of nineteenth-century brownstones just south of downtown. While ongoing news coverage of the "Murderapolis" controversy insisted that African Americans arriving from Chicago, Cleveland, Gary, and other rust-belt cities, and Hmong refugees fleeing the consequences of the U.S. war in Southeast Asia, were bringing the pathologies of concentrated poverty to Minneapolis, the *Star Tribune* offered the history of gay migration to Loring Park as a solution to these urban dilemmas. The story painted the Loring Park of the 1960s as "rough" and "dangerous," ridden with "drunks, crime, and decay." But after twenty years of a growing gay community "molding and shaping" Loring Park, the neighborhood had become a "bohemian" mix of nineteenth-century walkups and modern condo complexes. Gays and lesbians "stabilized tax bases" and "pumped money into the economy," gradually enhancing the neighborhood's attractiveness. The article noted that gay and lesbian businesses brought a "flavor" to the neighborhood otherwise absent, making Loring Park home to "the chic places" and "the trendy places," and the appreciating real-estate values that accompany them.[38]

Subsequent *Star Tribune* stories documenting the GLBT community as a driving force in rising home values, and the gay presence in the technology industry as a key to Minneapolis's economic stability, joined national coverage making similar arguments.[39] *New York Times* columnist David Brooks argued that "bourgeois bohemians"—hip urbanites consuming the grittiness of the city with money to burn and sounding strikingly like the gays and lesbians described in the *Star Tribune*—were transforming and invigorating urban spaces.[40] Similarly, Richard Florida's widely cited and publicized *The Rise of the Creative Class* insisted that robust gay and lesbian populations were signs of the innovative, flexible, and human capital–intensive economies that cities needed for success in the "New Economy."[41] All painted an urban portrait in which a gay community flourished amid marketization and deregulation while racialized, working-class populations floundered, dependent on a sinking, stagnated, "old" industrial economy.

An ascendant GLBT community that pumped money into the economy and heralded trendiness and chicness was immediately leveraged by the real-estate industry and others invested in urban economies. Real-estate sales professionals realized that fashionable gay urbanity would supplement and enhance sales to the growing "lifestyle market," recruiting those willing to pay a premium for a stylish, edgy, cosmopolitan experience intentionally deviating from suburban domesticity.[42] Project managers hired interior design consultants to decorate model condos to simulate the cosmopolitan lifestyles of hip young artists, dancers, actors, and fashionistas. Model homes were no longer simply aimed at demonstrating the functionality of a unit, as would test-driving a minivan or station wagon, but rather at simulating the lifestyle of an entire demographic group.[43] One project spent $160,000 on interior furnishings for the model of a line of small one-bedroom downtown units that would retail at a similar price. A nearby condo conversion project included a $300,000 lobby makeover to more clearly articulate the sophistication of potential new owners. The Sexton, a downtown Minneapolis condo project self-styled as "smart" and "cool," began its online marketing pitch with a social and cultural, rather than economic, hail to the urban elite:

> You are the entrepreneurs of today and the headline makers of tomorrow. You know that "dot.com" is no longer inextricably linked to the word "bub-

ble." You are cool, cosmopolitan, connected. You embrace the heartbeat of the city and you cherish its diversity. Your living space is as genuine and innovative as your lifestyle. You belong at Sexton.[44]

Selling the image of the fashionable, connected, downtown jet-setter, rather than simply the building she or he calls home, paid off beautifully for the real-estate industry in some cases. The Ivy, an elite brownstone redevelopment between downtown Minneapolis and Elliot Park offering twenty-four-hour concierge service and trendy food nouveau restaurants

Taking a gamble that sex sells to the gay market, advertisers for the Skyscape, a twenty-plus-story condominium complex on the corner of Tenth Street and Portland Avenue South in the Elliot Park neighborhood of Minneapolis ran this espresso-sipping hunk in a full-page spread in Lavender *in 2005. From* Lavender *(August 19, 2005): 93.*

for busy professionals, sold 90 percent of its units on the first weekend on the market, with many bringing in more than $2 million, and the average unit being a $750,000 1,500-square-foot unit with an association fee of more than $600 per month.[45] Lifestyle marketing at The Ivy and other projects allowed developers and investors to reap sales prices previously unimaginable on the Minneapolis condo market.

Yet, as more condominium projects have turned to the lifestyle market in attempts to maintain or enhance sales prices, narrower and more precise niches have been necessary for projects to maintain their distinctiveness. The Gay Land Rush politics embedded in the *Star Tribune*'s history of Loring Park—depictions of gay life featuring high disposable incomes, freedom from the expense and time constraints of child rearing, an insatiable demand for the arts and entertainment, and an innate eye for the hottest styles and trends in fashion, architecture, and home decor—has been a particularly effective aid to lifestyle marketing, offering a new mechanism to counteract both overbuilding and ongoing racialized and gendered fears of the city.

A Lifestyle of Boutiques, Banks, and BMWs

While the real-estate industry and individual home sellers scrambled to cash in on the "value add" of GLBT community, perhaps the most enduring and visible proponents of the Gay Land Rush were mainstream GLBT political institutions and media outlets. The linkage between the real-estate industry and GLBT community is most visible in *Lavender,* the only GLBT publication in regular print in the Twin Cities. Three of the first five pages of the October 28, 2005, issue, for example, are full-page advertisements for expensive real estate, ranging from the fifty-story steel and sandstone Nicollet in downtown Minneapolis, to The Lumen, a three-story boutique loft blocks from Lake Calhoun in Uptown, to a quaint nine-hundred-thousand-dollar bungalow in St. Paul's quiet Highland Park neighborhood. A particularly suggestive full-page advertisement features a tan, chiseled, oiled young man lying prone on a polished hardwood floor, wearing only a pair of designer white briefs. The only text on the page is the sentence "We are having a party, and you might be invited." Rather than an invitation to a sex party, the Web address at the bottom of the page takes the titillated reader to a sales site of The Sexton, the luxury high-rise heavily leveraging lifestyle marketing.[46]

In one 2006 issue, real-estate advertisements are peppered amid the results of the magazine's annual "Fab 50" awards, *Lavender*'s selection of the Twin Cities' hottest GLBT political organizations, entertainment experiences, neighborhoods, and consumer products. Although longtime GLBT cultural and political institutions are present among the winners, from grassroots activist Ann DeGroot to St. Paul's working-class, race- and gender-mixed Town House gay bar, the results are an homage to the most exclusive lifestyles in the Twin Cities. St. Paul's Grand Avenue, one of that city's two most expensive neighborhoods and home to a variety of high-end boutiques, won best place to shop and dine. Wells Fargo took best employer, implying that to be gay is to have an advanced degree in finance. And for "favorite car," *Lavender* selected none other than the BMW—not a BMW sold by a particular gay dealer, but because of "style points and reputation alone."[47]

The articulation of gay public life via boutiques, banks, and BMWs is by no means isolated to local gay presses or to the Twin Cities. Market-research experts Robert Witeck and Wesley Combs, via their partnership with marketing giant Harris Interactive, are working to cultivate patronage of a "gay market" that they argue is worth $641 billion annually. Witeck and Combs's book *Business Inside Out: Capturing Millions of Brand Loyal Gay Consumers* prescribes how to cash in on a market that is mushrooming while others stagnate. The text explains why "gay consumers have such a high potential for brand loyalty," offers contrasting strategies for both targeted and "gay-vague" marketing, and tracks emerging trends within the GLBT niche, including gay and lesbian parenting and retirement communities.[48]

Mainstream GLBT political organizations share Witeck and Combs's enthusiasm for gay niche marketing. The Human Rights Campaign (HRC), the largest national GLBT political advocacy and lobbying group, headlines its Web site with "Fight for Fairness While You Shop," trumpeting the release of the new consumer guide *Buying for Equality 2007*.[49] The HRC asserts that GLBT people will fight for their rights on holiday shopping trips guided by the organization's annual "corporate equality index." And although the corporate equality index opens an important dialogue about health insurance, retirement benefits, bereavement leave, and nondiscrimination around sexuality and gender identity or expression, HRC evaluation criteria consciously disarticulate the politics of sexuality from all other social and workplace issues. Thus, while the index requires that

In the 2005 "Pride" edition of Lavender, *Infinity Real Estate and Mortgage Services wagers that private property is the key to success—and political enfranchisement—for the GLBT "family." From* Lavender *(July 8, 2005): 19.*

companies allow employees to form a gay rights group without retribution, there is no mention of the right to organize a union. Although companies are docked points for discriminating based on sexual orientation, there is no consideration of workplace sexual or racial harassment policies. And although the index penalizes companies that lobby against gay rights, there is no penalty for supporting candidates who aim to end affirmative action, weaken workplace safety laws, or privatize Social Security.[50] The corporate equality index and "Fight for Fairness while You Shop" consciously conflate "gay rights" struggles with niche marketing, imagining boutiques, banks, and BMWs as primary sites of gay liberation, and encapsulating sexual politics within these elite white social spaces.

Trips to Williams-Sonoma to "Shop for Equality," brief-clad beauties splayed out by real-estate developers in magazines, and cocktail parties with the "Condo Queen" force a reconsideration of the relationship between the capitalist economy and GLBT community and identity. At first consideration, the notion of "GLBT community" seems to be far removed from the economy, offering a haven from the pressures of work, housing, health care, retirement security, or debt. Yet a deeper exploration of phenomena like the Gay Land Rush exemplifies feminist political theorist Miranda Joseph's argument that capitalism and "GLBT community" are deeply interwoven, depending on each other for survival. Joseph insists that community and capitalism exist in a *supplementary* relationship; that is, narratives of community fill in for what capitalism lacks, providing resources that capitalism itself cannot.[51] In the Twin Cities, the regressive economic reforms of the last thirty years—the termination of all public housing construction, eroding commitment to public schools and healthcare programs, and "the end of welfare as we know it," among others—have, in many cases, made city streets and neighborhoods into spaces of poverty, hunger, crime, homelessness, and misery. The "GLBT community" sold in *Lavender* magazine helps make up for this devastating void, filling it in with the beauty of designer kitchens, the fun of all-night dancing, and the chicness of apparel bought in boutiques. The arrival of exotic, exciting, and profitable gay lifestyles heralded by "Holiday Shopping Guides" and the Gay Land Rush allows the crises of capitalism in post-welfare Minneapolis to momentarily disappear.

The problem with this Gay Land Rush politics is that in the process "GLBT community" becomes an excuse to ignore, and even abet, intensifying poverty. The urban condominiums and cocktail parties of the Gay Land Rush allow the *Star Tribune* and elected officials to celebrate the "revitalization" and "renaissance" of urban neighborhoods while advocating further abandonment of public commitment to the health, housing, and education programs most critical to these landscapes and populations. Furthermore, this supplementary relationship between the "GLBT community" and regressive policy reforms transforms what it means to be gay, lesbian, bisexual, or transgender in problematic ways. If the arrival of gay populations helps neighborhoods "recover" from "blighted" periods, then groups blamed for "blight"—unwed mothers, families of color, African American youth, people on welfare, homeless people—are denied access to "GLBT community," effectively excluded from political movements surrounding sexuality.

The Gay Land Rush Goes Bust?

While the real-estate industry, policy makers, and mainstream GLBT political movements have worked in tandem to bolster the Gay Land Rush, queer city life may by no means be fully explained by its relationship to capitalism. A multiplicity of social networks, political interventions, and economic realities both exceed and contradict the GLBT community sold with boutiques, banks, and BMWs in *Lavender* magazine. For example, though *all* the gay and lesbian real-estate agents interviewed for this project heavily advertised in the gay press, *none* uncritically parroted the logic of the Gay Land Rush when describing their own careers, instead narrating connection between gay identity and home ownership with nuance and ambiguity. Jerry Fladmark, a white gay Minneapolis agent working out of a busy sales office on the shores of Lake Calhoun, argues that his glossy advertisements in Lavender allow him to connect three decades of gay activism to a new career in real estate:

> I had been director of volunteer services for the Aliveness Project, organized political campaigns focused around causes or getting people elected, and been president of the Twin Cities Gay Men's Chorus. I have such a long history going back into the 1970s in the gay movement. I don't have all those people's names and addresses. I just needed to make sure people knew I was selling real estate. For me, with the thousands of people I know, it turns out that marketing was the best way to stay in touch.[52]

"GLBT community" clearly does economic work for Jerry, helping him navigate an increasingly competitive marketplace by winning customers away from other agents who lack connections to the gay scene. Yet the dominant logic of the Gay Land Rush—where the GLBT community secures political rights by "Buying for Equality" and where GLBT community manages the anxieties of life in the post-welfare city by "revitalizing" "blighted" areas—is entirely absent in Jerry's logic. Social and political institutions, from precinct caucuses to the Twin Cities Gay Men's Chorus, are the center of gay identity for him, rather than the modern design, skyline balconies, and fashionable cocktail parties of elite condo complexes.

Jerry and other real-estate agents in his cohort insist that the majority of their GLBT clients are buying neither in rapidly gentrifying neighborhoods of color in the central city nor in new construction complexes aimed at the lifestyle market. Nancy Kelly, a white lesbian who also regularly advertises in *Lavender,* lives and works in Cottage Grove, a working- and middle-class suburb on the Twin Cities' southeastern fringe. Although she occasionally commutes to Minneapolis to frequent queer businesses and entertainment venues, both her lesbian social network and many of her lesbian clients have chosen suburban living to remedy a growing crisis of affordability in the region:

> I get calls from people who say, "I hear you are a mom, and my partner and I have a kid and we are looking in South St. Paul." They're moving out of Minneapolis. If you have a big cash flow, you can stay in the urban areas. If you have a lot less you have to go to the third or fourth ring. Their financial situation really determines the outcome.[53]

Nancy laughs when describing the queer stereotypes that are always part of industry banter—lesbians fixing up old Victorians with their power tools and gay men fussing over minimalist interior design. But she insists that home prices, rather than marketing to the gay niche, drive the real-estate decisions of the vast majority of her GLBT-identified clients.

Furthermore, while Nancy's analysis points to an increasing number of queer people who have been priced off the island of Gay Land Rush Minneapolis, there is no guarantee that these island-making gentrification strategies always succeed. In 2003, a group of gay investors and executives converted an abandoned Northeast Minneapolis warehouse into a gay entertainment complex that included the Boom! nightclub and Oddfellows restaurant.[54] The new complex, as well the gay-owned Italian fusion restaurant across the street, a pricey cocktail lounge next door, and a café and bookstore around the corner, garnered enough attention for the style and culture weekly *City Pages* to insist in 2004 that Northeast was on its way to becoming Minneapolis's "gayborhood," a trendy urban enclave linking GLBT identity, consumption, and domesticity. Real-estate agent Brad Palecek argued: "There is the potential for Northeast to become one large stretch that you can walk down, like Chicago's Boystown and DuPont

Circle in DC. And that's the fun. That's what people want. A six or eight block walk where they can parade themselves, good, bad, or indifferent."[55] Yet, as months went by it became increasingly unclear who really wanted to live, shop, or eat in the gayborhood. Four of the six gay establishments, including both restaurants and bars, had gone out of business by 2006. In the place of Boom! rose the Bulldog, a rather nondescript franchise of a South Minneapolis straight bar offering "plenty of beer choices plus Chicago style hot dogs."[56] Beer and hot dogs—echoing Northeast Minneapolis's Eastern European working-class roots—were a definite letdown for real-estate speculators who had hoped to cash in on a landscape of gay boutiques, bankers, and BMWs. But by 2006, the Gay Land Rush and a gayborhood full of tourists "Buying for Equality" seemed to be as much a fantasy of the real-estate industry and the HRC as an expression of the actual desires and agendas of queer Minneapolitans.

Conclusion: Queer Politics Contesting Accumulation by Dispossession

This chapter has worked to trouble the Gay Land Rush. It argues that policy makers and institutions—advocacy by liberal reformers, legislative initiatives by public officials, marketing efforts by real-estate agents, developers, and financiers, mainstream GLBT political organizations, major newspapers, and the gay press, among many others—have made sexuality a centerpiece of efforts to transform the city after the demise of the welfare state. They have done so by offering a raced and classed sexual formation—a "GLBT community" articulated with boutiques, banks, and BMWs—as a solution to the problem of urban poverty caused by the sexual pathologies of poor people and people of color. In the process, "GLBT community" has reinforced and intensified the process of accumulation by dispossession, as the value add of gays in the neighborhood becomes the alibi for further erosion of the public housing, public transportation, public education, unemployment insurance, and welfare programs.

As this chapter indicts the tactics of mainstream GLBT political movements, it must also address the question of what is to be done. If the Gay Land Rush will yield neither liberation for queer people nor a more sustainable urban future, then we must consider other ways to make sexuality in the city political. Before offering such suggestions, I must note what this chapter is *not* proposing. A critique of the Gay Land Rush must not be the basis for a guilt-driven narrative of victims and villains, where elite white gays and lesbians inevitably dispossess powerless women and people of color in gentrifying neighborhoods. Tales of guilt are not only paralyzing but once again reduce politics to the realm of individual consumer choices. Condemnations of home-buying gay and lesbian villains might insist, "Why don't those bourgeois gays and lesbians leave the city alone and spend their money in the elite white west suburbs where they belong?" In addition to assuming that to be gay is to be white and elite, such arguments reproduce the HRC's "Buying for Equality" agenda in which consumer choices—how you shop and eat and where you reside—are the only ways to politically shape the world we live in.

Instead, this essay demands that sexuality be the basis for new forms of political mobilization. A spectrum of activists and scholars have made these very demands for decades. For example, amid the racist, sexist, and homophobic vitriol culminating in "the end of welfare as we know it" in 1996, Angela Davis insisted that the intersection of gender, race, and sexuality should be the basis for new alliances. "One of the coalitions that should be encouraged is between welfare rights and gay and lesbian organizations. Both welfare mothers and gays and lesbians are directly targeted by conservative emphasis on 'family values,'" she insisted.[57]

Although Davis's argument might seem dated after a decade of mainstream GLBT political focus on marriage, military service, and "buying for equality," the coalitions she prescribes may be more likely than they seem at first glance. After all, a multiplicity of queer people—whether they identify as gay, lesbian, bisexual, or transgender, or whether they do not—are excluded from the multiple privileges that are interwoven through the nuclear family. As the nuclear family becomes the centerpiece of U.S. social policy after the demise of the welfare state, its constitutive elements—suburban home ownership, a male breadwinner as head of household, white racial privilege, marriage tax breaks, and privatized health services, education, and transportation—are increasingly necessary for economic stability.[58] This intensifying focus on the monogamous nuclear family life dispossesses—rather than emancipates and empowers—populations who deviate from the nuclear family's sexual and gender norms. Interrupting this dispossession by demanding a decoupling of monogamous nuclear family life from public policy prescriptions for education, labor, health care, and retirement is a task that queer political movements must take up.

This space for a queer intervention in public policy is increasingly evident in Minnesota. In early 2008, Minnesota U.S. Representative Michelle Bachmann heralded Minnesota as "America's Workingest State." A longtime militant foe of GLBT political movements, and especially of family benefits for GLBT workers, Bachmann turned her attention to Minnesotans' increasing propensity to work. "We're the workingest state in the country, and the reason why we are, we have more people that are working longer hours, we have people that are working two jobs."[59] Bachmann crafted the "workingest" concept to tout her prowess among Minnesota conservatives long aiming to trim welfare roles in a state once proud of its commitment to social programs. This anti-welfare agenda has sustained efforts to cut corporate taxes—evident in the 25 percent cut proposed in Bachmann's "workingest" speech—and enhance tax breaks for married couples in efforts to make family and work the centerpieces of social policy. Yet, as Bachmann exalts this brave new Minnesota, she admits that more people are working longer hours at more jobs for stagnant wages. Long hours on the job present new pressures for parents and the childless, for nuclear families and single people, and for straights and queers alike. Exposing the empty promises of family and work as the organizing principles of public policy—and exposing the complicity of Bachmann's framework with accumulation by dispossession—will be an increasingly productive horizon for queer politics.

Notes

Special thanks to the activists in the Twin Cities Welfare Rights Committee—and especially to Angel Buechner—for the conversation and dialogue that inspired this chapter. Thanks to Professors Lisa J. Disch and Martin F. Manalansan IV for their generous readings of multiple drafts of this chapter. Thanks to fellow graduate students, especially Lisa Arrastia, Jason Ruiz, Jason M. Stahl, and Alex Urquhart, for ongoing assistance with this project.

1 *State of the City 2000* (Minneapolis: City of Minneapolis Planning Department, 2001), 6–10.

2 "Lavender Night" took place on Nicollet Avenue at Franklin on October 26, 2005. The

event was open to the public and heavily advertised both on billboards in the Stevens Square neighborhood and in full-page ads in local GLBT periodicals.

3 I use the term "GLBT community" because it is the one most commonly used by both the real-estate industry and the gay and mainstream press when analyzing sexuality in urban neighborhoods. This catchall is able to mobilize multiple stereotypes and tropes about sexuality and domesticity, from gay male fabulousness to lesbian nesting to transnormative domesticity. In offering a homogeneous and universal GLBT urban experience, "GLBT community" obscures tensions and contradictions among these individual social locations. When I use *queer* in the text, it is meant to describe sexual spaces and practices that challenge dominant heterosexual and gender-normative standards. I use the term "community" to extend the critique of this category offered in Miranda Joseph, *Against the Romance of Community* (Minneapolis: University of Minnesota Press, 2002).

4 Manuel Castells, *The City and the Grassroots* (Berkeley: University of California Press, 1983).

5 My work on Minneapolis extends the critique of GLBT urban studies offered in Lawrence Knopp, "Some Theoretical Implications of Gay Involvement in the Urban Land Market," *Political Geography Quarterly* 9:4 (October 1990): 347.

6 Joseph, *Against the Romance of Community,* 2.

7 Ingrid Sunderstrom, "After Long Slide, Condo Prices Appear Stable," *Star Tribune,* January 26, 1991, 1R.

8 Terry Fiedler, "New Land Rush," *Star Tribune,* April 18, 2005, 1A.

9 Managers and agents at "Lavender Night" noted that they modeled their event on the overwhelmingly successful TV show *Queen for a Day.*

10 Ann Leviton, personal interview.

11 Ibid.

12 Brookings Institution, *Mind the Gap: Reducing Disparities to Improve Regional Competitiveness in the Twin Cities* (Washington, D.C.: Brookings Institution Metropolitan Policy Program, 2005), 8–9.

13 Brookings Institution, *Mind the Gap,* 11.

14 *State of the City 2000.*

15 Brookings Institution, *Mind the Gap,* 13.

16 Sanders Korenman, Leslie Dwight, and John E. Sjaastad, "The Rise of African American Poverty in the Twin Cities, 1980 to 1990," *CURA Reporter* 27:2 (1997): 6–7.

17 Gillian Partricia Hart, *Disabling Globalization: Places of Power in Post-Apartheid South Africa* (Berkeley: University of California Press, 2002), 39.

18 Ibid., 43.

19 See Grace Kyungwon Hong, *The Ruptures of American Capital: Women of Color Feminism and the Culture of Immigrant Labor* (Minneapolis: University of Minnesota Press, 2006), 33.

20 Jay Powell, "Twin Cities Homicides Dropped in 1999," *Star Tribune,* December 31, 1999, 1B.

21 Leonard Iskip, "Take Those City Rankings with a Healthy Grain of Salt," *Star Tribune,* December 3, 1996, 13A.

22 Dirk Johnson, "Ethnic Change Tests Mettle of Minneapolis Liberalism," *New York Times,* October 18, 1997, late ed., East Coast, A1.

23 James Walsh and Chris Graves, "Companies' Concerns about 'Murderapolis' Fuel Anti-Crime Tactics," *Star Tribune,* April 14, 1997, 1A.

24 Johnson, "Ethnic Change Tests Mettle of Minneapolis Liberalism."

25 Walsh and Graves, "Companies' Concerns about 'Muderapolis' Fuel Anti-Crime Tactics."

26 Johnson, "Ethnic Change Tests Mettle of Minneapolis Liberalism."

27 Edward G. Goetz and Lori Mardock, *Losing Ground: The Twin Cities Livable Communities Act and Affordable Housing* (Minneapolis: Center for Urban and Regional Affairs, 1998), 4–12.

28 Laura Briggs, *Reproducing Empire: Race, Sex, Science, and U.S. Imperialism in Puerto Rico* (Berkeley: University of California Press, 2002), 163.

29 Myron Orfield, *Metropolitics: A Regional Agenda for Community and Stability* (Washington, D.C., and Cambridge, Mass.: Brookings Institution Press and the Lincoln Institute of Land Policy, 1997), 3; emphasis added.

30 For a cogent critique of the way that racialized sexual pathologization shifts intellectual and political focus away from capitalist practices, see Briggs, *Reproducing Empire,* 165. Appraisals of urban poverty often use the presence of female-headed families and subfamilies as primary evidence of urban decline. See, for example, John S. Adams, Barbara J. VanDrasek, and Laura Lambert, *The Path of Urban Decline: What the 1990 Census Says about Minnesota* (Minneapolis: Center for Urban and Regional Affairs, 1995), 71–86.

31 Orfield, *Metropolitics,* 18.

32 Forced removal resulting from "deconcentration" policies officially affected only near-North Minneapolis residents living in the public-housing projects demolished pursuant to the *Hollman v. Cisneros* consent decree. However, the logic of deconcentration pervades much policy and scholarship, including the LCA, the transportation subsidy program for suburban Section 8 housing, and widely read literature of the mid-1990s such as Orfield, *Metropolitics.*

33 Edward G. Goetz, "Deconcentrating Public Housing in Minneapolis: *Hollman v. Cisneros,*" *CURA Reporter* 32:4 (2002): 1–8.

34 Angel Buechner, personal interview, July 7, 2006.

35 Parker Cohen, Jonathan Rogers, and Carlos Espinosa, "Midtown Global Market and the Sears Building: Small Business Incubators and Public/Private Investment," Senior Capstone Project, Macalester College Department of Urban Studies (St. Paul: Macalester College, 2006), 3.

36 For research on security perceptions, see ibid., 20.

37 Angel Beuchner, personal interview, July 7, 2006.

38 Kimberly Hayes Taylor, "Gays Returned Green to Loring Park," *Star Tribune,* September 25, 1994, 1B+.

39 Kim Palmer, "Out in the Market," *Star Tribune,* April 17, 1999, 4H+; Dirk Johnson, "Chicago Celebrates Gay, Lesbian Neighborhood," *Star Tribune,* August 31, 1997, 19A.

40 David Brooks, *Bobos in Paradise: The New Upper Class and How They Got There* (New York: Simon and Schuster, 2001).

41 Richard Florida, *The Rise of the Creative Class . . . and How It's Transforming Work, Leisure, Community, and Everyday Life* (New York: Basic Books, 2002).

42 For a cogent discussion of the role of the marketing of consumption in the urban political economy, see David Harvey, "From Managerialism to Entrepreneurialism: The Transformation of Urban Governance in Late Capitalism," in *Spaces of Capital: Towards a Critical Geography,* ed. David Harvey (New York: Routledge, 2001), 345–69. Harvey argues that elite consumption zones are particularly important as regions compete for private-sector investment amid public-sector austerity associated with neoliberal reforms. Cities compete for capital via postmodern political economic practices, selling "medium over message and image over substance." This analysis understands the Gay Land Rush as a practice of urban entrepreneurialism.

43 Claude Peck, "Supermodels," *Star Tribune,* September 14, 2005, 1H.

44 *Sexton,* Sexton Condominium Project, December 11, 2006. http://www.sextonlive.com.

45 Jim Buchta, "New Condos Offer Owners Luxury Hotel Pampering," *Star Tribune,* May 10, 2006, 1A.

46 *Lavender* (October 28, 2005).

47 "The Fab 50," *Lavender* (October 28, 2005): 22. The BMW was bumped out of first place in the 2006 poll by the even more expensive Mercedes-Benz.

48 "New Book First to Tell How to Tap into $641 Billion of Gay and Lesbian Spending Power," *Harris Interactive/News Room,* September 13, 2006, Harris Interactive, December 11, 2006; http://www.harrisinteractive.com/news/allnewsbydate.asp?NewsID=1091.

49 "This Holiday, Shop for Equality," HRC.com, 2006, Human Rights Campaign, December 11, 2006; http://www.hrc.com.

50 *Buying for Equality 2007* (Washington, D.C: Human Rights Campaign 2006). Statistics

used in this pamphlet and methodological information are from *Corporate Equality Index 2006* (Washington, D.C.: Human Rights Campaign, 2006), 11–13.

51 Joseph's argument depends on Jacques Derrida's notion of supplementarity in *Of Grammatology*. See Joseph, *Against the Romance of Community,* 2.

52 Jerry Fladmark, personal interview, November 14, 2005.

53 Nancy Kelly, personal interview, October 31, 2005.

54 For a history of Ferris Alexander's pornography operations, see Pamela Butler's contribution to this volume.

55 Dylan Hicks, "Boomtown," *City Pages,* July 7, 2004, 1.

56 "The Bulldog Restaurant—Citysearch," Twin Cities.Citysearch.com, 2006, Citysearch.com, December 11, 2006; http://twincities.citysearch.com/profile/37348835/.

57 Lisa Lowe, "Angel David: Reflections on Race, Class, and Gender," in *The Politics of Culture in the Shadow of Capital,* ed. Lisa Lowe and David Lloyd (Durham, N.C.: Duke University Press, 1997), 322.

58 See Lisa Duggan, *The Twilight of Equality?: Neoliberalism, Cultural Politics, and the Attack on Democracy* (Boston: Beacon Press, 2003).

59 Tom Elko, "Bachmann Proud Minnesota 'Workingest' State," *Minnesota Monitor* (January 16, 2008), Minnesota Monitor.com, May 9, 2008; http://www.minnesotamonitor.com/showDiary.do?diaryId=3047.

10. PRIVATE CURES FOR A PUBLIC EPIDEMIC

TARGET(ING) HIV AND AIDS MEDICATIONS IN THE TWIN CITIES

Alex T. Urquhart and Susan Craddock

On a predictably cold day in February 2005, the Minnesota HIV Services Planning Council held its monthly meeting at the Redeemer Missionary Baptist Church. The organization was, as usual, seeing to its primary mandate of allocating Ryan White Funds.[1] For those living with HIV, one of their most important functions was and is the allocation of this money to the AIDS Drug Assistance Program, more commonly known as ADAP, run by the Minnesota Department of Human Services (DHS). Over years of political and economic shifts, the council has faced a number of difficult decisions. But on February 8, 2005, the council, comprised of HIV-positive individuals, service providers, and administrators, began to plan for the day when money used to purchase HAART (Highly Active Anti-Retroviral Therapy) medications would no longer meet the demand of those in Minnesota in need of ADAP assistance.

The council was in the middle of an impossible dilemma. To disqualify participants, delay treatment, and even limit drugs is akin to a death sentence for those otherwise unable to afford their medications. Yet ADAP enrollments were continuing to grow and funds were not increasing at the same pace. The council needed a way to continue the program while containing the ever-growing costs. The decision emerging from this meeting was that the ethical dilemma was too much for it to decide alone. Instead, the Minnesota HIV Planning Council and the DHS hired an ethicist. In the year preceding the February meeting, this person evaluated possible solutions and developed a rationing plan that the council reviewed and accepted in June 2006. From that point on, some would get AIDS drugs while others would have to wait, hoping they moved up the list before opportunistic infections began to attack their bodies.

This emerging politics of scarcity is surprising in a number of ways. First and foremost, the struggle against HIV/AIDS would seem to have more allies than ever before. Just weeks before the adoption of a system that would "ethically" decide who would live and who would die, the Minnesota AIDS Walk—the most public face of HIV/AIDS prevention and services in the state of Minnesota—had multinational finance institutions, global retailers, and the University of Minnesota (one of the largest research universities in the world) literally lining up behind the cause. The most visible of these participants was Target, one of the largest retailers in the United States and a focal point of Twin Cities economic activity. Target's corporate headquarters lights up the skyline in colors announcing holidays, seasons, and even gay pride. With such powerful and wealthy allies, why was it becoming harder to access AIDS drugs?

This chapter attempts to explain the contradiction between these two phenomena. The first is a trajectory of scarcity represented by ADAP waiting lists and ethicists. The second is a narrative of abundance signified through corporate participation in the fight against AIDS in Minnesota, the United States, and globally. Our purpose is to demonstrate how the two are actually linked. We argue that the current political-economic constellation of AIDS activism, university research, corporate capital, and government policies has produced a world in which an amorphous commitment to fighting AIDS has simultaneously mandated increases in decisions of life and death.

In explaining the forces shaping this contradiction in Minnesota and beyond, we reject the idea that waiting lists and other manifestations of antiretroviral inaccessibility are inevitable results of shrinking state and federal budgets and rising cases of AIDS. Rather, we argue that they are the result of specific structures, relations, and policies that shape the way AIDS treatments are produced, while simultaneously obscuring ongoing university, governmental, and corporate relationships that maintain prohibitively high prices on antiretroviral drugs. While ethicists determine the most ethical, rational, and fair model of deciding who will live and who will die, our goal is to demonstrate that such agonizing decisions concerning the differential valuation of human lives should be unnecessary in the context of an ever-increasing number of antiretroviral drugs.

In drawing out the forces mandating these ethical quandaries, this chapter examines two case studies in the Twin Cities: the history of the Minnesota AIDS Walk as organized by the Minnesota AIDS Project (MAP) and the history of the conflict surrounding the University of Minnesota's HIV/AIDS drug Abacavir. Of specific importance is how these case studies manifest changing relationships to the state, community, queer politics, and disease. Using interviews, our own activist experiences, and archival research, we argue in the first case study that AIDS walks emerged as a way to raise awareness about HIV/AIDS, to make specific political and economic demands on the state for better funding and institutional support of prevention and treatment programs, and for expedited biomedical research on vaccines and antiretroviral drugs.[2] However, as AIDS walks have evolved, there has been a greater emphasis on their need to raise funds for HIV prevention programs from community agencies rather than the state. Integral to this shift has been a change in which bodies are made political and visible. In the second case study, what resides at the core of our analysis is the University of Minnesota's AIDS drug Abacavir. We examine the same dwindling visibility of AIDS as an issue relevant to a wide public constituency. Here our argument provides an illustration of a contentious relationship among university biomedical research, corporate dictate, and accountability to a nebulously defined public whose political validity is even more tenuous.

Central to these case studies is how a local, national, and global crisis of ethics is a product of a specific set of practices and ideologies organized around the mobilization of economic resources in the private sector, as opposed to demands that the state respond to a public health emergency, that has generated new conjugations of disenfranchisement and community politics that directly translate into increased AIDS morbidity and mortality. Using our two case studies, we explore some of the implications of this shift to a private paradigm: the changes in deployments and articulations of queer identities, how these identities and communities then make demands on the state and private-sector actors, and the politics of private versus public funding and its consequences for the AIDS pandemic in the Twin Cities and globally. In presenting these case studies, we want to highlight the often-invisible forms of violence inhering within the institutional and corporate relations we examine.

Broader-based critiques of the economic and social relations, what many scholars and activists call neoliberalism, have focused on the violence of welfare reform, structural adjustment programs, or low wages, but recently more studies are also focusing on neoliberalism's deleterious impacts on disease and suffering.[3] We add to this growing literature by arguing that the denial of AIDS drugs to the global South and to growing poor populations in the global North is unequivocally part of the coercive and violent manifestations of the imperative of profit under neoliberal capitalism that ultimately plays out in the death of millions.

Furthermore, we argue that the politics of AIDS walks and the dissemination of antiretrovirals exist in structures, institutions, and ideologies that both shape and emerge from these neoliberal politics as apparatuses at the core of changing relationships among government, the economy, social movements, and disease.[4] In exploring these case studies we hope to elucidate the inadequately explored question of why scientific achievement in the form of antiretrovirals and social interventions have not translated into better containment of an epidemic. In making this assertion, we believe that distinct new sets of identities around AIDS and queerness must be drawn upon to propel this transition from a politics based on the legacy of the welfare state to a neoliberal politics based on the privatization of public health infrastructure and the development of new or stronger relationships between private and public entities. In conclusion, we argue that these local politics and processes of the Twin Cities have a profound and lasting impact on the national and global geography of HIV and the landscape of disease.

ADAP, the Politics of Scarcity, and the Biosocial Reality of Disease

ADAP was designed to help those with and without private insurance who otherwise could not afford drug therapy. The seed money for these programs comes from the federal government, but the specificity of how it is allocated is largely defined by the states. In the mid-2000s, federal Ryan White money accounted for approximately a third of Minnesota's ADAP budget; the rest came from drug company rebates and the state of Minnesota. To qualify in Minnesota during this time period, a person had to be HIV-positive, have earnings equaling less than three times the federal poverty line, be uninsured or have an insurance program with prohibitive drug co-pays, and not be enrolled in another federal or state healthcare program. Until the beginning of the millennium, ADAP in Minnesota often had funding surpluses. By 2004, however, the program's surplus was spiraling toward deficit. Responding to the impending crisis, Minnesota enacted a policy whereby ADAP enrollees would "make monthly payments to continue participation in the program."[5] Those who failed to make these "cost-sharing" payments would be removed from the program, and by 2005 a number of AIDS patients were no longer receiving assistance. Individuals were removed from the program because they owed between five hundred and a thousand dollars. DHS Assistant Commissioner Loren Coleman, in defending this policy, stated in an interview with the *Star Tribune* that "Cost sharing has allowed us to avoid any waiting lists or changes in benefits."[6] The DHS was aware that, given the trends it was seeing, this was only the tip of the ethical iceberg ahead. In just four years since the dawn of a new millennium, "the number of patients in Minnesota's ADAP ha[d] grown by about 50 percent, while the state contribution ha[d] dropped by about 1 percent,"[7] and there was little sign that the trend would be reversed. By 2005, more than 1,200 individuals—approximately a fourth of all HIV cases in Minnesota—were receiving ADAP support.[8] Need for AIDS drugs was increasing at a rate far higher than new HIV cases. Given that demand was exceeding supply and the gap between them was only increasing, the 2006 adoption of an ADAP rationing system seemed the only solution.

This problem was new to Minnesota, but AIDS drug rationing is not new in the United States, and is standard in most of the global South. Minnesota was implementing what, as of 2005, eleven other states had already done. In the midst of crisis, the state was also considering other cost-saving measures implemented in other state ADAP programs. If rationing was not enough, the state was also considering reducing the number of drugs available through the program, capping enrollment on some of the more expensive drugs like Fuzeon, capping monthly expenditures per client, or instituting stricter eligibility requirements.[9]

As employers were slashing benefits to their employees, as more and more people were finding themselves in low-paying service jobs often with no health benefits, and as prescription co-pays and drug prices were continuing to rise, it was no surprise that ADAP was being inundated with new enrollees. Combined with the fact that HIV infections in Minnesota were on the rise, this trend foreshadowed a future in which Minnesota ADAP's minor deficits would transition into major shortfalls in funding. In the future, the state would be forced to make more and more hard decisions impacting the lives of Minnesotans living with HIV.

This precarious future of ADAP represents the current predicament facing AIDS services in Minnesota, the United States, and numerous countries in the global South, a predicament where life is as much a product of political and economic decisions as it is of the biological organism attacking the body. For epidemiologists, this crisis becomes a set of statistical representations of a biological event. They measure the severity of an epidemic in terms of morbidity (the frequency in occurrence of a disease or infectious agent in a place) and mortality (the number of people who die from that particular illness), but the political, economic, and social worlds in which disease agents spread and kill is always represented in these statistics. We can see this in the example of ADAP's cost-sharing policies. When DHS dropped the first three individuals from ADAP because of their failure to pay, the effect (likely, eventual death) will be represented in the mortality of HIV. The act itself will not. AIDS drugs serve as a technology that keeps people alive, but when policies stop providing them or categorically deny people access, these social acts become represented in AIDS mortality. The move to understand these social forces in terms of epidemiology is what Paul Farmer argues is understanding HIV as a biosocial reality.[10]

At the heart of this concept is that even though HIV is a biological agent that invades cells and destroys immune systems, how it spreads and whom it kills is as much a product of the social world as of the biological. Understanding HIV as a biosocial reality means examining how viruses are empowered by the social formations that produce poverty, in the same ways that they are curbed by technologies like AIDS drugs—which are themselves social formations. Prevalence of HIV in the global South in populations characterized by poverty, limited public health infrastructures, and global debt have translated into huge populations of the sick and the dying.[11] Similarly, social processes that force individuals into sexual lives rooted in economic dependence become represented in the frequency of HIV in a particular place. When who we have sex with and how we have sex becomes conditional on meeting our basic needs—food, shelter, clothing—negotiating AIDS risk becomes that much more difficult.

In Minnesota, the biosocial reality of the AIDS epidemic has changed significantly since the first infections in the early 1980s. Many of these changes have meant a dramatic diminution of both the morbidity and the mortality of AIDS. One of the most important developments has been the advent of HAART treatments. One of these, Abacavir, was developed at the University of Minnesota. There was also a significant activist response to HIV in Minnesota. This response included a small but committed ACT-UP cell, a proliferation of community-based social services and advocacy, and a substantial state response. The Twin Cities are home to the Minnesota AIDS Project (MAP), services that house people living with AIDS (PLWAs) such as Clare Housing, PRIDE Alive, the Rural AIDS Action Network, free food and delivery service to PLWAs through Open Arms of Minnesota, the African American AIDS Task Force, Red Door Clinic, and the American Indian AIDS Task Force. HAART and NGOs have prolonged lives and thwarted the rise of HIV infections and deaths from AIDS. Put simply, their interventions mitigated both the biological morbidity and the mortality of HIV by tirelessly working on prevention efforts and demanding the existence of programs like ADAP.

The future of ADAP, however, demonstrates that these positive forces can no longer hold the tide. While drugs have prolonged the lives of many, they did not, as Andrew Sullivan suggested, end the AIDS epidemic.[12] In fact, the story of ADAP and epidemiological tracking would suggest the opposite.[13] Just as a number of social forces worked to decrease the number of people with HIV and increase length and quality of life, the future of ADAP suggests that a number of social forces are now working against that trend. Most often blamed are new drug-resistant viral strains, changes in gay male sexual habits, changing U.S. demographics, and new recreational drugs. While these are indeed part of recent shifts in HIV/AIDS morbidity and mortality, they are insufficient to explain why the increase in ADAP enrollment outpaces rates of new infections. They do not account for the forces that are denying drugs to individuals who need them. In the course of this epidemic, other forces have shifted the biosocial epidemiology of HIV in a way that mandates more and more ethical quandaries regarding who will live and who will die. In the following two case studies, we account for this shifting biosocial epidemiology of HIV by examining the same activist organizations and AIDS drug policies that once positively impacted HIV/AIDS morbidity and mortality in the past and now are falling short.

A Change of Shirt for the AIDS Walk

The first AIDS Pledge Walk in the Twin Cities was on May 22, 1988. It was the capstone event to a week of activities and fund-raisers organized by the Minnesota AIDS Project. It launched under the title "From All Walks of Life" to raise money for care, research, and education.[14] The ten-kilometer event left Minnehaha Park—a beautiful site of open fields, historic buildings, a waterfall, picnic areas, and barbeque pits that bursts with life for as long as the often-harsh Minnesota winter allows. After leaving this pastoral setting, the Walk followed a path along the Mississippi River. The inaugural year saw more than a thousand participants and generated close to one hundred thousand dollars.[15] Organized by Pete Bissonette, MAP, and a number of volunteers, the Walk was a "usual pledge pitch for money, but the face-to-face appeal for understanding [was] more important: 'It's OK and safe to care about people with AIDS.'"[16] As the crowd marched, church bells rang in solidarity with the participants and radio stations played "That's What Friends Are For" and "Friends Everywhere."[17] The event was small and there was no corporate participation.

In the 1988 Walk, the bodies of people living with AIDS were on center stage. The papers reported PLWAs attempting the Walk, a challenge for many given low T-cell counts and a number of attendant illnesses. The image of a man crawling over a bridge, emaciated from opportunistic infections and obviously sick, was a way not only to draw attention to the disease, but also to highlight the lack of government and state response to a deadly epidemic.[18] The Walk projected the stark reality of HIV through the bodies of Minnesotans. Those with HIV who were still healthy politicized their bodies in other ways. Wearing T-shirts that marked themselves as HIV-positive was common, but in 1988 even embodying a queer aesthetic was enough to mark oneself as positive, or at least at risk. In the inaugural Walk, absent bodies were also used to make HIV a visible issue. Many held picket signs in memory of a friend, lover, or family member who had died. The absent body, the spectral body, conveyed the sense of loss as a tactic to heal, remember, and make the casualties of the epidemic indelible. In the early days of AIDS, the idea was to make the disease public and, more important, to publicize the shame of allowing people to die. Making HIV-positive bodies, ill bodies, and the spectral body hypervisible was thus an invaluable tactic to leverage access to drugs, public research, and services.[19]

In 2010, MAP launched its twenty-third Pledge Walk. Over the years, many features had remained the same, yet one can hardly believe that the first Walk and the one today share the same genealogy. It is still run by MAP, Minnehaha Park still acts as command and control, and it follows the same beautiful scenery along the Mississippi River. It also continues to be an important opportunity to take a stand against the stigma associated with the disease. People continue to march in remembrance of those who died from indifference and in solidarity with friends and family who continue to face the political/economic/personal challenges related to HIV/AIDS, just as they did in the inaugural Walk.

The Walk is, however, much bigger. It draws nearly ten times as many participants and generates a similar increase in gross revenue. Corporate booths now litter Minnehaha Park. The 2006 event lists Asian Pages, RBC Dain Rausher, Whole Foods Market, Radio K, *Lavender* magazine, Karell, KDWB101.3, the Rake, K102, Cities97, Ameriprise Financial, Bioscript Pharmacy, ING, Marshall Fields, Dex, Metro Transit, and last but not least, Target as corporate sponsors. Walkers are handed food, beverages, and advertiser merchandise at each mile. Other corporations sponsor groups of walkers but are not listed as official sponsors. These corporate "teams" sporting matching T-shirts trumpeting corporate commitment to fighting AIDS march alongside cohorts in matching T-shirts remembering a loved one. Today, the corporate T-shirts vastly outnumber the images of HIV status and the spectral body. At the first Walk, at center were absent loved ones and personal HIV status, whereas at the 2006 AIDS Walk the landscape was dominated instead by corporate America.

This new corporate visibility has definitively changed the politics of the Minnesota AIDS Walk. Many believe that this new visibility is a positive force because it adds validity and respectability to a disease closely aligned with social stigma. But in exchange for validity and respectability, corporate participation politicizes the body in a different way, or, more precisely, it politicizes a different body. Corporate America's participation and gift of "respectability" requires that a respectable body, abstracted from the realities of disease, supplant the ill, infected, and spectral bodies that once served to set the political message of the Walk.

The 1988 Walk did not have a message that worked for corporate America. HIV is a disease that is deeply embedded in images of intravenous drug use, sex work, blood, semen, rape, poverty, homelessness, racism, violence against women, and not being able to afford AIDS drugs, food, and rent. These are not images that sell the products of corporate America. In fact, the externalities of death, sickness, and exploitation are the very liabilities to corporate America that companies seek to distance themselves from via participation in community events like the AIDS Walk. So, in resisting the stigma of AIDS, in securing funding, and in exchange for validity and respectability, AIDS organizations in the Twin Cities and elsewhere often find themselves creating fund-raising events that, often unintentionally, reflect the needs of corporations. Therefore, the sick, dead, and dying body has been replaced in these partnerships so that the needs of community-service organizations (funding) can align with the needs of corporate America (profit). The Walk over the years has become corporation friendly.

Making the Walk corporate friendly is only possible if the bodies closely associated with the realities of HIV that dominated the 1988 Walk are erased or disciplined into the category of respectable. This is not necessarily an intentional act of repression, but a product of not directly addressing the forces that produce these acts of erasure and discipline. For example, Somali women, African American women, and queers of color were largely rendered invisible in the 2006 Walk.[20] Although these bodies make their appearance prominently in Minnesota HIV statistics, they are not part of the Walk. Highlighting the absence of racialized nonheteronormative bodies is not a call for an AIDS multiculturalism, but rather points to how corporate participation transforms the Minnesota AIDS Walk in particular ways. Although Somali women, African American women, and queers of color often work for the companies that now populate the Walk, racist and sexist social practices are far more likely to produce these workers as frontline employees.[21] Taking a weekend walk in a park has a different meaning for a "team member" who works in a high-rise for a salary than it does for a frontline checker who needs to work two jobs, including weekend shifts, to make ends meet. Wearing the mandatory red shirt for Target on a day off is different from putting it on for "fun."[22] Corporate salaried employees get to dress down while frontline employees are actually wearing a version of their uniform on their day off. Making the walk corporate friendly requires reproducing, as opposed to challenging, the social forces that shape the racialized workplace.

While people of color were often erased at the 2006 AIDS Walk, white gay men—the largest statistical HIV demographic in the state of Minnesota—remained. They were however, disciplined into a particular performance of gay erotic expression understood as "respectable." As a few younger, white, gay men half-joked about having sex in the bushes and getting AIDS at the AIDS Walk, a white Minnesota mother pushing a stroller and a white thirty-something gay male couple in Target T-shirts separately scoffed at what they perceived to be the tackiness of the comment. Similarly, a group of white women registered their disdain when a man rubbing his eye was asked by his effeminate male friend, "Cum in your eye?" to which he replied, "Little bit, little bit." These interactions highlight how a gay community is still part of the Walk, but one that is disciplined out of erotic expression. These types of performances, while acceptable in a gay bar, are not acceptable in the office. The gay men in Target T-shirts may indeed enjoy sex in the bushes, but speaking to that desire in front of coworkers is taboo. The act of making an AIDS Walk corporate friendly thus unintentionally reproduces the sexual regulations of the office that make being gay "respectable" in the workplace.

Corporate participation at the AIDS walk in many ways transplants what Lisa Duggan describes as a politics of homonormativity from the business world to what is often thought of as a gay community event. Duggan describes homonormativity as "a politics that does not contest the dominant heteronormative assumptions and institutions, but upholds and sustains them, while promising the possibility of a demobilized gay constituency and a privatized, depoliticized gay culture anchored in domesticity and consumption."[23] Making AIDS a respectable issue via homonormativity at the AIDS Walk, however, has actually reproduced an even more draconian erasure of erotic expression than Duggan describes. Retailers often seek association with, if not outright sponsorship of, Pride events because the glamorous and sexualized gay body on display in these venues helps the image of their products. Young gays joking sexually is what makes Pride interesting and edgy. Getting partnerships at the AIDS Walk requires something else.

Sponsoring Pride festivals provides an opportunity to brand a vanguard of young attractive gay men and high-end fashionable lesbians. Pride celebrations are filled with the edgy sexuality and even sex that corporate America often pays unbelievable amounts of money to an ad agency to produce. For example, the national Target advertising campaign in June 2006, the same time as Pride, was of a young, attractive, skinny man in muscle shirts and the same model wearing swimsuits with no shirt among Target products. In terms of visual images, there seems little difference between this and a group of gay men with well-chiseled and proportioned bodies sipping high-end vodka cocktails with their shirts off and a well-placed Target Pride tattoo adding to their sexual capital. A temporary target tattoo, however, is much cheaper than a national advertising campaign. At the AIDS Walk these same images in the context of HIV imply AIDS transmission, not a sexy and glamorous consumer lifestyle. Maintaining the alliance between corporate America and AIDS funding at the 2006 AIDS Walk required a white, gay male body, but one disciplined out of erotic expression.

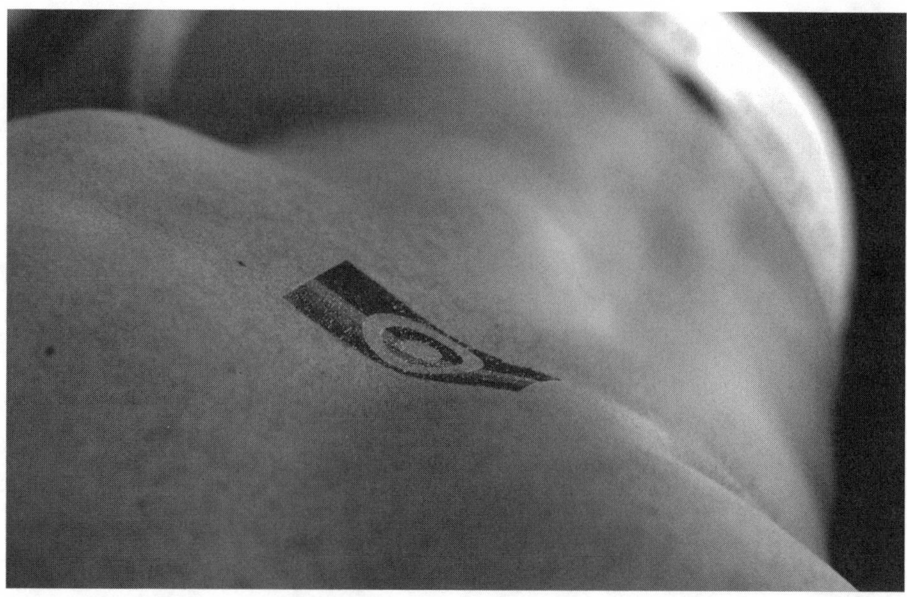

Tattoo of rainbow flag with Target logo distributed at Twin Cities Pride. Target volunteers use sponges to place thousands of these images on Pride participants every year. Photograph by Pamela Butler.

These acts of erasure and disciplining have fundamentally shifted the focus of the Walk away from the HIV-positive body, ill body, spectral body, or even at-risk body that fueled the 1988 Walk. What is on display at the Walk in 2006 is not even the homonormative body, but something new entirely: countless white, straight couples make out, snuggle on picnic blankets, herd children, and push strollers. Meanwhile, University of Minnesota cheerleaders perform high kicks in short skirts. In numbers and in exhibitionism, these are the bodies politicized at the 2006 AIDS Walk. Again, these bodies are symbols associated not with HIV transmission but with white, procreative, and productive domesticity. As a white Minnesota cheerleader kicks her leg into the air, her blond ponytail bouncing—the precise image of white, heterosexual, domestic purity that has long been proffered as the cure for AIDS—one does not imagine her life deeply embedded in the realities of HIV. Although she might indeed have an intense connection to the epidemic or be positive herself, neoconservative and public health rhetoric has long espoused the view that it is the choice not to embrace all that she represents that has caused the AIDS epidemic in the first place.[24] Her central presence, combined with the cultural legacies of the discourse of HIV, causes queer sex and its association with HIV to be replaced by heterosexual sexuality and heteronormative reproduction as the body on display at the 2006 AIDS Walk. The cheerleader is able to accomplish what the HIV-positive body and spectral body never could—it is an image of AIDS that makes you want to buy corporate products. The most unfortunate part of this transition is the equation that emerges at the 2006 AIDS Walk, namely, that the cure for AIDS is heterosexual sex and retail therapy.

While retail therapy and heterosexual sex may be more fun than multidrug cocktails, they are far less practical in fighting the AIDS pandemic. These domesticated gay bodies and normative straight bodies, unlike those that predated them, are necessary for "respectability" because they are not a site of contradiction to corporate policies and practices. It is a substitution to buy corporate participation, but these new bodies on display cannot be leveraged in the same ways the spectral and diseased bodies once were. The cheerleader demands smiles and dancing, not AIDS drugs and social services.

In fact, the new image at the center of the AIDS Walk actually obfuscates processes that are hindering the fight against HIV. As we watch the high-kicking cheerleader for the University of Minnesota, we forget the role her university has played in keeping drug prices high. As thousands walk around in corporate T-shirts, it is harder to see a history where corporations have continually sought to deprive workers of health-care benefits and lobbied for a structure that underfunds or eliminates much-needed social services.[25] As the ADAP dilemma shows, this antagonism is still alive and well in AIDS morbidity and mortality, just not in the staging of the AIDS Walk. The staging of the AIDS Walk instead hides the hand that corporate America has played in producing this very politics of scarcity. AIDS activist rhetoric has not changed, but the addition of corporate America makes it seem like just another activist has joined the cause. With a change of shirt, the politics of the Walk has changed.

"Price Check, Pharmacy Aisle"

Although the interests of corporate friendliness allow a new image of respectability to dominate the AIDS Walk, it is important to understand the price tag that accompanies this transition. To uncover this impact, the most fruitful site of interrogation is the dominant player at the 2006

Minnesota AIDS Walk. One might assume that MAP, the organizer of the event, would be this dominant player, but the evidence points elsewhere. From signs to brochures to people, all evidence points to the Target Corporation as the most significant contributor to the Walk. The Walk has become so corporate friendly that corporations eclipse the organizers.

Target's involvement in the AIDS Walk is predictable in Minnesota. In part, this is because the Target Corporation, headquartered in Minneapolis, has cast itself as a kinder, gentler corporation. It has pioneered the 5 percent rule, written into its bylaws in 1946 (when it was Dayton-Hudson), and has encouraged other corporations to follow.[26] This rule is guided by the principle that 5 percent of the corporation's gross revenue will be used for charitable causes. It funds schools, contributes to the arts, sponsors the Minnesota AIDS Walk, and attempts to integrate itself into the landscape and practices of community. Seemingly a call to Target's humanitarian goals, Target uses this 5 percent campaign to cast itself as the positive alternative to Wal-Mart, its largest competitor. In return, communities fight to exclude Wal-Mart, while Target is often recruited with tax subsidies and favorable zoning laws.[27]

Target may say it is kinder and gentler, but it follows industry standards and has a zero union density workforce that it vehemently works to maintain.[28] Part-time employees have no health benefits and full-time employees often cannot afford to enroll on the wages Target pays.[29] Under this model, any Target part-time employee working twenty hours a week and earning under thirty dollars an hour would qualify for ADAP in Minnesota.[30] Even at full time a frontline worker would need to make at least fifteen dollars an hour to not qualify for ADAP in 2006. These wages are calculated for someone with no dependents. Someone with two kids in the same scenario would need to earn more than twenty-five dollars an hour not to qualify for ADAP. Target's employment model, like that of most corporate retailers, produces employees who require ADAP assistance if they are HIV-positive.

Additionally, Target has one of the most advanced "loss recovery and prevention" departments in the world and regularly partners with and accepts contracts from the FBI. Its lab in the center of downtown Minneapolis is considered one of the leading forensic labs in the world, and part of its function is to develop techniques for policing its employees and customers. So, what does it mean to be a kinder, gentler corporate retailer? How do we understand this new friendly corporate world? Target is a leader in philanthropy, on the one hand, and the traditional mechanism of exploitation, on the other. How can Target be the cure for AIDS when it produces employees who on their own could not afford their treatment?

What generates and allows this contradiction to stand is Target's unmatched ability to brand itself and its products. And it is very good at it. Target wins more awards for branding than any other company. And it is not stopping with its logo. At the 2003 Retail Advertising Conference in Chicago, Target took home thirty-seven awards, more than any other company. A reporter covering the event highlighted this brand identity when he wrote:

> "We are no longer satisfied with owning the bull's-eye, now we want to own the color red." To show how committed the company is to this goal, he treated RAC attendees to an image of chairman and CEO Bob Ulrich dressed all in red, a portrait that hangs, said Francis, in the company's new corporate headquarters in Minneapolis. A building that itself is topped in red lights.[31]

Target's participation in the AIDS Walk must be understood as part of this larger branding campaign. The 5 percent branding campaign, however, is arguably more profitable than it is humanitarian. In 2001–2 Minneapolis participated in a nationwide protest against Wal-Mart, while the city of Minneapolis paid more than $100 million to open one Target store in downtown.[32] The 5 percent campaign brands Target as an activist in the same way that its corporate advertisers and marketers have a manifest destiny for the color red. At the AIDS Walk, its 5 percent branding campaign and the branding of the color red even align in disturbing ways. The branding of HIV—a red ribbon—is not far from a red Target logo, and in the corporation's trademarking of the color red it seemingly had its sights set on the red ribbon.

In fact, at the 2006 AIDS Walk, red ribbons, the symbol of an "AIDS community," were substituted for the Red Target—a symbol of Target's commitment to the free market, but the substitution often went unnoticed. The miracle for Target is that it has been able to litter the landscape of the AIDS Walk with corporate logos as a direct substitution for the activist red ribbon branding campaign. At the Target booth, "goodie" bags are passed out with Target-brand sunscreen, visor, and other Target products, along with a red T-shirt that is covered with Target logos on the front, and the back bannered with "Real Passion, Real Commitment, Real Difference."

Almost a fourth of the people at the Walk wear the shirt. Some wear shirts fresh out of the bag, while others brought the identical shirt from previous years. Dogs prance about with Target handkerchiefs tied around their necks. Children play with toys given to them at the Target booth and Target-logoed pinwheels are attached to strollers, bicycles, and backpacks. The beginning of the Walk is outlined by thousands of these same pinwheels. Red ribbons are actually hard to find in the sea of red Target gear and were only prominently visible on the outskirts of the park at the 2006 Walk.

In this visual scene of T-shirts and community rhetoric, corporate America—and Target in particular—is transformed into an AIDS activist. The community of PLWAs and their supporters that were symbolized by the red ribbon introduced in the early 1990s has been replaced at the Minnesota AIDS Walk by Target's red bull's-eye, understood not as a corporation but as a community with "Real Passion, Real Commitment, Real Difference." If Target now is understood as community, then it is not part of the violence of profit under capitalism that ensures that AIDS drugs are prohibitively expensive and complicated, fights unionism, fights fair wages, and demands conditions of poverty. Target is using the AIDS Walk to brand itself as an AIDS activist, the supposed antithesis to the politics of profit that proliferates with AIDS. In proclaiming a "Real Commitment" to fighting HIV/AIDS, Target is able to cast itself as the "good guy"—or "good buy"—in the fight against the epidemic.

This branding enterprise, however, needs a very particular community, a community of consumers, a community that is not associated with the realities of HIV and is instead centered on the trappings of heterosexual domesticity—something that is only possible if the AIDS Walk is made respectable and corporate friendly, as the 2006 Walk was. But are Target's manufacturing policies in the global South a commitment to end AIDS or a proliferation of AIDS? Does the antiunionism in the United States at Target stores help or hinder access to AIDS drugs?[33] Are Target's contributions to elected officials who support abstinence-only sex education both here and abroad a "Real Commitment" to fighting AIDS?[34] Recent Federal Election Commission (FEC) filings for contributions by Robert Ulrich and Target Corporation are almost exclusively to Republican candidates and the Republican National Committee. In funding Republican candidates, Target has financed the mandates of abstinence-only education and the gag rule. So, while it fights AIDS at the AIDS Walk, in other instances the proliferation of HIV serves its bottom line. Furthermore, it achieved this branding while contributing very little in terms of real money to fight HIV.[35] Not only is branding the AIDS Walk profitable, it is cheap.

The biggest question needs to be: is Target making a "Real Difference," as its T-shirt claims? The key is that these political configurations do help people, but only some people. Target's participation makes a "Real Difference" for some people with AIDS. The money it raises is very important for funding MAP and securing HAART treatments for people with AIDS in the Twin Cities. But we must remember just how small Target's contribution really is. This is often obscured because of how much time and energy corporations spend touting their philanthropic enterprises. It is well within the norm for corporations to spend significantly more money advertising their contributions to "community" than to give directly to those communities. If we judged proportionally how much Target means in the fight against AIDS based on the number of Target logos at the Walk, we would be led to believe that, yes, indeed, Target is going to save us and the world from AIDS. The reality, however, is that corporate donations represent only a small fraction of the Walk's revenue, and an even smaller fraction of MAP's total budget. More than 70 percent of MAP's funding comes from public, not private, sources, so Target's contribution is a small fraction of the total.[36] ADAP is entirely funded by the state and federal governments. The state role, however, in funding these organizations has been made invisible because of the hypervisibility of corporate participation. While the state is blamed for ADAP waiting lists, the visibility of corporate participation in an AIDS movement is increasing. The problem is that increases in corporate funding do not always correspond with increases in visibility. MAP receives millions of dollars from public sources, and as these public sources are removed, or become inadequate, private sources are unable—and often unwilling—to pick up the slack. Target has never offered to fix the funding disparity in Minnesota's ADAP program.

This is what branding is designed to do. It increases value beyond the use value of the product. What branding does for Target at the AIDS Walk is increase its surplus value in the commodity of activism. Target may be the new activist on the scene, but branding does little to put drugs in the hands of those who need them or offer wages that allow choice in negotiating informal and formal sexual economies. As corporations have branded AIDS activism and made it "respectable," HIV has only proliferated. Corporate participation is making a difference—just not the difference that

The pill organizer distributed by Target volunteers at the 2006 AIDS Walk. Photograph by Pamela Butler.

their branding campaign would have us believe. The Walk tells a fiction that Target is going to be the cure for AIDS. Meanwhile, corporations like Target continue to advocate the destruction of the tax base that funds these services.[37] As corporate lobbies have successfully sought to downsize state services, money to HIV/AIDS has shrunk. Services are shrinking at the hand of the very corporations that are being touted as saviors.

Target admits that the 5 percent campaign is a good business practice. It is good in terms of real money, reputation, assuaging shareholder guilt, and making Target look like a strong leader. Target's contribution is 5 percent. The Target store on the Nicollet Mall next to the corporate headquarters received $115 million in tax incentives, which is just slightly less than what it gave out to the entire country in 2006.[38] If we do the arithmetic, the 5 percent campaign is a net loss to tax revenue that could be used for social services in Minnesota.[39] The process of branding would have us believe otherwise, but the impact is real. Target's policies are creating people in need of ADAP at the same time that it is making the program harder to fund.

Target's branding of the 2006 Walk was so complete that it even distributed daily pill organizers to the crowd. Given out by attractive coeds in short shorts, at the center of the red seven-sided box is a white Target logo. Here, Target was not only branding the AIDS Walk but branding the experience of taking antiretrovirals. If the box were big enough, the treatment for AIDS would supposedly come out of a Target box—that is, if you could afford the drugs that go into that box. What must be made clear is that while Target may provide the box to hold antiretrovirals, its policies help produce waiting lists for those who need to fill that box. At the same time, by branding HIV activism in the Twin Cities, Target is transforming the corporation from something one might leverage in protest, boycott, and strike into one's friend and ally. All the while, the politics of profit remains the same. The example of Target at the AIDS Walk is an example of a low-cost public-relations campaign that has ensured Target's ever-increasing profitability and the continuation of HIV/AIDS.[40]

The University–Corporate Nexus

Indeed, the pill organizer handed out by Target representatives is, literally, an empty gesture—empty because, until recently (and at the time of the AIDS Walk), the box's handy compartments for daily pill consumption were too small to contain all of the pills needed for multidrug antiretroviral regimens available for those living in the United States and covered by health insurance, and because the compartments would remain empty for the vast majority of those living in low-income regions. Target's pillbox is in fact an unwitting symbol of the contradiction between scientific breakthroughs on chemical compounds able to keep PLWAs alive, on the one hand, and, on the other, the articulated set of national and global regulations keeping the marketed versions of those compounds unaffordable to the vast majority who need them. A compound developed by scientists at the University of Minnesota and subsequently marketed as the antiretroviral Ziagen illustrates the complex interplay of science, policy, and profit that has become costly in terms of lives as well as dollars. The University of Minnesota's discovery has also played a part in the international backlash against university–corporate relations embodying ethically tenuous practices in contradiction to the stated mission of public universities. The contours of this backlash, especially as it has played out at the University of Minnesota, illustrate in very different ways from the AIDS Walk the divergent definition of community, its relation to corporate practice, and the multiple roles of university, science, and government in determining the neoliberal canvas of treatment access regulations and activism.

In 1987, researchers at Minnesota discovered a compound that they called Carbovir, which was subsequently patented and licensed exclusively with GlaxoSmithKline, one of the world's largest pharmaceutical companies with its headquarters in Great Britain. Although originally supposed to be a cancer drug, Carbovir or Abacavir under its patented name, and Ziagen under its brand name, became instead a successful antiretroviral drug in the nucleoside reverse transcriptase inhibitor class. Under the usual terms of the exclusive licensing agreement, Glaxo has sole control over pricing decisions for Ziagen, and it consequently marketed the drug at $3,500 per year for wholesalers in 1998,[41] or up to $5,700 retail. As noted by Amanda Swarr in an April 2001 *Star Tribune* article, Ziagen's price guaranteed that it did not reach more than 90 percent of the people whose lives it could potentially save. As of 2001, Glaxo had earned $220 million off the sale of Ziagen, and the university had received more than $20 million of that profit.[42] Although the money coming in from Ziagen has consistently been used for public purposes such as to support graduate fellowships and the School of Pharmacy, the explicit privileging of "patents over patients" signaled by Ziagen revenues and exemplified by the relationship between the University of Minnesota and GlaxoSmithKline spurred a small but vocal activist movement against the university beginning in 2000.

The graduate students who began urging the University of Minnesota to pressure Glaxo to lower the price of Ziagen in low-income countries were in fact part of a growing national and international movement of similar groups pressuring their universities to change the exclusive nature of licensing agreements to private-sector industries. They were pushing back against relationships that emerged in 1980 with the passage of the Bayh–Dole Act, which for the first time allowed publicly funded universities to negotiate licensing agreements on new discoveries directly with private industry such as biotechnology firms or pharmaceutical companies. Before 1980, any discoveries made at research universities using National Institutes of Health (NIH) and other federal funding were automatically considered property of the federal government, which in turn assumed responsibility for marketing the new products. Yet a massive backlog of new discoveries occurred under this arrangement, resulting in significant delays in translating discoveries into commodities accessible to consumers.

Recognizing this inefficiency, Congress passed the Bayh–Dole Act, which was intended to create channels for more quickly getting new inventions—some of which had the potential to save lives or improve safety and well-being—under the control of a corporate sector far better equipped for large-scale manufacturing and marketing. By almost anyone's account, a greater efficiency has in fact occurred in the last two decades in getting new discoveries out of the laboratory and onto vendors' shelves. Yet there have been other consequences to the Bayh–Dole Act that are arguably less fortunate and that relate directly to the inappropriateness of the Target pill dispenser.

Two consequences of strengthening relations between research universities and private industry that have the most bearing here are a much greater influence by the private sector over what research scientists pursue within university laboratories, and new rules for regulating patentable products emerging from those laboratories. Biotechnology firms and pharmaceutical companies now regularly look to universities for potentially marketable new products, but in doing so they expect university scientists to be turning their attention to arenas with larger and more lucrative market potential and away from areas that promise low returns.[43] How much pressure pharmaceutical companies and other sectors of the biotech industry can place on academic scientists varies significantly, with one department chair at Minnesota claiming that he would not allow direct financial arrangements between industry and members of his department,[44] to research agendas in other departments being largely defined by grants from or contracts with private sector companies.

Pressure does not come just from industry, however. With major budget cuts occurring at most public universities over the past decade or so, university administrations have been forced to acknowledge that they can no longer count on state support to run their institutions and instead must look to the private sector for additional financial resources. One way to leverage this support is to capitalize, quite literally, on the channels opened by the Bayh–Dole Act by actively recruiting private-sector companies to take advantage of the research opportunities and resources offered by university science and technology departments. At a meeting on industry–university possibilities staged by the University of Minnesota and no doubt replicated across the country, audience members were first directed to listen to a number of scientists and corporate executives speak about the benefits of university–industry alliances, the various means by which these alliances could be formed, and the successful examples that could already be attributed to these alliances. Conference participants then were free to check out an enormous number of booths hosted by companies ranging from small, local startups to large multinational corporations embracing a similarly diverse range of research interests from agricultural to computer to pharmaceutical products. The message was obvious: if private industry was looking for good research opportunities to enhance the pipeline of new products, the university was looking for new bases of capital and opportunities for financial reward.

Although such opportunities for financial gain through scientific research are still not predictable, they are increasingly being realized in the form of licensing agreements. A second consequence of the Bayh–Dole Act of relevance here is that universities themselves stand to gain in kind, and not just status, from new discoveries produced in their own labs. The result of stronger ties with private industry is that promising new entities are rapidly patented by new technology transfer offices that have sprung up since 1980 and then licensed for use with a particular company. As with Ziagen, these licensing agreements are almost always "exclusive," meaning that only one company gets to produce and market the promising new product; and as exclusive, noncompetitive arrangements usually go, the company holding the licensing agreement has monopoly control over pricing the new commodity. Under terms of the negotiated agreement, universities as patent holders then receive a certain percentage of profits from sale of the new product. Depending, of course, on the nature of the product, its price, and its market, universities have made millions of dollars from licensing agreements. Indeed, the number of university-based patents and licenses has exploded over the past two decades, and revenue from licensing agreements between 1991 and 1997 went from $186 million to $725 million.[45] Patentable discoveries have thus become critically important players in the new corporate-driven model of university finance and governance.

While licensing agreements thus have been proliferating since 1980, the appalling breadth of the AIDS epidemic and the advent of antiretrovirals in the mid-1990s made especially visible the contradictions, and even more, the human rights abuses, embedded in contracts defining the appropriation and market regulation of life-saving new discoveries. The activist group Universities for Access to Essential Medicines (UAEM) was launched with the intention of intervening in these contradictions by urging universities to incorporate what is often called equal access or humanitarian clauses in licensing agreements—that is, agreements that would allow pharmaceutical companies under contracts negotiated with the patent holder and licensor to manufacture cheaper versions of expensive new drugs and other technologies for sale in low-income countries. By 2001, students at the University of Minnesota had successfully brought some degree of visibility to the issue of Ziagen with articles in local papers such as the *Star Tribune, Minnesota Daily,* and *City Pages;* they also had procured a statement from the university's administration suggesting that it would welcome a price reduction of Ziagen in areas like sub-Saharan Africa, even though it might mean a reduction in royalties.[46]

The public yet nonbinding nature of this achievement illustrates the contradictory position in which the university administration found itself. Interviews with members of the technology transfer office made the contradiction even more explicit: there was no attempt to hide the fact that the licensing agreement between the university and Glaxo contravened the promise as articulated in the university's mission statement to apply the outcomes of university-produced knowledge "to benefit the people of the state, the nation, and the world."[47] On the other hand, however, there was an acknowledgment that the university—including members of the technology transfer office—depended on successful licensing agreements for financial support as well as jobs. There was also the perception, however accurate, that the university held very little leverage vis-à-vis powerful pharmaceutical corporations in brokering agreements even when the university was sitting on potentially lucrative patents. As one technology transfer officer asserted, if Minnesota tried to start demanding contingencies such as humanitarian clauses in licensing agreements that already took months if not years to broker, then pharmaceutical companies would simply walk away and refuse to negotiate.[48]

Over the next four years, a core group of UAEM members, together with a larger but fluctuating constituency of graduate and medical students, continued to campaign for incorporation of humanitarian clauses in licensing agreements for essential medicines. One track of the campaign attempted to broaden the base of support by increasing visibility of the issue through World AIDS Day talks at the medical school and other venues, and by getting students, staff, and faculty to sign petitions of support. The other track made more direct attempts at changing the structure of licensing agreements through presentations at the various committees responsible for overseeing and approving university policy, and through meetings with high-level administrators.

During this time, the sway of powerful multinational pharmaceutical corporations over research institutions such as Minnesota became clear, indicating a relationship that was fraught at the same time that it was considered unavoidable. One example of this tension was the initial reluctance of university administrators to make changes in licensing agreements that UAEM members determined to be a win–win situation. Implementing licensing clauses that would allow generic competition in low-income regions, contrary to the university's suggestion, would not threaten royalty payments because these come overwhelmingly from sales in high-income countries; they would, however, enable drugs like Ziagen to reach countless more individuals in low-income regions by drastically reducing prices. The reasons posited for not wanting to make a change in licensing agreements ranged from the business logic that one university could not go it alone in demanding contingencies from powerful pharmaceutical companies; to a frequently expressed attitude that it was the federal government and not universities that was responsible for regulating access; to the problematic and racialized sentiment expressed by one high-level administrator that African officials were corrupt anyway and couldn't be expected to properly administer antiretroviral drugs to their populations.[49]

Another frustration was the transitional nature of UAEM's members; before any substantive changes got made at the university, the primary group responsible for initiating the campaign at Minnesota and for undertaking the majority of its organizational and tactical endeavors finished their dissertations and went on to academic jobs outside the state. Indeed, the vast majority of UAEM members across the United States, Canada, and Great Britain are medical, law, and graduate students, resulting in similar fluctuations in the number and names constituting each institutional chapter. For faculty members of UAEM, professional pressures to write grants, publish, teach, and serve on multiple committees made sustained activism difficult. The contradiction of this positionality—that is, the relative privilege conferred on faculty through grants and other resources available through the university, on the one hand, and the time-consuming responsibilities concomitant with these privileges, on the other—makes for an uneasy relationship to and with the university–corporate nexus. Even while struggling to change some components of this nexus, in other words, simultaneous participation in it is all but inevitable.

Unlike the AIDS Walk, where corporate visibility is heightened, for most faculty and students at the university, close ties with private companies and the increasing corporate subsidization of university resources remain obscured. Similar to the AIDS Walks, the far-reaching impact of corporate practices on the lives of individuals inside, and especially outside, of the global North is invisible—indeed, the devastating repercussions of university–pharmaceutical pricing policies for millions living with AIDS and other diseases globally seemed until recently beyond the capacity and/or willingness of even those university administrators forging these policies to recognize. Or, if they did recognize downstream repercussions, they embraced the more myopic view that any potential costs to the university of disrupting normative corporate relations had to be prevented, even if this meant maintaining longer-term but more easily ignored costs to the countless poor living with AIDS in distant regions.

In the last few years, however, some change can be seen occurring at Minnesota and other universities. With a change of personnel within the administration at Minnesota came a shift in attitude about the ability of Minnesota to "go it alone" in implementing humanitarian, or equal access, clauses within the university's licensing agreements. Although never cited as a direct reason, the increasing global controversy over AIDS treatment access at the very least served as a backdrop—if not a more significant public-relations onus—spurring policy change at the university level. In meetings that began in the fall of 2005, university administrators, lawyers, technology transfer officers, and UAEM members began discussing specifics of how the university should incorporate changes in licensing agreements. Given the range of models for increasing access in low-income countries to patented products, even this was a difficult endeavor, but one that was aided by well-vetted legal models produced by UAEM lawyers. These meetings continued through the spring of 2007, in many ways unfolding into a success story: the university—at least in the form of several relevant administrators, technology transfer personnel, and lawyers—articulated commitment to implementing equal access clauses in future licensing agreements with the private sector, and doing so in a way that "had teeth," as one administrator put it. The suggestion was even embraced that Glaxo be approached about retroactively changing its licensing agreement on Ziagen so that it would be available at much reduced prices in low-income countries.[50] One administrator even critiqued the UAEM model licensing contract for not going far enough in its dedication to equal access by not incorporating language ensuring access for all PLWAs in the United States. With multidrug antiretroviral regimens costing upwards of ten thousand dollars a year and the federally funded ADAP suffering major budget cutbacks, individuals in low-income countries are not the only ones facing curtailed access to AIDS drugs in the near future. The one remaining frustration in this scenario, as is usually the case when large bureaucracies are concerned, is the glacial pace at which change happens. Indeed, Ziagen went off patent before Glaxo could even be approached.

Although this case study is in some ways more of a success story than the AIDS Walk, in other ways it also exemplifies the shifting, if not invisible, landscape in which struggles for social change take place, and the conditional nature of change when and if it comes. If the conflation of community and corporate strategy in the AIDS Walk case is evident, for example, community in the drug access campaign has sometimes been difficult to even locate at the local level. Access to AIDS drugs has been a globally visible and volatile issue for years now, galvanized in part by the ethical travesty of thirty-nine pharmaceutical companies pressing charges against South Africa for attempting to pass a law allowing production of generic antiretroviral drugs (ARVs) in 1998,[51] and in part by the inequalities structured into the World Trade Organization's Trade Related Aspects of Intellectual Property agreement determining global patent regulations and drug prices. In combating the powerful multinational pharmaceutical industry, its government supporters (such as the United States), and the transnational regulatory bodies determining drug pricing policies, the larger access campaign has been similarly transnationally constituted by an assortment of grassroots organizations such as South Africa's Treatment Action Campaign, transnational NGOs such as Oxfam and Doctors Without Borders, and national NGOs like Health Gap. UAEM's well-focused aim to change licensing policies between universities and pharmaceutical and biotech industries, together with the considerable talents and drive of its founding members, has led to a degree of strength, organization, and visibility at the national and international levels, as evidenced for example by the WHO's mention of UAEM in its Commission on Intellectual

Property Rights 2005 Report and its recommendation that universities follow the initiative of UAEM in incorporating equal access clauses into licensing agreements.[52]

Yet, as Raymond Smith and Patricia Siplon mention in their overview of the drug access campaign, initiative is harder to sustain when the object of change is localized and diffuse, and the access campaign at Minnesota is no exception.[53] For one thing, unlike the AIDS Walk, where corporate presence is everywhere, even if portrayed as a beneficent player, in the access campaign the corporate presence is largely hidden and its relationship to the university, and to drug access, not widely known. And though it would be difficult for the pharmaceutical industry to pose as a positive player in the access debate, opinions on its role in intellectual property questions are actually more variable at the university level. One scientist, for example, was thrilled that the university increased its ability to patent more discoveries and license them to the private sector, because finally the products of his successful scientific efforts would make it out of the laboratory and into the domestic market.[54] Although not all scientists agreed with the direction in which increased patenting was going,[55] none of the scientists interviewed for this project had considered the implications of patent regulations or university licensing agreements on the availability of their discoveries outside the United States and Europe. Not surprisingly, they were not even participants in licensing negotiations even when their own discoveries were involved.

The university itself plays more than one role in the access campaign, acting as multiple institutions and agencies under one overarching rubric. On the one hand, the boundaries between university and corporation are difficult to determine as private-sector financing, interests, and governance are increasingly mapped onto preexisting university practices or are increasingly superseding them. On the other hand, the university has displayed flexibility in its official administrative position by embracing UAEM rhetoric, if not actual policies of equal access licensing, and actually expanding the contours of desired change from essential medicines to health and agricultural products broadly defined. Yet this flexibility is limited: the university has still not officially incorporated equal access clauses as a matter of course into its licensing agreements, and for now the pressure to do so has diminished.

Unlike the AIDS Walk, the drug access issue is not a "feel good" campaign where activism comes in the form of a nice stroll on a spring day "for the cause." It is a constant and largely tedious effort in which keeping focus on the end result can take stamina. Rather than just needing to be aware that a particular disease kills, the drug treatment campaign also requires at least nominal mastery over complex and ever-shifting intellectual property laws that—as one frustrated UAEM member indicated on the listserv—can be off-putting to more active and informed participation. Unlike early AIDS activism among gay communities in the United States or current campaigns in South Africa and Brazil, the implications of not having widespread access to AIDS drug treatment are also not explicitly visible in the Twin Cities. The very direct link through university–corporate licensing between Minneapolis and Harare, Mumbai, or Port-au-Prince is thus effectively elided.

The same connections linking preventable deaths from AIDS to U.S. industry and trade policies needs scrutiny. In rationalizing support for pharmaceutical pricing strategies, U.S. administrators rely on tropes of market adjustment and the ultimate, if chimerical, benefits of technology transfers through intellectual property regulations. Yet, outlining Brazil's stance on intellectual property regulations regarding essential medicines highlights the cultural boundedness of the U.S. position. As evidenced in the anthropologist João Biehl's account of Brazil's campaign for universal access to antiretrovirals, the roles played by government, science, neoliberal, and civil constituencies are starkly different.[56] While Biehl talks about a Brazilian government committed to health as a human right and the subsequent integration of state and NGO movement toward universal access, the U.S. government until very recently has shown equal commitment to market forces determining access to health care or lack thereof, and an antagonism toward any equal treatment access campaigns, whether these target affordable drugs for the elderly or affordable antiretrovirals for PLWAs inside and outside of the United States. Whereas Brazil has managed to open its economy to neoliberal policies while strengthening its national pharmaceutical industry and employing it in the production of low-priced ARVs, the U.S. government, universities, scientists, and multinational corporations have all worked together in creating regulatory structures directly benefiting them while circulating life-saving biotechnologies so high-priced that only a relative few can afford them. Brazil is characterized by public-sector science supported by a highly mobilized civil society, whereas science in the United States increasingly submits to private-sector interests, while civil society of almost any definition is relatively uninterested in "articulating a novel concept of patient citizenship" defined through pharmaceutical access.[57] Indeed, though positive change might in fact happen in the future at Minnesota and at research universities around the country, the fundamentally close relations between private industry, university administrations, government, and science will remain essentially the same.

Conclusion

As evidenced by both case studies, AIDS politics today cannot be understood outside of a deliberation of government, institutional, and public practices—in other words, outside of particular conjugations of neoliberal practices. But if neoliberalism in the form of strong corporate presence, tenuous boundaries between public, private, and governmental interests, and increased visibility of nonprofit and civil sectors is evident in the nature of AIDS walks and access to ARVs, so is the violence of its impacts on those vulnerable to or living with HIV/AIDS. New biotechnologies clearly hold promise for effective interventions into the AIDS epidemic, but that promise has been largely diminished through policies that effectively curtail distribution of drugs through the privileging of corporate profit over public health, or that obfuscate the contradictory ways in which institutional, governmental, and private agendas significantly contribute to coordinates of suffering and vulnerability in the AIDS epidemic while purporting to make positive interventions.

Again, the alliance between Target and MAP at face value does a wonderful thing, but the violence of profit as a social force complicates that relationship, demands that people no longer have access to ADAP, and forces people to work in conditions that multiply social vulnerability to HIV infection and its progression to AIDS. It is equally important that the University of Minnesota be able to produce one of the essential medicines to fight HIV and raise money to fund more research, but in order for that money to exist in the way that it does, people must go without these drugs. Working to remedy this is a commendable and necessary step, but it fails to reverse the years in which millions have been systematically deprived of Ziagen through the "successful" partnership of Glaxo and the University of Minnesota.

What is occurring and what we argue against in this chapter is the notion that equivalent extensions of community to corporations, university mission statements, and fun-friendly walks in the park cannot serve as an alibi for the deaths of millions. If we are going to celebrate the neoliberal politics of the university and AIDS NGOs, then we cannot erase the price we pay for this relationship. Milton Friedman and Friedrich von Hyek believed that the free market was the only way to guard against tyranny, and from this genealogy stems the idea behind much of what we have discussed—that the free market is the best mechanism for intervening in AIDS. This logic originates with the assumption that capitalism is fundamentally interested in emerging markets and the death of millions is the death of millions of consumers; the death of consumers is in turn a closure of markets. What this does not account for is that the AIDS epidemic itself provides biotech, pharmaceutical, insurance, and health-care industries, as well as retail investment capital firms among many others, ample opportunities for economic growth, while the deaths of millions gains visibility only as a glaring failure of public health interventions rather than the calculus of global policy and corporate interest. Under its current coordinates, in other words, the free market is underwriting the AIDS epidemic rather than mitigating its devastations.

Notes

We would like to thank Roderick Ferguson, Kevin Murphy, and Michael Franklin for reading versions of this chapter and for their extensive feedback. Alex Urquhart would also like to thank his dissertation group—Ryan Murphy, Jason Stahl, and Lisa Arrastia—for their support and comments. In addition, he would like to thank Sean Kennedy and Dan Hanson for providing inspiration along the way.

1 DHS (database online), Minnesota, cited January 20, 2008. Available from http://mnhivplanningcouncil.org/.

2 Steven Epstein, *Impure Science: AIDS, Activism, and the Politics of Knowledge* (Berkeley: University of California Press, 1996).

3 Paul Farmer, *Pathologies of Power: Health, Human Rights, and the New War on the Poor* (Berkeley: University of California Press, 1999); Paul Farmer, *Infections and Inequalities: The Modern Plagues* (Berkeley: University of California Press, 2003); Alan Ingram, "The New Geopolitics of Disease: Between Global Health and Global Security," *Geopolitics* 10 (autumn 2005): 522.

4 Drawing from Bruno Latour and Miranda Joseph, one of our agendas in tracing these changes is to illuminate the inseparability of community politics and corporate prac-

tice in the constitution of biocapitalism—capitalism and the creation of surplus value at the intersection of our life processes—as defined by the centrality of new biotechnologies and disease responses to an array of private and government policies. See Miranda Joseph, *Against the Romance of Community* (Minneapolis: University of Minnesota Press, 2002), and Bruno Latour, *The Pasteurization of France* (Cambridge: Harvard University Press, 1988).

5 Glenn Howatt, "State may drop some from HIV program; officials say the law permits action against those owing co-pays, but patient advocates say the move affects the neediest," *Star Tribune*, December 7, 2005, section B.

6 Ibid.

7 Stuart Rennie, "Prioritizing Title I and II Funds for HIV/AIDS Services in Minnesota: An Ethical Analysis of the 2006 Process" (report, Minnesota HIV Services Planning Council, 2006), 9.

8 Ibid., 8.

9 Ibid., 34.

10 Farmer, *Pathologies of Power.*

11 As Bruno Latour and other science-studies scholars point out, pathogens themselves play critically important roles in the choreography of epidemic response and contestation. Depending on the pathogen in question and the sociopolitical environment in which it is translated from the laboratory into national and global policy arenas (Latour, *The Pasteurization of France*), the contours of nationalism, citizenship, political alliances, and geopolitical relations pivot around the interpretive lexicon of pathogen, and pathogenic, behavior. For HIV, focus on gay communities and the pathologization of sexual practices in early epidemiological interpretations within the United States generated lethargic governmental and scientific responses to the epidemic through the 1980s (Epstein, *Impure Science*). The consistent, if expanded, ascription of HIV to marginalized populations from gay to injection drug using to ethnic and global poor has in turn closed the door to high-level political and funding commitments even while generating productive nongovernmental political alliances across community and national borders. Despite highly visible moves by the U.S. government in the last few years to address AIDS globally, the widespread interpretation of HIV as a sexually transmitted virus and its association with deviant populations has had critical impact on national responses to AIDS over the past twenty years.

12 When medical advances provided the first truly effective treatments for HIV, Andrew Sullivan, in an article appearing in the November 6, 1996, issue of the *New York Times*, announced the end of the AIDS plague. Sullivan, a self-proclaimed right-wing HIV-positive gay activist, saw these new antiretroviral treatments signaling the end of an epidemic and he proclaimed it a victory hard won by activists and scientists. In his

article, the gay community had rallied its cultural and economic resources to end AIDS once and forever. It is a story of the gay community and private enterprise championing an epidemic made possible by homophobia and delayed government responses. But clearly, AIDS is far from over. It not only persists more than a decade after Sullivan's prediction, but it continues to worsen in many parts of the world. For Andrew Sullivan, AIDS drugs, won by a gay community working with private industry, "ended" the plague for many of the white, wealthy gay men he sees as his audience, but his assertion does not account for a global pandemic that has intensified for people of color, women, and the poor. The narrative of AIDS in the Twin Cities could similarly be told as a story of success. AIDS services in the Twin Cities are numerous and fairly comprehensive, and research at the University of Minnesota has produced one of the essential treatments for the management of HIV, Abacavir. But these successes must be seen in light of the diminished political capital available to HIV/AIDS activists, as seen most consistently in reduced state and federal funding for prevention and treatment, lack of coverage in the media, and the reduced visibility of activism itself. See Andrew Sullivan, "When Plagues End," *New York Times,* November 6, 1996, section 6.

13 Ron Stall, "Re-emerging HIV Epidemics among MSM in the United States and Other Industrialized Nations: Evidence and Insight," Toronto, Canada, 2006; http://www.aids2006.org/pag/PSession.aspx?s=150.

14 "Over 1,000 Join AIDS Benefit March," *Star Tribune,* May 23, 1988, metro edition.

15 Ibid.

16 Jim Klobuchar, "OK to Care about Those with AIDS," *Star Tribune,* May 15, 1988, metro edition.

17 Barbara Flanagan, "Albrechts on Nicollet Mall Is Expanding," *Star Tribune,* May 13, 1988, St. Paul edition; http://www.proquest.com/ (accessed April 24, 2008).

18 "Over 1,000 Join AIDS Benefit March."

19 For a discussion of ACT-UP and the group's politics, see Brett C. Stockdill, *Activism against AIDS: At the Intersection of Sexuality, Race, Gender, and Class* (Boulder, Colo.: Lynne Rienner, 2003).

20 When asked why the Rural Action AIDS Network was unable to court corporate dollars, Linda Brandt stated simply: "We can't produce a large enough population to be advertised to" (personal correspondence with Linda Brandt). In rural Minnesota, Target gains nothing by sponsoring AIDS prevention; there are not enough possible customers to bear witness to the company's heroics. The executive director of the African American AIDS Taskforce, in response to a similar question, stated: "I think we could get the money, we just have not asked," but later said that she would refuse to litter her office or the group's posters with corporate logos. In view of this statement, it is

debatable whether or not she really could get the money from Target. Target is courting a certain image, and so is the African American AIDS Taskforce. Target symbols next to or on African art hanging on the walls would change the feeling of the group's office and the interventions it is able to make. It would change Target's image and whom it markets to as well.

21 Saskia Sassen, *The Global City* (Princeton, N.J.: Princeton University Press, 2006).

22 Salaried employees can at least consider this part of their loyalty to the company and something that they may be rewarded for in the future. Some companies even pay salaried employees through compensated "volunteer" days.

23 Lisa Duggan, *The Twilight of Equality? Neoliberalism, Cultural Politics, and the Attack on Democracy* (Boston: Beacon Press, 2003), 50.

24 While almost every history of HIV contends with this political and medical rhetoric, a number of scholars also offer historical accounts of how disease under liberalism has become a powerful tool for policing the boundaries of normalcy. See Nayan Shah, *Contagious Divides: Epidemics and Race in San Francisco's Chinatown* (Berkeley: University of California Press, 2001); Alan M. Kraut, *Silent Travelers : Germs, Genes, and the "Immigrant Menace"* (Baltimore: Johns Hopkins University Press, 1995); Allan M. Brandt, *No Magic Bullet: A Social History of Venereal Disease in the United States since 1880* (New York: Oxford University Press, 1985).

25 David Harvey, *A Brief History of Neoliberalism* (New York: Oxford University Press, 1985); David Harvey, *Spaces of Capital: Towards a Critical Geography* (Edinburgh: Edinburgh University Press, 2001); David Harvey, *The Limits to Capital* (London: Verso, 1999).

26 Target Corporate Responsibility Report, 2007; accessed January 8, 2008. The report reads: "Since 1946, we have contributed 5 percent of our annual income to programs that serve our communities. Today, this long-standing tradition means that more than $3 million every week goes to education initiatives that inspire children to learn, make it possible for families to experience the arts and to partner with a variety of social service agencies, families and communities across the country."

"Our financial support is just the beginning. Team members across the country regularly offer hands-on help to nonprofit organizations, volunteering hundreds of thousands of hours of their time and talent, and immeasurable amounts of heartfelt generosity. The philosophy of giving, sharing and helping is embraced at every level of our organization, it's part of our DNA" (5).

27 "Voter's Guide, General Election, City Council, Minneapolis," *Star Tribune,* October 31, 2001, metro edition; http://www.proquest.com/(accessed April 25, 2008); "Tiff over TIF: How Should Cities Renew Themselves," *Star Tribune,* June 13, 2001, metro edition; http://www.proquest.com/(accessed April 25, 2008); Dan Wascoe Jr., "How

Much Help Can City Afford to Give? As Minneapolis Continues to Embrace the Development Subsidy Known as Tax-increment Financing, Some at City Hall are Raising Red Flags about the Overall Impact," *Star Tribune,* April 10, 2000, metro edition; http://www.proquest.com/(accessed April 25, 2008); Ann Merrill, "FYI ; Union Members to Protest Wal-Mart," *Star Tribune,* November 21, 2002, metro edition; http://www.proquest.com/(accessed April 25, 2008).

28 Target argues that its antiunion stance as actually a commitment to community. Its Corporate Responsibility Report in 2007 reads: "Target believes in solving issues and concerns by working together with the help and input of all team members. Target wants to continue to create the kind of workplace where team members don't want or need union representation to resolve issues. We don't believe that a union or any third party representative would improve anything, not for our team members, guests or the company. There are a lot of great things that go along with being a Target team member, and our team members don't need to go to an outside party to get them" (14).

29 Chris Serres, "Teflon Target; While Wal-Mart Is Seen as the 'Evil Empire,' Target Has a Sterling Image. But Labor Groups Say the Two Giants Treat Their Workers Much the Same," *Star Tribune,* May 22, 2005; http://www.proquest.com/(accessed April 25, 2008).

30 Calculated by using federal poverty guidelines of $10,400 and standard hours one would work at Target and be considered part-time in 2006.

31 Laura Heller, "Target Plans to 'Own' Red to Keep Business in Black--Campaign around Its Signature Bulls-eye Has Been Successful; Wins Awards at Retail Advertising Conference," *DSN Retailing Today,* February 24, 2003.

32 "Voter's Guide, General Election, City Council, Minneapolis"; "Tiff over TIF"; Wascoe, "How Much Help Can City Afford to Give?"; Merrill, "FYI."

33 Serres, "Teflon Target."

34 Federal Election Commission filings of Robert Ulrich, Target chairman and CEO, and FEC filings for Target Corporation, Target Stores, and Dayton Hudson.

35 Target is a community partner for MAP listed at the ten thousand–dollar level, but its team does not even make the top ten for money raised at the AIDS Walk, despite its being by far the largest presence. The biggest "team" continues to be MAP itself.

36 Lorraine Teal, executive director of the Minnesota AIDS Project, personal correspondence, 2005.

37 Included in Target's Corporate Responsibility Report (2007) is a statement on political activities by the corporation, which reads: "At Target, governmental policy initiatives closely align with our business and corporate reputation needs, helping to make Target an active political presence with an influential voice in the deliberations, decisions and activities of our federal, state and local governments." The report goes on to

state: "Target contributes to political candidates, caucuses and causes in a non-partisan manner based strictly on issues that directly affect our retail and business interests. We do this through corporate contributions where legally permissible as well as through the Target Citizens PAC, which is funded through the voluntary efforts of our team members" (29).

38 Art Hughes, "Minneapolis Target Store Opens, but Controversy Doesn't End," Minnesota Public Radio, October 9, 2001.

39 While TIF does increase tax revenue, many places have seen increases in tax rates in order to pay for TIF projects.

40 Yet, particularly within those arenas of capitalism centered on new biotechnologies, neoliberal politics extends beyond standardized calculations of a government–market nexus to encompass larger assemblages of institutions, individuals, scientific understandings, global regulatory networks, geographic inequalities, and even viruses, thereby denuding "free market politics" of meaning and generating greater unpredictability in the negotiation, impact, and outcome of biocapitalist practices (see Latour, *The Pasteurization of France*; Stephen J. Collier and Aihwa Ong, "Global Assemblages, Anthropological Problems," in Aihwa Ong and Stephen J. Collier, eds., *Global Assemblages: Technology, Politics, and Ethics as Anthropological Problems* (London: Blackwell, 2005), 3–21. If, as its ideologues argue, the free market is going to bring about an end to AIDS, then how do we account for HIV's unbelievable mobility and increased mortality within the free market? In other words, we can recognize that the term "neoliberal" is a relatively empty one when used to designate a particular political, economic, and historical moment.

41 Marua Lerner, "AIDS Drug Puts 'U' in Debate over Access in Africa; Activists Want a Drug Developed at the U of M to Be Sold Cheaper in Africa. But the School Says It Has No Control over Global Marketing," *Star Tribune*, April 2, 2001, 1A.

42 Ibid.

43 Hence the rise of what are called "neglected diseases" such as malaria and tuberculosis that primarily affect populations from low-income regions. Since 1975, out of more than 1,300 new molecular entities marketed, fewer than 1 percent targeted "tropical" diseases (Ellen t'Hoen, "TRIPS, Pharmaceutical Patents and Access to Essential Medicines: Seattle, Doha, and Beyond," WHO.int/intellectualproperty/topics/ip/tHoen.pdf, 2003).

44 Personal communication, 2000.

45 Annetine C. Gelijns and Samuel O. Their, "Medical Innovations and Institutional Interdependence: Rethinking University–Industry Connections," *JAMA* 281:1 (2002): 72–77.

46 University of Minnesota statement on Ziagen license, April 19, 2001. The assumption

of diminished royalties under humanitarian licensing clauses is a common misunderstanding, in that more than 80 percent of worldwide drug sales come from the United States, the European Union, and Japan, and given that under negotiated humanitarian licensing agreements, more drugs are sold and more royalties are earned by the patent holders (see www.essentialmedicines.org).

47 Subdivision I, Mission Statement, University of Minnesota, Board of Regents Policy, adopted January 14, 1994.

48 Personal communication, 2003.

49 These views were articulated by various faculty and administrators in committee and private meetings during the course of 2002–3.

50 Glaxo has already made Ziagen available to the least-developed countries at $986 for a year's supply, but greater competition would reduce this price much further. See Médecins Sans Frontières, "Untangling the Web of Price Reductions," December 2002, 7.

51 Under an intense international public-relations backlash, the pharmaceutical companies withdrew their suit in 2000.

52 The report can be found at www.who.int/intellectualproperty; accessed August 3, 2006.

53 Raymond Smith and Patricia Siplon, *Drugs into Bodies: Global AIDS Treatment Activism* (New York: Praeger 2006).

54 Personal communication, 2002. This scientist worked on reducing the side effects of antiretroviral drugs that were already available.

55 One scientist, for example, bemoaned what she considered not only overpatenting, but inappropriate patenting by people not scientifically trained. The result was a diminished ability to do research when access to various models, data, and other things was impeded by patent regulations.

56 João Biehl, "Pharmaceutical Governance," in Adriana Petryna, Andrew Lakoff, and Arthur Kleinman, eds., *Global Pharmaceuticals: Ethics, Markets, Practices* (Durham, N.C.: Duke 2006), 206–39.

57 Ibid., 229.

11. GAY WAS GOOD PROGRESS, HOMONORMATIVITY, AND ORAL HISTORY

Kevin P. Murphy

From the very beginning, the development of *Queer Twin Cities* faced a number of significant challenges. One important challenge stemmed from the interdisciplinary nature of the collective, which includes not only historians, but sociologists, geographers, and those working in the interdisciplinary fields of American studies and gender, women, and sexuality studies. These individuals brought with them not only varying methodological approaches but a diverse range of intellectual interests; some shared a queer theoretical stance that was skeptical of the empirical underpinnings of social history. We engaged in generative debates, for example, over the ways in which our project might lead to the reification of categories of sexual identity given our protocol for soliciting interviewees (framed around discrete identities) and the ways in which language used early on about "recovering" an undocumented history might overdetermine a linear and progressive narrative. In response, we ultimately broadened our approach to include a much wider array of narrators and of questions posed to those narrators.

A second, related challenge involved the stated goals of the project; we were all committed to producing a volume that would be accessible to those outside of the academy, and especially to residents of the Twin Cities metropolitan region. Yet we struggled with the fact that many collaborative local histories produced for a general audience in the past two decades have relied on the same tropes of progress and community formation that we challenged. We wanted to bring more complicated analyses to bear on our treatment of queer history and oral history—analyses that dealt with issues of narrativity, the uneven and complicated history of identity formation, and ones that looked at sexuality more broadly as a historical category of social organization. Some prospective readers of the book asked explicitly for a transparent, linear, and "representative" community history; others expressed concern that we would not be able to produce a truly accessible book built around a self-reflexive and complex analysis of sources that brought a critical and theoretical lens to LGBT politics and community.

The political dimensions of this problematic have proven especially vexing, but ultimately extremely productive. Underlying some of the strong suggestions that we produce an accessible and chronologically organized narrative documenting a move from invisibility (or at least marginality) and oppression to visibility and social and political power in the post-Stonewall period was a long-standing assumption that such a narrative would validate and empower those still struggling against very real issues of homophobic discrimination and even violence and thereby produce a stronger community in the present. As we discussed this assumption as a group, our rejection of this position was based not only on theoretical and methodological grounds, but on the exigencies of the political present as well. In the Twin Cities, as elsewhere in the country, prominent LGBT organizations and leaders have been advocating a decidedly neoliberal form of equality, one that focused on corporate inclusion and the accrual of social provision through claims to a privatized model of "gay marriage"—in short, embracing what Lisa Duggan has called "the new homonormativity . . . a politics that does not contest dominant heteronormative assumptions and institutions but upholds and sustains them."[1] The genealogy of this politics is a complicated one, but rests, at least in part, on a form of public memory that recasts past struggles as progressing toward privatized forms of normalcy and belonging. As a growing number of queer scholars have argued, this form of public memory elides a long history of radical queer challenges to the regime of the normal and to the embeddedness of identity categories (and some forms of identity politics) and the concept of "community" in a capitalist political economy structured by social and economic inequalities.[2]

As we developed the project, one key shared objective focused on the production of a text—and the deployment of oral histories—in order to offer a critical historical analysis of homonormativity and, to the extent that the project intervened in the concerns of the present, offered an alternative vision of queer identities, communities, and political organizing.

We've addressed this challenge in a number of ways. One strategy has been to adopt a concept of queerness that transcends particular identity categories like gay and lesbian and instead analyzes struggles over categories of sexual normativity and dissidence, to produce a history that encompasses a variety of historical actors stigmatized and marginalized as outside normative heterosexuality—a history of "punks, bulldaggers, and welfare queens," to borrow Cathy Cohen's formulation.[3] This strategy led to the multivalent approach evident in the chapters that comprise this volume.

When we described to people the development of this project, we were often met with skeptical questions about its reception locally. Most common is the question about whether critical analyses of local LGBT community politics will be unwelcome; namely, that the book will be perceived as dangerous and counterproductive at a time when homophobia and transphobia continue to run rampant. We've wrestled with these concerns collectively and, while we do anticipate objections to our analyses, we remain committed to the idea that complex, critical analysis will ultimately prove generative to public debate about queer futures, especially in the face of the politics of homonormativity that we wish to counter. Concern about reception is most crucial in relation to our respondents, who contributed their stories to our project and to whom we bear an ethical commitment. I should note, however, that, in many ways, the critical analysis we offer emerges from our respondents themselves (the majority of whom do not identify as activists). Indeed, as chapter 1 argues, from the very beginning, individuals contributing to this project often refused or complicated seemingly stable identity categories like "gay" and "lesbian." As we conducted more oral histories for this project, we were also struck by the ambivalent interpretations of our respondents to the historical developments of the recent past and to the historical trajectory of LGBT community and politics. As well, we were surprised by the ways in which the narratives put forth by our respondents bore a complex and uneasy relationship to tropes of progress, inclusion, and normalization.

It is this oral history testimony, and especially its fraught relationship with a narrative of progress, that I'd like to address in the remainder of this chapter. I will consider some examples from our respondents before analyzing how recent queer scholarship on the relation between emotion and politics might help us understand what is important and politically generative in narratives about the queer past that resist progressive or utopian frames.

First, as might be expected, testimony from the individuals we have interviewed support the findings of recent queer historiography in countering the notion that the Stonewall Riots of 1969 represent a singularly transformative moment. Our respondents challenged the centrality of Stonewall in a number of ways. Many told us that they had not even been aware of Stonewall until considerably after the event and also effectively challenged what George Chauncey has called three myths of pre-Stonewall gay life: isolation, invisibility, and silence.[4] One respondent, a gay man named Robert, for example, responded as follows when asked about the impact of Stonewall: "I have trouble remembering what year it was . . . '69? No, we were too busy partying at the Gay 90's, and Sutton's, and Tony's [bars frequented by gay men and, in the case of Tony's, lesbians]. We weren't harassed by the cops." Robert's testimony was echoed by many others, who described social opportunities in bars and cruising grounds throughout the Twin Cities in a time that has been characterized as one of profound repression.

Even our narrators who were politically aware and active downplayed the importance of Stonewall, citing a local activist organization FREE, a university-based group founded in April 1969—two months before Stonewall—with close ties to the antiwar New Left and countercultural movements. Interestingly, FREE organized not strictly around discrete sexual identities but around a broader challenge to regimes of sexual normativity—the acronym stands for "Fight Repression of Erotic Expression." Although FREE's founders, Koreen Phelps and Steven Ihrig, formed the group to fight for "homosexual emancipation," they linked the oppression of homosexuals to broader structures of inequity and aligned the group with the civil rights and women's movements. Similar to the more famous Gay Liberation Front, established in New York months later, FREE members advocated a "Gay Power" revolution aimed at celebrating and legitimating difference rather than advocating assimilation. "The main difference between a gay person and a hip gay person is self acceptance," said Ihrig in a student newspaper interview. "A hip gay person is not ashamed of what he is."[5] In another interview, he asserted: "One of our main functions as a group is to acclimatize the straight public to our existence—to our reality."[6] The brash tactics of FREE were evident in member Jack Baker's successful campaign for student body president at the University of Minnesota; his campaign poster featured him wearing a pair of women's high-heeled shoes.[7] This early radical movement, which also emphasized the economic causes and effects of antigay sentiment, established a

14

FREE: A Photo Glimpse

FIGHT REPRESSION OF EROTIC EXPRESSION

Koreen Phelps (1969)

Stephen Ihrig (1970)

FREE Protest Picket (1970)

FREE
Robert Halfhill
$5.00

FREE Dance at U of M (1969)

FREE ("Fight Repression of Erotic Expression"), a group formed at the University of Minnesota in April 1969 (two months before the Stonewall uprising in New York), posed a broad challenge to regimes of sexual normativity. Fight Repression of Erotic Expression memorial page from the Twin Cities Pride Guide, *1989; courtesy of the Twin Cities Pride Collection, Tretter Collection in GLBT Studies, University of Minnesota Libraries.*

local framework for understanding gay liberation that extended beyond a moderate claim to belonging. This legacy encouraged the rejection of a homonormative vision for some of our respondents.

Even more interesting, many narrators, while recognizing positive changes associated with the gay and lesbian movement of the 1970s, resisted a characterization of the preceding period as "repressive." For example, like many of those we interviewed, Lynda, a sixty-year-old white lesbian, looked back with nostalgic longing to the 1950s and 1960s: "Well, I think it's unfair to just say that was a repressive time. I mean, I lived in that time and I know it was a warm and sweet and tender time." Others spoke of some perceived losses that attended the "post-Stonewall" period. Tom, a fifty-nine-year-old white gay man, referred to some of the costs of gay visibility and the negative consequences of a politics of "coming out":

> When you're known and you're out you can also be an easier target for people's homophobia, whereas in years gone by when people were closeted, maybe they could sneak through without getting the homophobic reaction. I mean, look at all the born-again Christians that are much more hostile to homosexuals than maybe they ever would have been in the past. Don't you think that's a part of what we're dealing with now?

Judy, a fifty-nine-year-old lesbian, spoke about positive changes that emerged from identifying as lesbian and as a feminist, but also ruminated with some ambivalence about the consequences of the gay liberation and women's movements. When asked about the challenges for younger generations, she responded:

> Well, I think there are many, many more choices and life is consequently much more difficult because there are more choices to make. I followed a path that I thought I didn't have any choice about and so I didn't agonize about whether to have kids or not. They happened to me. And then I took care of them. And I loved them. So it's a blessing and a curse to be nineteen now. More choices and more choices to make.

This ambivalence about the past was even more pronounced in testimony that dealt with changes in queer politics and culture over the past several decades. Some interviewees spoke of a decline in community feeling and politics. Judy, for example, answered a question about changes in the "lesbian community" over the previous twenty-five years as follows:

> I don't know that there really is much of a community anymore. I think people are scattered and integrated more. The whole idea, we were very downwardly mobile at the time. It was not okay to be middle-class or above. You were to be working-class. You were not to be making a lot of money. That has changed dramatically. People are allowed to make a lot of money. It's valued. People are allowed to dress in a variety of costumes. People are allowed to

> be feminine or not. People are allowed to change genders, for that matter. People are well regarded if they raise children, if they stay together. This is all different. People are home. And family is important where before it was dancing and drinking and politics. Political action. There isn't a lot of political action now.

For Judy, the stakes of losing a coherent community politics are high: "It'll be too bad if we let our community splinter. You know, if it happens that our freedom start[s] being taken from us, we're not going to have a way to fight that. And it could happen. It's happened before."

Judy was not the only narrator who tied a process of "integration" to a loss of community or to assert the serious dangers of such a loss. Jean, a gay activist and archivist, invoked a long history of homophobic violence and stated the need for communal politics in stark terms: "Surely, we have to hang together because we shall certainly all hang separately." For Jean, a self-defined essentialist, the dangers of "integration" manifest not only in an embrace of "mainstream" popular and political cultures, but also in the work of "queer theorists" and "social constructivists," whose theoretical destabilization of "GLBT identity," he fears, will lead to a form of assimilation unable to counter antigay violence and persecution. Other respondents, while invoking the dangers of "integration" or "assimilation" in the recent past, cite different causes and consequences. Tom, for example, identifies a politics of "assimilation" as part of a broader, and alarming, conservative embrace of "security" that works against the liberatory and communal goals of queer life on the Left in the 1970s:

> So, I mean, it really was a time that just seems like a far-off land or another culture. You know, people that were living in communes; I think a lot of people at that time thought of themselves as bisexual because they were experimenting with sex with men and women. You know, maybe orgies or communes where groups of people would have sex.... And in some ways it seems like now that we're in the land of George Bush, it seems in a way almost horrifying how much people are oriented toward security now and towards what I feel are latching onto value systems that are not really going to save us. They're actually going to destroy us out of the need for security.

For her part, Claire identifies commercialization and corporatism as the engines of declension, as evinced by her comparison of early Twin Cities "Pride" events with those that took place decades earlier:

> Of course, now it's [Twin Cities Pride] just a mega-event. I think much too orchestrated, and much too commercial, in my opinion. In the early '70s, there still was a sense of this kind of special, secret community, and there was something about the secrecy that was actually kind of appealing because it was—it was like a family, in kind of a way. And the other interesting thing is that you were thrown in with people of different socioeconomic groups than yourself, people with different interests than yourself, different professional areas, different races—in a way that you might not have been elsewhere.

Claire is not alone in recalling the excitement of secrecy and of claiming an outsider status. In a 2004 newspaper interview about early Pride events, for example, gay activist Gregg White recalled, "Back then, being out was scandalous and exciting, and walking into a gay club was almost revolutionary."[8]

These narratives of loss are, of course, no more transparent or reliable than are narratives of progress. Queer oral historian Nan Alamilla Boyd reminds us that "[w]hen researchers depend on the voices of historical actors to narrate the history of sexual identities, that is, how individuals understood their sexual selves in relation to larger social forces, the meaning of their self-disclosure is always constructed around historically specific norms and meanings. . . . The narrators' voices must, therefore, be read as texts, open to interpretation, and their disclosures should be understood as part of a larger process of reiteration."[9] The interviews collected for this project, like all oral history interviews, represent a collusion between interviewer and respondent. Our questions often prodded the people who spoke to us to position themselves vis-à-vis dominant narratives about the "progress" of gay liberation over the past several decades and testimony must be understood as being explicitly framed in this way. Moreover, all testimony about the past involves selective remembering and narrating; we tell stories about the past that comport with the ways we see ourselves—and the ways we wish others to see us—in the present. In telling the story of our lives, we construct our own identity as well as a particular vision of the world we live in.

Given that the interviews must be understood as texts, it is useful to call attention to the ways that testimony differs from other narratives of the past, as well as from historical evidence culled from other sources. In particular, the descriptions Claire and others offered about the transition from a period of greater activism, diversity, and community feeling in the earlier years of the movement to a present that seems more safe, homogeneous, and commercialized elide some of the cleavages in the late 1960s and early 1970s that emerge from an examination of written accounts of the period. For example, historian Anne Enke has shown that lesbian bars and other queer public spaces during this period, while often comprising significant diversity in terms of socioeconomic background and cultural style, were often almost exclusively white. Moreover, contemporary reporting about FREE and early Pride events suggests significant tensions between gay men and lesbians, with many women complaining about being excluded or marginalized, as well as criticisms of participants who performed gender in nonnormative ways.[10]

Perhaps the most powerful narrative about the past as "better"—in particular the activist past of the early gay and lesbian movement—involves the movement away from a more coherent and authentic "community" toward a present characterized by inauthentic market-driven social formations. This trajectory is most clearly reflected in narrators' descriptions of annual Pride festivals as at first organic and politically meaningful only to become co-opted by superficial and commercial interests in later years. The point here is not to argue that this trajectory is entirely fabricated; scholars have demonstrated beyond a shadow of a doubt, for example, that corporate interests have increasingly viewed gay men and lesbians as desirable consumers and have developed corresponding marketing strategies beginning in the 1980s.[11] Evidence of this transformation abounds in the contemporary Twin Cities, where the Pride event is underwritten by corporate interests such as Target and Saturn and the leading GLBT publication is a glossy lifestyle magazine replete with advertisements for loft condominiums and depilation services. Rather, this narrative is problematic in that it occludes evidence of commercialization in the past. Scholar Miranda Joseph argues that "community" has often been embraced as a romantic other to modern capitalism, when in fact "community is deployed to shore up and facilitate the flow of capital."[12]

Historians have demonstrated the extent to which capitalism has animated the development of GLBT communities and political organizing in the twentieth-century United States. Nan Alamilla Boyd's study of San Francisco, for example, argues that San Francisco's material interests in promoting a strong tourist economy led to the emergence of a queer commercial culture—including bars, dance halls, and venues for sexual entertainment—and that the postwar queer movement developed to defend those institutions from policing. Her argument is not that this movement was co-opted or inauthentic because it was embedded in commercialism, but rather that political community is necessarily tied to commerce in a capitalist society.[13]

Although the economy of the Twin Cities has historically been less dependent on tourism, the history of queer life has followed a similar path, as is made evident in the third chapter of this volume. Anne Enke has shown that the market remained foundational to the development of queer community and politics even during the more radical movement years of the 1970s. She shows, for example, how the owner of the Town House bar in St. Paul, in danger of going out of business, courted a gay clientele and that ultimately the Town House functioned as the epicenter of lesbian life in the Twin Cities of the early 1970s. The other central institution for lesbians in this period was the Amazon Bookstore, founded in a West Bank commune in 1970 but run as a profitable business by 1975. Enke argues that, for decades, Amazon served as a business that used "conventional market relations toward the radical end of providing space for a feminist movement that it helped define."[14] Although many lament that more radical or equitable types of business ventures exemplified by Amazon have declined, a narrative of "co-optation" can obscure the place of commerce within earlier formations of community by implying that it is capitalism per se, rather than the pernicious form of neoliberal capitalism in ascendance over the past several decades, that has proven so deleterious to egalitarian goals.

That these oral histories are constructed does not mean that they are devoid of historical meaning. Testimony about the past yields important insights not only into the meanings attached to sexual identities and communities but also into political values and goals. Stories about what is lost speak directly to what is desired; as such, they can be deployed to animate struggles for social equity.

So, what are we to make of the expressions of ambivalence and loss in these oral histories—these narratives that complicate trajectories of political and social progress? And why, in particular, are they important elements of a community history project? To diagnose narratives of declension in the post-Stonewall period as the product of internalized homophobia or to dismiss assertions of a more communal and productive sexual politics in the early 1970s as manifestations of "Left Melancholy"—to use a concept developed by Walter Benjamin—would not only do violence to those who contributed their life stories to our project but also elide important interpretive possibilities.[15] Recent work by queer scholars has argued that queer identities and politics emerged not only from a utopian impulse, but also from an array of negative emotions that index the injuries of marginalization. As cultural critic Heather Love asserts, "feelings such as nostalgia, regret, shame, despair, ressentiment, passivity, escapism, self-hatred, withdrawal, bitterness, defeatism, and loneliness . . . are tied to the experience of social exclusion and to the historical 'impossibility' of same-sex desire."[16] Love and others, notably Anne Cvetkovich and Judith Halberstam, have asserted that rather than disappear in the post-Stonewall period, such negative feelings can become even more shameful, given the rhetorical power of "pride" to gay politics and culture.

Following these scholars, I'd like to propose that these narratives of decline, disappointment, and loss might be read as expressions of the melancholy of homonormativity—as speaking to the psychic and political costs of moving from a position of exclusion to one of belonging in a realm that Gayle Rubin has described as the "charmed circle" of sexual normalcy.[17] These costs are significant and many. As Heather Love puts it, "'Advances' such as gay marriage and the increasing media visibility of well-heeled gays and lesbians threaten to obscure the continuing denigration and dismissal of queer existence. One may enter the mainstream on the condition that one breaks ties with all those who cannot make it—the nonwhite and the nonmonogamous, the poor and the genderdeviant, the fat, the disabled, the unemployed, the infected, and a host of unmentionable others."[18]

The costs of homonormativity are abundantly evident throughout this volume; Alex Urquhart and Susan Craddock demonstrate in chapter 10, for example, that mainstream GLBT leaders' advocacy for a domestic partnership provision involved capitulation to a more extensive and repressive policing of less prosperous and respectable queer people. Several chapters have pointed to the ways in which the deployment of stable identities like "gay" and "lesbian" elide or stigmatize differing sex/gender systems among communities of color. The costs of homonormativity accrue heavily to transgender people as well. Historian Susan Stryker points to a conception of homonormativity dating to the 1990s that articulated "the double sense of marginalization and displacement experienced within transgender political and cultural activism."[19] The trans people who participated in our project spoke pointedly of this double marginalization, noting that the "T" in "LGBT" has often masked a continued prejudice against and marginalization of trans people. Barbara, a transgender activist, offered the following story:

> The only negative experience [using a bathroom] I've ever had as a transgender woman was around the bathroom and was in a gay bar. I was asked to leave the bathroom by the owner saying I wasn't in the right [place]. . . . She was a lesbian. Were you born a woman? Nope. Then you don't belong here. And this is a bar that is thought of as being a GLBT bar. And was very happy to take money from GLBT patrons. . . . The only significant issue came from a place where I thought I wouldn't ever have an issue. Sort of the sanctuary of the gay bar.

Barbara asserted that, in the name of respectability and a misguided attempt to remain profitable, the bar owner resorted to more oppressive gender policing than she had encountered anywhere else in the Twin Cities.

Reading these oral histories this way does not necessarily lead to a politics of cynicism and inaction. Rather, an understanding of the costs and losses of homonormativity might help to further a politics of rupture with the neoliberal agenda of the mainstream GLBT movement. In the specific context of this local project, we are calling attention to the very ubiquity of expressions of disenchantment with, and estrangement from, a dominant gay politics that locates equality in terms of marriage and the corporation. Moreover, an analysis of the melancholy of homonormativity, and a corresponding call to look and feel backwards, might help to disrupt an overarching narrative of "progress," the end point of which is inclusion within a "mainstream" defined by homonormative and neoliberal free-market values, and to open up possibilities for developing a coalitional politics that, rather than insisting on "pride" and "progress," galvanizes feelings of exclusion, alienation, and disaffection to critique the injustices of neoliberal governance from the margins.

Notes

1 Lisa Duggan, *The Twilight of Equality? Neoliberalism, Cultural Politics, and the Attack on Democracy* (Boston: Beacon Press, 2003), 50.

2 In addition to Duggan, see also, for example, Kevin P. Murphy, Jason Ruiz, and David Serlin, eds., "Queer Futures," a special issue of *Radical History Review* 100 (winter

2008); David L. Eng, Judith Halberstam, and José Esteban Muñoz, eds., "What's Queer about Queer Studies Now," a special double Issue of *Social Text* 23:3-4 (fall–winter 2005).

3 Cathy J. Cohen, "Punks, Bulldaggers, and Welfare Queens: The Radical Potential of Queer Politics?" *GLQ: A Journal of Lesbian and Gay Studies* 3:4 (1997): 437–66.

4 The ways in which our project engages and challenges popular narratives about Stonewall, and also challenges the three myths of pre-Stonewall gay life characterized by Chauncey, is addressed in chapter 1. See George Chauncey, *Gay New York: Gender, Urban Culture, and the Making of the Gay Male World, 1890–1940* (New York: Basic Books, 1994), 1–32.

5 S. Jane Albert, "Free U Starts 'Homosexual Revolution,'" *Minnesota Daily,* June 20, 1969.

6 "Homosexuals Intend to Integrate 'U' Dance," *Minneapolis Star,* February 5, 1970.

7 On the history of FREE, see John D. Wrathall, "'What Are You After?': A History of Lesbians, Gay Men, Bisexuals, and Transgender People at the Twin Cities Campus of the University of Minnesota, 1969–1993," in *Breaking the Silence: Campus Climate for Lesbians, Gay Men, Bisexuals and Transgender People, Final Report of the Select Committee on Lesbian, Gay, and Bisexual Concerns,* University of Minnesota, November 1, 1993, 54–56. On the radical politics of the Gay Liberation Front, see Terence Kissack, "'Freaking Fag Revolutionaries': New York's Gay Liberation Front, 1969–1971," *Radical History Review* 62 (spring 1995): 104–34. On the broader history of gay politics in the postwar United States, see John D'Emilio, *Sexual Politics, Sexual Communities: The Making of a Homosexual Minority in the United States, 1940–1970* (Chicago: University of Chicago Press, 1983).

8 Dylan Hicks, "Pride: How the Twin Cities Pride Fest Helped Turn Minneapolis into the San Francisco of the Wheat Belt," *City Pages,* June 23, 2004. This "anecdotal history of Pride and the local GLBT activism associated with it" includes interviews with a number of local GLBT activists and offers a fascinating portrait of the early movement.

9 Nan Alamilla Boyd, "Who Is the Subject? Queer Theory Meets Oral History," *Journal of the History of Sexuality* 17:2 (May 2008): 179–80.

10 Enke's account of the Town House bar in St. Paul in the 1970s points to an overwhelmingly white clientele. Anne Enke, *Finding the Movement: Sexuality, Contested Space, and Feminist Activism* (Durham, N.C.: Duke University Press, 2007), 38–49. On gender conflicts in the movement, see Wrathall, "'What Are You After?'" and Hicks, "Pride."

11 See, for example, Alexandra Chasin, *Selling Out: The Gay and Lesbian Movement Goes to Market* (New York: Palgrave, 2000), and Katherine Sender, *Business, Not Politics: The Making of the Gay Market* (New York: Columbia University Press, 2005).

12 Miranda Joseph, *Against the Romance of Community* (Minneapolis: University of Minnesota Press, 2002).

13 Nan Alamilla Boyd, *Wide Open Town: A History of Queer San Francisco to 1965* (Berkeley: University of California Press, 2003).

14 Enke, *Finding the Movement,* 70.

15 Walter Benjamin, "Theses on the Philosophy of History," in *Illuminations: Essays and Reflections,* trans. Harry Zohn (London: Fontana, 1982), 257–58. See also Wendy Brown, "Resisting Left Melancholy," in David L. Eng and David Kazanjian, eds., *Loss: The Politics of Mourning* (Berkeley: University of California Press, 2003).

16 Heather Love, *Feeling Backward: Loss and the Politics of Queer History* (Cambridge: Harvard University Press, 2007), 4. See also Anne Cvetkovich, *An Archive of Feelings: Trauma, Sexuality, and Lesbian Public Cultures* (Durham, N.C.: Duke University Press, 2003), and Judith Halberstam, *In a Queer Time and Place: Transgender Bodies, Subcultural Lives* (New York: New York University Press, 2005).

17 Gayle Rubin, "Thinking Sex: Notes for a Radical Theory of the Politics of Sexuality," in Carole Vance, ed., *Pleasure and Danger* (New York: Routledge and Kegan, Paul, 1984).

18 Love, *Feeling Backward,* 10.

19 Susan Stryker, "Transgender History, Homonormativity, and Disciplinarity," *Radical History Review* 100 (winter 2008): 145–57.

CONTRIBUTORS

Charlotte Karem Albrecht is a graduate student in feminist studies at the University of Minnesota.

Pamela Butler is a PhD candidate in American studies, with a minor in feminist studies, at the University of Minnesota.

Brandon Lacy Campos is the development and marketing manager at *Words without Borders,* an international literary magazine dedicated to translated literature. He is the author of *It Ain't Truth If It Doesn't Hurt.*

Susan Craddock is associate professor in the Department of Gender, Women, and Sexuality Studies and the Institute for Global Studies at the University of Minnesota. She is the author of *City of Plagues: Disease, Poverty, and Deviance in San Francisco* (Minnesota, 2000) and coeditor of *HIV and AIDS in Africa: Beyond Epidemiology.*

Michael David Franklin is a PhD candidate in American studies at the University of Minnesota.

Jessica Giusti is a PhD candidate in feminist studies at the University of Minnesota.

Larry Knopp is professor and director of Interdisciplinary Arts and Sciences at the University of Washington at Tacoma. He was professor of geography at the University of Minnesota, Duluth for twenty years, with additional academic and administrative appointments at the University of Minnesota, Twin Cities.

Megan L. MacDonald is a doctoral candidate in American studies at Purdue University.

Kevin P. Murphy is associate professor of history at the University of Minnesota. He is the author of *Political Manhood: Red Bloods, Mollycoddles, and the Politics of Progressive Era Reform.*

Ryan Patrick Murphy is a doctoral candidate in American studies at the University of Minnesota.

Jennifer L. Pierce is professor of American studies and a former director of the Center for Advanced Feminist Studies at the University of Minnesota. Her publications include *Telling Stories: The Use of Personal Narratives in the Social Sciences and History* (with Mary Jo Maynes and Barbara Laslett) and *Gender Trials: Emotional Lives in Contemporary Law Firms.* She coedited *Feminist Waves, Feminist Generations: Life Stories from the Academy* (Minnesota, 2007) and *Is Academic Feminism Dead? Theory in Practice.*

Jason Ruiz is assistant professor of American studies at the University of Notre Dame and cofounder of the Twin Cities GLBT Oral History Project. He is coeditor of a special issue of the *Radical History Review,* "Queer Futures."

Mark Soderstrom is assistant professor in the Center for Graduate Programs at SUNY Empire State College in Syracuse, New York.

Amy M. Tyson is assistant professor in history at DePaul University in Chicago.

Alex T. Urquhart is a doctoral candidate in American studies at the University of Minnesota.

INDEX